# Introduction to Data Structures
# and Algorithms with C++

## Glenn W. Rowe

PRENTICE HALL

London   New York   Toronto   Sydney   Tokyo
Singapore   Madrid   Mexico City   Munich

First published 1997 by
Prentice Hall Europe
Campus 400, Maylands Avenue
Hemel Hempstead
Hertfordshire, HP2 7EZ
A division of
Simon & Schuster International Group

Typeset from author's disks by Dorwyn Ltd, Rowlands Castle, Hants

Printed and bound in Great Britain by
Hartnolls Ltd, Bodmin, Cornwall

---

Library of Congress Cataloging-in-Publication Data

---

Rowe, Glenn. (Glenn W.)
  Introduction to data structures and algorithms with C++ / Glenn W.
Rowe
    p.  cm.
  Includes index.
  ISBN 0-13-579178-2
  1. C++ (Computer program language) 2. Computer algorithms.
  3. Data structures (Computer science)  I. Title.  II. Series
QA76.73.C153R68   199
005.13'3 — dc20                                              96-18767
                                                               CIP

---
---

British Library Cataloguing in Publication Data

---

A catalogue record for this book is available from
the British Library

ISBN 0-13-579178-2

---

1 2 3 4 5   01 00 99 98 97

# Contents

# Contents

# Contents

# Preface

## Motivation

As there are already a large number of books on C++, another large number on data structures and algorithms, and an increasing number on the two topics together, the prospective reader of this book may well ask "Why another book on this topic?"

To answer this question we need a bit of history. If we go back a decade or more, the average computer science student was expected to have, upon graduation, an understanding not only of the practical aspects of hardware and software design, but also of the theoretical aspects of computing. This meant that the student would be required to take courses on such topics as computability and complexity and formal languages. Data structures such as trees and graphs, and algorithms for searching, sorting and hashing were studied not only with a view to their application in 'real' software projects, but also in order to derive formulas giving their complexity measures.

Many universities and colleges are now trying to attract students without a mathematical background, yet still train them to be competent computer scientists. The degree programmes for which these students enrol contain courses with more emphasis on practical application (skills such as teamwork, oral presentation, documentation, and software maintenance, for example) and less on theoretical and mathematical aspects of the subject. Most of the textbooks on data structures and algorithms, no matter what computer language they use, still expect their readers to have significant mathematical ability. With the advent of these new, non- or low-mathematical courses in these areas, a new book which caters to these requirements is needed.

In recent years, object oriented programming, or OOP, has become increasingly popular. The most commonly used OOP language is C++, so many computer science programmes feature courses in object oriented programming using C++. There has been much debate over whether C++ is a 'proper' object oriented language. Since C++ was designed to be backwardly compatible with C, any C program is (in principle) also a C++ program. This backwards compatibility means that it is possible to write C++ programs where classes and objects are never used or, arguably a more grievous sin, programs where some of the code is encapsulated in classes and some consists of free-floating modules. A 'pure' treatment of object oriented programming should probably use a language such as Smalltalk, Eiffel, or the recently developed Java (from Sun Microsystems), since these languages insist that all code be properly encapsulated inside classes and objects. However, these languages are not (or at least not yet) used much outside their own circle of devotees. For better or worse, C++ is the most common language in which 'proper' object oriented code can (with some effort at times) be written, so that is the language we shall use in this book.

In summary, then, this book is designed to meet two needs: an introduction to object oriented programming using C++, and an introduction to the study of data structures and algorithms from a non-mathematical point of view.

## Background expected of the reader

This book assumes that the reader has already had a course in computer programming using some procedural or imperative language such as C or Pascal. Students are expected to be familiar with the basic program structures such as functions, operators, conditional statements, loops, and input/output. Some experience at designing, writing, and debugging small programs is also assumed.

Readers are not expected to have used either C++ (or C) or any other object oriented programming language before. Similarly, readers are not expected to be familiar with data structures and algorithms beyond simple, built-in data structures such as arrays and records.

Since one of the main aims of this book is to provide a non-mathematical treatment of data structures and algorithms, readers are not expected to be familiar with any mathematics beyond very elementary algebra (if you can solve the equation $4x = 24$ for $x$, you should be safe). Although logarithms are used in some discussions of the running time of algorithms, they are explained heuristically before they are used.

## Plan of the book

The book divides roughly into two main sections. The first section introduces the idea of object oriented programming and illustrates how object oriented programs may be written using C++. The second section introduces the main data structures and algorithms used in modern software engineering. There is no clear division between the two sections of the book since some data structures are used to illustrate the concepts of OOP and C++ in the early chapters, and some new C++ syntax and programming techniques are introduced in the later chapters of the book.

Many texts on C++ begin with a lengthy introduction to the low-level syntax of the language and delay the mention of object oriented concepts until much later. I believe this to be a flawed approach. The OOP paradigm is a totally new way of approaching a programming problem. If your goal is to write properly constructed object oriented programs, you *must* think in terms of classes and objects right from the start. Trying to become familiar with the detailed syntax of C++ before you have any idea what classes or objects are leads you into writing procedural programs in C++ and then trying to patch them up later on to turn them into some semblance of object oriented code. The result is, at best, a flawed object oriented design and, at worst, a disaster.

The first two chapters of the book are therefore devoted to an understanding of object oriented programming, classes and objects, with minimal reference to C++ syntax.

Chapter 3 surveys the nuts and bolts of the C++ language and illustrates these features by fleshing out the classes developed in the first two chapters. Chapters 4 and 5 introduce constructors, destructors, and function and operator overloading. Chapter 6 studies inheritance.

Chapter 7 introduces the first data structures in the book: stacks and queues, implemented using arrays. The stack and queue are each implemented as a class, and some applications are given.

Chapter 8 introduces the C++ template feature. The difficulty of writing a stack or queue class which may be used to store arbitrary data types is used as the motivation for defining templates for these structures. Many of the remaining chapters in the book develop templates for other data structures.

Chapters 9 and 10 introduce sets and linked lists and implement them in C++.

The study of algorithms begins in Chapter 11, where two searching algorithms (binary and sequential search) are examined. The experimental method of analysing algorithm efficiency is also introduced here. Computer experiments are done to count the number of steps required by an algorithm as a function of the amount of data it has to process. The results of these experiments on the two searching algorithms are used to motivate a general discussion of the efficiency of algorithms using the big-oh notation. All of this is done without using any mathematical arguments; computer experiments and qualitative reasoning allow a clear discussion of the efficiency of algorithms that should be understandable by a student will minimal mathematical background.

Chapter 12 continues the study of algorithms by looking at several sorting algorithms. The remaining three chapters examine hashing, trees, and graphs.

The book is designed to be read through from the beginning, but for those lacking the time or the perseverance to do this, it is recommended that the first two chapters be read to gain a grounding in object oriented programming before any other section of the book is attempted. To understand the C++ code in the later chapters, Chapters 3, 4, 5, 6, and 8 must be read first. The other chapters (7, and 9 through 15) are reasonably independent of each other, since each chapter introduces a different data structure or set of algorithms. Some of the later chapters do make use of stacks, queues, linked lists, and sets, however.

I have tried to cover the main concepts to give the reader a good grounding in each area. If more information is required, readers may consult some of the numerous textbooks that treat these topics in more depth.

As to the amount and nature of the C++ code that appears in the text, I have tried to provide *complete, working* C++ programs to illustrate the topics in each chapter. The source code for these programs should eventually be available free of charge at a public ftp site.

The type of exercises provided at the end of each chapter varies with the topics covered in that chapter. In the early chapters in which the C++ language is developed, the exercises are more abundant and aim to develop the student's understanding of the finer points of the language. In the later chapters, the programming exercises tend to be larger, involving either modifying the examples given in the preceding chapter, or else writing a new program more or less from scratch. I have not tried to provide exercises that are 'tricky', or that introduce topics not covered in the text itself. Some of the programming exercises may be fairly challenging, but they can all be solved by applying the principles stated in the main body of the book.

## Acknowledgements

Since this book is based on the course notes that I have used over the past few years in my second year course at the University of Dundee, I would like to thank those members of the classes (too numerous to list here) who have made helpful comments and criticisms. Thanks are also due to Gareth Thorburn for many helpful ideas (some of which I actually used). Last but not least, I would like to thank Jackie Harbor, Derek Moseley, and the staff at Prentice Hall who have done a masterful job of producing the finished volume.

# CHAPTER 1

# Object oriented programming

## 1.1 Procedural languages

In your first exposure to programming, you most likely studied programming using a *procedural language*, such as Pascal, C or some form of BASIC. In a procedural language, the steps followed in designing a program usually follow a pattern such as:

1. Describe, in words, the problem to be solved by writing the program. This stage is often provided for you by someone else as, say, a programming problem in a course, or a customer requesting a software package from a commercial software house.
2. Write out, in some precise form, the steps to be followed by the computer to solve the problem. These steps comprise an *algorithm*, that is, a precise sequence of steps which lead you from the initial step in the program through all possible paths the program can take, to the final statement in the program.
3. Decide which language to use for the program.
4. Decide on appropriate variables and data structures to represent the quantities and methods being used in the program.
5. Apply the method of stepwise refinement, or top-down design, to determine the various functions and procedures that will make up the program.
6. Starting with the topmost level, write each module.
7. Test each module as it is written.
8. Refine and debug each module to correct any mistakes found in step 7.

In this sequence of operations, the driving force is the *algorithm*, the sequence of steps that the program must follow. Everything else in the planning, design, implementation, and testing of the code is determined by the algorithm being used.

You might think that such an approach is the only way a program *could* or even *should* be written. After all, if you don't know the precise steps a program is to follow, how can you write the code?

In one sense, of course, this is quite correct: in order to program a computer, you must know the algorithm with which it is to be programmed. The important point here, however, is not whether or not we need the algorithm (of course we do), rather it is whether or not everything in the design and execution of the program should be centred around it.

Since you probably don't know any other way a program could be written, this concept may be hard to grasp. Let us illustrate the situation with an example.

## 1.2 An automatic teller machine (ATM) - procedural version

You will probably have used an automatic teller machine, or ATM, at some point. Virtually all banks, or other institutions that will safeguard your money, provide these machines so that you can withdraw or deposit cash, check the balance in your accounts, and perhaps perform several other operations. A real ATM has a relatively simple interface. There is a slot into which you insert your bank card, a few buttons which you use to issue commands, a slot out of which your cash comes when you make a withdrawal, and possibly another slot into which you place an envelope containing cash when you make a deposit. However, despite the simplicity of the design, real ATMs are connected to sophisticated computer networks. Most bank cards will work not only in an ATM provided by the same bank that issued the card, but in many other ATMs provided by other branches of the same bank, and by other banking firms. In some cases, a card can be used in ATMs over the whole country. The programs required to keep all the records straight, prevent fraudulent withdrawals, and so on, are substantial.

To keep things simple, let's consider an ATM which can handle only those accounts belonging to a single customer. We will allow the customer to have several accounts, possibly of different types, such as chequing and saving. The customer will only be allowed to use the one ATM that is attached to the specific branch where their account is deposited, so we can ignore the complexities of a network of ATMs and just concentrate on one. Our task is to write a program that handles the various transactions the customer might make.

If we design this program using a procedural approach, we will follow the steps given above. First, we need to give a description of the problem in ordinary English.

The ATM should allow the user to enter their card, punch in their code number, and then make a choice of action from the set of buttons present on the console, provided that the code number was correct. The actions allowed are:

1. Check balance (the balance is displayed on the screen).
2. Withdraw cash, provided that sufficient funds are available in the account. If cash is withdrawn, the amount withdrawn is subtracted from the balance.
3. Deposit cash. The amount deposited is added to the balance of the account. (We'll trust the customer to actually deposit the amount of cash they say

they have by putting it in an envelope and inserting it in the deposit slot in the machine. No *real* bank, of course, would be so foolish.)

We would like the program to be designed in such a way that more features can be added easily later on. We might want to add features such as transferring cash from one account to another, requesting a bank statement for the last month, and so on.

We will assume that the hardware interface of the ATM consists of 10 numbered buttons labelled from 0 to 9, and three other buttons, one for each action listed above. There may be other buttons present, but they are inactive, as they are just there to allow for future expansion of the facilities.

Next, we need to consider the algorithm as a precise sequence of steps. To do this, we need to start at the beginning of the program and provide a step-by-step guide through the logic of the program to show all possible paths a user might take. One sequence is as follows.

1. Wait for user to enter card and punch in code.
2. Is code correct? If yes, go to step 3; if no, go to step...
3. Display menu. If user selects "Withdraw", go to step 4; if user selects "Deposit", go to step 7; if user selects "Check balance", go to step 8.
4. Request amount to withdraw.
5. Is there enough money in the account? If yes, go to step 6; if no, go to step 9.
6. Subtract the amount withdrawn from the balance; dispense cash. Go to step 9.
7. Request amount to deposit; accept the cash; modify the balance. Go to step 9.
8. Retrieve and display the balance.
9. Eject card; go to step 1.

1¡Here¡, we have omitted many error checks or convenience options that a real ATM would have. For example, if the customer punches in the wrong code after inserting their card, the ATM simply quits without giving our hapless customer a second chance to get the code right. (Writing truly user-friendly programs which anticipate most of the errors a user might make and providing sensible actions when an error occurs is a difficult and time-consuming process, so we will keep things simple for the moment.)

Once the algorithm is fully specified, either as pseudocode or as a data flow diagram, we would proceed to the design of the data structures. A list of quantities that we will need may include:

- A record to hold details of each account, such as the balance, type of account (chequing or savings), an array or linked list for storing the transactions, and so on.

- A variable to hold the number code as read from the bank card.
- A variable to hold the number punched in by the customer.
- A variable to hold the choice of transaction as selected by the customer.
- A variable to hold the amount of withdrawal or deposit requested by the customer.

Of these variables, only the record holding details of a customer's account is a compound data structure; the others are all single variables. We might therefore define the record as a new, user-defined data type in this program and content ourselves with using built-in data types such as integers and reals for the other variables.

Having finished our survey of data structures and variables, we proceed to the top-down design of the modules to be used. If we have done a good job of describing the algorithm, this part of the analysis is usually not too difficult, since we have already identified the main sections in the program. The module structure here would follow that in the pseudocode above quite closely. Each step in the algorithm would correspond to one module in the code.

Since an ATM is designed to give 24-hour access to the customer's accounts, the main module takes the form of an infinite loop. The loop begins by printing a welcome message on the ATM screen, prompting the user to insert their card. The machine waits for a card to be inserted. Once the card is present, the next module (called from main) requests the code number. After the code has been punched in by the user, a module is called to check the number against that read from the card. The return value from this module is used as a switch to determine the next action. If the number is wrong, the card is ejected and the ATM returns to its waiting state. If the number is correct, a module is called to process the user's choices.

The module in which a user's choices are processed also contains an infinite loop, since we do not know in advance how many actions the user will want to do. (A real ATM, of course, has a time limit for the user to enter their choice. If no action is taken after, say, 30 seconds, the card is ejected and the transaction is terminated. We won't bother with that complication here.) The module waits for a choice, with the result being used as a flag in a switch statement. Pressing 'Withdraw Cash', for example, will cause the WithdrawCash module to be called. The process continues until the user presses 'Exit', at which point the loop (and the module containing it) is terminated, so that the ATM returns to its waiting state, ready for the next customer.

We won't go any further in our analysis of this program, since hopefully the point has been made. We begin with a verbal or written description of the problem to be programmed. This description is often (in the real world of industry) given by a customer who knows little about computers. The description is therefore often vague and incomplete. The specification is then converted into a precise algorithm (by someone who knows something about computers). Data structures are designed, and a modular structure is created for the program structure. Then the code itself is written, tested, and modified until both the author of the code and the customer for whom it was written are satisfied.

# 1.3 The object oriented approach - classes and objects

The procedural approach to designing the program for an ATM is probably the way you are used to writing a program. The algorithm, that is, the *sequence of actions*, is the central consideration. Now we'll have a look at the *object oriented* approach to writing a program.

In the object oriented, or OO, approach to writing a program, the *actions* to be performed by the program take second stage to the *objects* upon which the actions occur. This philosophy must be realized and understood right from the beginning of the design process, since the entire approach you take to the project, even from the initial translation of the verbal description of the project into more precise language, must reflect the OO approach.

To understand how object oriented programming works, we need to introduce a few terms commonly used in the trade. First, we need to understand what is meant in object oriented programming by *classes* and *objects*. Classes and objects are terms that, by their very nature, must be defined in a vague, abstract way unless we use the strict syntax of formal computer languages. However, since we are not expecting the reader to have any grasp of such formal syntax, we will have to try to convey the idea in ordinary English.

A *class* is a collection of attributes (properties and actions) which collectively describe an entity. An *object* is a particular instance of a class. Since these two statements don't usually mean much the first (or even the tenth) time you read them, we really need some examples.

Let us try to define a class which can be used to describe cars. Some of the *properties* of a car are things like:

- colour
- engine size
- manufacturing company
- model
- year of manufacture
- mileage
- capacity of the petrol tank
- current contents of the petrol tank.

Some of the *actions* that can be performed on a car are:

- driving
- parking
- putting it in a garage
- servicing
- repainting
- filling the petrol tank.

You can see that the properties of a car are quantities that can be used to describe it. In a computer language, these properties can be represented by variables such as integers, floats, and user-defined data types such as records and arrays.

The actions, on the other hand, describe things that can be done *to* the car. Some of these actions may change some of the properties. For example, driving the car or filling the petrol tank will change the current contents of the petrol tank.

In general, you can think of the properties of a class as *adjectives*: they are quantities that describe the class. The actions can be thought of as *verbs*: they describe things that the class can actually do. The class itself can be thought of as a *noun*: it is an entity which can have properties that describe it, and which can participate in actions.

The description of the car class that we have given, however, does not refer to any specific car. The properties and actions are things that can be used to describe any car you like. To actually use the car class, we must define an *instance* of it. The reason for this is that, in a computer language like C++, a class is just a new kind of data structure, like an integer or a character. When you define a class to describe a car, you are merely saying what properties and actions the data structure should have. You have not actually declared a particular instance of that data structure. For example, if you describe the integer data type by giving the rules by which integers are stored in computer memory, you can now use that definition to declare some specific instances of integers, using, say, the Pascal declaration:

```
var
   i,j : integer;
```

or the C declaration:

```
int i,j;
```

In each case, the data type is an `integer` or `int`, and `i` and `j` are particular *instances* of integers. In the case of the car class, the lists of properties and actions that we have given above define the data type. We can use this type in an object oriented language such as C++ to declare particular instances of this type. (We will see how this is done in the next chapter.)

Just as with ordinary data types like integers, an instance of a class need not have any values assigned to its properties (you can declare an integer as we did above without giving it any initial value). Thus we could declare an instance of a car class without assigning values to its properties such as colour, mileage, and so on. These properties can be filled in later as the need arises in the program. However, it is more typical that a particular instance of a class will have values assigned to its various properties when it is defined. It is good programming practice to do this anyway. The C++ language provides a special mechanism, called a *constructor function*, for initializing property values when an instance is declared.

A particular instance of a class is called an *object*. As you might guess from the name 'Object Oriented Programming', classes and objects are the central features in the OO style. In order to design an OO program, you must first identify the classes which the program will use. Only after this is done should you think about what is actually to be done with the classes you have just created.

The contrast between the procedural approach and the OO approach can be summarized as follows. In the procedural approach, the first stage in the analysis is to work out the algorithms to be used by the program. Following this, the data structures are designed and the modules are constructed. In the OO approach, the first stage in the analysis is to work out the classes that will be used. Properties and actions are associated with each class. Once the classes are constructed, the actions for each class are written as individual modules. The overall algorithm is then implemented by arranging for the individual objects to act on each other, using the actions associated with each class.

We will study classes and objects in more detail, including their implementation in C++, in the next chapter. For now, we will examine how an object oriented model of the ATM might be constructed.

# 1.4 The ATM - an object oriented approach

In writing an OO version of the ATM program, we need to start our design by thinking of the ATM as a class, and ask ourselves what its attributes (properties and actions) are. An initial stab at such a list might result in something like:

**Properties**
- card code (the code stored in the magnetic stripe on the card)
- entered code (the code punched in by the user)
- account balance

- account number.

**Actions**
- display welcome message
- read card
- check entered code
- offer menu of actions from which user chooses
- withdraw cash
- deposit cash
- check account balance
- check account number.

We could construct a class with these attributes and label it `atm`, or some similar name. We could then proceed to determine what data types would be appropriate for each of the properties (for example, the card code is probably an integer, the account balance is a real number, and so on). Then we could write each of the actions as separate functions which altered the values of the properties in appropriate ways. For example, the check entered code function would compare the card code property to the entered code property to determine if the user has entered the correct code. The withdraw cash function would check the account balance property to ensure that enough money is in the account and, if so, would subtract the withdrawn amount from the account balance property and produce the cash. The whole ATM program would then consist of a main routine which called these various functions in some appropriate order.

However, if we think about this situation, we will see that it is not the best way of designing the class. We have confused the properties and actions associated with the ATM with properties and actions more logically associated with individual accounts. For example, the account balance is not a property of the ATM; it is a property of a particular account. The withdraw cash function does not operate on the ATM; it operates on an account. It would make more sense, then, to define another separate `account` class, which may have the following contents:

account class

**Properties**
- account balance
- account number.

**Actions**
- withdraw cash
- deposit cash
- check account balance
- check account number.

Since these attributes have been assigned to a separate class, the atm class now becomes:

atm class

**Properties**
- card code (the code stored in the magnetic stripe on the card)
- entered code (the code punched in by the user)
- list of accounts managed by the ATM.

**Actions**
- display welcome message
- read card
- check entered code
- offer menu of actions from which user chooses.

The atm class contains only those properties and actions which relate specifically to the ATM. One of the properties of the ATM is a list of accounts, which could be represented as an array of account objects, each element of which is an *instance* of the account class defined above. The properties and actions which apply specifically to *accounts* are now contained in the account class, and not in the atm class.

This example illustrates that designing classes may require more than one attempt. There is usually no one correct way of doing it: various class designs are equally good for modelling a particular system. There are, however, definitely some inefficient or incorrect ways of designing classes. Our first attempt at an ATM class is an example of such an incorrect method: we hadn't thought through the logical structure of the system before attempting to write out the class structure.

In OO design, it is absolutely vital that you take the time to think through the problem and make sure you understand exactly what it is that your program is to model *before* you attempt to design any classes. Even with this forethought, you will probably find that several attempts are needed before an acceptable set of classes emerges. To an even greater extent, it is important to think through the class design before you start writing any C++ code. A properly structured C++ program, with logically designed classes, can be much easier, in the long run, to write and maintain than procedural code written in C or Pascal, but it does take care and understanding to produce correct C++ code.

# 1.5 Procedural versus object oriented - why bother?

By this time, you may be wondering whether all the effort required to produce a good object oriented design is really worth it, especially if you have some experience as a procedural programmer. At first glance, the object oriented way of writing programs seems to add yet another layer of complexity on top of the top-down design method that is used for a properly designed procedural program.

While it is true that a good object oriented design usually requires more planning than a procedural design, the long-term benefits of object oriented programming can outweigh the short-term advantage of a procedural program.

The idea of encapsulating your data structures into classes where the data fields and their associated actions are all grouped together under one roof is a more logical and neater way to design code. In languages such as C and Pascal, there is no easy way of linking the actions (which would have to be written as separate functions) exclusively to the data fields on which they act. As we will see, in C++, this is an easy and natural thing to do.

The object oriented structure of C++ makes it possible to define *class libraries,* that is, collections of classes for commonly used data structures and algorithms that are not built into the C++ language.[1] Once you have written some libraries you can reuse this code by simply including it in future programs.

Finally, the use of classes and objects allows many powerful programming features (such as operator overloading, templates, and inheritance) that are not available in non-OOP languages. More of this in later chapters.

## 1.6 Exercises

### Review questions

1. What is the main feature of a *procedural* programming language?
2. What is an *algorithm*?
3. What is the main idea behind *object oriented programming* (OOP)?
4. What is meant by a *class* in OOP?
5. What are the two main types of attributes a class may have?
6. What is the relation of an *object* to a *class*?
7. Compare procedural and object oriented programming methods, listing advantages and disadvantages of each method.

---

[1] Unfortunately, there is little uniformity in the class libraries that are available at the moment, since everyone tends to design their own, with standards that are different from everyone else's. Hopefully as the C++ language evolves, there will eventually be sets of standard libraries.

## Problems

1. The following list contains attributes of a television set. Specify which of the attributes are properties and which are actions. Try to identify any groups of attributes which could form their own separate class.

- turn on
- turn off
- can receive teletext
- select channel
- current channel number
- channel is a satellite channel
- turn off sound (use the mute function)
- repair television
- current channel's sign-off time
- list of channels received by television.

2. List some properties and actions that may be included in a class designed to represent a house. Critically examine your list to see if there are some properties and actions that could form a separate class, in the same way that we created the account class in this chapter.

3. Suppose you wanted to write a computer program which simulated a customer's visit to a supermarket. The program should simulate the events from the time the customer arrives at the door of the supermarket, through the various events that occur during a normal visit (collecting a trolley, selecting items from shelves, ordering something from the butcher or delicatessen, and so on) up to the checkout. Finally the customer should leave the store.

Outline how you might design (i) a procedural and (ii) an object oriented approach to such a problem. The procedural design should list the main functions you would use, and indicate in what order and combination these functions would be called. The object oriented design should begin with a specification of the classes involved, followed by an indication of how these classes (and their associated actions) would be used to run the simulation.

CHAPTER 2

# Classes and objects

## 2.1 Introduction

To emphasize our approach to object oriented programming, we shall begin our survey of the C++ language by examining its facilities for implementing *classes* and *objects*, since, as we saw in Chapter 1, it is the classes and objects which are of central importance in an OO language.

Many books that concern themselves with teaching the C++ language tend to begin with a survey of the syntactical features of the language: operators, loops, conditional statements, and so on. Classes and object oriented programming are only mentioned after several chapters on the 'basics' of the language, and are treated as 'advanced' features of C++ programming. This approach is fundamentally flawed, since it emphasizes the procedural aspects of the language and has the effect of training you to write procedural programs which must be patched up later to convert them into proper object oriented packages. Although C++ was designed as a 'better C' (the name C++ is derived from the ++ operator in C, which increments its argument by 1), and therefore shares much of C's syntax, it is a mistake to attempt to write C-style programs in C++. The difference between C and C++ is much larger than that between C and another procedural language, such as (non-object oriented) Pascal.

We therefore begin learning C++ by actually constructing some classes to represent some data. Of course, to actually write the detailed code that will be run by these classes, we need to understand the syntax of C++, but it is important that you understand that the *first* thing you should do in designing a C++ program is to design the classes. The detailed code that will be inserted into the functions belonging to these classes is something we can worry about later.

Having said this, however, we do still need to understand the built-in data types allowed by C++, since we must ultimately base all our classes on these data types. We will therefore have a look at these before proceeding to our first C++ class.

## 2.2 The basic data structures in C++

The syntax in C++ for declaring simple data types is:[2]

---

[2] The convention used in code listings in this book is as follows. Code will be printed in a typewriter font (where all characters take up the same horizontal space) so that the code will look much the same as it would in an editor that you might use to write it. Any text in a code listing that appears in italics (such as the line given here) is to be interpreted as a description

```
data-type list-of-variables;
```

There are only a few fundamental data structures in C++. They are:

- `int`: the integer data type. Integers come in a variety of flavours in C++. If you simply declare a variable as

```
int testint;
```

it represents a signed integer, defined using the standard two's complement representation in memory. However, the range of integers allowed by an `int` declaration is not constant from one system to another, so that the `int` declaration should be used with some caution. You can rest a little more easily if you use one of the alternative declarations for an integer:
- `short` and `long`: a short integer is typically allocated 2 bytes of storage, so that it allows integers in the range –32,768 to +32,767. A long integer is typically allocated 4 bytes, allowing the range –2,147,483,648 to +2,147,483,647. Prefixing the declaration by the keyword `unsigned` means that all integers are non-negative (either positive or zero), so that the range of an `unsigned short` is from 0 to +65,535, and of an `unsigned long` from 0 to +4,294,967,295. However, these limits are not guaranteed, as some compilers may allocate different numbers of bytes to the various forms. All you can be certain of is that a `long` integer is no shorter than a `short` integer! If you are planning on using integers of any size, it is a good idea to investigate the limits of the various forms in order to avoid some difficult bugs in your programs. C++ provides no overflow checks to warn you when your integers are going out of bounds.
- `float` and `double`: the floating point representations. Again, the precisions offered by various compilers may vary, but in any sensible implementation, a `double` will provide roughly twice the accuracy of an ordinary `float` variable. If you are planning on relying on the precision of a floating point variable, it is a good idea to do some preliminary tests to determine the accuracy on the system you are using.
- `char` is a 1-byte ASCII character variable. Beware that an ordinary `char` is signed, just like an ordinary `int`, so if you intend to store ASCII codes larger than 127 in a `char`, you may get curious results when you access

---

of the various components that would be typed in a real program. For example, the phrase *data-type* in the line given here means that some actual C++ data type (such as `int` or `float`) should be typed in its place.

them again. You can avoid this problem by prefixing the `char` declaration with the `unsigned` keyword.

## 2.3 Aspects of classes in OOP

Before we get around to writing any C++ code, we should consider the class/object concept in a bit more depth than in Chapter 1. We have seen that the idea of defining classes to represent the entities in the program is central to OO programming. A class has two main components: the *properties* of the class and the *actions* which may be carried out on these properties. The properties in a C++ class are represented by variable declarations such as `int`s, `float`s, and `char`s, or by user-defined data types. The actions are represented by functions which can change some of these variables.

Although the distinction between properties and actions is fundamental to OOP, there is another distinction which is just as important. In most classes of any size, there are certain properties and actions that describe or affect only internal parts of the class. That is, there are certain properties and actions in the class whose values and actions are of no concern to anything outside the class. For example, if we are designing a class to represent a car, we probably don't care about such details as the sizes of the various nuts and bolts that hold the car together, although such information is vital to the proper functioning of the car. The average car driver cares only about such things as how fast the car is moving, how much petrol is in the fuel tank, and so on. Similarly, there are many actions inside a car that are not of direct interest to the driver, such as the motions of pistons in the engine, the actions of various gears in the drive shaft, and so on. The driver is interested in actions such as putting his foot on the accelerator or brake, and not in what internal actions occur as a result of where his feet are.

The designer of a car class then can divide the total set of properties and actions, or *fields* as the two together are collectively known, into two groups:

1. Those fields that need only be known to the interior of the class. These fields are called *private* fields.
2. Those fields which need to be known outside the class. These fields are called *public* fields.

Another way of thinking about the distinction between private and public fields is that the public fields provide an *interface* between the inside of the class and the outside world. In a car, for example, the actual speed of the car depends on how fast the wheels are turning. The interface between this internal state of the car and the outside world (the driver) is given by the reading on the speedometer. The speedometer can therefore be regarded as a public function whose action is to measure the rotation speed of the wheels and whose return value is the speed of the car. In order for this function to be able to calculate the speed, it must have access to the private fields of the car so that it can translate the rate at which the wheels are turning into a needle position or digital readout on the face of the meter.

This separation of fields into public and private is more than just a cosmetic feature of OOP. In order to define a class properly, you need to collect together all the properties and actions appropriate to the entity that the class is being used to represent. Once you have done this, you need to ensure that access to these fields is controlled so that only those fields that *should* be accessible to the outside world actually *are* accessible. This principle is known as *encapsulation*.

A good guideline is that *all* property fields should be private, so that the only way to change them is through a public interface function. In terms of the car analogy, this could be interpreted as the idea that the only way to change a property of the car is to use one of the interfaces provided by the manufacturer. For example, to change the speed of the car, you have to use the accelerator pedal, which is an 'interface function' to those internal parts of the car that are used to increase the speed.

It is a common feeling amongst novice programmers that this preoccupation with 'proper design' of computer code is more trouble than it is worth. There is a strong urge to cut corners by not giving much thought to how classes should be designed, to which fields should be public or private, or to which properties belong in which classes. It may seem easier to write code without spending some time away from the computer planning out the structure of the program. However, any programmer who takes the trouble to learn the proper techniques of program design is more than repaid by being able to produce code that is easier to write, debug, document, and maintain.

The design of a class in an object oriented programming project is no small matter. A great deal of planning should be done to determine what the best fields (both properties and actions) are to describe a system, and which of these fields should be public and which private. The study of the proper design of classes is a subject in its own right, called *object oriented analysis and design*. For large systems (and OOP really comes into its own in very large programming projects), there may be hundreds or thousands of classes, many of which interact with each other through mechanisms that we will consider in later chapters. There are various diagrammatic schemes for picturing the relationships between the classes that may be used to ease the process of object oriented design. Some 40 or 50 such schemes are in use at present, though their use is beyond the scope of this book. You should know, however, that many industries that write large-scale object oriented programs make use of computer packages known as CASE tools (for Computer Assisted Software Engineering) which allow you to design your classes graphically on the screen. Some CASE tools will also generate the code for you in a language of your choice after you have designed the diagrams.

Before you get into such sophisticated computer tools, though, you should understand how to write object oriented code yourself without their aid. Let us therefore examine some simple classes in C++.

## 2.4 A class in C++

To introduce the idea of a class in C++, let's return to the ATM (automatic teller machine) model we discussed in Chapter 1. To keep things simple at this stage, we wish to construct a class that can represent an ATM which allows three operations on an account:

1. check account balance
2. withdraw cash
3. deposit cash.

At the moment, we will allow only one type of account. Later we will see how to generalize this so that different types of accounts (such as chequing and saving) are allowed. A first try at a class in C++ may look like this:

```
const int MAXACCOUNTS=10;
typedef int BOOL;
enum {FALSE, TRUE};

class account
{
private:
  float Balance;
  int AccountNumber;
public:
  BOOL Withdraw(float Amount);
  BOOL Deposit(float Amount);
  float CheckBalance();
  int CheckAccountNumber();
};

class atm
{
private:
  int EnteredCode;
  int CardCode;
  account Account[MAXACCOUNTS];
public:
  void DisplayWait();
  void ReadCard();
  BOOL CheckCode();
  void ProcessChoice();
};
```

Let us explain this code step by step, starting from the top. The first line is

```
const int MAXACCOUNTS=10;
```

This declares the name MAXACCOUNTS as a constant int, with the value 10. It is always good programming practice to define clear names for constants, rather than using 'bare' or 'magic' numbers in your programs. It is often difficult to figure out what these numbers mean. For this reason, we will endeavour to give each such number a name by using a const identifier at the beginning of a program.[3] The general syntax for a const declaration is:

```
const datatype parameter_name = value;
```

Following the const definition, we introduce a typedef to define a Boolean data type for convenience. The BOOL data type is simply an int with the special values TRUE and FALSE defined by the following enum statement.

We now see two class definitions. The syntax for a simple class definition in C++ is:

```
class classname
{
private:
  private_fields
public:
  public_fields
};
```

The keyword class must be followed by a name for the class. This name becomes a new data type which may be used to declare variables, just like int and char. Following the class name is the body of the class definition. The keywords private and public introduce the fields of each type. Neither of these keywords is required in the definition of a class, but if the type of field is not specified, it is private by default. For example, if we declared a class such as:

```
class PrivateClass
{
  int field1;
  float field2;
};
```

---

[3] Pascal programmers will be familiar with the const keyword for declaring constants. C programmers may be used to using the #define syntax to declare constants. The const keyword is superior to #define, since it defines a genuine parameter that can be tracked by a debugger, and also allows type-checking by the compiler.

both fields would be private. We'll see in a minute that a class in which all fields are private is essentially useless, because none of its data are accessible to anything else in the program.

We could omit the private keyword but include public, to get a class like:

```
class PublicClass
{
  int field1;
  float field2;
public:
  char PublicChar;
};
```

Here the last field is public, but the first two are private.

It is good programming practice (although not followed in all textbooks) to always place the private fields before the public fields in a class definition. The reason for this is that private fields can be accessed only by functions declared within the class itself, while public fields are generally accessible to any other part of the program. The whole reason for making private fields private is that they cannot be accessed, and therefore modified, by any functions except functions actually belonging to the class in which they are defined. If you are in the habit of putting public fields before private ones in your class definitions, and one day inadvertently leave out the private keyword, then all your fields in that class will become public. This could cause a number of subtle (where 'subtle' means 'very hard to find') errors in the program due to fields which you *thought* were private being accessed and modified by functions that really shouldn't have any access to them. If you are in the habit of putting private fields before public ones, on the other hand, and forget to include the public keyword, all your fields will be private. This will cause the compiler to complain stridently when you compile the program, since any time you attempt to access a field that you *thought* was public (but is in fact, erroneously private) in a function defined outside the class, the compiler will generate an error. These sorts of errors are easy to fix.

The rest of the class definitions for the ATM class should be fairly obvious from what we have said up to now. The first class definition is for a bank account. The class name is account. A brief explanation of the naming convention for classes may be useful here.

You can, of course, call your classes anything you like, but to preserve some form of order, it is a good idea to decide on a consistent naming convention. We will adopt the standard that all class names begin with a lowercase letter, to make them consistent with already existing data types such as int and float. Frequently, you want to use the same word as that used for the data type when you define a variable of that type. In such a case, we will begin the variable name with a capital letter. For example, in the definition above for the `atm` class, a variable named `Account` of data type `account` is declared.

We have defined two private fields: `Balance` and `AccountNumber`. You might object to this, since you obviously need to have outside access to your account's balance, and you wouldn't mind knowing the account number either. This brings out an important point about object oriented programming. Although you may wish to know your account's balance, you wouldn't want anyone else to know it. You therefore want some way of controlling access to this data. This is where the idea of hiding certain parts of the class away from the outside world, and only allowing access through carefully defined interface functions, comes into play. The account balance is declared as private, and only certain functions are allowed access to the balance. These interface functions may be public or private, depending on their purpose. For example, in the `account` class, there are three public interface functions which will be allowed access to the balance: `Withdraw()`, `Deposit()`, and `CheckBalance()`. Although we haven't written the functions yet, we know that only the first two will be allowed to change the balance; the last function is only allowed to read the value of the balance.

If we had made the `Balance` field a public variable, we could still have defined these three interface functions to take care of withdrawals, deposits, and viewing the amount in the account. However, any other functions, either within other classes, or just independent functions not connected to any class, could also access the balance field. The control of the `account` class over the balance field is lost. The whole point of setting up a class for a bank account is to define an independent entity within which the data fields and the operations permissible on them can be encapsulated. Any other part of the program that wants to access any of the data stored within a bank account class *must* do so through one of the interface functions.

You might be thinking to yourself at this point: "Well, OK, but isn't this all rather a lot of effort to go to just for the sake of nicely organized code? I *know* that the only operations that are allowed to alter the balance are withdrawals and deposits so I'll just make sure that those are the only functions in my program that do it. Why do I need to declare a special interface function just to *look at* the value of the balance?" Initially, it may seem like a lot of extra typing just to properly encapsulate your data, but in the long run, it is the only way of making code readable, reducing the debugging time, and generally conforming to the object oriented way of doing things. Most programmers come up with a similar objection the first time they are forced into writing properly structured procedural code. "Why do we need to break everything up into separate functions, when it is easier to just type in a program as one long list of statements?" The reason is much the same: what works for short programs collapses in a tangled mess for longer ones. The idea of top-down design is essential for writing long procedural programs.

The idea of proper data encapsulation is essential for writing long object oriented programs.

The `atm` class follows the same principles as the `account` class. There are three private fields: one for storing the code number read from the card inserted by the customer, one for the code number punched in by the customer, and an array of `account` classes. Note that class `account` is being used here as a new data type for the purpose of declaring a new variable.

For simplicity, we will assume the code number is the same as the account number, and that this account number is also the array index in the `Account` array.

The interface functions implement the operations necessary for running the ATM. There are functions for displaying the 'waiting for next customer' message, reading the code from the inserted card, checking the code with that punched in by the user, and displaying and processing the various operations requested by the user.

## 2.5 Summary

The features of C++ introduced in this chapter were:

- the fundamental data types `int`, `short`, `long`, `float`, `double`, and `char`;
- the `const` declaration;
- the syntax of a `class` definition;
- the keywords `private` and `public`.

The key concepts introduced were:

- class fields are divided into *properties* and *actions* (nouns and verbs);
- class fields are also divided into *private* and *public* fields;
- private fields are accessible only to class functions;
- public fields are accessible to any functions;
- data encapsulation groups all related aspects of a class together;
- data encapsulation insulates those fields from access by any function outside the class;
- interface functions provide the only means of access to private fields.

## 2.6 Exercises

### Review questions

1. What are the differences between the `int`, `short`, and `long` data types for representing integers?

2. What are the differences between the `float` and `double` data types for representing real numbers?

3. Why is the `const` declaration to be preferred to the `#define` method for defining a constant parameter?

4. What parts of a program have access to a `private` data field in a class?

5. What is the rationale for separating class fields into private and public sections?

6. What is *data encapsulation* and why is it useful?

7. Why might a private class *function* be useful?

8. What is the main role of an interface function?

## Problems

1. For each of the problems in Chapter 1 (concerning the television set, house, and supermarket), separate the fields you defined for each of your classes into private and public sets. Justify your choices.

2. Write C++ class definitions for the classes you identified in Chapter 1.

CHAPTER 3

# The elements of C++

## 3.1 Introduction

In Chapter 2 we began our study of C++ by looking at how it implements the class concept. We saw how to specify properties and actions of classes, and how to divide up the fields in a class into private and public members.

We cannot progress any further in a study of OOP, however, without seeing how we can make the C++ language actually do something for us. To that end, we now begin a survey of the commands and operators available in C++.

In this survey, we are assuming that you have already learned how to program in some procedural language such as Pascal or C. You should, therefore, be familiar with the basic concepts of procedural programming such as loops, conditional statements, functions, arithmetic and logical operators, and so on. We therefore will not treat these topics in great depth.

After we have introduced the elements of C++ commands and operators, we will apply them to flesh out the `atm` class introduced in Chapter 2.

## 3.2 Declarations, definitions, statements and functions

You have already met the basic data types used in C++ in Chapter 2. As mentioned there, all other data structures in C++ are built up from these fundamental types, although sometimes the breadth and depth of these compound structures may get so large it is hard to believe that they are all based on these few building blocks. You were also told in Chapter 2 that the design of any C++ program should begin with a description of the classes of which it will be composed. We must now consider how a functioning C++ program is to be constructed.

A properly constructed C++ program should consist primarily of class definitions, such as those given in Chapter 2, and associated code for the functions that are defined in these classes. If the object oriented philosophy of program design has been followed, virtually all of the functions in the program should be members of the classes. This will no doubt be something of a departure from the procedural programming techniques with which you may be familiar, where each function or procedure that you wrote was an independent entity, connected to other functions only through those parameters passed to it in its argument list.

### 3.2.1 Code organization

Before we consider how to declare and code functions that are members of classes, it is worth considering how such functions should be stored on disk.

If you have only written relatively small programs so far, you may have written the entire code for the program in a single file. At the beginning of the file will be any global data type and variable declarations, function declarations, and so on. Following this will be the individual functions making up your program. Putting everything in a single file like this has the advantage that it is easy to compile the program, since you only need to issue a single command. However, once your programs get beyond a certain length (usually more than about 40 or 50 lines), it becomes very difficult to keep track of everything if the entire program is written in a single disk file. Some guidelines for storing and managing large programming projects follow.

• Create a separate directory or subdirectory for each programming project. Separate declarations, data type definitions, function declarations, and so on, into an independent header file. This file should have suffix of .h. For example, the header file for the ATM model may be called `atm.h`. The header file is then included in all other files requiring the definitions that it contains, using the `#include` directive:

```
#include "atm.h"
```

• In larger projects, there will usually be more than one header file in which classes and functions are defined or declared. Some header files may even include other header files. Since C++ does not allow you to define a class or function more than once during compilation, you should take precautions to ensure that the same header file is not included more than once in any other file. The easiest way to do this is to use `#ifndef` and `#define` directives built in to C++. Begin every header file with the lines

```
#ifndef HEADER_FILE_LABEL
#define HEADER_FILE_LABEL
.... header file statements ....
#endif
```

For example, with the file `atm.h`, we should begin with the statements:

```
#ifndef ATM_H
#define ATM_H
```

and end with the `#endif` directive.

The `#ifndef HEADER_FILE_LABEL` statement means "if the symbol *HEADER_FILE_LABEL* is not defined, then continue with the next statement, otherwise, skip to the `#endif` statement". The `#define HEADER_FILE_LABEL` statement defines the symbol *HEADER_FILE_LABEL*, and then continues with the statement on the next line. The first time the `atm.h` header file is processed by the compiler, the symbol ATM_H will not be defined, so the statement #ifndef ATM_H will not cause the contents of the header file to be skipped. However, on the next line, the symbol ATM_H is defined, so that if the same file is included again later on, its contents will not be recompiled, thus avoiding any duplicate definition errors.

It is good programming practice to insert the #ifndef ... #define ... #endif statements in *all* header files, even if you know they are not included more than once in any of your code. In future expansion of your program, or if your header files are used in other programs later on, such multiple inclusion *could* occur, and by placing these statements in the file when you first design it, you are avoiding potential errors for all time.

• Write each function or group of related functions in a separate file. Give the file the same name as the function or as close as your operating system will allow. For example, if you are programming in Windows or MS-DOS, you are restricted to filenames with up to 8 characters in the prefix and 3 characters in the suffix, so you may need to condense a function name if it is longer than 8 characters in your C++ code.

• Use a *makefile* or a *project file* to manage the compilation of your code. If you are using a stand-alone C++ compiler that does not have its own project management facilities (such as the public domain g++ compiler popular on many UNIX systems), a makefile is the most convenient way of managing the project. The makefile specifies what files form part of your project, how they should be compiled and linked, and which files in your project depend on which other files. Once you have seen the outline of a typical makefile for one C++ project, it is easy to modify this file to serve in virtually any other project on the same computer system.

If you are using a professional C++ development package such as Borland C++ or Microsoft's Visual C++, you can make use of its project management facilities which handle the file dependencies and compilation options more or less automatically.

Whatever system you are using, you should consult the documentation (or ask your systems administrator) for more information on makefiles or project files.

All the code in this book was developed and tested using Borland's C++ compiler, version 4.0.

### 3.2.2 Declaring class functions

Recall from Chapter 2 the definition of the account class:

```
class account
{
private:
    float Balance;
```

```
      int AccountNumber;
public:
    BOOL Withdraw(float Amount);
    BOOL Deposit(float Amount);
    float CheckBalance();
    int CheckAccountNumber();
};
```

The functions in the public section of this class have been *declared* (the compiler is informed of their existence when it reads these lines) but not *defined* (the code for each function has not yet been written). The declaration of each function includes:

- The return value of the function. For example, the Withdraw() function returns a BOOL. For the most part, a function may return any data structure that has been defined in the context of the program: one of the built-in data types such as int or float, or one of the user-defined ones. A function may also return nothing at all, in which case it is declared as a void function.
- The *name* of the function.
- A list of *arguments* to the function. The Withdraw() function contains a single argument Amount, while the CheckBalance() function has no arguments. Note that, even if a function has no arguments at all, it is still necessary to include a pair of empty parentheses to indicate that it is a function.

The actual code for these functions will be written elsewhere. It may follow the class declarations in the same file, but it is more likely (and better practice) that the code for each function (or group of functions) is in a separate file. The syntax for defining a class function separately is:

```
return_datatype classname::function_name(arguments)
{
    statements
}
```

For example, the CheckBalance() function may be defined in a separate file as:

```
float account::CheckBalance()
{
    return Balance;
}
```

25

The notation tells the compiler that CheckBalance() is a member function of class account, and therefore has access to all fields of that class. The double-colon operator : : is a *scope resolution operator*; it relates a class field to the class of which it is a member.

We may therefore refer to any field from the class account without any further ado, as we do here when we refer to the Balance field. This function is particularly simple, in that all it does is return the value of Balance. We will develop the other functions in both the account and atm classes towards the end of this chapter.

### 3.2.3 Declarations and definitions

As stated earlier, all variables and functions must be *declared* before being used. However, they must also be *defined*. The distinction between the two terms is delicate, but important. Let us consider the difference as applied to functions first.

A function *declaration* is a description of the function containing its name, return type, and argument list (and, if they belong to a class, which class they belong to). For example, for a function which is not a field of a class, a declaration may be written as:

```
int intfunction(float floatarg, char chararg);
```

The body of the function, that is, the statements that are executed when the function is called, is not included in the declaration. It is understood by the compiler that the function body will be supplied elsewhere in the code, possibly later in the same file, or in another file. At this stage, the function is *declared*, but not yet *defined*. The definition of the function occurs when the actual statements it executes are encountered by the compiler.

Functions that form part of a class are declared when they are written as part of the class definition. Thus the functions listed in the account class above have been declared, since their name, return type, argument list, and owner class are all given, but the body of the function is located in a separate file.

It is possible to declare and define a function simultaneously. This may be done by simply giving the full function, including its body, when it is first encountered by the compiler. In fact, this is probably what you have done in the short procedural programs you have written up to now. However, in a language like C++, which is designed for writing large programs, it is a good idea to get used to separating the declaration and definition of your functions. Also, if a function is defined in one file and used (called by another function) in another file, the second file must include a declaration of the function being called. The best way to do this is to declare all your functions in a header file and #include this file in any other file that needs it.

It is also possible, though less common, to declare variables and define them in a separate place. The distinction between a declaration and a definition in the case of a variable is that a variable *declaration* only informs the compiler that the variable exists, without reserving any memory space for it, while the *definition* of the variable actually reserves the space. Separate declarations and definitions of variables should occur very rarely in C++, because the language's object oriented structure should mean that all your variables are encapsulated inside classes. The class defines a new data type, so that no memory is actually reserved by the compiler until a variable of that new data type is defined. Occasionally, however, you may find a use for a global variable (a variable that is accessible to every function in your program). A global variable must be known to all functions in all files in your program, so it is best to declare it in the header file that is included in all these other files. However, although the variable is accessible to all files, it should only be *defined* once, since we only wish to allocate memory for the variable once.

This can be accomplished by declaring the global variable in the header file using the `extern` keyword. The definition of the variable may then be placed, for example, in the file containing the `main()` function (the function with which all C++ programs begin execution; see next section), but *outside of any functions in that file*. For example, if we wish to declare a global variable `globvar`, we would include the line

```
extern int globvar;
```

in the header file, and write the file containing `main()` so that it has the form:

```
#include "header.h"
int globvar;

int main() {....}
```

The point of doing things this way is that the `extern` declaration in the header file informs the compiler that the variable `globvar` exists without actually allocating any memory for it. Since this header file is included in every other file in the project, every function is informed of the existence of this global variable. The actual definition of the variable occurs in the file containing `main()`, which is only processed once by the compiler, so that space is reserved only once.

As mentioned above, the object oriented structure of C++ should virtually eliminate the need for global variables, making them as obsolete as the dreaded `goto` statement, which you have no doubt been told to avoid like the proverbial plague. If you ever consider using a global variable (or even a variable that is not a member of class), you should give some serious thought as to whether your program structure is correct.

### 3.2.4 The `main()` function

There is one function that must be present in every C++ program, and which is not part of any class: the `main()` function.[4] The `main()` function is where every C++ program begins. Its syntax is:

```
int main()
{
  declarations

  statements
}
```

The purpose of the `main()` function (besides starting the program) should be to define the top-level objects in the program (as instances of the classes you defined in the header files), and then to run the main blocks of the program by calling the appropriate functions.

When writing a program containing several functions, it is a good idea to test each function as it is written. During program development, the `main()` function can be used to make test calls to the various class functions as you write them.

### 3.2.5 Example - filling out the ATM project

Let us illustrate the concepts of this section by applying them to the ATM program. First of all, we place the `const` definitions, data type definitions and class definitions in a file named `atm.h`:

```
#ifndef ATM_H
#define ATM_H
#include<iostream.h>

const int MAXACCOUNTS=10;
typedef int BOOL;
enum {FALSE, TRUE};

class account
{
```

---

[4] A common notation used in books on C and C++ to refer to functions in the main text is to give the function name followed by a pair of parentheses, as in `main()`. The parentheses serve solely to indicate that the object under consideration is a function and not a variable name or some other object. Although the function, when used in the C++ program itself, may have some arguments passed to it, these arguments are omitted when it is written in-line in the text of the book. Thus, when the `main()` function is used in a real program, it may have arguments such as `main(int argc, char **argv)`, but these are not included in the textual description.

```
private:
    float Balance;
    int AccountNumber;
public:
    BOOL Withdraw(float Amount);
    BOOL Deposit(float Amount);
    float CheckBalance();
    int CheckAccountNumber();
};

class atm
{
private:
    int EnteredCode;
    int CardCode;
    account Account[MAXACCOUNTS];
public:
    void DisplayWait();
    void ReadCard();
    BOOL CheckCode();
    void ProcessChoice();
};
#endif
```

This file contains the class definitions introduced earlier. It also contains (as its third line), a #include statement, which includes the system header file iostream.h. This file contains declarations of items necessary for input/output (I/O) routines for writing data to the screen and reading input from the keyboard. We shall need these routines when we get around to writing the class function definitions.

You will find that you will need to include various system files depending on what library functions you use in your programs. Practically every program will have need for I/O functions, however, so you will almost always need to include the iostream.h system file.

Next, we need to define the functions in each of the classes. First, we place the functions for the account class in a file named account.cpp[5]:

```
#include "atm.h"

BOOL account::Withdraw(float Amount)
{
    cout << "Withdraw called." << endl;
}

BOOL account::Deposit(float Amount)
```

---

[5] The actual suffix used for C++ source files depends on the compiler. The suffix .cpp used in this book is that required by the Borland compiler. Other compilers may expect your C++ source files to have a different suffix, such as .cc or .C. Check the documentation for your system.

```
{
    cout << "Deposit called." << endl;
}

float account::CheckBalance()
{
    cout << "CheckBalance called." << endl;
}

int account::CheckAccountNumber()
{
    cout << "CheckAccountNumber called." << endl;
}
```

Since we haven't covered enough C++ syntax to actually write the code for most of the functions yet, we have shown only skeleton versions of some of the functions to illustrate how they would be arranged in files apart from the header file atm.h. Each of these functions merely prints out a line indicating that it has been called. The line

```
    cout << "CheckBalance called." << endl;
```

for example, will print out the message CheckBalance called. followed by a carriage return on the screen. We will consider the input/output routines of C++ in more detail later; for now it would be better if you just accepted that these are output statements.

We have placed all four functions in the same file, since they logically belong together (they are all class functions of the account class), and they will not be very long once they are written out. If the total length of the functions in a file is less than around 50 lines, it is perfectly acceptable to keep them together in the same file. When functions or groups of functions exceed this length it is advisable to separate them into different files.

We can insert the functions for the atm class in a file named atm.cpp:

```
#include "atm.h"

void atm::DisplayWait()
{
    cout << "DisplayWait called." << endl;
}

void atm::ReadCard()
{
    cout << "ReadCard called." << endl;
}

BOOL atm::CheckCode()
{
```

```
        cout << "CheckCode called." << endl;
}

void atm::ProcessChoice()
{
    cout << "ProcessChoice called." << endl;
}
```

Finally, we would write a `main()` function and place it in the file `main.cpp`:

```
#include "atm.h"

void main()
{
    atm autobank;

    while(1) {
        autobank.DisplayWait();
        autobank.ReadCard();
        if (autobank.CheckCode())
            autobank.ProcessChoice();
        else
            cout << "You have entered the incorrect code.\n";
    }
}
```

We have jumped ahead a little here, in that a couple of C++ features (`while` and `if...else`) have been used before we have formally discussed them. However, you should recognize these language features from other programming languages you have studied. The `main()` function defines an *object* called `autobank` which is an instance of the class `atm`. The central `while` loop is actually an infinite loop (the statement `while(1)` says that the loop should continue as long as the expression in the parentheses is true; in C++, the numerical value 1 is always 'true'). The infinite loop ensures that the ATM is always available to customers.

The statements within the loop indicate how the various class functions are called. The first thing we want to do is display the "Welcome" message and wait for a customer to insert their card. The `atm` class function `DisplayWait()` is what will do this (once we write the code for it, that is), so that is the function that should be called first. The specific ATM object which should display the "Welcome" message is the one represented in the program by the `autobank` object, so we want that object to be the one that calls the `DisplayWait()` function. This is accomplished by the statement

```
autobank.DisplayWait();
```

The general syntax for a class function call is:

```
object.class_function(class_function_arguments);
```

where `class_function()` is a function in the same class as that to which `object` belongs.

The `DisplayWait()` function will return control to `main()` only when a card has been inserted into the ATM. At this point, the `ReadCard()` function is called, which waits for the customer to type in the code number. When this is done, the `if` statement compares the entered code with the code stored on the card itself, and returns a flag indicating whether or not the customer typed in the correct code. If so, the `ProcessChoice()` function is called, which will offer the customer a menu of choices. If not, an error message is printed, and the ATM returns to the waiting state by displaying the "Welcome" message again.

Our project at this point consists of four files:

1. `atm.h`: header file containing class definitions and other declarations and definitions.
2. `account.cpp`: C++ source code containing definitions of the `account` class functions.
3. `atm.cpp`: C++ source code containing definitions of the `atm` class functions.
4. `main.cpp`: C++ source code for the `main()` function.

The program as given above could actually be compiled and run, though the presence of the infinite loop in `main()` would cause an endless stream of messages from the various skeleton functions to be printed on the screen. We could comment out the `while` loop during this initial test of the program so that we can see whether one cycle of the loop is executed correctly.

The final stage of setting up the files should consist of writing a makefile or defining a project file to organize the compilation procedure. As explained earlier, this step depends on which compiler you are using.

It is good programming practice to get into the habit of testing your code as early in the development process as you can, and to continue testing it as each new function is added. Running the ATM program in its current state, for example, will test that classes have been properly defined in the header file, that the `#include` statements are in their proper places, that no duplicate declarations occur, and that the `main()` function is calling the correct class functions. If you can satisfy yourself that all this is working properly at this stage, you can proceed to writing the code for the class functions with a reasonable amount of confidence that the first stage of the program is correct.

## 3.3 Arithmetic operators

The standard operators are available in C++. For those of you familiar with C,
C++ includes all the C operators in the same form. They are:

- Assignment (=). The assignment operator assigns a value to a variable, as in
  the statement

```
sum = num1 + num2;
```

  which assigns the sum of num1 and num2 to the variable sum.

- Arithmetic operators (+, -, *, /) for addition, subtraction, multiplication
  and division, respectively. They operate on any form of integer or floating
  point variable or constant. The data type of the result returned by these
  operators is always the highest precision of that used in the operands. For
  example, if you add an int and a float, the sum will be a float. The
  usual caution about integer division applies here as well. An expression of
  the form *int/int* will return an *integer* quotient which is the greatest
  integer less than or equal to the actual quotient. In particular, in an
  expression like i/j, if i is smaller than j, the quotient will be zero.

- The modulus operator (%) when applied between two integers returns the
  remainder when the first integer is divided by the second. For example, 13
  % 2 returns 1, 53 % 7 returns 4, and so on.

- The increment and decrement operators (++, --). These are unary operators
  (operators that take only one argument instead of two). The ++ operator[6]
  increments the value of its argument by 1; the -- operator decrements the
  value of its argument by 1. Although these operators are frequently used in
  isolation, it is important to realize that besides affecting their operand, they
  also return a value. For example, if all you want to do is to increment the
  value of the variable num by 1, the stand-alone statements

```
num++;
```

  or

```
++num;
```

  will both suffice. The statements

```
othernum1 = num++;
```

---

[6] The ++ operator is, as you might have guessed, the origin of the name of the C++ language.
The original intent of C++ was as a 'better version of C', so the name C++ means 'an
increment on the C language'. This is an unfortunate name, since as this book attempts to
demonstrate, the approach to programming in the two languages is very different.

and

```
othernum2 = ++num;
```

are also valid C++ syntax. However, while the two statements num++ and ++num on their own both have the same effect, the two assignment statements just shown do *not*. The reason is that if the ++ operator comes *after* its operand, as in num++, the value returned is the value of num *before* the increment is applied. If the ++ operator comes *before* its operand, as in ++num, the increment is applied *first*, then the incremented value is returned. For example, consider the following set of statements:

```
num = 5;
othernum1 = num++;
othernum2 = ++num;
```

After these statements had executed, the value of num would be 7, the value of othernum1 would be 5, and the value of othernum2 would be 7.

- The -- operator works in a similar fashion.
- Many binary operators (operators requiring two operands) in C++ have a matching 'convenience' form when the return value from the operator is to be applied to one of the operands. For example, a statement like:

```
num = num + othernum;
```

is of this form because num is both one of the operands, and the variable to which the return value of the sum is to be assigned. Expressions such as this occur frequently in programming, and can be tedious to write, especially if the operand concerned is long. For this reason, C++ introduces convenience forms for any binary operator where this situation can arise. The above statement can be written as:

```
num += othernum;
```

Similarly, the expression

```
num = num - othernum;
```

can be written as
```
num -= othernum;
```

and so on.

## 3.4 Logical operators

The standard logical operators are:

- >, <, >=, <=, ==,!=, which stand for greater than, less than, greater than or equal to, less than or equal to, equal to, not equal to, respectively. All these operators are binary operators, requiring two operands. The operands may be any expressions evaluating to a standard data type such as integer, floating point, and so on. The value returned by any of these operators is either true or false (actually 1 or 0), and is usually used in a conditional statement (see next section). Note in particular that the logical operator for testing equality is a *double* equal sign (==), *not* a single equal sign. This is a common mistake, even among experienced C++ programmers, and can have disastrous consequences, as we will see in the next section.
- Other logical operations supported are the *not* operation, logical *or* and *and*, represented by the operators !, | |, and &&, respectively. The ! operator is unary, returning false if the expression to which it is applied is true, and true if the expression is false. For example, the expression

```
!(x > y)
```

will return true if x is not greater than y. It is equivalent to the expression

```
x <= y
```

The | | and && operators are binary. The | | operator returns true if either of its operands is true, while the && operator returns true only if *both* its operands are true.

## 3.5 Conditional expressions

A conditional expression is one where a choice must be made to determine what statement is to be executed next. The standard if-else statement is the prototype of a conditional statement, but there are several other forms available in C++.

### 3.5.1 The **if** statement

The if statement has the form:

```
if (condition)
    single_statement
```
or
```
if (condition)
{
    block_of_statements
```

```
}
```

Note a few things about this statement. The *condition* *must* be enclosed in parentheses. The condition itself can be any constant or expression. A condition is true if it is non-zero, false if it is zero. Any of the logical operators in the last section can be used as a condition, but any other expression can also be used. For example, the expressions

```
if (x > y) ...
if (x) ...
if (++x) ...
if (x++) ...
if ((x % y) + 7) ...
```

are all legal `if` statements. In fact, a useful form of the condition is to use an assignment as the expression being tested, as in

```
if ((x = y+z) > 0) ...
```

To understand what this statement is doing, you need to remember that the assignment operator (=) returns the value assigned. In this `if` statement then, the sequence of operations is as follows:

1. The assignment $x = y+z$ is carried out, returning the value assigned to x.
2. The new value of $x$ is compared with the constant 0, and, if it is greater than 0, the condition is true.

It is important to realize that *the assignment statement is executed whether or not the resulting comparison is true or false.*

It is worth pointing out another subtle error that is possible at this point. Although using an assignment statement as a conditional expression can be convenient, you must be sure this is really what you mean to do, and not an equality test instead. For example, if you wanted to insert a condition testing if $x$ is equal to $y$, you might write by accident:

```
if (x = y) ...
```

instead of

```
if (x == y) ...
```

Beware that both of these statements are syntactically correct in C++, but they have very different effects. The first statement will assign the value of $y$ to $x$ and then use the new value of $x$ as the condition. It will therefore be false only if x has just been assigned the value 0. The second statement simply compares the values of x and y, and will return true if they are the same.

### 3.5.2 The `if-else` statement

The `if` statement can be extended to cope with multiple choices by adding one or more `else` clauses. The general syntax is:

```
if (condition1) {
    statements
} else if (condition2) {
    more_statements
} else if (condition3) {
    even_more_statements
} else {
    final_set_of_statements
}
```

The number of `else if` blocks is arbitrary, but there can be at most one `else` (without an associated `if`) block at the end. The program will check each condition in the order it is given in the code, and execute the statements corresponding to the first condition that evaluates to true. Note that if more than one condition is true, only the statements corresponding to the first true condition will be executed. The final set of statements corresponding to the `else` block at the end will be executed only if all the preceding conditions are false.

### 3.5.3 The `switch` statement

If you have a long series of conditions to check, a large block of `if..else` statements can get tiresome and confusing to write (and read, later on). For this reason, C++ provides the `switch` statement. The general syntax is:

```
switch (expression) {
case value1:
   statements
   [break;]
case value2:
   statements
   [break;]
....
default:
   statements
}
```

An expression is evaluated in the first line of a switch statement, and its value is used to determine the action or actions to take. The value of the expression is compared in turn with each value listed next to a `case` statement. If a match occurs, the statements following that `case` statement are executed. The break statement (shown in square brackets to indicate that it is optional; the square brackets are not actually part of the code), if present, causes the switch statement to be terminated after the statements in the current case block are executed. That is, control will pass to the statement immediately after the final brace ending the switch statement without any further case statements being tested. If the break statement is *not* present, the next case statement will be checked as well. In other words, a switch statement offers greater flexibility that an if..else statement in that it allows more than one block of statements to be executed. For example:

```
switch (number) {
case 0:
    number++;
    break;
case 1:
    number += 5;
case 2:
    number--;
    break;
default:
    number *= 2;
    break;
}
```

If number is 0, only the number++ statement in the case 0 block will be executed before the break is encountered, which terminates the switch statement. If number is 1, the statement number += 5 under the case 1 block will be executed, but because there is no break statement following this, execution will continue with the statements in the case 2 block. Thus, if number has the value 1 upon entry to the switch statement, it will have the value 1+5–1 = 5 upon exit. If number has the value 2 on entry, only the number-- statement will be executed before a break is encountered. Finally, any other value for number will result in the default block being executed.

A common error in using switch statements is omitting a break in a case block. As with so many features in C++, the presence or absence of a break will not be detected by the compiler, since both are correct syntactically. However, if you omit a break, you must remember that not only the code for that particular case block will be executed, but all code in all succeeding case blocks until a break is encountered. It is good programming practice to place a break after the statements in the default block as well, even if it is the last block in the switch statement, because you might add more blocks to the switch statement in a new version of the program.

### 3.5.4 The conditional operator ? :

Because the conditional operation `if(expression)` `result1` `else` `result2` is so common in programs, C++ provides a special operator for this case. The operator is unusual in that it is a *ternary* operator (it takes three operands). The syntax is:

```
condition ? expression1 : expression2
```

The initial condition is any expression or constant that evaluates to a quantity that can be taken as true or false. If the condition is true, the value of `expression1` is returned by the operator, otherwise, `expression2` is returned.

The conditional operator may be used to return the maximum of two numbers a and b:

```
maxnum = (a > b) ? a : b;
```

## 3.6 Loops

C++ provides three loop structures: `for`, `while`, and `do..while`.

### 3.6.1 The `while` loop

The `while` loop is the simplest looping construct in C++. Its syntax is:

```
while (expression) {
   statements
}
```

If there is only a single statement in the body of the loop, it is permissible to omit the braces:

```
while (expression)
   single_statement
```

The loop will continue executing the statements in its body until the expression evaluates to false or zero. An alternative way of breaking out of a `while` loop is to use the `break` statement somewhere in the loop's body. This will cause an immediate transfer of control to the statement immediately following the loop.

For example, the following loop calculates the sum of the numbers from 1 to 100:

```
int number = 1;
int sum = 0;
while(number <= 100) {
   sum += number;
```

```
   number++;
}
```

An alternative method of calculating the same sum using only a single statement in the loop is:

```
int number = 1;
int sum = 0;
while (number <= 100)
   sum += number++;
```

Recall that the ++ operator increments the value of number *after* its value has been added to sum, because the ++ operator was placed *after* its operand.

### 3.6.2 The do..while loop

In a while loop, the expression being used as the termination condition for the loop is always evaluated *before* the loop body is executed. In some cases, it is more convenient to do the test after the execution of the loop body. C++ provides the do..while construct for this purpose. Its syntax is:

```
do {
   statements
} while (expression);
```

The loop for summing the numbers from 1 to 100 can be written in this form as follows:

```
int number = 1;
int sum = 0;
do {
   sum += number;
   number++;
} while (number <= 100);
```

As with the while statement, if the body of the loop consists of a single statement, the enclosing braces are not necessary. The above example can therefore be rewritten as:

```
int number = 1;
int sum = 0;
do
   sum += number;
while (++number <= 100);
```

Note that this time we have applied the ++ operator *before* its operand, so that number is incremented *before* being compared with the constant 100.

### 3.6.3 The comma operator

This is an appropriate place to introduce the C++ comma operator, since it is most frequently used in loop control statements. The comma is a binary operator in C++, with the syntax:

```
statement1 , statement2
```

Its effect is to execute `statement1`, followed by `statement2`, and to return whatever value is returned by `statement2`. The returned value from `statement1` is simply discarded. Using the comma operator, we may write the sum routine as follows:[7]

```
int number = 1;
int sum = 0;
while(sum += number, ++number <= 100);
```

A caution to Pascal programmers is in order at this point. If you are used to writing two-dimensional arrays in Pascal as `arr[i,j]` beware that this same syntax is legal C++, but it does *not* describe an element from a two-dimensional array. It is a good exercise for the reader to work out just what this notation does describe in C++, though you may have to wait a few minutes until we get to the section describing arrays in C++.

### 3.6.4 The `for` loop

The final looping structure available in C++ is also the most powerful. The syntax of the `for` statement is:

```
for (expression1; expression2; expression3) {
    statements
}
```

The expression `expression1` is an *initialization* expression. It is executed only once for any loop: the first time the `for` statement is encountered. The expression `expression2` is the *termination test*. It is checked on every iteration through the loop and, as long as it remains true, the loop continues. It is also checked *before* the first iteration of the loop is done, so if `expression2` is false at the beginning of the loop, the statements within the body of the loop are never executed. The expression `expression2` is executed after each iteration of the loop.

The sum routine can be written as a `for` statement:

---

[7] The existence of such operators as the comma operator and the ternary conditional operator leads me to believe that it is possible to write any C++ program as a single statement, if you are clever enough. However, a certain amount of clarity in programming style would be sacrificed in doing so, so I don't recommend it.

```
int number;
int sum = 0;
for(number = 1; number <= 100; number++)
  sum += number;
```

We can use the comma operator to combine the initializations of `number` and `sum`:

```
int number;
int sum;
for(sum = 0, number = 1; number <= 100; number++)
  sum += number;
```

In fact, we can use the comma operator to eliminate the body of the loop entirely, although this is probably getting a bit silly:

```
int number;
int sum;
for(sum = 0, number = 1;
    number <= 100; sum += number, number++);
```

As you can see from these examples, there are many ways in which loops can be written in C++. To a certain extent, how you do it is a matter of personal taste and style, but whatever you prefer to do, make sure it does not sacrifice the clarity of the program. For example, a good guideline is that the first expression in a `for` loop should contain *only* statements that directly pertain to initializing variables to be used in the loop body, the second expression should contain *only* statements that directly pertain to the termination condition of the loop, and the third expression should contain *only* statements that alter those variables used in the termination condition given in the second expression. From this standpoint, the second to last example given above is acceptable, since both `sum` and `number` are initialized in the first expression, the second expression contains only the termination check (`number <= 100`), and the third expression contains only the alteration to `number` which will eventually cause the termination condition to become false. The last example, in which the statement `sum += number` is added to the third expression, is not good programming style, because `sum` is not used in the termination check and therefore should not occur in the third expression.

## 3.7 Arrays

C and C++ are both fairly primitive in their handling of arrays. One-dimensional arrays are fairly easy to use, but two and higher dimensional arrays can cause problems. Fortunately, for the most part, we only need one dimensional arrays in this book.

### 3.7.1 One-dimensional arrays

Arrays may be declared for any data type, either built-in or user-defined. We will illustrate arrays with the `int` data type, but the examples all generalize directly to any data type.

An array is declared by a statement like:

```
int IntArray[100];
```

which declares an array of 100 `int`s. When the compiler encounters this declaration, it reserves a *contiguous* block of memory sufficiently large to store 100 integers.

One peculiarity of C++ arrays is that the first element *always* has an index of 0, and the last element an index of one less than the size of the array. Thus for the array declared above, the first element would be referenced with the notation `IntArray[0]`, and the last by `IntArray[99]`. This contrasts with other languages such as Pascal and Fortran, where the range of indexes used by an array may be explicitly specified in the declaration. In Pascal, for example, an array of 100 elements may begin with the index 50 and end with the index 149.

The reason for the seemingly perverse array notation in C++ is that C++ treats an array as a *pointer* with an associated *offset*. That is, the name of the array (`IntArray` above) on its own (without any [ ...] following it) represents a pointer to the *first* element of the array. The index of the array indicates how many elements along from the pointer you are referring to. Thus the notation `IntArray[0]` means that you go to the location pointed to by the pointer `IntArray`, and then move 0 elements along from it; in other words, you access the element to which `IntArray` points, which is the first element in the array. The second element in the array is one element along from the first one, so if you start at the location pointed to by `IntArray`, you need to move along one element to reach the second element: that is, an offset of 1 element from the starting point. This is written as `IntArray[1]`. In general, to access the $n$th element in the array requires an offset of $n-1$ elements from the initial pointer.[8]

The fact that the name of an array is also a pointer to the first element in the array allows some flexibility in the method by which array elements can be referenced. In standard C++ syntax, if a variable such as `IntPointer` is a pointer to an `int`, the data stored at the location to which `IntPointer` points can be accessed using the notation `*IntPointer`. That is, the contents

---

[8] Arrays in other languages such as Pascal work the same way, of course, but these other languages provide an interface which allows arbitrary index ranges to be mapped down to the 0 to $n-1$ range in which all arrays are represented.

of a pointer variable can be accessed by prefixing the variable name with an asterisk (known as the *dereferencing* operator in this context).

Applying this to the array `IntArray[]` above, an alternative way of referring to the first element of the array is then `*IntArray`. C++ allows limited arithmetic to be done on pointers, so that the second element in the array can be referenced by the expression `*(IntArray + 1)`, and the *n*th element by the expression `*(IntArray + n - 1)`. In this way, for example, a routine to add up all the elements in an array might be written:

```
int sum = 0;
for (int i = 0; i < 100; i++)
   sum += *(IntArray + i);
```

Which notation you use is up to you, though the more traditional notation of `IntArray[i]` is more common, and easier to read. In some cases, however, the explicit pointer representation makes more sense, so you should be aware of it.

### 3.7.2 Two-dimensional arrays

A two-dimensional array in C++ is implemented by constructing an array of one-dimensional arrays. The syntax for declaring a two-dimensional array is

```
data_type array_name[dimension1][dimension2];
```

For example, a 2 by 4 array of `int`s is declared as:

```
int IntArray[2][4];
```

Note that it is *not* correct to declare a two-dimensional array using the notation `int IntArray[2,4]`. Recall from section 3.6.3 that the comma is a binary operator in C++ which has the effect of evaluating its first argument, discarding the result, and then evaluating and returning its second argument. This declaration would therefore have the effect of declaring a *one-dimensional* array with 4 elements.

Two-dimensional arrays may be used in the normal way in a C++ program. For example, to add up all the elements in `IntArray`, you could write:

```
for(i = 0; i < 2; i++)
   for(j = 0; j < 4; j++)
      sum += IntArray[i][j];
```

Since two-dimensional arrays are implemented as arrays of one-dimensional arrays, though, we could also write:

```
for(i = 0; i < 2; i++)
  for(j = 0; j < 4; j++)
    sum += *(IntArray[i] + j);
```

though this is not as clear as the first method.

If you plan on using two-dimensional arrays extensively in C++, you should consult a reference text on the C++ language, since there are several finer points about the use of such arrays that we will not cover here.

## 3.8 Comments

Comments are an essential part of good programming style. There are two ways of writing comments in C++ code:

1. A comment of any length (over several lines, if desired) may be defined by enclosing a block of text between the strings /* and */. For example:

```
/* The following statements sum the integers
   from 1 to 100
*/
for(sum = 0, i = 1; i < 100; i++)
  sum += i;
```

2. The double slash // indicates that all characters following it on the same line are to be regarded as a comment. The double slash cannot be used to indicate a comment of more than one line in length. For example:

```
// Sums integers from 1 to 100
for(sum = 0, i = 1; i < 100; i++)
  sum += i;
```

Getting the content and quantity of comments right is something of an art form, and is to a large extent a matter of personal taste. The need for comments within functions can be reduced or even eliminated if sensible names are used for variables and classes, and code is written in a neat, ordered fashion (proper indentation of loops and conditional statements, blank lines between logical sections of the code, and so on). A good guide is to provide a line or two of comments at the beginning of each function definition, and to comment each variable declaration and class definition if their purposes are not obvious from the variable names used. If any complex or obscure algorithm is used, this should be explained with comments as well.

Putting in too many comments can be almost as annoying as not including enough comments. Don't comment lines whose function is obvious or trivial, and try to condense comments so that they occur only in key places in the code.

## 3.9 Input and output

Although standard C++ at the time of writing (1995) does not come with many built-in classes, it does have a powerful suite of routines for input and output. We will mention only the basics in this section, and leave some of the more powerful features to later chapters.

If you have done any programming in C, you will be familiar with the library functions `printf()` and `scanf()` for output and input, respectively. Although these functions may also be used in C++, it is advisable to use the *stream* classes provided with C++ instead, as they provide much more flexible and powerful features.

At its simplest level, data may be read from the keyboard using the standard input stream `cin` and the operator >>, and written to the screen using the standard output stream `cout` and the operator <<. For example:

```
#include <iostream.h>
int IntNum;
float FloatNum;

cout << "Enter an integer and a float: ";
cin >> IntNum >> FloatNum;
cout << "You entered " << IntNum << " and "
  << FloatNum << endl;
```

Note that you must `#include` the system header file `iostream.h` to use these stream classes.

The first statement after the declarations prints the string

```
Enter an integer and a float:
```

on the screen. The next statement reads an integer from the keyboard, assigns it to the variable `IntNum`, then reads a float and assigns it to the variable `FloatNum`. The final output statement prints these two variables, along with some explanatory text, onto the screen. The final item (`endl`) printed is a carriage return (which may also be written as `"\n"`).

No special formatting is required for either input or output: the stream operators << and >> take care of this for you, at least for the built-in data types in C++. If you want to read in or print out objects from your own classes, the unmodified << and >> operators will not do it. However, it is possible to *overload* these (and indeed, almost all) operators so that they can handle any data type. More on this in a later chapter.

Users of `printf()` and `scanf()` in C will know that these functions allow you to specify elaborate formatting for data. You can print out strings and numbers in neatly formatted columns, set numbers of digits, and so on. There are a great many library functions that allow you to format data with the C++ stream classes as well. We will not have any need for these formatting features in this book, so if you have an overwhelming desire to produce fancy output, you should consult a reference book on C++ which contains information on the iostream libraries.

## 3.10 Example: the ATM class functions

We will now illustrate some of the concepts introduced in this chapter by fleshing out the class functions declared in the account and atm classes earlier. Recall that we had completed the header file atm.h and had written skeleton versions for all the class functions. We now need to consider what these functions look like. We shall begin by examining the functions in the account class.

### 3.10.1 The account class functions

The withdrawal function must test that the balance is sufficient before carrying on with the withdrawal. The function is as follows:

```
BOOL account::Withdraw(float Amount)
{
   if (Balance >= Amount) {
     Balance -= Amount;
     return TRUE;
   } else {
     return FALSE;
   }
}
```

We test that the Balance in the account is sufficient for the requested withdrawal. If so, we subtract the requested Amount from the Balance and return the value TRUE to indicate that the function succeeded in making a withdrawal. If insufficient funds are present, we return FALSE immediately. Note that we have not included any error message if the withdrawal failed: this is the job of whatever routine calls this function.

The Deposit operation is:

```
BOOL account::Deposit(float Amount)
{
   Balance += Amount;
   return TRUE;
}
```

Since it is impossible (from both the bank's and the customer's point of view) for an account to contain too much money, no test on the balance is included here. However, the function is defined as returning a Boolean value to allow for some future error test to be included, if desired.

The function that checks the balance in the account is very simple:

```
float account::CheckBalance()
{
    return Balance;
}
```

In this case, the return value is a float, since the balance is a floating point number such as 255.34, indicating a balance of £255.34.

Finally, a function to return the account number:

```
int account::CheckAccountNumber()
{
    return AccountNumber;
}
```

This function is used in verifying the code entered by the customer.

You may complain that the last two functions are unnecessary since all they do is return a single value, without doing any tests or calculations. It may seem a lot easier if we just made the Balance and AccountNumber fields public so we could access them directly, rather than having to define special interface functions as we have done. However, as we mentioned earlier, allowing data fields to be public violates the object oriented philosophy: the data fields should be private, with access to them allowed only through interface functions. After all, if Balance, say, were public, then any external function could alter it; not a good idea from the customer's point of view!

## 3.10.2 The atm class functions

We now consider the actions of the atm class. The first action an ATM will perform is to display its invitation to the customer to insert a card. The function looks like this:

```
void atm::DisplayWait()
{
    char card='\0';

    while (card != 'c') {
        cout << "Please insert your card.\n";
        cout << "Testing: enter 'c' and hit return"
        cin >> card;
    }
    cout << "Please enter code on card: ";
    cin >> CardCode;
}
```

In a real ATM, you must actually insert a plastic card into a slot and wait for the machine to read your personal code from the magnetic strip on the back of the card. Since you are attempting to simulate this operation on an ordinary desktop computer, you obviously cannot actually insert a card into the machine. This function simulates the insertion of a card by asking the user to type the letter c into the terminal.

The next thing that needs to be done after inserting the card is to read the code number from the back of the card. Since you aren't actually inserting a card into the computer, we will have to fake this operation too. We will simulate the reading of the code by asking the user to type in a code number and take that number as that read from the card.

At this point in a real ATM transaction, the machine would have loaded your card and read the code number from it. The ATM would now ask you to enter your code using the numeric keypad. This is something we *can* simulate directly with our program, so we have the next function ask the user for the code:

```
void atm::ReadCard()
{
   cout << "Please enter your personal code: ";
   cin >> EnteredCode;
}
```

Admittedly, it would be pretty difficult for the user to get the code wrong in our simulation, since they just had to enter the code that was 'stored' on the back of the card before having to enter the same code number again. However, in the absence of a real ATM on which to run our program, this is the best we can do.

Now that we have both the card's code number and that punched in by the user, we must compare them to ensure that the user is to be allowed access to the account. The function is:

```
BOOL atm::CheckCode()
{
   return EnteredCode == CardCode ? TRUE : FALSE;
}
```

Here we have used the ternary conditional operator to test that the codes are the same. The Boolean value returned is TRUE if the codes match and FALSE if they don't.

Assuming that the codes match, we now want to present the user with a menu so that they may choose which action to perform on the account. The function for this is:

```
void atm::ProcessChoice()
{
```

```cpp
int choice;
float amount;

do {
  cout << "Select an option:\n";
  cout << "Withdraw cash -- Press 1\n";
  cout << "Deposit cash  -- Press 2\n";
  cout << "Check balance -- Press 3\n";
  cout << "Quit          -- Press 0\n";
  cin >> choice;
  if (choice < 0 || choice > 3)
    cout << "Invalid choice. Try again.\n";
} while (choice < 0 || choice > 3);
switch (choice) {
case 0:
  return;
case 1:
  cout << "Enter amount to withdraw: ";
  cin >> amount;
  if (Account[CardCode].Withdraw(amount))
    cout << "Transaction successful.\n";
  else
    cout << "Balance insufficient for withdrawal.\n";
  break;
case 2:
  cout << "Enter amount to deposit: ";
  cin >> amount;
  if (Account[CardCode].Deposit(amount))
    cout << "Transaction successful.\n";
  else
    cout << "Transaction unsuccessful.\n";
  break;
case 3:
  cout << "Current balance of account is: ";
  cout << Account[CardCode].CheckBalance() << endl;
  break;
  }
}
```

The menu is printed on the screen and the user is asked to enter an integer to specify a choice. A switch statement is used to choose the correct action for the selection. It is here that the various functions from the account class are called. Notice the syntax that is used. The CardCode is used as the account number (this is not, of course, what is done in a real ATM, but it will serve our purpose here). The account number is also the index in the Account array. Since each element of this array is a variable of data type account, we can call the functions from the account class for each of these array elements. The syntax for calling a class function is:

*variable_name.function_name(function_arguments)*

For example, if the customer wishes to withdraw cash from the account, the routine above requests an amount, and the `Withdraw` function from the account class is called for the account by the statement:

```
Account[CardCode].Withdraw(amount);
```

Here, the variable name is `Account[CardCode]`, the function name is `Withdraw`, which is a member of the class of which the variable `Account[CardCode]` is an instance, and the function argument is `amount`. The `Withdraw` function is called and applied to the particular instance of the account class which calls it. In other words, this call will attempt to withdraw the amount specified from the account with account number `CardCode`. The other cases work in a similar fashion.

It is important to realize the hierarchy inherent in this type of notation. In a procedural language such as Pascal or C, the function assumes primary importance, and the variables on which it operates assume secondary roles. For example, in a procedural language you would probably pass the account number as an argument to the `Withdraw` function along with the amount to be withdrawn, as in `Withdraw(CardCode, amount)`. In the object oriented approach, however, the *object* (the account) assumes the primary role and the *action* (the `Withdraw` function) assumes a secondary role. The notation reinforces this ordering: the `Withdraw` function is written as a component of the account, rather than the account being written as an argument passed to the `Withdraw` function.

### 3.10.3 Putting it all together

We have now filled in all the code for the class functions, so for completeness we will show you how the entire program looks when all the parts are put together. We will store the code in four files: the header file `atm.h` for the class definitions, a file `account.cpp` for the `account` class function definitions, a file `atm.cpp` for the `atm` class definitions, and a file `main.cpp` for the main function, which we have already written earlier.

The header file `atm.h` is:

```
#ifndef ATM_H
#define ATM_H
#include<iostream.h>

const int MAXACCOUNTS=10;
typedef int BOOL;
enum {FALSE, TRUE};

class account
{
private:
```

```
        float Balance;
        int AccountNumber;
    public:
        BOOL Withdraw(float Amount);
        BOOL Deposit(float Amount);
        float CheckBalance();
        int CheckAccountNumber();
    };

    class atm
    {
    private:
        int EnteredCode;
        int CardCode;
        account Account[MAXACCOUNTS];
    public:
        void DisplayWait();
        void ReadCard();
        BOOL CheckCode();
        void ProcessChoice();
    };
    #endif
```

The file `account.cpp`:

```
    #include "atm.h"

    BOOL account::Withdraw(float Amount)
    {
      if (Balance >= Amount) {
        Balance -= Amount;
        return TRUE;
      } else {
        return FALSE;
      }
    }

    BOOL account::Deposit(float Amount)
    {
      Balance += Amount;
      return TRUE;
    }

    float account::CheckBalance()
    {
      return Balance;
    }

    int account::CheckAccountNumber()
    {
      return AccountNumber;
    }
```

The file atm.cpp:

```cpp
#include "atm.h"

void atm::DisplayWait()
{
  char card='\0';

  while (card != 'c') {
    cout << "Please insert your card.\n";
    cout << "Testing: enter 'c' and hit return"
    cin >> card;
  }
  cout << "Please enter code on card: ";
  cin >> CardCode;
}


void atm::ReadCard()
{
  cout << "Please enter your personal code: ";
  cin >> EnteredCode;
}

BOOL atm::CheckCode()
{
  return EnteredCode == CardCode ? TRUE : FALSE;
}

void atm::ProcessChoice()
{
  int choice;
  float amount;

  do {
    cout << "Select an option:\n";
    cout << "Withdraw cash -- Press 1\n";
    cout << "Deposit cash  -- Press 2\n";
    cout << "Check balance -- Press 3\n";
    cout << "Quit          -- Press 0\n";
    cin >> choice;
    if (choice < 0 || choice > 3)
      cout << "Invalid choice. Try again.\n";
  } while (choice < 0 || choice > 3);
  switch (choice) {
  case 0:
    return;
  case 1:
    cout << "Enter amount to withdraw: ";
    cin >> amount;
    if (Account[CardCode].Withdraw(amount))
      cout << "Transaction successful.\n";
    else
```

```
          cout << "Balance insufficient for withdrawal.\n";
        break;
      case 2:
        cout << "Enter amount to deposit: ";
        cin >> amount;
        if (Account[CardCode].Deposit(amount))
          cout << "Transaction successful.\n";
        else
          cout << "Transaction unsuccessful.\n";
        break;
      case 3:
        cout << "Current balance of account is: ";
        cout << Account[CardCode].CheckBalance() << endl;
        break;
      }
  }
```

Finally, the file main.cpp:

```
#include "atm.h"

int main()
{
  atm autobank;

  while(1) {
    autobank.DisplayWait();
    autobank.ReadCard();
    if (autobank.CheckCode())
      autobank.ProcessChoice();
    else
      cout << "You have entered the incorrect
        code.\n";
  }
}
```

   This program presents the outline of an ATM model. There are still a few important aspects missing from it. For example, the balance in each account managed by the ATM is not initialized when autobank is defined. Some compilers initialize all data fields to zero automatically, others simply reserve the space for the variable and do not check to see what is stored in that space. As a result, if you run this program on your own computer, you may get some rather curious behaviour unless you insert an initialization statement somewhere. This would be easy enough to do by defining another action in the atm class which is called as the first statement in main(). However, because initialization is such a common requirement for a newly defined variable, C++ provides a special mechanism, called a *constructor function*, for doing this. We will consider constructor functions in Chapter 4.

## 3.11 Summary

The concepts introduced in this chapter were:

- Code should be organized so that class definitions are in header files, and each function or related group of functions is in its own file.
- Header files should always be bracketed with `#ifndef` ... `#define` ... `#endif` statements.
- *Declaring* a function or variable informs the compiler of its existence; *defining* the function provides the code for it; defining a variable reserves space for it.
- All C++ programs begin with the `main()` function.
- The standard arithmetic and logical operators are provided in C++.
- C++ provides the `if`, `else if`, `else`, `switch`, and `?:` features for dealing with conditional statements.
- C++ provides `while`, `do...while`, and `for` loops.
- The comma operator executes two statements and returns the value of the second one.
- C++ arrays are available in one- and two-dimensional forms. The array index always begins at 0. Arrays are treated as a pointer with an offset.
- C++ comments use either the `/* ... */` notation or the `//` notation.
- Simple input and output can be implemented using `cin` and `cout`, together with the `<<` and `>>` operators.

## 3.12 Exercises

1. Consider the three C++ variables declared as:

```
int num1, num2, num3;
```

a. What value does `num3` have after the statements:

```
num1 = 6;
num2 = 13;
num3 = num2 / num1;
```

b. What value does `num3` have after the statements:

```
num1 = 6;
num2 = 13;
num3 = num1 / num2;
```

c. What value does `num3` have after the statements:

```
num1 = 6;
num2 = 13;
num3 = num1 % num2;
```

d. What value does num3 have after the statements:

```
num1 = 6;
num2 = 13;
num3 = num2 % num1;
```

2. Assuming all variables are ints, answer the following:

a. What value does othernum have after the statements:

```
num = 10;
othernum = num++;
```

b. What value does num have after the statements:

```
num = 10;
othernum = ++num;
```

c. What value does thirdnum have after the statements:

```
num = 10;
thirdnum = (othernum = --num);
```

d. What value does thirdnum have after the statements:

```
num = 10;
thirdnum = (othernum = --num);
fourthnum = (thirdnum += othernum++);
```

e. What value does fourthnum have after the statements:

```
num = 10;
thirdnum = (othernum = --num);
fourthnum = (thirdnum += othernum++);
```

f. What value does othernum have after the statements:

```
num = 10;
thirdnum = (othernum = --num);
fourthnum = (thirdnum += othernum++);
```

3. Assume all variables are ints and answer the following:

a. What is the value of othernum after the statements:

```
num1 = 5;
num2 = 15;
othernum = (num1 *= (++num2));
othernum /= (num2 -= 10);
```

b. What is the value of othernum after the statements:

```
num1 = 5;
num2 = 15;
othernum = (num1 *= num2++);
othernum /= (num2 -= 10);
```

c. What is the value of othernum after the statements:

```
num1 = 5;
num2 = 15;
othernum = (num1 *= num2++);
othernum %= (num2 %= 10);
```

4. After the statements:

```
num1 = 10;
num2 = 20;
if (num2 > num1 && !num1)
    num3 = num1 + num2;
else if (!(num2 - 2*num1))
    num3 = num1 - num2;
```

what is the value of num3?

5. After the statements:

```
num1 = 10;
num2 = 20;
num3 = 0;
if (num2 = num1)
    num3 = num1 + num2
```

what is the value of num3?

6. After the statements:

```
num1 = 10;
num2 = 20;
num3 = 0;
```

```
if((num2 = 3*num1) < 0)
   num3 = num1 + num2
```

what is the value of num2?

7. After the statements:

```
num1 = 10;
num2 = 20;
num3 = 0;
if((num2 = 3*num1) < 0)
   num3 = num1 + num2
```

what is the value of num3?

8. After the statements:

```
num1 = 10;
num2 = 20;
num3 = 0;
if(num1 == num2 && num1 = num2)
   num3 = num1 + num2
```

what is the value of num1?

9. After the statements:

```
num1 = 10;
num2 = 20;
num3 = 0;
if(num1 = num2 && num1 == num2)
   num3 = num1 + num2
```

what are the values of num1 and num3?

10. After the statements:

```
num1 = 10;
num2 = 20;
num3 = 0;
if(num1 == num2 || num1 = num2)
   num3 = num1 + num2
```

what are the values of num1 and num3?

11. After the code:

```
cin >> num1;
num2 = 20;
num3 = 30;
switch(num1) {
case 1:
   num3 = num1 + num2;
   break;
case 2:
   num3 = num1 + 2*num2;
case 3:
   num2 -= num1;
   num3 = num1 + 4*num2;
case 4:
   num2 += num3;
   num3 = num1 + 5*num2;
   break;
default:
   num3 = 0;
   break;
}
```

find the values of num2 and num3 if num1 is (a) 1; (b) 2; (c) 4; (d) 5.

12. Consider the statements:

```
cin >> num1;
num2 = 20;
num3 = (2*num1 == num2) ? num1 + num2 : num1 - num2;
```

what is the value of num3 if num1 is (i) 10; (ii) 60?

13. Consider the nested conditional operator statement:

```
num1 = (num2 >= num3+num4) ?
   (num3 > num4 ? num4 : num3)
   : (num2 > 2*num3+num4 ? num2 : 2*num2);
```

a. What value is num1 if num2, num3, and num4 are all set to 1?
b. What value is num1 if num2 is 1, num3 is –1, and num4 is 2?
c. What value is num1 if num2 is –2, num3 is –2, and num4 is 1?

14. Consider the following loop:

```
int num1 = 2;
int result = 0;
while(num1 <= 10) {
   result += num1;
   num1 += 2;
}
```

What are the values of result and num1 after the loop finishes?

15. The following loop is proposed to provide a shorter version of the loop in the previous question (the line numbers are used in the questions which follow; they are not part of the code):

```
1.  int num1 = 2;
2.  int result = 0;
3.  while (num1 <= 10)
4.     result += (num1 += 2);
```

a. What are the values of result and num1 after the loop finishes?
b. Which of the following changes to this code would give the same value for result as in question 14?

A. Replace line 1 with int num1 = 0;
B. Replace line 2 with int result = 2;
C. Replace line 3 with while (num1 < 10)
D. (A) and (C) together.

16. Another form for this loop is as follows:

```
1.  int num1 = 0;
2.  int result = 0;
3.  do {
4.     result += num1;
5.     num1 += 2;
6.  } while (num1 <= 10);
```

a. What are the values of result and num1 after the loop finishes?
b. How many iterations of the loop are done?
c. Which of the following changes will allow the number of loop iterations to be reduced while retaining the same final values for result and num1?

A. Replace line 1 with int num1 = 2;
B. Replace line 2 with int result = 2;
C. Replace line 4 with result += (num1 += 2); and delete line 5.
D. Replace line 6 with while (num1 < 10);

17. What value does num have after the statements:

```
int num, num1, num2;
num = (num1 = 25, num2 = ++num1);
```

18. A common habit of Pascal programmers new to C or C++ is to write a two-dimensional array in C++ as array[i,j]. Assuming that array has been declared as a pointer to an int in a C++ program, what does the notation array[i,j] denote?

19. Consider the following loop:

```
int num1, result;
for (result = 1, num1 = 1; num1 < 6; num1++)
    result *= num1;
```

What values do result and num1 have when the loop finishes?

20. Consider the code fragment:

```
for (num1 = 10, sum = 0;
    num1 != 0 && sum/num1 >= 0; --num1)
    sum += num1;
```

a. What are the values of sum and num1 when the loop finishes?
b. If the termination condition in the for loop is changed to:

```
sum/num1 >= 0 && num1 != 0
```

which of the following is true?

A. The values of sum and num1 after the loop finishes are unchanged.
B. One extra iteration of the loop will occur.
C. The loop becomes an infinite loop.
D. A run-time error due to division by zero will occur.

21. Consider the nested loops:

```
int num1, num2, sum = 0;
for (num1 = 1; num1 < 6; num1++)
    for (num2 = 1; num2 <= num1; num2 += 2)
        sum += num1 + num2;
```

a. What are the values of sum, num1, and num2 after the statements finish?
b. How many times is the statement sum += num1 + num2; executed?

22. Consider the array declaration:

```
int IntArray[10];
```

a. What notation refers to the first element of this array?
b. What notation refers to the last element of this array?
c. To what does the notation `IntArray` refer?
d. To what does the notation `*(IntArray + 3)` refer?

23. Consider the code:

```
int IntArray[50];
int index;

for (index = 0; index < 50; index++)
   IntArray[index] = 2*index;

index = 0;
while ( *(IntArray + index++) < 50);
```

a. What is the value of `index` after the `while` loop?
b. What is the last value of `index` for which the condition

```
*(IntArray + index++) < 50
```

in the `while` loop is satisfied?
c. How many array elements are examined by the `while` loop?

24. Write a code fragment which will determine the length of a string stored in the `char` array `String[]`, storing the length in the `int` variable `Length`.

25. The program shown below contains a class with a single public function `Hello()`, which should print the message

```
Hello world!
```

on the screen. Write a function definition at the location indicated. Type in and run the program on your computer.

```
class hello
{
public:
   void Hello();
};

// Enter your function definition here

int main()
{
   hello Message;
```

```
    Message.Hello();
    return 0;
}
```

26. Define a C++ class `ascii` which provides fields for an ASCII character and its corresponding decimal code. The class should contain two functions: `Input()`, which reads in an integer code, stores this value as the decimal code for an ASCII character, and assigns the correct character to the `char` field, and `Print()` which prints out the ASCII character after first testing that the character is, in fact, printable (ASCII codes from 0 to 31 are usually not printable). Write a `main()` function which uses your class to read in a series of ASCII codes and then prints out the character string to which these codes correspond.

27 a. Write a definition for a C++ class to represent a calendar date. The class should include data fields for `DayOfWeek`, `Day`, `Month` and `Year`, and also declarations for the functions `IsWeekend()`, which determines if the date is either a Saturday or a Sunday by examining the `DayOfWeek` field, `Load()`, which reads (from the keyboard) values for all data fields in the class, and `Print()`, which prints out the data fields in a neat format. The `DayOfWeek` should be a character string, all other data fields should be numbers. For each field, decide if it should be `private` or `public`. Write a `main()` function which tests all the functions in your class.

b. Add a function `ValidMonth()` to your date class which checks that the entered month is valid (that is, a number from 1 to 12). Decide if the function should be public or private, and what return value the function should have. Modify the `Load()` function so that it makes use of `ValidMonth()`, printing out the message "Invalid month" if an incorrect month number is entered.

c. In this part, you will use your `date` class as a data field in another class. Define a new class called `diary`. The diary class should contain an array of three `date` objects (you can make the array larger if you like, but it will get tedious typing in the data) and functions for reading in (called `Load()`) and printing out (called `Print()`) the entire array. The reading and printing functions in the `diary` class should make use of the corresponding functions in the `date` class. Note that you cannot write `diary` class functions that access the private fields of the `date` class anyway, so you must use the interface functions in the `date` class to access these fields. Finally, write a `main()` function which declares a `diary` object, reads in the three dates in this object, and then prints them out on the screen.

CHAPTER 4

# Constructors and destructors

## 4.1 Introduction

In Chapter 3, we built our first complete object oriented C++ program. We observed at the end of the chapter that there were a few loose ends with this program. These loose ends will be used as motivation to introduce the topics of this chapter, although the ideas behind constructor functions and destructor functions are of great importance in C++ programming in general.

## 4.2 Constructor functions

We noted at the end of Chapter 3 that we hadn't initialized any of our variables before using them, which is bad programming practice. We could, of course, simply insert some code into the main() function, or even define a separate initialization function to do this, but C++ provides a better way. Because initialization is so commonly required in programming, there is a special C++ feature, called a *constructor function*, or just *constructor* for short, whose job it is to do this. To see how a constructor works, consider again the ATM classes in Chapter 3:

```
class account
{
private:
  float Balance;
  int AccountNumber;
public:
  BOOL Withdraw(float Amount);
  BOOL Deposit(float Amount);
  float CheckBalance();
  int CheckAccountNumber();
};

class atm
{
private:
  int EnteredCode;
  int CardCode;
  account Account[MAXACCOUNTS];
public:
  void DisplayWait();
  void ReadCard();
  BOOL CheckCode();
  void ProcessChoice();
};
```

There are several fields in these classes that should be initialized before the classes are first used. For example, we should initialize the balance in an account. We might also like to determine the maximum number of accounts to be handled by the ATM dynamically, that is, to specify the value of MAXACCOUNTS when the program is run, rather than before it is compiled.

We can insert a constructor function into the class to do these things. A constructor *always* has the same name as the class to which it belongs, and *never* has a return type specified (not even void). Since a constructor must be accessible outside the class, it must be a public function. For example, the class account could have a constructor defined for it, so that the new definition of the account class is:

```
class account
{
private:
   float Balance;
   int AccountNumber;
public:
   account();        // Constructor
   BOOL Withdraw(float Amount);
   BOOL Deposit(float Amount);
   float CheckBalance();
   int CheckAccountNumber();
};
```

The actual definition of the constructor itself can be deferred to a separate file, just like any other class function. The general form of a constructor (if it is defined in a separate file, or in a separate location in the same file) is:

```
ClassName::ClassName(arguments) : InitializationList
{
   statements
}
```

This form is similar to the form for any other function, apart from three main points:

1. There is no return type specified. A constructor may contain a return statement without an argument, but any attempt to return any type of value from a constructor is an error.

2. The name of the constructor function is the same as the name of the class.

3. An (optional) initialization list may follow the name and arguments of the constructor. The list is a comma-separated list of class members with associated initial values. The list is separated from the argument list by a single colon.

The initialization list contains those class members that you wish to initialize, together with the values to which they are to be initialized. These initial values may be constants, or they may be variables derived from the argument list to the constructor itself. For example, if we wished to initialize the Balance and AccountNumber fields in the account class, we may use a constructor defined as follows:

```
account::account()  :  Balance(0.0),  AccountNumber(-1)  {}
```

To make use of this constructor, we must declare a new instance of an account variable. The conventional declaration:

```
account Account;
```

*automatically* calls the constructor. In fact, in the version of this program that we used in Chapter 3, where we hadn't explicitly written any constructor at all, the compiler *generated* its own argumentless constructor which is called by any such declaration. This default constructor wouldn't actually do anything, but is required by the compiler. If all you want to do, therefore, is to initialize all fields in a class variable to some constant value every time such a variable is declared, you can define your own argumentless constructor which will automatically be called for each declaration.

In this case, no arguments are passed to the constructor, the balance is always initialized to 0.0, and the account number is always initialized to –1. Usually we would like to be able to specify initial values for variables when they are declared, rather than always initializing them to some constant value. To do this using a constructor, we need to define a constructor which accepts arguments. We can do this for the account class by adding a constructor with two arguments:

```
class account
{
private:
  float Balance;
  int AccountNumber;
public:
  account();        // Argumentless constructor

          // Constructor with 2 arguments
  account(float NewBalance, int NewAccount);
  BOOL Withdraw(float Amount);
  BOOL Deposit(float Amount);
  float CheckBalance();
  int CheckAccountNumber();
};
```

with external definition:

```
account::account(float NewBalance, int NewAccount) :
    Balance(NewBalance), AccountNumber(NewAccount) {}
```

In this form of the constructor, the arguments `NewBalance` and `NewAccount` are passed to the constructor and used to provide initial values for the class fields `Balance` and `Account` respectively. Arguments are passed to constructors by adding them to variable names in a declaration. For example, to declare two `account` variables `Account1` (with an initial balance of 10 and account number 1) and `Account2` (with an initial balance of 50 and account number 2), we would say:

```
account Account1(10, 1), Account2(50, 2);
```

These two constructors contain no actual statements after the initialization list (hence the pair of empty braces `{}`). Alternatively, we could avoid the initialization list altogether and include the initializations as assignments in the constructor body:

```
account::account(float NewBalance, int NewAccount)
{
   Balance = NewBalance;
   AccountNumber = NewAccount;
}
```

It is considered better C++ style to use the initialization list, however, especially as there are some situations in which this is the only way that initializations can be done.

You may have wondered whether it is legal for us to have two constructors in the same class, as we did above, since both constructors have the same name (`account`). Languages such as C would complain about this sort of thing, saying that you have a duplicate definition of the function. In C++, though, we are allowed to define as many constructors as we like, provided that the argument lists for all of them are different. In this case, one of the constructors is argumentless and the other has two arguments, so we are OK. The compiler decides which one to use in a variable declaration by matching up the number and type of the arguments.

For example, the declaration:

```
account Account;
```

will call the argumentless constructor, while the declaration:

```
account Account(2.50, 17);
```

will call the constructor with two arguments. If a declaration is given with anything other than zero or two arguments, or if we tried to pass the wrong type of data (for example, some user-defined data type) as arguments in the second declaration, it will be flagged as an error.

There are a few things it is important to understand about constructors in order to avoid many hours of painful debugging:

- If you don't define any constructors at all for a class, the compiler will generate an argumentless constructor for you, although it won't do anything.
- If you define *any* constructors for a class, the compiler will *not* provide a default, argumentless constructor, even if all the constructors you have defined have arguments attached to them. This can cause some confusing compiler errors if you don't realize what is happening. For example, if we had defined only the constructor with two arguments for the `account` class, and then attempted to declare a variable with the statement:

```
account Account;
```

the compiler would flag an error, because no argumentless constructor exists. To correct this error we must either provide our own argumentless constructor, or else *delete* all other user-defined constructors. The first action is, of course, preferable!

- It is possible to define default values for some or all of the arguments in a constructor. For example, we could have combined the two constructors for the `account` class into one by using the declaration

```
account(float NewBalance = 0.0, int NewAccount = -1);
```

in the `account` class, with associated external definition:

```
account::account(float NewBalance, int NewAccount) :
    Balance(NewBalance), AccountNumber(NewAccount) {}
```

Note a few things about default values:

1. If the constructor is declared within the class and defined externally, the default values are given in the class declaration only.
2. The default values are used only if the constructor is called without some or all of its arguments.
3. If a constructor with default values for its arguments is called with fewer arguments, the arguments passed to it override the default values, while the default values are used for the remaining arguments.

4. If only some of the arguments are to have default values, *all* arguments without default values must *precede* all arguments with default values.

For example, the declarations

```
account Account;
account Account(10.50);
account Account(10.50, 5);
```

are all legal. In the first case, `NewBalance` is set to 0.0 and `NewAccount` is set to −1, since these are the default values given in the definition of the constructor, and no arguments are provided in the declaration of the variable name to override these defaults. In the second case, the single argument overrides the *first* default value in the argument list (`NewBalance`), and the second argument (`NewAccount`) is given the default value of −1. In the third case, both default values are overridden.

It is permissible to supply default values for only some of the arguments. However, *all* arguments with default values must follow *all* arguments without default values. For example, if we had decided to provide a default value for the new account number, but not for the balance, we could declare the constructor as:

```
account(float NewBalance, int NewAccount = -1);
```

but *not* as

```
account(int NewAccount = -1, float NewBalance);
```

If this constructor were the only constructor defined for the `account` class, all declarations would have to contain either one or two arguments, and *no argumentless constructor would be defined*.

It is a good idea to provide an argumentless constructor for every class, even if it does nothing, and you don't plan to use it yourself. Some implicit operations in C++ require such a constructor to be present.

A special kind of constructor, called a *copy constructor*, is required in certain cases. We will return to this after we have discussed dynamic allocation of memory.

## 4.3 Dynamic memory allocation

In all the examples we have considered so far, all variables have been defined at compilation time. This means, for example, that the number and type of variables used in each function must be decided when the code is written, that all arrays must have predetermined sizes, and so on. Frequently it is useful to be able to define new variables or decide the size of an array while the program is running. In order to do this, we must be able to allocate memory for these variables and arrays *dynamically* (during the execution of the program), rather than *statically* (when the program is compiled).

For example, considering the ATM program again, we declared an array of `account` objects to hold details of customers' accounts. We do not know in advance how many customers a bank will have, so it would be convenient to be able to specify the array size when the program is running. That way, we could use the same program in different branches with different numbers of customers. If we had to specify the array size in advance, we would have to guess the largest number of customers a branch could have and declare the array to be of that size. If our guess is too large, we waste computer memory by reserving space for array elements that will never be used. If our guess is too small, we won't have enough space to store information on all the customers at the branch.

C++ provides a built-in operator for dynamic memory called `new`. In order to understand how `new` works, we will need to understand something about pointers in C++.

## 4.3.1 Pointers in C++

The easiest way to view a *pointer* is as a memory address. Every variable, of whatever data type, must have a location in memory in order for it to be accessed and used by the program of which it is a part. A pointer to a variable is the address at which the variable is stored. Since a memory address can always be written as an integer, a pointer is, in effect, just an integer. This means that, no matter how large the data structure whose address is stored at the pointer location, the amount of memory required for storing the *address* itself is always the same.

In C++, a pointer to a variable can be denoted in several different ways. This particular aspect of C++ syntax is unfortunately somewhat confusing. Most of the syntax was inherited from C to conform to the requirement that all C syntax must also be legal C++ syntax. The notation that is used to denote a pointer depends on the context in which it is used. If you wish to declare a pointer to a particular data type, the variable name in the declaration must be prefixed with an asterisk. For example:

```
int *IntPointer;
```

declares `IntPointer` to be a *pointer* to an integer. It is important to realize that a declaration such as this reserves space in memory *only* for the pointer, and *not* for the object which it may ultimately point to.

The second way in which a pointer can be denoted is to prefix the name of an ordinary variable with an ampersand (`&`). For example, if a variable is declared as:

```
float RealNumber;
```

then a pointer to `RealNumber` can be obtained using the notation `&RealNumber`. To illustrate the difference between the two methods of referring to pointers, consider the following code fragment:

```
float RealNumber;
float *RealPointer;

RealNumber = 3.14;
RealPointer = &RealNumber;
cout << "The quantity " << *RealPointer <<
   " is stored at memory location " << RealPointer;
```

Here, `RealNumber` is declared as an ordinary `float` variable, and `RealPointer` as a pointer to a `float`. The float `RealNumber` is given the value 3.14. The memory address at which this value is stored is assigned to `RealPointer`. The output statement uses yet another notation for referring to pointers. If `RealPointer` is a pointer, the data stored at the location pointed to by `RealPointer` can be accessed by prefixing the variable name with an asterisk, as shown in the `cout` statement. The * operator used in this context is called a *dereferencing* operator.

This dual use of the asterisk-prefix notation can cause some confusion initially. It is best to remember that any variable prefixed by an asterisk must be a pointer variable, both in a declaration statement and in ordinary code. The meaning in the two cases is different, to be sure: in the declaration, a pointer is being defined, while in a C++ statement, the contents of the location pointed to by the variable are being accessed.

### 4.3.2 The **new** operator

In the previous section, we saw how to declare pointers, and how the memory address of another variable can be assigned to a pointer variable using the ampersand prefix notation. These examples did not, however, use dynamic memory allocation, since all variables were declared and defined explicitly in the code. Let us consider now how to dynamically allocate memory and associate it with a previously defined pointer variable.

Consider the code fragment:

```
float *RealPointer = new float;
int *IntPointer = new int(24);

*RealPointer = 2.342;
cout << "Pointer: " << RealPointer << "; Value: " <<
*RealPointer << endl;
```

```
cout << "Pointer: " << IntPointer << "; Value: " <<
   *IntPointer << endl;
```

Note that only the two pointers, one to a `float` and one to an `int`, were explicitly declared. In the case of `RealPointer`, space was allocated for a `float` variable by the code `new float`. The operator `new` is intelligent enough to examine the data type it is given as an argument (in this case, `float`), determine how much space is required for that data type, find a free section in memory with enough space, reserve the space, and return the address of that space. This return value is assigned to `RealPointer` by this statement so that the pointer now contains the address of this space in memory. It is now safe to refer to the location pointed to by `RealPointer`, as we do in the statement `*RealPointer = 2.342`.

The second definition is similar, except that a pointer to an `int` is defined, space is reserved for this pointer to point to, and the `int` at this location is initialized to the value 24. Invoking the `new` operator calls the constructor for the data type concerned. In the first case, where we allocated memory for a `float`, the default argumentless constructor provided by the compiler was called. Since this constructor doesn't do anything (on some compilers it may initialize the value to 0), this has no effect on the space allocated by the `new` statement. In the second case, the `int` constructor is called to initialize the value of the `int` to 24. (All built-in data types like `int`, `float`, and so on have both a default argumentless constructor that either does nothing or sets all bits to zero, and a default single-argument constructor that will initialize the value of the variable to that argument.)

### 4.3.3 Dynamic allocation of arrays

The `new` operator can also be used to allocate space for arrays dynamically. If we want to reserve space for an array of 100 `ints`, for example, we can use the statement:

```
int *IntArray = new int[100];
```

In this case, the pointer `IntArray` is declared, and the `new` operator is used to allocate space sufficient for 100 consecutive `ints`. The address of the *first* `int` in the array is returned, and assigned to the variable `IntArray`. This statement is equivalent to the static array declaration:

```
int IntArray[100];
```

so that individual elements of the array can be referred to in the usual way. The first element is `IntArray[0]`, the 50th is `IntArray[49]`, and the last is `IntArray[99]`. The difference between the two declarations is that, in the second, traditional way of declaring an array, the size of the array (100 in this case) must be a constant. In the first case, where we used the `new` operator, the size of the array could have been a variable which is calculated while the program is running, thus allowing the size of the array to be determined by other parameters in the program.

For static array declarations, it is possible to call constructors other than the argumentless one for each array element. For example, we can declare an array of 10 `int`s and initialize the elements of the array to the integers 1 through 10:

```
int Numbers[10] = {1,2,3,4,5,6,7,8,9,10};
```

If we provide fewer numbers in the initialization list than are in the array, the argumentless constructor is called for the remaining numbers. For example, using the `account` class with the two-argument constructor, we could declare an array of 5 `account`s, and initialize the first 3:

```
account Account[5] =
   {account(10,1), account(25,2), account(50,3)};
```

The last two `Account` elements will be initialized by calling the argumentless constructor. (Note that if no argumentless constructor exists, the compiler will generate an error here.)

If the array is declared dynamically, however (using the `new` operator), *only* the argumentless constructor is called for each array element. It is not possible to call any other form of constructor for the elements in a dynamically allocated array. This is a rather annoying feature of C++, since it removes a lot of the flexibility that is present for declaring single variables, where you can specify initial values for the variables as part of the declaration.

# 4.4 Argument passing in function calls

## 4.4.1 Passing by value and reference

Dynamic memory allocation using the `new` operator, as in the last section, is only one instance in which dynamic allocation occurs. The other instance is more subtle, and happens more often than you might expect. This occurs when data are passed to functions as arguments. Let us review some of what happens when a function is called.

A function such as:

```
int IntFunction(int Arg1, float Arg2) { ..... }
```

expects two arguments, one `int` and one `float`, and returns an `int`. Such a function is called from another function with a statement like:

```
ReturnedInt = IntFunction(Int1, Float2);
```

where `Int1` and `ReturnedInt` have been declared previously as `int`s, and `Float2` as a `float`. The arguments `Arg1` and `Arg2` in the function's argument list are variables *local* to the function. That is, the space for them is allocated when the function is called and released when the function returns. The space for the argument `Arg1`, for example, is allocated *dynamically* when the function is called, the value passed to that argument (`Int1`) is *copied* to the space just allocated, the variable is used within the function in whatever manner the function's statements dictate, and then the memory is deallocated (freed up for later use by the same program or any other program running on the same machine) when the function terminates, and control passes back to the routine that called the function in the first place. This method of passing arguments to a function is known as *passing by value*, because only the *value* of the variable is passed to the function, not the address of the variable. Any changes made to the local copy of the value within the function do not affect the original variable in the calling routine.

C++ provides a second way of passing a variable to a function called *passing by reference*. The syntax for this is:

```
int RefFunction(int &Arg1, float &Arg2) { .... }
```

Note that each argument is prefixed by an ampersand. Such a function is called in exactly the same way as one where the arguments are passed by value:

```
ReturnedInt = RefFunction(Int1, Float2);
```

The difference between `IntFunction` and `RefFunction` is that the *addresses* of the arguments are passed in `RefFunction`, and not the actual values. As such, no extra memory is reserved within the function, since no copy of the arguments needs to be made. The variable `Arg1` within the function and the variable `Int1` passed to it are identical: they share the same address in memory. In this case, any change made to `Arg1` within the function will also affect `Int1` in the calling routine.

It is important to note that there is no way of telling from the function call whether your variables are being passed to the function by value or by reference: you can only tell this if you examine the function declaration or definition itself. For this reason, some purists do not like the reference passing facility in C++ (which is not present in C), preferring to actually make explicit the fact that they are passing a pointer to a variable by using the syntax:

```
int PointerFunction(int *Arg1, float *Arg2) { .... }
```

for defining the function, and the syntax:

```
ReturnedInt = PointerFunction(&Int1, &Float2);
```

for calling it. In this case, the syntax in the function definition is the same as that used when declaring pointers to variables: the asterisk prefix indicates that the variable name is a pointer. In the function call, the variable Int1 was declared as an int, and the ampersand prefix indicates that a pointer to this variable is being passed. Thus the fact that pointers and not values are being passed is made explicit in both the function definition and the function call.

All of this is very nice, but if the values of the arguments Arg1 and Arg2 are used within the function body (and if they're not, why pass them in the first place?) they must always be prefixed by an asterisk to access the values stored at the address locations that have been passed. This can lead to cumbersome code that is difficult both to write and to read. Unless there is some special circumstance for using this notation, we will not use it from now on.

Some textbooks make the case for *always* passing variables by reference and *never* by value. Their reason for doing this is that passing a variable by value requires that a copy of the variable be made, which takes up both space and time, especially if the variable is an instance of a complex data class with many fields. Passing by reference requires transferring only the pointer to the variable's location, and no copy need be made.

This sounds like a good reason to always pass by reference, but if you are awake, you should spot a danger here. Remember that one difference between the two methods of passing a variable is that in one case, any changes made to the variable within the function have no effect on the calling routine, while in the other case, the changes *do* affect the variable in the calling routine. If you pass a variable by reference and inadvertently make changes to it within the function that you don't intend to be reflected in the calling routine, this could spell disaster. Fortunately, C++ has a mechanism that allows you to protect against such an error, even if you pass the variable by reference.

### 4.4.2 The const keyword

We have met the const keyword already as a way of defining a constant value which can be used in place of a raw number within your program. The const keyword has several other uses in C++, particularly in relation to function definitions. Consider the function definition:

```
int ConstArgs(const int &Arg1, const float &Arg2)
{ .... }
```

The const keyword before each argument tells the compiler that although these arguments are being passed by reference, they are not allowed to be modified within the function body. They become, in essence, 'read-only' objects: their values may be accessed but not altered. Thus, the following function definition would give rise to a compile-time error:

```
int ConstArgs(const int &Arg1, const float &Arg2)
{
    Arg1 *= 2;
}
```

A general rule is: if you agree with those people who tell you to pass arguments by reference whenever possible (and I'm not saying that you should, although the argument does have its merits), you should carefully consider whether each variable *should* be changed within the function to which it is being passed. If not, you should ensure that it is declared as a const parameter in the function definition. This is purely a safeguard against subtle errors; if your program is written correctly, it won't make any difference whether the const is there or not, but if you make a mistake and attempt to alter a variable within a function where it shouldn't be altered, the prefix const just might save you hours of debugging.

Another use of the const keyword is *after* a function declaration in a class. For example, in the class definition:

```
class ConstClass
{
private:
  declarations
public:
  int ConstFunc( args ) const;
};
```

the const after the declaration of ConstFunc() states that ConstFunc() is not allowed to change any fields of the object that calls it. For example, with the code fragment:

```
ConstClass Object;

Object.ConstFunc();
```

the call to ConstFunc() must not alter any of the values of any of the data fields of Object. This is another safety feature in C++ designed to help you catch programming errors early. If you declare a function as const in this fashion and then inadvertently insert some statements into the definition of that function that alter some of the fields of the object calling the function, the compiler will flag an error. It is therefore a good idea to think carefully about whether or not a function *should* be allowed to alter any data fields and, if not, declare it as const.

### 4.4.3 Copy constructors

We observed above that whenever you pass a variable to a function by value, a copy of the variable is made for local use by the function. The space in which this copy is stored is dynamically reserved by the function being called. You will remember that, when we reserved space for a variable using the new operator, one of the constructors for the data type corresponding to the variable was called. You might have guessed, therefore, that some sort of constructor is called whenever a variable is passed to function by value. This is, in fact, the case, though the constructor is not one of those we have considered so far. The particular kind of constructor is called a *copy constructor*.

The reason that a constructor is needed at all is not immediately obvious. After all, constructors are used primarily for initializing values of variables, and when we pass a variable by value to a function, the value that is to be assigned to the copy is *always* the same as the value in the calling routine. You might think, therefore, that the mechanism for copying the source variable into the function could be built in to the language and need not concern the programmer further.

To a certain extent, this is true. In those cases where we have passed variables to functions in examples in earlier chapters, these variables have been passed by value and no problems have occurred. To see where a problem can arise, we need to consider a class with a special kind of field.

We can use this opportunity to redesign the atm class slightly. One of the things we mentioned earlier as being desirable is that the array of accounts should have a size that is determined when the program is run, not when it is compiled. Consider the new forms for the account and atm classes:

```
class account
{
private:
   float Balance;
   int AccountNumber;
public:
   account(float balance = 0.0, int accountnumber = -1);
   BOOL Withdraw(float Amount);
   BOOL Deposit(float Amount);
   float CheckBalance();
   int CheckAccountNumber();
};
```

```
class atm
{
private:
  int EnteredCode;
  int CardCode;
  int NumAccounts;
  account *Account;
public:
  atm(int numaccounts = 10);
  atm(const atm& Copyatm);
  ~atm();
  void DisplayWait();
  void ReadCard();
  BOOL CheckCode();
  void ProcessChoice();
};
```

A constructor has been added to the account class, with default values for the balance and account number. The constructor is defined in a separate file (the file account.cpp would be appropriate):

```
account::account(float balance, int accountnumber) :
  Balance(balance), AccountNumber(accountnumber)
{ }
```

The main changes are in the atm class, however. We now wish to define the number of accounts in an atm object when it is declared, rather than hard-wire it into the class definition. The field NumAccounts, for storing the maximum number of accounts (the size of the Account array), has been added. There are now two constructors, and a curious looking function named ~atm(). The latter function is a *destructor* function, which we will get to in the next section. The first constructor function is a normal constructor which initializes the value of NumAccounts, and reserves space for the Account array:

```
atm::atm(int numaccounts) : NumAccounts(numaccounts),
    Account(new account[NumAccounts])
{}
```

The second constructor is a *copy constructor*. Its form is:

```
atm::atm(const atm& Copyatm)
  : NumAccounts(Copyatm.NumAccounts),
    EnteredCode(Copyatm.EnteredCode),
    CardCode(Copyatm.CardCode)
{
  Account = new account[NumAccounts];
  for (int i = 0; i < NumAccounts; i++)
```

```
        Account[i] = Copyatm.Account[i];
}
```

To understand what is going on here, we need to understand the reason a special form of constructor is needed. A copy constructor is called whenever a variable is passed by value to a function. If a variable of class atm is passed to a function, all its fields must be copied into a local atm class variable within the function. If we did not define our own copy constructor to do this, the compiler will generate its own copy constructor (which is, in fact, what happened in our previous examples where we passed simple data types like ints to functions). This default copy constructor performs what is known as a *shallow copy*. This means that only the fields of a class are copied, and *not anything those fields may point to*. In other words, if the class object being copied contains only non-pointer fields, such as the first version of the atm class declared back in Chapter 2, the default copy constructor will be fine. However, in our new version of the atm class, we have replaced the array field with a pointer to an account object. As a result, the default copy constructor will copy only this pointer when it passes an atm object to a function, with the result that both the local copy in the function and the original variable in the calling routine will be pointing to the same memory area for the Account array. In other words, even though you may think you are passing the atm object by value, part of it (the array) is actually being passed by reference. If you don't realize this, you might think it is safe to change values of some of the array elements without affecting the corresponding values in the original array. This is wrong, and can lead to some fiendishly difficult-to-find bugs.

To get around this problem, you need to define your own copy constructor which explicitly allocates memory for a copy of the array, and then explicitly copies the source array into the local array within the function. Having done this, the copy of the atm object within the function is truly local, and any changes made to the copy will not affect the original object.

Copy constructors always have the syntax:

```
ClassName::ClassName(const ClassName& VariableName) :
    InitList
{
    statements
}
```

The copy constructor has exactly one argument: a reference variable of the same class as the class to which the copy constructor belongs. This is the reference to the source object which is to be copied. It is vitally important that this argument be a *reference* variable and *not* a variable passed by value. The reason for this is that, had you used a non-reference variable (which is easily done in error by omitting the ampersand), you would require a copy of the variable to be passed to the copy constructor. To do this, the program will call the copy constructor to create the copy, which requires *another* copy of the variable to be made, which results in another call to the copy constructor, which... In other words, omitting the ampersand will trap you in an infinite recursion.

Note also that the argument is declared as a `const` argument. This ensures that no changes to the original variable can be made by the copy constructor. This is essential, since the copy constructor is invoked only when a variable is passed to a function by value, and the whole point of doing that is to avoid making any changes to the original variable.

Hopefully, the operation of the copy constructor above for the `atm` class is now fairly obvious. The non-pointer fields of the object are copied using the initialization list. In the body of the function, the `new` operator is used to reserve space for the copy of the `Account` array, and a `for` loop is used to copy the fields over from the original `atm` object to the new, local one. It is important to remember that if you are defining your own copy constructor, you need to handle *all* the copying required, and not just the pointer fields that the default constructor can't handle. As with the ordinary constructor, the compiler will only supply a default copy constructor if you don't provide your own. Once you have defined your own copy constructor, you must ensure that it does everything required.

Strictly speaking, a customized copy constructor is only really necessary if your class contains pointer fields which point to dynamically allocated memory, as with the `Account` array in the new `atm` class. If your class contains no data fields other than standard value types, the default copy constructor is perfectly adequate. Some C++ purists advocate supplying a copy constructor with every class, so that if you add a pointer field to a class later on, you will not have any problems. However, others are content to add a copy constructor only when such a pointer field is added.

Writing your own copy constructors is a useful exercise because it makes explicit the amount of extra work done every time you pass a variable by value to a function. If you pass a variable by reference, no copy constructor is required, since only the pointer to the object is passed to the function.

Copy constructors are also used whenever a function returns an object as its return value. For example, if we declared an external function which returned an object of class `atm`, such as

```
atm GetATMData();
```

we might use it in a `main()` routine as follows:

```
int main()
{
```

```
    atm TestATM = GetATMData();
    // Other statements
    return 0;
}
```

Here, the copy constructor is used to copy the returned `atm` object from the call to the `GetATMData()` function into the variable `TestATM`.

### 4.4.4 Initializations versus assignments

Note that although the = operator is used to initialize the value of `TestATM` in the example just given, this is *not* an assignment statement! C++ distinguishes between the use of the = operator for initializations (as in the example given here, or in the simpler case of a declaration and initialization statement such as `int num1 = 3;`) and its use for genuine assignments, where the value of one variable is copied to another variable, as in a statement such as `num1 = num2`. Copy constructors are used for initializations and the assignment operator = is used for assignments. If you wish to define a specialized form of the assignment operator = for one of your own classes, you must explicitly write an overloaded version of the = operator. We will consider this in the next chapter.

If you are confused about when a copy constructor is called, it is a good idea to experiment by writing a few simple programs that use copy constructors in various situations, and put an explicit statement such as

```
cout << "Copy constructor called.\n";
```

in the copy constructor so you can see when it is being used.

## 4.5 Destructors

The space allocated for a local copy of a variable in a function must be released when the function returns. If the variable is of a data class with only simple data fields (no pointers), this is handled automatically by the C++ language. However, whenever the `new` operator is used to reserve space for a variable, this space is never released unless the programmer provides instructions to do so. If you don't delete the memory allocated by a copy constructor, each call to a function which invokes the copy constructor will allocate more memory. If the function is called frequently, you may eventually exhaust the memory available in the computer. It is therefore important to release the memory after each function call. C++ provides a special function called a *destructor* for doing this.

The syntax for a destructor definition is:

```
ClassName::~ClassName()
{
```

```
    statements
}
```

As with a constructor, a destructor takes the same name as the class to which it belongs. The name is always prefixed by the tilde (~) character. Destructors have no return value, and take no arguments.

The destructor ~atm() declared in the new form of the atm class above has the form:

```
atm::~atm()
{
    delete [] Account;
}
```

The destructor makes use of the C++ keyword delete, which has the opposite effect to that of the new operator: it frees up memory. The empty square brackets following the delete keyword indicate the following variable name (Account) is a pointer to an array, and that all elements of this array should be removed. If Account had been a pointer to a single variable, and not an array, the square brackets are not necessary, but it doesn't hurt to put them in anyway.

A destructor will be called automatically for any local variables in a function when the function returns. However, you can call a destructor explicitly by using the delete command yourself. For example:

```
int *IntArray = new int[50];
atm *ATMPointer = new atm;

statements using variables

delete [] IntArray;
delete ATMPointer;
```

An array of 50 ints and a single atm object are allocated using new, used for various calculations, and then deleted.

A few points about destructors that you should remember:

- The operand of the delete operator *must* be a pointer. You cannot deallocate memory reserved for non-pointer variables. For example, the code:

```
int i;

delete i;
```

will produce an error, since i is not a pointer.

- The memory released is only the memory that is pointed to by the pointer. The pointer itself still exists.
- The basic data types such as `int`, `float` and so on have default destructors defined for them.
- If you don't provide a destructor for a class, the compiler will generate a default destructor, but if your class contains any dynamically allocated memory, this default destructor will not release it. It is therefore essential that you define your own destructor for any such class.
- Destructors are called recursively. For example, in the case above where we called the `atm` destructor, the statement within this destructor will call the destructor for each element of the `Account` array. Since the `account` class has no explicit destructor defined for it (since it contains no pointer fields), the compiler will generate a default destructor which will simply remove the data fields for each `account` object.

## 4.6 Summary

The main points introduced in this chapter are:

- **Constructors**
  - A *constructor* is used to initialize the fields in a newly declared object.
  - A constructor always has the same name as the class to which it belongs.
  - A constructor has no return type (not even `void`).
  - Data fields may be initialized using an *initialization list*.
  - Constructor arguments may have default values.
  - It is permissible to have more than one constructor for each class, provided that the argument lists of all constructors are different.
  - If no constructors are defined by the user, the compiler will generate a default *argumentless* constructor, which does nothing.
  - If *any* constructors are defined by the user, the compiler will *not* generate an argumentless (or any other kind of) constructor.
- **Dynamic memory allocation**
  - Dynamic memory is allocated while the program is running.
  - Pointers are *declared* using the `*` operator, and *referenced* using the `&` operator.
  - Memory can be dynamically allocated using the `new` operator.
  - Arrays can be dynamically allocated using `new type[size]`.
- **Argument passing in function calls**
  - Arguments may be passed by *value* or by *reference*.
  - Passing by value requires copying the object to the function.
  - Passing by reference passes only a pointer to the function.
  - Passing by value will not alter the object in the calling function; passing by reference will.

 – Use the `const` keyword to protect objects when calling by reference.
 – Use the `const` keyword to protect object fields in a class function.
 – Provide a *copy constructor* to allow dynamically allocated fields to be copied when an object is passed by value to a function.
- **Destructors**
 – A *destructor* is used to deallocate dynamically allocated memory when the associated object goes out of scope.
 – A destructor always has the same name as the class to which it belongs, prefixed by the ~ symbol.
 – A destructor takes no arguments, and has no return type.
 – Use the `delete` operator to deallocate memory.
 – Use `delete []` *ArrayPointer* to deallocate arrays.

## 4.7 Exercises

1. Consider the class definition:

```
class testType
{
private:
  int num1, num2;
  float real1;
public:
  testType() : num1(5), num2(9) {}
};
```

After the declaration:

```
testType Object1;
```

a. what are the values (if any) of num1, num2, and real1?
b. Using the same class definition, the declaration

```
testType Object2(12);
```

is made. What are the values of num1, num2, and real1 after this declaration?

2. Consider the following code:

```
class testType
{
private:
  testType() {}
public:
  int x;
};

main()
{
```

```
    testType ObjectTest;
}
```

a. Describe the result if an attempt is made to compile and run this program. Try to predict the result before you actually compile it.

b. Change the class definition so that the declaration

```
testType ObjectTest;
```

will properly declare an object ObjectTest in which the value of x is initialized to 10. Propose at least two different ways this may be done.

c. Change the class definition so that the declaration

```
testType ObjectTest;
```

still declares an object in which the value of x is initialized to 10, but the declaration

```
testType OtherObject(5);
```

declares an object in which x is initialized to 5. Propose at least two ways this may be done.

3. Consider the code:

```
class testType
{
private:
   int num1;
   float real1;
public:
    testType(int Num1Start, float Real1Start = 3.14) :
        num1(Num1Start), real1(Real1Start) {}
};
```

Describe what effect (in either compilation or execution) each of the following declarations will have:

a. testType TestObject;
b. testType TestObject(32, 9.45);
c. testType TestObject(42);
d. testType TestObject(52, 7.43, 12);

4. a. In the following program, write a constructor for the class widget that initializes num1 to 47 and real1 to 2.718. Write a main() routine that

declares an object of type `widget` and uses the `PrintData()` function to print out the field values.

```
class widget
{
private:
    int num1;
    float real1;
public:
    // Insert constructor here.
    void PrintData() { cout << "num1 = " << num1 << ";
        real1 = " << real1 << endl; }
};
```

b. Modify the constructor for the class `widget` so that the user may specify initial values for `num1` and `real1`. `real1` should have no default value, but `num1` should have a default value of 100. In the `main()` function, declare two objects of type `widget`, named `Object1` and `Object2`. In `Object1`, initialize `real1` to 47.231 and accept the default value for `num1`. In `Object2`, initialize `real1` to 107.89 and `num1` to 53. Write a `main()` routine that prints out the fields of both objects.

c. Modify the `widget` class so that it contains *two* constructors: an argumentless constructor that does nothing except print out the message "Argumentless constructor called.", and a second constructor which requires two arguments (neither with a default value), used to initialize the values of `num1` and `real1`. Write a `main()` routine that declares and prints objects of this class using various types of declarations. In particular, you should try declaring objects with no, one, and two arguments to see what happens. Try to predict what will be printed before you run the program in each case.

5. Write a *single* C++ statement which declares a pointer to a `float` object and uses the `new` operator to allocate memory for this pointer to point to. The value stored in this location should also be initialized to 9.43.

6. Write a declaration using the `new` operator which defines an `int` pointer named `IntArray` and reserves space for an array of 25 `int`s pointed to by `IntArray`.

7. Consider the C++ function:

```
void StringFunction()
{
    char *String = new char[50];
    // Other statements....
}
```

a. What does the pointer `String` represent?

b. What happens to the memory allocated by the new operator when StringFunction() finishes?

8. Consider the two following declarations, which are intended to declare an array of 64 floats:

```
int ArraySize = 64;
float *Array = new float[ArraySize];
```

and

```
int ArraySize = 64;
float Array[ArraySize];
```

Which (if either) of these two declarations is correct? What is wrong with the declaration(s) that is/are incorrect?

9. It is stated in the text that it is not possible to use a constructor to initialize the individual elements in an array when the memory for these array elements is allocated using the new operator. Describe some methods by which such initialization might be done.

10. a. In the following class, write a constructor for the class wotsit which uses the new operator to assign an array of 10 integers to the int pointer IntArray. The constructor should have a single argument which is used to assign an initial value to each array element. The default value for the argument should be 10. Write a main() routine which declares a testArray object and uses the PrintData() function to print out its IntArray field.

```
class testArray
{
private:
   int *IntArray;
public:
   // Define constructor here
   void PrintData();
};

void testArray::PrintData()
{
   for (int Index = 0; Index < 10; Index++)
     cout << IntArray[Index] << ' ';
   cout << endl;
}
```

b. Add a private int field named ArraySize to the testArray class, and another constructor which initializes the field ArraySize and uses the new operator to allocate to the IntArray pointer an int array of size

ArraySize. The constructor should have two arguments: one for the value of `ArraySize` and another giving the initial value of each array element. Modify the `PrintData()` function so that it prints out the entire `IntArray` array, for any value of `ArraySize`. Write a `main()` routine to test your answer.

11. Consider the following C++ program:

```cpp
void SumFunction(int AddNumber)
{
  AddNumber += 10;
}

void main()
{
  int TestNumber = 20;
  SumFunction(TestNumber);
  cout << "TestNumber = " << TestNumber << endl;
}
```

a. What will be printed by the `cout` statement?
b. If the function is modified as follows:

```cpp
void SumFunction(int& AddNumber)
{
  AddNumber += 10;
}
```

what is printed by the `cout` statement?

c. If the function is further modified as follows:

```cpp
void SumFunction(const int& AddNumber)
{
  AddNumber += 10;
}
```

what effect will this have?

12. Consider the class definition:

```cpp
class testConst
{
private:
  int Num1, Num2;
public:
  testConst(int num1 = 1, int num2 = 2) :
    Num1(num1), Num2(num2) {}
  void NumFunc1() const;
```

```
   void NumFunc2() const;
};

void testConst::NumFunc1() const
{
   Num1 += Num2;
}

void testConst::NumFunc2() const
{
   cout << Num1 + Num2 << endl;
}
```

What error(s) will be reported by the compiler?

13. Consider the code:

```
class testClass
{
private:
   int *ArrayPtr;
   int ArraySize;
public:
   testClass(int arraysize = 10) :
      ArraySize(arraysize), ArrayPtr(new int[arraysize])
      { for(int i=0; i < arraysize; i++)
         ArrayPtr[i] = 0; }
   void ChangeArray()
      { for(int i=0; i < ArraySize; i++)
         ArrayPtr[i] += 10; }
};

void TestFunc(testClass FrisObj)
{
   FrisObj.ChangeArray();
}

int main()
{
   testClass FunObj(5);
   TestFunc(FunObj);
}
```

a. What value will each of the elements of the array `ArrayPtr` have at the end of `main()`?

b. The copy constructor:

```
testClass(const testClass& Source) :
   ArraySize(Source.ArraySize),
   ArrayPtr(new int[Source.ArraySize])
   { for (int i=0; i < ArraySize; i++)
      ArrayPtr[i] = Source.ArrayPtr[i]; }
```

is added to the class testClass. Now what value will each element of the array IntArray have at the end of main()?

14. The program below defines a class containing two pointer fields which point to dynamically allocated arrays. Before you answer the question that follows, you should type in and run this program on your computer without modifying it. Observe that even though the object TestdynArray is passed by value to the function ChangedynArray(), its array elements are still changed.

```
#include <iostream.h>
class dynArray
{
private:
   int IntArraySize, FloatArraySize;
   int *IntArray;
   float *FloatArray;
public:
   dynArray(int intarraysize=5, int floatarraysize=3);
// Add a copy constructor here
   void UpdateArrays();
   void PrintArrays();
};

void ChangedynArray(dynArray Source);

dynArray::dynArray(int intarraysize,
   int floatarraysize) :
   IntArraySize(intarraysize),
   FloatArraySize(floatarraysize),
   IntArray(new int[intarraysize]),
   FloatArray(new float[floatarraysize])
{
   for(int i=0; i < IntArraySize; i++)
     IntArray[i] = 10;
   for(i=0; i < FloatArraySize; i++)
     FloatArray[i] = 3.14;
}

void dynArray::UpdateArrays()
{
   for (int i=0; i < IntArraySize; i++)
     IntArray[i] += 25;
   for(i=0; i  < FloatArraySize; i++)
     FloatArray[i] *= FloatArray[i];
}

void dynArray::PrintArrays()
{
   for (int i=0; i < IntArraySize; i++)
     cout << IntArray[i] << ' ';
```

```
    cout << endl;
    for(i=0; i < FloatArraySize; i++)
      cout << FloatArray[i] << ' ';
    cout << endl;
  }

  void ChangedynArray(dynArray Source)
  {
    Source.UpdateArrays();
  }

  int main()
  {
    dynArray TestdynArray(4,5);

    cout << "Before ChangedynArray:\n";
    TestdynArray.PrintArrays();
    ChangedynArray(TestdynArray);
    cout << "After ChangedynArray:\n";
    TestdynArray.PrintArrays();
    return 0;
  }
```

Now add a copy constructor to the class dynArray so that the object passed to the function gets its own copies of the two arrays. When you run the program this time, you should see that the object TestdynArray in main() remains unchanged by the call to ChangedynArray().

15. The program below defines a class with two fields: an int, and a pointer to an int which is initialized by the constructor to point to an array. The main() function does nothing more than declare two objects of type Snowflake.

a. Write a destructor for this class. To convince yourself that the destructor is actually being called, place an output statement in it that prints out the message "Destructor called." on the screen. Run the program to test it.

```
#include <iostream.h>
class Snowflake
{
private:
  int Sides;
  int *Shapes;
public:
  Snowflake();
  // Insert destructor here
};

Snowflake::Snowflake() : Sides(6), Shapes(new int[10])
{}
```

```
int main()
{
  Snowflake Flake1, Flake2;
}
```

b. Add the class definition given below to the program in part a. Write a destructor for the `blizzard` class which deallocates the memory in the `Flake` array. Before you run the program, predict how many times the message "Destructor called." will appear.

```
class blizzard
{
private:
  Snowflake *Flake;
  int NumFlakes;
public:
  blizzard(int numflakes = 10) :
    NumFlakes(numflakes),
    Flake(new Snowflake[numflakes]) {}
  // Insert destructor here
};

int main()
{
  blizzard Storm;
}
```

# CHAPTER 5

# Function and operator overloading

## 5.1 Introduction

We have spent considerable time discussing features of C++ that have no obvious connection with its object oriented properties, so it is time for a reminder of some of the principles of OOP. Recall that the central dogma of OOP states that programs should be designed around the idea that everything can be represented in terms of classes, in which properties and actions related to the class can be grouped together, fields that are relevant to the class only can be hidden from the outside world, and all interactions with other classes and objects are carried out through interface functions.

As we delve deeper into OOP, we will see that one feature that is required for a proper implementation of OOP is the ability to define functions and operators with the same name, but different effects depending on their context. This is known as *function overloading*.

We have already met an example of function overloading when we discussed constructor functions in the previous chapter. We saw there that it is possible to define several different constructors for the same class, as long as the argument list was different for each constructor. The compiler is able to sort out which constructor is the correct one by examining the list of arguments being passed to it.

In much the same way, almost any function or operator in C++ can be overloaded. By *operator overloading* we mean that operators such as +, *, +=, and so on may all be generalized so that their operands can be objects based on user-defined classes. Since operator overloading is really just a special case of function overloading, we will consider function overloading first.

## 5.2 Function overloading

The main rule for function overloading is: two (or more) versions of a function with the same name are allowed provided that the function *signature* is different for each version. The function signature is just the argument list of the function. For example, the following functions have the same name but different signatures:

```
int Func();
int Func(int Arg1);
int Func(float Arg2);
int Func(int Arg1, float Arg2);
```

The argument lists must differ either in the number of arguments, the type of arguments, or both. The return type of a function is *not* part of its signature, so you cannot overload a function merely by changing its return type. For example:

```
int Func(int Arg1);
float Func(int Arg1);
```

is not allowed, since the argument lists of both functions are the same. This will generate a "redeclaration of function" error from the compiler.

Note that the actual data types of the arguments must be different to overload a function. You can't get around this requirement by using a typedef, as in:

```
typedef int NewInt;

void Func(int Arg1);
void Func(NewInt Arg1);
```

Because the data type NewInt is equivalent to an int, the compiler will also flag this as an error.

Despite these restrictions, it *is* possible to have two different functions with identical signatures and the same name, *provided that each function belongs to a different class.* In this case, there is no possibility of confusion, since class functions can only be called with reference to an instance of that class. For example, we could add a function print() with no arguments to each of the account and atm classes, which prints out in some pretty format all the fields in each class. Had we done this, we could call these functions as follows:

```
atm ATMobj;
account AccountObj;

// statements setting up the fields, etc.

ATMobj.print();
AccountObj.print();
```

The correct print() function is called for each object.

## 5.3 Operator overloading

An operator such as + is really just a special kind of function. Operators come in several forms, as discussed in Chapter 3. Unary operators, such as ++, − −, and the unary − take only a single operand. Binary operators, such as the arithmetic operators +, *, / and so on, take two operands, and the conditional operator ? : is a ternary operator, taking three operands. Most operators in C++ can be overloaded. In fact, the built-in versions of some of these operators already are overloaded.

Take the + operator as an example. It can be used to add two floats, two ints, or a mixture of the two forms. On the binary level, floating point numbers are stored in a very different form to integers, so the addition procedure required on the bit level must also be different. The fact that a single operator (+) can be used to add together two different data types is a form of operator overloading: one operator can act on different data types to produce different results.

The rules for overloading operators in C++ are quite liberal, but there are a few restrictions. You can only overload an operator if at least one of its operands in the overloaded version is an object from a user-defined class. For example, you cannot overload the + operator so that it has a different effect than the built-in function when applied to two ints. (You can't overload + so that i+j produces the *difference* between i and j, for example.) You also can't change the "arity" of an operator: unary operators must still be unary, binary operators must remain binary. Other than that, almost anything goes.

As an example, suppose we wanted to overload the += operator in the account class so that it can replace the Deposit() function. That is, to deposit an amount Amount in an account object with name Account, we can write

```
Account += Amount;
```

instead of what we have written up to now:

```
Account.Deposit(Amount);
```

To do this, we make the following declaration as a public field in the account class definition:

```
BOOL operator+= (float Amount);
```

This is actually a function definition just like any other in the class. The function's name is operator+=, its argument is float Amount, and its return value is of type BOOL. The body of this function is *exactly* the same as that given earlier for the Deposit() function.[9]

We can overload the -= operator to duplicate the Withdraw() function in a similar way. We insert the public declaration

```
BOOL operator-= (float Amount);
```

---

[9] In fact, we can call this function in the same way as any other class function: the statement Account.operator+=(Amount) has the same effect as the statement Account += Amount, though it looks less elegant.

in the definition of the class account. Again, the body of this function is exactly the same as that given earlier for the Withdraw() function. If we wanted to test the return value of this operation (for example, to ensure that sufficient funds were in the account for the withdrawal to take place) we can use the statement:

```
if (Account -= Amount)
  cout << "Transaction successful\n";
else
  cout << "Insufficient funds for withdrawal\n";
```

In other words, the only difference between the earlier form where we used an explicit function call such as Account.Withdraw(Amount) and the operator overloaded form is in the method we use to write the statement. All the calculations done by both methods are identical, as is the return value.

Having seen a couple of examples of operator overloading we can now state the rules that must be followed. We begin with the rules for overloading binary operators (such as += and -=):

- The declaration is of the form

```
return_type operator operator_symbol(right_operand);
```

The term operator is a reserved word in C++. Only the right operand of the binary operator is given in the argument list. The left operand is always assumed to be an object of the class in which the overloaded operator is defined. For example, in the above illustration, the left operand of the += operator was an object of class account.
- A binary operator can only be overloaded when the left operand is an object of a user-defined class. The right operand (the argument of the operator) can be of any data type (user-defined or built-in).
- One operator can be overloaded as often as is desired, as long as the two operands are not the same for any two overloadings. For example, we could overload the += operator twice within the account class, once for a float right operand, and once for an int right operand.

Unary operators can be overloaded in a similar fashion. For example, suppose we wished to overload the ++ operator in the account class so that it added £1 to the specified account (that is, it represented a deposit of £1). We would add the following public declaration to the account class:

```
float operator++();
```

In this case, the function has no arguments, since its only operand is an object of class `account`. We have given the overloaded operator a return type of `float`, but this could have been anything. A possible definition of this function is:

```
float account::operator++() {
   return (Balance += 1);
}
```

and a possible use of this operator is:

```
account Account;

cout << "Balance:" << ++account << endl;
```

Note that this way of overloading the ++ operator overloads only the *prefix* version of the operator (that is, the form where the ++ precedes the operand). It is also possible to overload the postfix version. To do this, we add a dummy `int` argument to the function. The following example overloads the postfix form of ++ so that it deposits £2 into the account:

```
float account::operator++(int dummy) {
   return (Balance += 2);
}
```

It can be used as follows:

```
account Account;

cout << "Balance:" << account++ << endl;
```

Note that this overloaded version of the postfix form of ++ differs from the ordinary form of the operator as it is applied to an `int`. Recall that the difference between `++IntVar` and `IntVar++`, where `IntVar` is an int variable, is that the returned value from the `++IntVar` operation is the value of `IntVar` *after* the ++ operator has been applied, while the returned value from the `IntVar++` operation is the value of `IntVar` *before* the ++ operation. In our example of overloading ++ in the `account` class, the return value is the value of the `Balance` field *after* the operation in both cases. This was entirely our decision, of course; we could equally as well have adhered to the original convention.

There are many more things we could do with operator overloading. For example it is even possible to overload the square brackets [ ] ordinarily used to denote an array element, the round brackets ( ) used for enclosing function arguments, the `new` operator, and so on. However, these are fairly esoteric features of C++ which we will not have need of in this book. If you are interested in these features, you should consult a reference book on C++.

## 5.3.1 The overloaded assignment (=) operator

There is, however, one final overloaded operator which we do need to consider: the overloaded assignment operator =. The reason this is important is the same as the reason we needed a copy constructor. If we have two variables Atm1 and Atm2 of class atm, say, the statement

```
Atm1 = Atm2;
```

means "copy the fields of Atm2 into the corresponding fields of Atm1". An overloaded version of the = operator is provided automatically by the compiler when you apply it between two variables of the same user-defined class. However, just as with the default copy constructor, this form of the = operator only performs a shallow copy; any dynamically allocated memory attached to pointer fields will not be copied. As a result, it is possible to have two different variables that share the same address space for some of their fields, leading to disastrous consequences.

The overloaded = operator for the atm class could be declared and defined as follows. In the public section of the atm class definition, we add:

```
atm operator=(const atm& SourceAtm);
```

and elsewhere, we give its definition:

```
atm atm::operator=(const atm& SourceAtm)
{
  if (this == &SourceAtm)
    return (*this);
  if (NumAccounts != SourceAtm.NumAccounts) {
    cout << "Error in assignment:
      different array sizes.\n";
    return 0;
  } else {
    EnteredCode = SourceAtm.EnteredCode;
    CardCode = SourceAtm.CardCode;
    for (int i = 0; i < NumAccounts; i++)
      Account[i] = SourceAtm.Account[i];
    return (*this);
  }
}
```

This function duplicates, for the most part, what the copy constructor did earlier for the same class. There are a few things to note however.

First, we have specified the return value of this operator to be of type atm, because we plan to follow the convention in C++ of having the = operator return its left operand after the operation.

Second, we have made use of another C++ reserved word that we haven't met up to now: the keyword this. The keyword this is always a *pointer* to the specific object which invoked the function in which it is found. For example, if this overloaded = operator were invoked by the statement:

```
atm Atm1, Atm2;

Atm1 = Atm2;
```

then the left operand of the = operator (the variable Atm1) invoked the function call, so this becomes a pointer to Atm1, and *this becomes the actual value of Atm1 itself. The first thing the overloaded = operator does is compare the pointer to the left operand (given by this) with the pointer to the right operand (given by &SourceAtm). If they are equal, this means that you are attempting to assign a variable to itself, so no action need be taken other than to return the value of the variable, which is done by the return(*this) statement.

The main difference between the overloaded = operator and the copy constructor is that the = operator assumes that its left operand already exists (including any dynamically allocated parts), while the copy constructor assumes that it must create a new instance of the class before it does any copying. In the overloaded = operator given here for the atm class, we require that the array sizes of the two operands are equal before we allow any copying to take place. If this is true, then the = operator copies all the fields from SourceAtm to the left operand, and returns the value of the left operand.

This isn't the only way we could have written the overloaded = operator. We might, for example, have decided that the assignment should always take place, regardless of the relative sizes of the Account arrays in the two operands. In this case, we could delete the array elements in the left operand and then reallocate memory to make the array in the left operand the same size as the array in the right operand. The code for this is:

```
atm atm::operator=(const atm& SourceAtm)
{
  if (this == &SourceAtm)
    return (*this);
  if (NumAccounts != SourceAtm.NumAccounts) {
    delete [] Account;
    Account = new account[SourceAtm.NumAccounts];
    NumAccounts = SourceAtm.NumAccounts;
  }
```

```
  EnteredCode = SourceAtm.EnteredCode;
  CardCode = SourceAtm.CardCode;
  for (int i = 0; i < NumAccounts; i++)
    Account[i] = SourceAtm.Account[i];
  return (*this);
}
```

Which of these two methods (or some other method, if you like) you decide to use for the overloaded = operator depends, of course, on the context in which it is to be used.

A good general rule is that an overloaded assignment operator is required whenever a copy constructor is, since they both achieve essentially the same ends, although the contexts in which each is required are different.

## 5.4 Summary

The main points introduced in the chapter are:

- **Function overloading**
    - Two or more functions within the same class may have the same name, provided their *signatures* (argument lists) are different.
    - The return type of the function is *not* part of the signature.
    - Two functions with the same name and identical signatures may exist, provided that the functions are fields in different classes.
- **Operator overloading**
    - Most operators may be *overloaded* for use with user-defined classes.
    - At least one of the operands of an overloaded operator must be a user-defined object.
    - The arity (unary or binary) of an operator cannot be changed.
    - Use the syntax `ReturnType operatorSymbol(Argument)` to define an overloaded operator.
    - The prefix and postfix versions of the ++ and -- operators may both be overloaded. Provide a dummy `int` argument for the postfix version.
    - The assignment operator = must be overloaded for any class containing dynamically allocated memory in its fields.

## 5.5 Exercises

1. For a class named `MultClass`, write a *declaration* for an overloaded form of the * operator in which both operands are of type `MultClass`, and the return type is `float`.

2. Write declarations for overloaded forms of the unary -- operator (both prefix and postfix versions) for a class named `BigMinus`.

3. The program given below provides an example of an overloaded + operator. Copy the program to your own directory and run it to see how the overloaded + operator works. Note that it adds together the two `int` fields in each object and returns an object of class `Object`.

```
#include<iostream.h>
class Object
{
private:
   int Field1, Field2;
public:
   Object(int field1=0, int field2=100) :
     Field1(field1), Field2(field2) {}
   void Print() {
     cout << "Field1 = " << Field1 << "; Field2 = "
     << Field2 << endl; }
   Object operator+(Object& SecondObject);
};

Object Object::operator+(Object& SecondObject)
{
   Object LocalObject;

   LocalObject.Field1 = Field1 + SecondObject.Field1;
   LocalObject.Field2 = Field2 + SecondObject.Field2;
   return LocalObject;
}

int main()
{
   Object Obj1(5,10), Obj2(15,20), Sum;

   Sum = Obj1 + Obj2;
   Sum.Print();
   return 0;
}
```

a. Add a second overloaded operator for the – operation, which subtracts the `Field1` and `Field2` fields of the second operand from the corresponding fields in the first operand. Add code to the `main()` function to use this operator on `Obj1` and `Obj2`, and print out the result using the `Print()` function.

b. Add an overloaded version of the += operator which adds the `Field1` and `Field2` fields of its right operand to the corresponding fields of its left operand and returns the left operand. (That is, it works the same way as the += operator on an `int`, except that it operates on both fields of the object.) Add a couple of lines to the end of the `main()` function to apply this operator in the form `Sum += Obj1`, then print out the result.

c. Add an overloaded version of the unary ++ operator which adds 1 to both the fields Field1 and Field2. Overload the ++ operator only in the prefix version, so it can be applied in the form ++Obj1. The operator should return its operand *after* it has added 1 to both fields (that is, it should work in the same way as ++i does when i is an int). Add a couple of lines at the end of the main() function applying this operator to Sum, and print out the result.

d. Add a second overloaded version of the unary ++ operator which adds 1 to both the fields Field1 and Field2, except this time overload the ++ operator in the *postfix* version, so it can be applied in the form Obj1++. The operator should return its operand *before* it has added 1 to both fields (that is, it should work in the same way as i++ when i is an int). The main() function provided tests out the two versions of the overloaded ++ operator by saving the return value in a variable Plus. The comments in the code explain what values Plus should have in each case. Use this main() function (or something similar) to test your answers.

```
int main()
{
    Object Obj1(5,10), Obj2(15,20), Sum, Plus;

    Plus = ++Sum;    //Plus should be Sum AFTER ++
    Sum.Print();
    Plus.Print();
    Plus = Sum++;    //Plus should be Sum BEFORE ++
    Sum.Print();
    Plus.Print();
    return 0;
}
```

4. Select *all* statements in which an assignment occurs:
   A. int NewNum = 34;
   B. NewNum = 34;
   C. if (x = y) cout << "Statement is true.\n";
   D. float NewReal(2.34);
   E. float RealArray[10];
   F. float *RealArray = new float[10];

5. Select *all* statements in which an initialization occurs:
   A. float real1 = 3.57;
   B. real1 = 3.57;
   C. int num1(90);
   D. int num1;
   E. int numarray[25];
   F. int *numarray;
   G. int *numarray = new int[10];

6. An overloaded version of the = operator for the class oddClass is declared as:

```
oddClass operator=(const oddClass& Source);
```

Select all cases where this operator would be used (all variables are of type oddClass):

A. `oddClass Object1 = Object2;`
B. `Object1 = Object2;`
C. `if (Object1 == Object2)`
     `cout << "Objects are equal.\n";`
D. `oddClass *ObjectArray = new oddClass[13];`
E. `ObjectValue = FunctionThatReturnsoddClass();`
F. `oddClass ObjectValue =`
     `FunctionThatReturnsoddClass();`

7. Reread question 14 in Chapter 4, in which the class dynArray was defined. Using the class definition from that question, run the following main() function. Notice that both TestArray1 and TestArray2 are initialized to the same values. The two objects are printed to show that they are the same at the start of main(). Then an assignment operator is used, followed by the UpdateArrays() function being applied only to TestArray1. You should find, however, that when the arrays are printed, they both show the same values.

a. Explain why this happens.

b. Write an overloaded = operator for the dynArray class that will fix this problem. Run the program again to test that it works.

```
void main()
{
   dynArray TestArray1(4,5), TestArray2(4,5);

   TestArray1.PrintArrays();
   TestArray2.PrintArrays();
   TestArray2 = TestArray1;
   TestArray1.UpdateArrays();
   cout << "After using operator= and updating:\n";
   TestArray1.PrintArrays();
   TestArray2.PrintArrays();
}
```

# CHAPTER 6

# Inheritance

## 6.1 Code reuse

One of the great advantages of OOP, its proponents claim, is the ability to reuse large amounts of code. This claim should arouse a bit of suspicion in you, since all well-written code should be reusable to a certain extent. Part of the idea of top-down design in a procedural language such as C or Pascal is to identify blocks of code which can stand on their own and be plugged into new programs without any changes. This principle has been used to build up libraries of functions for various languages (such as the C libraries available in UNIX, or the libraries of Windows functions available on PCs).

The idea of code reuse in an OOP language, however, goes deeper than this. The introduction of the class/object concept means that not only individual functions, but entire classes can be reused. For example, if you write banking programs that use ATMs, you can simply transplant the atm class we defined earlier into another program and proceed from there.

Once you get into the habit of doing this, it won't take you long to discover that although the ability to lift classes out of one program and drop them into another is very handy, it would be even more convenient if you could add on some extra fields to a previously defined class, without having to write out the existing fields again. This is one of the reasons that *inheritance* was introduced into OOP languages.

To illustrate what we mean, suppose we consider the account class we have been using to represent the details of a bank account. Up to now, we have only considered one type of account, and have allowed only very basic information (the balance and the account number) to be stored about each account. Banks usually have several types of account available to their customers: chequing accounts, savings accounts, high interest, restricted access accounts, and so on. All of these different types of accounts still have balances and account numbers associated with them, and allow deposits and withdrawals, so if we wanted to define classes to represent them, we would like to use the same (or similar) fields and functions that we have defined for the simple account class we have used so far.

One way of doing this would be to use an editor to duplicate the code that we have already written and add in the extra fields that we need for each special type of account. This will rapidly become tedious, and will cause the amount of code to grow very quickly through the duplication. The inheritance mechanism in OOP allows us to *derive* new classes that *inherit* all the fields (properties and actions) from another class, called a *base class*.

Before we get into the details of how this is done in C++, it is worth emphasizing a few things about inheritance.

- Inheritance is used in a situation where we can define a general class of things (such as bank accounts), and we wish to define more specific classes based on this general class. In other words, inheritance is appropriate when we can identify several classes that are *special cases* of a more general class, such as chequing and savings accounts which are special cases of a more general bank account. For this reason, the relation between the base class and derived classes in inheritance is often referred to as a *type-of* relationship: each of the derived classes is a *type of* the base class.

- A common mistake made by those new to inheritance is to attempt to use it in a situation where a class *contains* one or more instances of another class. For example, the `atm` class we have been using to represent an ATM contains an array (or a pointer to an array) of `account` objects. It is *not* correct to use inheritance in this case: you cannot construct a correct model by attempting to have the `atm` class inherit the `account` class. This should become clear if you realize that an ATM is *not* a special type of account. The two classes are quite distinct. The only connection between an ATM and an account is that an ATM is used to provide access to an account.

- It is also not correct to use inheritance to allow access to the fields of one class by the functions in another class, if those two classes do not form a type-of relationship as described earlier. For example, if we defined a class `customer` to represent someone with an account at our bank, it is not correct to define the `customer` class as a derived class of the `account` class in order to allow the functions in the `customer` class to access private fields in the `account` class. If the customer wished to deposit some money into the account, the proper way to do it is for the `customer` object to call the public `Deposit()` function for the `account` object into which the money is to be deposited, and *not* for one of the functions in the `customer` class to directly access the private `Balance` field in the `account` class.

  If you find yourself tempted to use inheritance to provide access to private fields in one class by functions in another, unrelated, class, this is a sure sign that your OO design is flawed. Different classes that do not share a 'type-of' relationship should *only* communicate with each other through their public interface functions, and *never* by directly accessing each other's private data fields.

- Inheritance provides a cornerstone in OO design because it allows you to construct hierarchies of classes. These hierarchies can be reused as blocks in various programs, and have extra fields added to them to enlarge the hierarchies in other programs. The concept of code reuse thus expands from simply reusing individual functions to reusing entire data constructs. A complete data description can be designed, coded, and tested, and then inherited by another application with the confidence that that block of the design has been thoroughly debugged.

# 6.2 Inheritance in C++

The syntax for declaring a derived class which inherits a base class is:

```
class DerivedClass : public BaseClass {
  statements
};
```

The notation signifies that the class DerivedClass inherits the class BaseClass. This means that all the *public* fields of BaseClass are available in DerivedClass just as if they were defined in DerivedClass (we'll worry about private fields in BaseClass in a minute). The keyword public after the colon signifies that the public fields of BaseClass are also public fields in DerivedClass, meaning that they are accessible by functions outside those contained in BaseClass and DerivedClass in the usual way. If we had used the keyword private instead of public, the public fields in BaseClass would become *private* fields of DerivedClass. This means that DerivedClass functions could still access these fields, but functions not contained in DerivedClass could not.

As an example, let us use the account class as a base class and define two derived classes, one for chequing accounts and one for savings accounts.

```
class account
{
protected:
  float Balance;
  int AccountNumber;
public:
  account(float balance = 0.0, int accountnumber = -1);
  BOOL Withdraw(float Amount);
  BOOL Deposit(float Amount);
  float CheckBalance();
  int CheckAccountNumber();
};

class chequing : public account
{
private:
  float Overdraft;
public:
  chequing(float overdraft = 0.0);
  BOOL CashCheque(float  Amount);
};

class savings : public account
{
```

```
private:
    float InterestRate;
public:
    savings(float InterestRate = 5.0);
    void AddInterest();
};
```

There are several points to note about these definitions:

- The `private` keyword in the base class `account` has been replaced by the keyword `protected`. A `protected` field is one that is accessible to class functions from the class within which it is defined, and in all classes derived from that class. Thus `Balance` and `AccountNumber` are available directly to the base class and to both derived classes in this example, but could not be accessed directly by any code outside these classes.
- The fields defined in each derived class are added to those inherited from the base class. For example, if the `chequing` class were written out in full, it would look like:

```
class chequing
{
private:
    float Balance;
    int AccountNumber;
    float Overdraft;
public:
    // The constructor is a special case - see below
    chequing(float overdraft = 0.0);
    BOOL Withdraw(float Amount);
    BOOL Deposit(float Amount);
    float CheckBalance();
    int CheckAccountNumber();
    BOOL CashCheque(float  Amount);
};
```

If both the `account` class and the `chequing` class were defined separately, without using inheritance, not only would the definition of the `chequing` class be much longer, as is shown here, but all the class functions would have to be redefined (all the code would have to be written out again), even for those functions that are identical in both classes.

## 6.2.1 Constructors and inheritance

Both the base class and the derived class can have their own constructor functions. This causes a few complications. When an object of class `chequing` is defined, the derived class constructor is called first, followed by the constructor for the base class. For example, a possible constructor for the `chequing` class is:

```
chequing::chequing(float overdraft)  :
  Overdraft(overdraft)  {}
```

The constructor merely initializes the value of the `Overdraft` field in the derived class. However, even though no explicit mention is made of the fields inherited from the base class, the argumentless constructor for the `account` class will be called by default. Herein lies a problem: if you have neglected to define an argumentless constructor for the base class, but you *have* defined a constructor *with* arguments, the constructor for the `chequing` class will attempt to access an argumentless constructor from the base class, fail to find it (remember that the compiler will *not* generate an argumentless constructor if you have defined any constructors on your own), and flag an error. There are two ways around this problem:

1. Make sure the base class has an argumentless constructor defined for it.
2. Make an explicit call to one of the existing base class constructors in the derived class constructor.

The first solution is easy enough, but may not do what you want. For example, you might not want to accept the default initialization values for all your fields. The second solution can be implemented by including a call to the base class constructor as part of the initialization list in the derived class constructor:

```
chequing::chequing(float overdraft)  :
  Overdraft(overdraft), account(25.50, 34) {}
```

This form of the constructor initializes the `Overdraft` field in the derived class by means of an argument to the constructor, and then initializes the two inherited fields to constant values of 25.50 and 34. In the most general case, you probably want to have control over all the values used for initialization. To do this, you need to expand the argument list in the `chequing` constructor. The most general form must first be declared in the definition of the class:

```
chequing::chequing(float overdraft = 0.0,
  float balance = 0.0, int accountnumber = -1);
```

and then defined:

```
chequing::chequing(float overdraft,
  float balance, int accountnumber)  :
  Overdraft(overdraft), account(balance, accountnumber)
  {}
```

The function `CashCheque` in the `chequing` class was included merely to show that a derived class can add functions of its own to those it inherits from the base class. No new techniques are required to define this function, which is left as an exercise for the reader.

The other derived class, `savings`, may be defined and modified in exactly the same way as the `chequing` class. In particular, the constructor given for this class contains only one argument to allow explicit initialization of the new `InterestRate` field defined in the derived class. If this constructor is used, the argumentless constructor from the `account` class will be called by default. Just as with the `chequing` class, an explicit call to the `account` constructor with arguments can be made.

## 6.3 Function overloading in derived classes

The examples of inheritance we've seen so far have assumed that any functions declared in the base class will be inherited and used in the derived classes in exactly the same form. In some cases, this may not be what the user wants.

Returning to our example using the various types of bank accounts, some banks only allow withdrawals larger than a certain amount from savings accounts, and make an administration charge if a withdrawal is made from a chequing account. We would like to incorporate these extra conditions in the derived classes, but it would be convenient if whatever function we defined for making withdrawals could still be called `Withdraw()` no matter what type of account it is connected to.

C++ allows you to do this by permitting any function in the base class to be overloaded in the derived classes. This kind of function overloading is a bit different from that which we discussed in Chapter 5, because in this case, a function in the derived class is allowed to have exactly the same *signature* (recall that the signature of a function consists of its name together with the data types of its argument list) as a function in the base class. It is possible to do this because the compiler can tell which function to apply by examining the class of the object calling the function.

Let us see how function overloading works by providing overloaded versions of the `Withdraw()` function for both chequing and savings accounts:

```
class account
{
protected:
  float Balance;
  int AccountNumber;
public:
  account(float balance = 0.0, int accountnumber = -1);
  BOOL Withdraw(float Amount);
```

```
  BOOL Deposit(float Amount);
  float CheckBalance();
  int CheckAccountNumber();
};

class chequing : public account
{
private:
  float Overdraft;
  float AdminCharge;
public:
  chequing(float overdraft = 0.0, float balance = 0.0,
    float accountnumber = -1,
    float admincharge = 0.50);
  BOOL CashCheque(float  Amount);
  BOOL Withdraw(float Amount);
};
```

Here we have copied out the definitions of the base and the derived classes from earlier in the chapter. The base account class is unchanged. We have added an identical declaration of the Withdraw() function to the derived chequing class. A private field AdminCharge, which is the administration charge for making a withdrawal from a chequing account, has been added to the derived class as well. The constructor has also been modified to allow initialization of this administration charge. The default value is 50p.

A possible definition of the overloaded form of the Withdraw() function is:

```
BOOL chequing::Withdraw(float Amount)
{
  if (Balance >= (Amount + AdminCharge)) {
    Balance -= Amount + AdminCharge;
    return TRUE;
  } else {
    return FALSE;
  }
}
```

The main difference between this definition and that of the original Withdraw() function for the account class, is that the class name (chequing) has been used to identify which class the function belongs to. The administration charge has been added to the amount debited from the account when a withdrawal is made.

## 6.4 Pointers and virtual functions

While the above method for overloading functions in derived classes is simple and straightforward, it is not as flexible as we would like in certain conditions. To see why, consider the following situation. Suppose you are managing several bank accounts of various types (savings or chequing). Every so often, you need to review the accounts and send out letters to the customers if there is something amiss. Let us say that you deem it necessary to send out a letter to the holder of a chequing account if that account has an overdraft, and to the holder of a savings account if the balance in the account is less than £1. You could do this by adding a function to the `chequing` derived class in which you test to see if the account has an overdraft, and another function to the `savings` derived class in which you test to see if the balance is less than £1. You would then need to call the appropriate function depending on which class the account belonged to.

All of this can get rather cumbersome, requiring separate variables for the different account types, and separate sections of code to arrange the correct function call. A much cleaner solution would be to store *all* the accounts in a *single* array, and then just loop through this array once, calling the appropriate function for each array element, depending on which account type it is.

Like many other languages, it is not legal to declare an array in C++ where the elements are different data types (since all elements of the array are supposed to take up the same space, which is what gives arrays their efficient data access). However it *is* legal to declare an array of *pointers* in C++ where each pointer points to a different type of object. This still allows the array elements to all be the same size, since all pointers are just integers. Let us take a look at the C++ syntax for assigning a pointer to different data types.

If we have a base class (like `account`) and a derived class (like `chequing`), we can declare a pointer to the base class, as in:

```
account *AccountPtr;
```

We can now allocate some memory for this pointer to point to, but unlike a pointer to an ordinary data type such as `int`, the pointer is allowed to point either to an object of the class for which it was declared (in this case, `account`) *or* to an object of any class derived from this class (such as `chequing` or `savings`).

We can extend this idea by declaring an array of pointers:

```
account *AccountPtr[3];
```

and having each element of the array point to a different class:

```
AccountPtr[0] = new account(50,12);
AccountPtr[1] = new chequing(0,25.50,15);
AccountPtr[2] = new savings;
```

Element 0 of the array points to an object of the base class `account`, element 1 to an object of the derived `chequing` class, and element 2 to an object of the derived `savings` class.

Before we can take full advantage of the capability, we need to introduce the concept of a *virtual function*. When we overloaded the `Withdraw()` function above, we simply duplicated the declaration of the function in each of the derived classes, then provided different function bodies for each version of the function. The following code fragment illustrates how the different versions of the `Withdraw()` function can be accessed:

```
account Account(50);
chequing Cheque(0,100);

Account.Withdraw(10);
Cheque.Withdraw(10);
```

The variable `Account` is defined to have an initial balance of 50, and the variable `Cheque` has an initial overdraft of 0 and an initial balance of 100. All other variables are given the default values listed in the declaration of the constructors for each class. In particular, the chequing account has an administration charge of 50p. If you run this code, printing out the balance of each account before and after the withdrawal, you will see that the functions called are different: only £10 is withdrawn from `Account` but £10.50 is debited from `Cheque`.

With pointers to base and derived classes, things aren't quite so straightforward. First, we need a bit of new notation. If we have declared a pointer to a class such as:

```
account *AccountPtr = new account(50);
```

where we have initialized the space it points to in the declaration, we can access the fields of this object by using an arrow `->` in place of the conventional dot that is used when the variable is declared directly to be an object of a particular class. For example, we can access the `Balance` field of the object pointed to by `AccountPtr` using the notation

```
AccountPtr->Balance
```

Similarly, we can call the `Withdraw()` function for this object using the notation `AccountPtr->Withdraw(10)`.

Now suppose we declare an array of pointers to the `account` base class and initialize them to point to different classes as before:

```
account *AccountPtr[3];
```

```
AccountPtr[0] = new account(50,12);
AccountPtr[1] = new chequing(0,25.50,15);
AccountPtr[2] = new savings;
```

This time, if we try to apply the withdrawal function to each of these accounts, we might try

```
AccountPtr[0]->Withdraw(10);
AccountPtr[1]->Withdraw(10);
AccountPtr[2]->Withdraw(10);
```

However, if you insert cout statements into each of the Withdraw() functions to trace which function is called in each case, you will find that all three calls are handled by the Withdraw() function belonging to the base class account. The reason why there is a difference between which function is called when we are dealing with pointers to classes and when we are dealing directly with objects is that in the pointer case we are using dynamic memory allocation: the actual class to which the pointer points is not determined until the program is actually run. In the case where we are dealing directly with the object (no pointers), the fields of the object are *bound* to the variable at compile time. In the pointer case, no fields are bound to the pointer, since the object to which the pointer is to be assigned need not be determined when the program is compiled.

We can ensure that the function appropriate to the class is called by declaring that version of the function in the base class as a *virtual function*. This is done simply by adding the keyword virtual before the function declaration. The account class definition thus becomes:

```
class account
{
protected:
  float Balance;
  int AccountNumber;
public:
  account(float balance = 0.0, int accountnumber = -1);
  virtual BOOL Withdraw(float Amount);
  BOOL Deposit(float Amount);
  float CheckBalance();
  int CheckAccountNumber();
};
```

No changes are necessary to the functions in the derived classes, unless these classes are in turn inherited by other classes, in which case the functions in these classes should also be declared as virtual.

With this alteration, we can now apply the `Withdraw()` function to a field of a pointer to any class (base or derived) and get the correct response. We can, for example, process the entire array by using a loop:

```
account *AccountPtr[3];

AccountPtr[0] = new account(50,12);
AccountPtr[1] = new chequing(0,25.50,15);
AccountPtr[2] = new savings;

for (int i = 0; i < 3; i++)
  AccountPtr[i]->Withdraw(10);
```

# 6.5 Destructors and virtual destructors

We have seen that a constructor for an object of a derived class automatically calls the constructor for the base class. What about destructors?

In simple inheritance, where objects of the derived class are declared directly (without using pointers), the destructors are called in reverse order to the constructors (that is, base class first, then derived class). If we are using dynamic allocation to create derived objects, we need to use *virtual destructors* to ensure that the correct destructors are called.

Consider the following code fragment:

```
account *ChequeAcct = new chequing(0,25,15);
delete ChequeAcct;
```

This definition declares a pointer to the base class and initializes it as pointing to a derived class. The `delete` statement, however, will call only the destructor for the *base* class, *unless* that destructor is declared as virtual, and another destructor is provided in the derived class. The virtual destructor in the base class will be called by the destructor in the derived class before the commands in the derived destructor are themselves executed. In other words, the destructors are called in the reverse order to the constructor functions, as you would expect.

For example, consider the base and derived classes shown:

```
class account
{
protected:
  float Balance;
  int AccountNumber;
public:
  account(float balance = 0.0, int accountnumber = -1);
  virtual ~account();
  virtual BOOL Withdraw(float Amount);
  BOOL Deposit(float Amount);
  float CheckBalance();
```

```
   int CheckAccountNumber();
};

class chequing : public account
{
private:
   float Overdraft;
   float AdminCharge;
public:
   ~chequing();
   chequing(float overdraft = 0.0, float balance = 0.0,
      float accountnumber = -1,
      float admincharge = 0.50);
   BOOL CashCheque(float  Amount);
   BOOL Withdraw(float Amount);
};
```

A statement such as delete ChequeAcct will result in the account destructor being called first, followed by the chequing destructor. If the account destructor had not been declared virtual, it would have been the only destructor called.

## 6.6 Inheritance in OO design

Inheritance is often difficult to get used to for someone coming to an OO language after some time using a procedural language like C or Pascal. As a result, some programmers tend to avoid it because it doesn't fit naturally with their way of thinking. If you are going to write proper OO programs, however, you really need to use inheritance whenever it is appropriate. You will find that inheritance fits more naturally into your design if you begin your analysis of the problem to be solved by listing all the classes in the model. Then, go over your list attempting to identify those classes which are "special cases" of a more general class (for example, chequing and savings accounts are specific types of bank accounts). All such classes may be derived from a base class which contains those properties and functions common to all members of the group. Certain actions may have variations in each derived class, but this can be handled in C++ using the virtual function mechanism.

After some practice analysing problems this way, you should find that it becomes natural to think of models in terms of classes and class hierarchies, rather than as individual, disconnected functions as is necessary in a procedural language.

## 6.7 Summary

The main points introduced in this chapter are:

- Inheritance allows a new class to *inherit* the fields of another class, and use them as its own.

115

- The original class is the *base class*, and the new class is the *derived class*.
- Inheritance is appropriate if the new class is a specialized type of the base class.
- Inheritance is used in a "type-of" relationship.
- Inheritance allows a class or set of classes to be designed and tested, and then inherited in other code.
- The inheritance syntax in C++ is:

```
class DerivedClass : public BaseClass {...};
```

- A *private* field in a base class is not accessible to a derived class.
- A *protected* field in a base class is accessible to a derived class, but not to any other class.
- The derived class constructor is called first, then the base class constructor.
- A function in the base class may be overloaded (with the same signature) in a derived class.
- A *pointer* declared as pointing to a base class object is allowed to point to an object from a class derived from this base class.
- A derived class function may be accessed through such a pointer provided that the corresponding function in the base class is declared as `virtual`.
- The virtual function feature allows arrays of pointers to different object types to be processed in the same way.

## 6.8 Exercises

1. Consider the class definitions:

```
class BaseClass
{
protected:
   int Num1;
public:
   BaseClass() : Num1(0) {}
   void TestFunc() { Num1 += 10; }
};

class DerClass : public BaseClass
{
public:
   void TestFunc() { Num1 += 20; }
};
```

a. After the code:

```
BaseClass Object1;
Object1.TestFunc();
```

what is the value of `Object1.Num1`?

b. After the code:

```
DerClass Object2;
Object2.TestFunc();
```

what is the value of `Object2.Num1`?

c. After the code:

```
BaseClass *Object3 = new BaseClass;
Object3->TestFunc();
```

what is the value of `Object3.Num1`?

d. After the code:

```
BaseClass *Object4 = new DerClass;
Object4->TestFunc();
```

what is the value of `Object4.Num1`?

e. The declaration of `TestFunc()` in `BaseClass` is now replaced by the line:

```
virtual TestFunc() { Num1 += 10; }
```

After the code:

```
BaseClass *Object5 = new DerClass;
Object5->TestFunc();
```

what is the value of `Object5.Num1`?

2. What is wrong with the following code?

```
class BaseClass
{
protected:
   int Num1;
   float Real1;
public:
   BaseClass(int num1, float real1) :
     Num1(num1), Real1(real1) {}
};

class DerClass : public BaseClass
{
private:
   char Thingy;
public:
   DerClass(thingy = 'x') : Thingy(thingy) {}
};
```

3. Consider the C++ code shown:

```
#include<iostream.h>
class BaseClass
{
protected:
   int Num1;
public:
   BaseClass() : Num1(42)  {}
   void Print() { cout << "Num1 = " << Num1 << endl; }
};

// Insert DerClass here

int main()
{
   BaseClass BaseObj;
   DerClass DerObj;

   BaseObj.Print();
   DerObj.Print();
   return 0;
}
```

a. Starting with the code below, write a second class called DerClass which inherits BaseClass. DerClass should contain a private int field called Num2, a constructor which initializes Num2 to the value of 104, and a Print() function which prints out the values of Num1 and Num2. (Note that Num1 should be inherited from the class BaseClass). Modify BaseClass as necessary.

Note that the Print() function is being overloaded: the same name and same signature is used in both classes, but the compiler decides which function to call based on which object calls it.

b. Modify the BaseClass constructor by giving it a default value for Num1. Modify the DerClass constructor by having it initialize Num1 by calling the constructor for BaseClass, *not* by using a statement of the form Num1(98) in the DerClass constructor.

c. Now alter the constructor in DerClass so that it allows the user to input values for the initial values of Num1 and Num2.

d. Using your two classes after answering part (c), use the following main() routine and run the program without any further modifications. Note that the main() function uses dynamic allocation to declare two objects: one of type BaseClass and the other of type DerClass. A pointer to type BaseClass is used for both declarations.

You should find that the Print() function from BaseClass is called for both objects, even though Obj2 is an object of class DerClass. Change the program so that the statement Obj2->Print() calls the Print() function from DerClass. (Do *not* change anything in main() to do this.)

```
int main()
{
    int num1, num2;
    BaseClass *Obj1 = new BaseClass;
    cout << "Enter initial values for Num1 and Num2: ";
    cin >> num1 >> num2;
    BaseClass *Obj2 = new DerClass(num1,num2);

    Obj1->Print();
    Obj2->Print();
    return 0;
}
```

4. The code below gives two class definitions, both of which contain a dynamically allocated array. Write definitions for all the functions declared in the classes so that they perform the following tasks:

- The BaseClass constructor should use its argument to initialize BaseArraySize, and to allocate memory (using new) for BaseArraySize ints in the array BaseArray. The array elements should be initialized to 0. The DerClass constructor should do the same thing for DerArraySize and DerArray.
- The destructor for each class should deallocate the memory for the array in that class.
- The Print() function for each class should print out the array size followed by the complete contents of the array for that class.

In the main() function, an object of DerClass and a pointer to BaseClass which is initialized to point to an object of class DerClass are declared. Use this main() function to test your code, without making any modifications to either the class definitions or the main() routine as given below. Note that when DerPtr is deleted, only the BaseClass destructor is called, and that DerPtr->Print() calls the Print() function from BaseClass (insert extra output statements as necessary to verify this).

Alter the class definitions so that deleting DerPtr calls both destructors, and DerPtr->Print() calls the DerClass Print() function.

```
class BaseClass
{
protected:
```

```
  int *BaseArray;
  int BaseArraySize;
public:
  BaseClass(int basearraysize=10);
  ~BaseClass();
  void Print();
};

class DerClass : public BaseClass
{
protected:
  int *DerArray;
  int DerArraySize;
public:
  DerClass(int derarraysize=5);
  ~DerClass();
  void Print();
};

void main()
{
  DerClass DerObj;
  BaseClass *DerPtr = new DerClass;

  DerPtr->Print();
  delete DerPtr;
  DerObj.Print();
}
```

5. Design a class hierarchy which represents methods of transportation. As an example of what you might try: at the top level should be a single base class containing properties common to all modes of transport. On the next layer, derive classes from this base class to represent transport on land, water, in the air, and in space. On land, you might consider walking, car, bus, and so on. You may further subdivide the car class by considering different types of cars. Carefully consider what properties and actions are appropriate at each level. Translate your description into C++ class definitions, using the features of inheritance discussed in this chapter. (You do not need to actually write the function definitions in order to construct a class hierarchy, although you may wish to do so, and hence obtain a fully working program which simulates various forms of transport.)

# CHAPTER 7

# Stacks and queues

## 7.1 Data structures and algorithms in C++

Up to now, we have concentrated entirely on object oriented programming and its implementation in the C++ language. OOP is a big subject, and it will take you time to master its intricacies and to learn to design and write properly constructed object oriented programs. We will continue to give examples of object oriented code in what follows, but we must now shift our focus slightly to accommodate the other main topic of this book: data structures and algorithms.

Although future versions of C++ will no doubt have a standard class library containing most of the data structures which are studied in this book, the current version has relatively few built-in data structures and classes. Beyond the syntax of the language itself, a standard C++ installation will have an input/output library (as exemplified by the `cin` and `cout` operations), a mathematical library (including functions from trigonometry, exponentials and logarithms, and so on), and possibly a few other libraries for more mundane tasks such as string handling and interaction with the operating system. You cannot count on finding any other data structures such as stacks, queues, sets, linked lists, tables, trees, or graphs, despite the fact that these data structures are commonly used in many program designs.

Some commercial compilers provide class libraries containing some of these data structures. Even if you are fortunate enough to have access to one of these compilers, it is a good idea to understand how these data structures and their associated algorithms are defined and used, so that you can make an intelligent choice of data structure and algorithm for your particular programming problem.

We will begin our survey of data structures with two of the simplest and most commonly used: stacks and queues.

## 7.2 Stacks

### 7.2.1 The stack data structure

To get a feel for what a stack is, and why it might be useful, suppose you wanted to design an algorithm for reversing a string of characters. If the characters are stored in an array, the simplest way to reverse them might be to locate the end of the string and just list the characters from that point back to the beginning of the array, using a simple `for` loop. However, suppose you don't know in advance how many characters there are in the string. This might be the case if you are reading the characters in, one at a time, from the keyboard or a file. One particularly simple method of reversing such a string might be the following:

1. Read in a character.
2. Place the character 'on top' of any previously read characters.
3. Repeat steps 1 and 2 until no more characters are presented for reading.
4. Remove the top character from the pile you created in the first part of the algorithm.
5. Print the character to the right of any previously printed characters.
6. Repeat steps 4 and 5 until all the characters have been printed out.

If you try this algorithm for a string of your own devising, you will see that it produces as its output the original string in reverse order. The pile of characters that you created by repeated application of steps 1 and 2 is an example of a *stack*.

The main features of a stack are:

• Access is allowed at one end (the *top* of the stack) only. Data are added and removed at this end.

• The action of adding a data element to a stack is called *pushing*.

• The action of removing a data element from a stack is called *popping*.

• Stacks handle data in a *last-in-first-out*, or LIFO, fashion: the last item pushed onto the stack is always the first item popped off the stack.

## 7.2.2 Implementing a stack

Since some standard versions of C++ will not have stacks as a built-in data type, we must consider how they can be coded in terms of lower level data structures. There are two main ways of doing this: arrays and linked lists. We will consider the linked list version later, after we study how linked lists are coded in C++. For the purposes of this chapter, we will concentrate on arrays.

If we wanted to implement stacks directly from their definition, we might try the following implementation in terms of arrays. First, we reserve some specific data value (such as ASCII 0, if we are storing characters on a stack) which we know will never form part of the valid data that are to be stored on the stack. We fill the array with this value to indicate an empty stack.

To push an item onto an empty stack, we insert it at array location 0 (since all C++ arrays start at 0). To push the next item onto the stack, we must first move the item at location 0 over to location 1 to make room for the new item, which is placed at location 0. We can continue pushing items onto the stack in this fashion: first move all previously added items over one location to make room for the new item, then store the new item at location 0.

Popping data from the stack works just like pushing in reverse. We remove (or read) the item at location 0, test to see if it is the special character indicating an empty stack and, if not, move over all the other items in the stack to fill in the gap left by removing the top element. We can continue popping data from the stack until we encounter the special character indicating that all the data have been removed from the stack.

While this method of doing things follows the definition of a stack very closely, it is also highly inefficient. Every time we push data onto or pop data from the stack, we must move all the other elements in the stack to compensate. If the type of data we are storing is complex, or if there are a lot of data on the stack (or both), this can be very costly in terms of computing time. It turns out that there is a much more efficient way of doing things.

Rather than defining the top of the stack to be at location 0 in the array, we will define the *bottom* of the stack at that location. The stack will then grow into the array, so that the location of its top (in terms of the array index) depends on the amount of data in the stack. The first item added to an empty stack is therefore added at location 0, the next at location 1, the next at location 2, and so on.

Doing things this way obviously requires that we keep track of where the top of the stack is after each push and pop. This is easily done by defining an auxiliary integer variable known as the *stack pointer*, which stores the array index currently being used as the top of the stack. We therefore have algorithms for pushing and popping data:

**Push:**
1. If stack is not full then:
2. add 1 to the stack pointer,
3. store item at stack pointer location.

**Pop:**
1. If stack is not empty then:
2. read item at stack pointer location,
3. subtract 1 from the stack pointer.

In an array with `StackSize` elements, the array locations are indexed from 0 to `StackSize - 1`. A full stack will therefore have its stack pointer pointing to location `StackSize - 1`, and an empty stack will have a stack pointer of $-1$.

### 7.2.3 A stack class in C++

Since a stack is a data structure with attributes (its size and the data stored in it) and associated actions (push and pop), it should be encapsulated as a class. Let us consider what features we would like our stack class to have.

First, we need to decide how many items the stack will be allowed to store (the size of the array). To maximize the flexibility of the class, we can allow the user to specify the size as an argument to the constructor, and then use dynamic allocation to reserve space for the array. We should provide a default value for the array size as well.

One problem that we won't be able to solve until the next chapter is that of finding an efficient way of defining a stack so that it can store any type of data. For example, if we decide that we want our stack to store characters, we must hard-wire this choice into the class definition by declaring an array of type char. If we also want a stack that stores integers, we must rewrite the definition to include an array of type int. We will see when we study templates in the next chapter that they provide a way to declare the stack class only once, yet allow us to define stack objects which store any data type.

Having chosen the array size and the data type, we can add interface functions that implement the push and pop operations, and provide tests for empty and full stacks. All data fields should be private. The interface functions are public.

Since a stack is a general data type, it is highly likely that some future application will require a more specialized version of a stack for some, as yet unknown, purpose. This new application will probably want to add extra interface functions, or modify the versions of popping and pushing functions we define here. The logical way for this future application to implement a specialized stack is to define a new class that inherits the basic stack class in this chapter. To allow for this extension, we should use protected fields instead of private fields, and declare the interface functions to be virtual.

With these considerations, the class charstack (for storing chars) may be defined as follows. The class definition may be stored in a file named charstak.h (the unusual spelling is due to the 8-character limitation of MS-DOS files - if you are using another operating system such as UNIX or Windows 95, you may want to change the header file names).

```cpp
#ifndef CHARSTAK_H
#define CHARSTAK_H
#include <iostream.h>
typedef int BOOL;
enum{FALSE, TRUE};

class charstack
{
protected:
   int StackSize;
   char *Element;
   int StackPointer;
public:
   BOOL Empty() const;
   BOOL Full() const;
   charstack(int stacksize = 10);
   virtual ~charstack();
```

```
    virtual BOOL Pop(char& TopElem);
    virtual BOOL Push(const char& NewElem);
};
#endif
```

The pointer `Element` will have `StackSize` locations allocated to it in the constructor, and will be used to store that actual data in the stack. The `Empty()` and `Full()` functions are declared as `const`, since they should not alter any of the stack's data fields. The `Pop()` and `Push()` functions return a `BOOL` parameter, which indicates whether the operation was successful or not. Remember that a pop will fail if the stack is empty, and a push will fail if the stack is full. If the pop succeeds, the value of the top stack element is placed in the reference variable `TopElem`. Note that the argument of the `Push()` function is declared as `const` since merely pushing data onto the stack should not change the data. Both `Push()` and `Pop()` pass their data by reference.

The functions may be defined in a file `charstak.cpp`:

```
#include "charstak.h"

charstack::charstack(int stacksize,
    char emptyelement) :
    StackSize(stacksize),
    Element(new char[stacksize]),
    StackPointer(-1)
{}

charstack::~charstack()
{
    delete [] Element;
}

BOOL charstack::Empty() const
{
    return StackPointer == -1 ? TRUE : FALSE;
}

BOOL charstack::Full() const
{
    return StackPointer == StackSize + 1 ? TRUE : FALSE;
}

BOOL charstack::Pop(char& TopElem)
{
    if (!Empty()) {
        TopElem = Element[StackPointer--];
        return TRUE;
    } else {
        cout << "Stack empty: pop failed.\n";
        return FALSE;
```

```
    }
}

BOOL charstack::Push(const char& NewElem)
{
   if (!Full()) {
     Element[++StackPointer] = NewElem;
     return TRUE;
   } else {
     cout << "Stack full: push failed.\n";
     return FALSE;
   }
}
```

These functions implement the algorithms for stack operations given earlier. The constructor allocates memory for the Element array and initializes the other data fields to define an empty stack. The Pop() function copies the value of the top of the stack into TopElem if the stack is not empty, and returns TRUE to indicate success; otherwise it prints an error message and returns FALSE.

The Push() function increments the stack pointer and stores the new data, or else prints an error message if the stack is full.

As an example of a main() function which uses the charstack class to reverse a character string, we present the following:

```
#include "charstak.h"

int main()
{
   charstack CharStack(20);
   char ReadChar;

   cout << "Enter a string: ";
   cin.get(ReadChar);
   while (ReadChar != '\n') {
     CharStack.Push(ReadChar);
     cin.get(ReadChar);
   }
   cout << "Reversed string: ";
   while (!CharStack.Empty()) {
     CharStack.Pop(ReadChar);
     cout << ReadChar;
   }
   cout << endl;
   return 0;
}
```

A character stack is initialized to contain up to 20 chars. We have introduced a new feature of the cin operation to read in the characters. The input parameter `cin` is actually an instance of the `istream` class, which is provided in the standard C++ input/output library. The `istream` class has several class functions which perform various specialized forms of input. We have used the class function `get()` to read in single characters from the keyboard. Characters are read and pushed onto the stack until an end-of-line (\n) character is read. Then characters are popped off the stack until the stack is empty, and printed out as they are popped, thus giving a reversed version of the string.

We used the `cin.get()` method of reading characters instead of the seemingly more straightforward `cin >> ReadChar` method, since the latter method ignores whitespace (blanks, tabs, and carriage returns).

This `main()` program tests all the class functions we have defined earlier, although it doesn't do anything particularly exciting with them. It is a good idea, when writing your own code, to get into the habit of testing every function (or set of related functions) as soon as you write them. You should ensure that your tests reach every statement in the code you have written. In this example, the constructor is called with an argument, then all the stack functions are tested in the body of the main function. The functions `Full()` and `Empty()` are tested in the process of pushing and popping items from the stack. The destructor is called automatically by the program when `main()` finishes.

# 7.3 Postfix notation

### 7.3.1 Computer arithmetic

Most humans are used to doing simple arithmetic using what is known as *infix* notation. An addition problem, such as the sum of 5 and 4, is written using the + operator as 5 + 4. The + operator is a *binary* operator, as it requires two *operands* (here, the 5 and the 4 are the operands) on which to operate. In infix notation, a binary operator is placed between its operands.

Doing things this way, however, has its problems. For example, given the problem 5 + 4 * 8 (where the * operator represents multiplication), is the answer found by doing the sum or the product first? If we do the sum first, we get 9 * 8 = 72, while if we do the product first, we get 5 + 32 = 37. You have probably been trained always to do multiplications and divisions before additions and subtractions, but there is no particular reason why this must be the case. If you want to give multiplication a higher precedence than addition, you must state this as an extra rule in your system of arithmetic. Furthermore, if you ever want to perform an addition before a multiplication, you have to introduce extra notation in the form of brackets to indicate this. For example, if you really did want to add the 5 and 4 before doing the multiplication in the problem 5 + 4 * 8, you would have to put brackets around the 5 + 4: (5 + 4) * 8.

Using infix notation therefore requires us to introduce two extra concepts into arithmetic: precedence of operators, and brackets to override this precedence if necessary.

It turns out that there is a simpler way of writing arithmetic expressions which eliminates the need for both operator precedence and brackets. This notation, known as *postfix* notation (or *reverse Polish notation* (RPN)), is used to store arithmetic instructions in a compiled computer program. That is, although in a C++ program you would write arithmetic expressions in the standard infix notation, the C++ compiler translates your infix expressions into postfix expressions before the program is executed. The reason for this is that postfix expressions are easier and faster to run than their infix counterparts.

### 7.3.2 Evaluating a postfix expression

Postfix notation, as its name implies, puts the operator *after* its operands, rather than between them as with infix notation. For example, the infix sum 5 + 4 would be written 5 4 + in postfix.

It is probably not obvious how this simple change can result in a system of arithmetic which eliminates the need for operator precedences and brackets. In order to see how this can be done, we need to introduce the algorithm for evaluating a postfix expression. The algorithm makes use of a stack. The input is assumed to consist of individual *tokens*, which can be either operators (such as +, *, etc.) or operands (numbers). The algorithm works as follows:

- Initialize an empty stack.
- While tokens remain in the input stream:
    - read next token;
    - if token is a number, push it onto the stack;
    - else, if token is an operator, pop top two tokens off the stack, apply the operator, and push the answer back onto the stack.
- Pop the answer off the stack.

For example, consider how we would evaluate the expression 5 4 + 8 *. In Fig. 7.1, the state of the stack is shown at each stage of the algorithm. The first token (5) is read and pushed onto the stack. The next token (4) is read and pushed onto the stack. The third token (+) is an operator, so the top two tokens (4 and 5) are popped off the stack, the operator is applied to them producing the sum (9), which is pushed back onto the stack. The next token (8) is a number, so it is pushed onto the stack. The last token (*) is an operator, so the top two tokens are popped, the operator applied to generate the product of 9 and 8, and the answer pushed back onto the stack. The final step of the algorithm pops the answer (72) from the stack, leaving an empty stack.

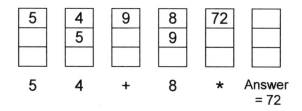

Fig. 7.1. Using a stack for postfix arithmetic.

Notice that we were able to do the infix problem (5 + 4) * 8 without the use of operator precedence or brackets. If we wished to do the infix problem 5 + (4 * 8), we could write this in postfix as 5  4  8  *  + (try it and see), again without precedence rules or brackets.

The algorithm we have given above assumes that the postfix expression on which it operates is a legal one. It makes no allowances for what to do if we should input, say, an expression such as 5  4  8  + (where there are too few operators) or 5 + 4  8  * (where the + operator has only a single operand on which to operate). Error checks are quite easy to build into the algorithm, however.

In the first case (as you can verify by going through the algorithm yourself), if we have too few operators for the number of operands, we will always have an extra number on the stack after the answer is popped off at the end. We must therefore check the state of the stack at the end of the algorithm to ensure that it is empty.

In the second case, where we have too few operands for an operator, we will attempt to pop an operand from an empty stack. Thus we must insert a check in the part of the algorithm where an operator is applied to its operands to ensure that at least two operands are present on the stack.

In either of these cases, an error message should be printed and the algorithm should stop.

### 7.3.3 A postfix evaluator in C++

As an illustration of how we can use stacks in a practical program, we will now examine a complete program which reads in a postfix expression, evaluates it, and prints out the answer (or an error message if the postfix expression is illegal).

To keep things moderately simple at this stage, we will assume that the numbers in the expression are all single digit, non-negative integers. We make this assumption since the postfix expression will contain a mixture of numbers and operators, so that the program must read the expression in as a character string and sort out the numbers from the operators internally. If we allow multiple-digit or negative integers, things get a bit more complicated.

Before we start writing any code, we should plan out the structure of the program in some detail. Since the central data structure needed for evaluating postfix expressions is a stack, we must construct this first. The stack class we defined in the last section was designed to store `chars`, but we will need to store `ints` here. It is a fairly straightforward process to copy out the stack class and replace the appropriate `char` data types by `int`.[10] The results are stored in the header file `intstack.h` and the function definition file `intstack.cpp`. The file `intstack.h` is:

```
#ifndef INTSTACK_H
#define INTSTACK_H
#include <iostream.h>
typedef int BOOL;
enum{FALSE, TRUE};

class intstack
{
protected:
  int StackSize;
  int *Element;    // Stores stack's data
  int StackPointer;
public:
  BOOL Empty() const;
  BOOL Full() const;
  intstack(int stacksize = 10);
  virtual ~intstack();
  virtual BOOL Pop(int& TopElem);
  virtual BOOL Push(const int& NewElem);
};
#endif
```

The file `intstack.cpp` is:

```
#include "intstack.h"
BOOL intstack::Empty() const
{
  return StackPointer == -1 ? TRUE : FALSE;
}

BOOL intstack::Full() const
{
  return StackPointer == StackSize + 1 ? TRUE : FALSE;
}

intstack::intstack(int stacksize) :
  StackSize(stacksize),
  Element(new int[stacksize]),
  StackPointer(-1)
```

---

[10] As you will no doubt notice, it is a tedious process to have to duplicate a class and change only a few data fields and function signatures when we want the same data structure to deal with different data types. We will see in the next chapter that the C++ template provides a more efficient way of doing this.

```
{}

intstack::~intstack()
{
   delete [] Element;
}

BOOL intstack::Pop(int& TopElem)
{
   if (!Empty()) {
     TopElem = Element[StackPointer--];
     return TRUE;
   } else {
     cout << "Stack empty: pop failed.\n";
     return FALSE;
   }
}

BOOL intstack::Push(const int& NewElem)
{
   if (!Full()) {
     Element[++StackPointer] = NewElem;
     return TRUE;
   } else {
     cout << "Stack full: push failed.\n";
     return FALSE;
   }
}
```

These two files are identical to `charstak.h` and `charstak.cpp` given in the previous section, except that the data type of the `Element` array has been changed from `char` to `int`, and all other references to data stored in this array have been changed similarly.

We now have an integer stack ready for use. We can turn our attention to constructing a class to handle the postfix operations.

This class must have the following data fields:

- an integer stack for storing the operands
- a field for the answer
- a `char` array for storing the initial postfix expression
- an `int` for storing the size of the postfix expression array

All these data fields should be private (or protected), since we will define interface functions for accessing them.

The actions that are performed on this class are:

- read the postfix expression into the array
- evaluate the postfix expression

- print out the answer

These three functions (and the constructor and destructor) are the only functions that need to be public. The reading and printing operations are quite simple and will not need to call any other functions. The evaluation process, however, is a bit involved, and could do with some subsidiary operations. We may therefore consider defining the following auxiliary functions, all of which should be private since they are called only by the evaluation routine:

- test a token to see if it is an operator or a number (or some erroneous character);
- apply an operator to the top two operands on the stack (and report an error if there are insufficient operands).

The remaining operations performed by the evaluation routine are all simple enough (or are already expressed in terms of other class functions) that we do not need to break down this routine any further.

The class `intpost` is defined in the file `intpost.h` as follows:

```
#ifndef INTPOST_H
#define INTPOST_H
#include "intstack.h"

class intpost
{
private:
   int Answer;              // Stores final answer
   intstack NumStack;       // Stack for storing operands
   char *PostfixExpr;       // Postfix expression
   int PostfixExprSize;     // Size of PostfixExpr

            // Is token an operator?
   BOOL Operator(const char token) const;
            // Apply operator to top 2 operands
            // and report errors
   BOOL ApplyOperator(const char Operator);
public:
   intpost(int StackSize = 10, int postfixexprsize = 50);
   ~intpost();
   void Read();
            // Evaluate postfix expression
            // and report errors
   BOOL Evaluate();
   void PrintAnswer() const;
};
#endif
```

The definitions of these class functions are in the file `intpost.cpp`:

```
#include "intpost.h"

intpost::intpost(int StackSize, int postfixexprsize) :
  NumStack(StackSize),
  PostfixExpr(new char[postfixexprsize]),
  PostfixExprSize(postfixexprsize)
{ }

intpost::~intpost()
{
  delete [] PostfixExpr;
}

// Read in the postfix expression to be evaluated
void intpost::Read()
{
  cout << "Enter postfix expression: ";
  cin.getline(PostfixExpr, PostfixExprSize);
}

// Test if current token is an operator
BOOL intpost::Operator(const char token)  const
{
  if (token == '*' || token == '+' ||
      token == '-' || token == '/')
    return TRUE;
  return FALSE;
}

// Apply operator to top two stack tokens
// Return TRUE if operation successful,
// FALSE if insufficient operands on stack
BOOL intpost::ApplyOperator(const char Operator)
{
  int operand1, operand2;

  // Pop two operands off stack
  if (!NumStack.Pop(operand1)) return FALSE;
  if (!NumStack.Pop(operand2)) return FALSE;

  switch (Operator) {
  case '*':
    NumStack.Push(operand2 * operand1);
    break;
  case '+':
    NumStack.Push(operand2 + operand1);
    break;
  case '/':
    NumStack.Push(operand2 / operand1);
    break;
  case '-':
    NumStack.Push(operand2 - operand1);
```

```
      break;
    default:
      return FALSE;
    }
    return TRUE;
}

BOOL intpost::Evaluate()
{
    int token = 0;

    while(PostfixExpr[token]) {
      if (Operator(PostfixExpr[token])) {
        if (!ApplyOperator(PostfixExpr[token])) {
          cout << "Error: too few operators\n";
          return FALSE;
        }
      } else if (int(PostfixExpr[token]) >= int('0')
        && int(PostfixExpr[token]) <= int('9'))
        NumStack.Push(int(PostfixExpr[token])
          - int('0'));
      token++;
    }
    if (!NumStack.Pop(Answer)) {
      cout << "Error popping answer.\n";
      return FALSE;
    } else if (!NumStack.Empty()) {
      cout << "Error: too many operands.\n";
      return FALSE;
    }
    return TRUE;
}

void intpost::PrintAnswer() const
{
    cout << "Answer = " << Answer << endl;
}
```

These functions implement the algorithm described in the previous section in a straightforward manner. The constructor initializes all the numerical fields except the Answer field, since the answer is assigned later in the calculation. The array PostfixExpr is allocated space, and its size is stored in the field PostfixExprSize. Note that the intpost constructor calls the intstack constructor directly to initialize the NumStack field.

The destructor frees up the PostfixExpr array. The destructor for the intstack class is also called implicitly whenever an object of type intpost is deleted, so that the space reserved for the stack is correctly deallocated.

The Read() function uses the getline() action of the istream class mentioned earlier to read in the postfix expression.

The Operator() function tests to see if the current token is one of the four operators we are accepting in this program.

The ApplyOperator() function attempts to pop two operands off the stack, returning FALSE if either attempt is unsuccessful due to the stack being empty. Remember that the Pop() function from the intstack class returns a BOOL value indicating whether the pop operation was successful; it is this return value that is used by ApplyOperator(). The remainder of ApplyOperator() applies the corresponding operator to the operands, returning TRUE if one of the four operators was found, and FALSE if the token was not a recognized operator.

The Evaluate() function reads successive tokens from the postfix expression until it encounters the ASCII 0 character that ends the string. It then calls the Operator() function to see if the current token is an operator. If so, it then calls ApplyOperator() to apply the operator to the top two operands on the stack. If this operation fails, an error message is printed, and the function returns. If the current token is not an operator, Evaluate() then tests to see if it is a number, by testing to see if the ASCII value of the token lies between the characters '0' and '9'. If so, the number is converted to int format and pushed onto the stack.

If the entire postfix expression is processed without an error, Evaluate() then attempts to pop the answer from the stack. If this is successful, and the stack is empty after the answer is popped, the value of the answer is assigned to the Answer field, and the function returns TRUE.

Finally, the PrintAnswer() functions simply prints out the Answer field. A simple main() that ties all of this together is in the file evalpost.cpp:

```
#include "intpost.h"

int main()
{
    intpost Postfix;

    Postfix.Read();
    if (Postfix.Evaluate())
        Postfix.PrintAnswer();
    return 0;
}
```

# 7.4 Queues

## 7.4.1 The queue data structure

A queue is used in computing in much the same way as it is used in everyday life: to allow a sequence of items to be processed on a first-come-first-served basis. In most computer installations, for example, one printer is connected to several different machines, so that more than one user can submit printing jobs to the same printer. Since printing a job takes much longer than the process of actually transmitting the data from the computer to the printer, a queue of jobs is formed so that the jobs print out in the same order in which they were received by the printer. This has the irritating consequence that if your job consists of printing only a single page while the job in front of you is printing an entire 200-page thesis, you must still wait for the large job to finish before you can get your page.[11]

From the point of view of data structures, a queue is similar to a stack, in that data are stored in a linear fashion, and access to the data is allowed only at the ends of the queue. The actions allowed on a queue are:

- creating an empty queue
- testing if a queue is empty
- adding data to the tail of the queue
- removing data from the head of the queue

These operations are similar to those for a stack, except that pushing has been replaced by adding an item to the tail of the queue, and popping has been replaced by removing an item from the head of the queue. Because queues process data in the same order in which they are received, a queue is said to be a *first-in-first-out* or *FIFO* data structure.

## 7.4.2 Implementing a queue

Just as with stacks, queues can be implemented using arrays or lists. For the present, we will consider the implementation using arrays. If we attempt to follow the algorithm for adding and removing data from a queue directly, we might try to implement a queue using an array as follows.

Define a class containing an array for storing the queue elements, and two markers: one pointing to the location of the head of the queue, and the other to the first empty space following the tail. When an item is to be added to the queue, a test to see if the tail marker points to a valid location is made, then the item is added to the queue and the tail marker is incremented by 1. When an item is to be removed from the queue, a test is made to see if the queue is empty and, if not, the item at the location pointed to by the head marker is retrieved and the head marker is incremented by 1.

This procedure works well until the first time when the tail marker reaches the end of the array. If some removals have occurred during this time, there will be empty space at the beginning of the array. However, because the tail marker points to the end of the array, the queue is thought to be 'full' and no

---

[11] All of which illustrates that Murphy's law applies equally well to the computer world as to the 'real' world, where, when you wish to buy one bottle of ketchup in a supermarket, you are stuck behind someone with a trolley containing enough to stock the average house for a month.

more data can be added. We could shift the data so that the head of the queue returns to the beginning of the array each time this happens, but shifting data is costly in terms of computer time, especially if the data being stored in the array consist of large data objects.

A more efficient way of storing a queue in an array is to 'wrap around' the end of the array so that it joins the front of the array. Such a *circular array* allows the entire array (well, almost, as we'll see in a bit) to be used for storing queue elements without ever requiring any data to be shifted. A circular array with QSIZE elements (numbered from 0 to QSIZE − 1, as usual for C++ arrays) may be visualized as shown in Fig. 7.2.

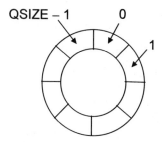

Fig. 7.2. A circular array.

The array is, of course, stored in the normal way in memory, as a linear block of QSIZE elements. The circular diagram is just a convenient way of representing the data structure.

We will need head and tail markers to indicate the location of the head and the location just after the tail where the next item should be added to the queue, respectively. An empty queue is denoted by the condition head == tail, as shown in Fig. 7.3.

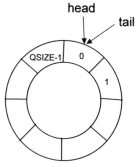

Fig. 7.3. An empty queue.

At this point, the first item of data would be added at the location indicated by the tail marker, that is, at array index 0. Adding this element gives us the situation shown in Fig. 7.4.

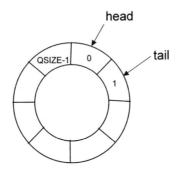

Fig. 7.4. A queue containing one element.

Let us use the queue until the `tail` marker reaches `QSIZE - 1`. We will assume that some items have been removed from the queue, so that `head` has moved along as well (Fig. 7.5).

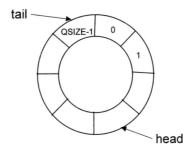

Fig. 7.5

Now we add another element to the queue at the location marked by `tail`, that is, at array index `QSIZE - 1`. The `tail` marker now advances one step, which positions it at array index 0. The `tail` marker has wrapped around the array and come back to its starting point. Since the `head` marker has moved along, those elements at the beginning of the array from index 0 up to index `head - 1` are available for storage. Using a circular array means that we can make use of these elements without having to shift any data.

In a similar way, if we keep removing items from the queue, eventually `head` will point to array index `QSIZE - 1`. If we remove another element, `head` will advance another step and wrap around the array, returning to index 0.

We have seen that the condition for an empty queue is that `head == tail`. What is the condition for a full queue? If we try to make use of all the array elements, then in a full queue, the tail of the queue must be the element immediately prior to the head. Since we are using the `tail` marker to point to the array element immediately *following* the tail element in the queue, `tail` would have to point to the same location as `head` for a full queue. But we have just seen that the condition `head == tail` is the condition for an *empty* queue. Therefore, if we try to make use of all the array elements, the conditions for full and empty queues become identical. We therefore impose the rule that we must always keep at least one free space in the array, and that a queue becomes full when the `tail` marker points to the location immediately prior to `head`.

We may now formalize the algorithms for dealing with queues in a circular array.

- Creating an empty queue: set `head = tail = 0`.
- Testing if a queue is empty: is `head == tail`?
- Testing if a queue is full: is `(tail + 1) % QSIZE == head`?
- Adding an item to a queue: if queue is not full, add item at location `tail` and set `tail = (tail + 1) % QSIZE`.
- Removing an item from a queue: if queue is not empty, remove item from location `head` and set `head = (head + 1) % QSIZE`.

Recall that the `%` operator is the modulus operator in C++. This ensures that `head` and `tail` wrap around the end of the array properly. For example, suppose that `tail` is `QSIZE - 1` and we wish to add an item to the queue. We add the item at location `tail` (assuming that the queue is not full) and then set `tail = (QSIZE - 1) + 1 % QSIZE = QSIZE % QSIZE = 0`.

### 7.4.3 A queue in C++

Having specified the algorithms we will use for implementing a queue using a circular array, it is straightforward to write the C++ code. We will store `int`s in the queue for the example here, but as with the stack data structure, it is a simple matter to replace the type of data stored in the queue by changing a few data types. If this seems too tedious, you can read the next chapter and then implement the queue as a template.

We write the class definition in the file `intqueue.h`:

```
#ifndef INTQUEUE_H
#define INTQUEUE_H
#include <iostream.h>
typedef int BOOL;
enum{FALSE, TRUE};

class intqueue
{
protected:
    int QSize;          // Size of the Element array
    int *Element;       // For storing queue contents
```

```
    int Head, Tail;     // Locate head and (tail+1)%QSize
public:
  BOOL Empty() const;
  BOOL Full() const;
  intqueue(int queuesize = 10);
  virtual ~intqueue();
  virtual BOOL Remove(int& TopElem);
  virtual BOOL Add(const int& NewElem);
};
#endif
```

We have allowed for this class to be inherited by using the `protected` keyword instead of `private`, and we have declared the class functions as virtual.

The definitions of these functions are in the file `intqueue.cpp`:

```
#include "intqueue.h"
BOOL intqueue::Empty() const
{
  return Head == Tail ? TRUE : FALSE;
}

BOOL intqueue::Full() const
{
  return (Tail + 1) % QSize == Head ? TRUE : FALSE;
}

intqueue::intqueue(int queuesize) :
  QSize(queuesize),
  Element(new int[queuesize]),
  Head(0), Tail(0)
{}

intqueue::~intqueue()
{
  delete [] Element;
}

BOOL intqueue::Remove(int& TopElem)
{
  if (!Empty()) {
    TopElem = Element[Head];
    Head = (Head + 1) % QSize;
    return TRUE;
  } else {
    cout << "Queue empty: Remove failed.\n";
    return FALSE;
  }
}

BOOL intqueue::Add(const int& NewElem)
{
```

```
  if (!Full()) {
    Element[Tail] = NewElem;
    Tail = (Tail + 1) % QSize;
    return TRUE;
  } else {
    cout << "Queue full: Add failed.\n";
    return FALSE;
  }
}
```

Everything in these functions should be clear from our discussion of the algorithms above.

In order to test this class and provide a simple application of inheritance, we will define a derived class `testqueue` which inherits `intqueue` and adds a few specialized functions useful for testing the queue. In particular, we will add a function `Print()` which traverses the queue, starting at `Head` and stepping through the queue until it reaches the item just before `Tail`. In doing so, it follows the circular array around its end if necessary. We also provide a function `Menu()` which prints a menu of options for testing the queue. The whole package is used in a `main()` function.

The `testqueue` class is defined in the header file `testque.h`:

```
#ifndef TESTQ_H
#define TESTQ_H
#include "intqueue.h"

class testqueue : public intqueue
{
public:
  testqueue(int queuesize = 10);
  void Print() const;
  int Menu() const;
};
#endif
```

The definitions of the new functions are in `testque.cpp`:

```
#include "testque.h"
testqueue::testqueue(int queuesize)
  : intqueue(queuesize)
{}

void testqueue::Print() const
{
  if (Empty())
    cout << "Queue is empty.\n";
  else
    for (int marker = Head; marker != Tail;
       marker = (marker + 1) % QSize)
```

141

```
      cout << marker << ' ' <<
          Element[marker] << endl;
}

int testqueue::Menu() const
{
  int Choice;

  cout << "--------------------------\n";
  cout << "Select from:\n";
  cout << "1. Add integer to queue\n";
  cout << "2. Remove item from queue\n";
  cout << "3. Print queue contents.\n";
  cout << "0. Quit.\n";
  cout << "Your choice: ";
  cin >> Choice;
  return Choice;
}
```

The main() function is in queue.cpp:

```
#include "testque.h"

int main()
{
  testqueue Queue(5);
  int Choice, Item;

  while (Choice = Queue.Menu())
    switch(Choice) {
    case 0:
      return 0;
    case 1:
      cout << "Enter item to add: ";
      cin >> Item;
      Queue.Add(Item);
      break;
    case 2:
      if (Queue.Remove(Item))
        cout << "Item " <<
          Item << " removed.\n";
      break;
    case 3:
      cout << "Contents of queue:\n";
      Queue.Print();
      break;
    }
}
```

A queue of size 5 was chosen so that it would be small enough to allow
easy testing of the wrap-around feature of the circular array. You should run

this program and convince yourself that it will accept at most four elements, and that the circular array does its job.

## 7.5 Summary

This chapter has introduced our study of data structures in C++ by examining stacks and queues.

The *stack* is a *last-in-first-out* or *LIFO* data structure. It is used in situations where data must be stored temporarily, then used in the opposite order to that in which they were stored. An application of stacks to postfix arithmetic, the most commonly used arithmetic algorithm in computers, was given.

The *queue* is a *first-in-first-out* or *FIFO* data structure. It is used to process data which are stored temporarily and then used in the same order as that in which they were generated.

No new features of C++ were introduced in this chapter.

## 7.6 Exercises

1. Given an initially empty stack which accepts single characters, the following operations are performed:

      Push T
      Push E
      Push X
      Pop
      Push R
      Push V
      Pop
      Push Y
      Pop
      Pop

   a. Write out the composition of the stack after these operations.
   b. What sequence of letters was popped off the stack?

2. The string MOUSE is subjected to the following sequence of stack operations, beginning with M and working left to right:

     push push pop push push pop pop pop push pop

What string is produced by the output from the pops off the stack?

3. The string SMOKESTACK is to be rearranged to give the string MSOSEKCATK. Give a sequence of stack operations (push or pop) that would give the desired reordering, assuming that the string SMOKESTACK is

to be processed left to right, i.e. beginning with the first S and ending with the last K.

4. An algorithm for converting a decimal (base 10) number into binary (base 2) is:

- Let the decimal number be $D$.
- While $D > 0$:
    - Let $R = D$ mod 2 (that is, $R$ is the remainder when $D$ is divided by 2, so that $R = 1$ if $D$ is odd, and 0 if $D$ is even). Write $R$ to the left of any previous values of $R$.
    - Let $D = D/2$.
- The binary number is the number constructed by writing down the values of $R$.

Try this algorithm on paper for several small numbers, like 2, 5, and 10. Note that what you are doing is saving the series of remainders and writing them down in reverse order.

Use the `intstack` class in this chapter to write a C++ program which will read in a decimal number and produce the equivalent number in binary.

5. Modify (use inheritance if appropriate) the postfix evaluation program in this chapter so that it can handle non-negative numbers with more than one digit. To do this, you will need a subsidiary routine that can read in a string of ASCII characters representing the digits 0 to 9, and convert this string into an `int` variable. Various methods exist, but in the spirit of this chapter, use this algorithm:

- Initialize empty stack.
- While character is a number:
    - push number onto a stack.
- Initialize $N$ to 0; initialize $P$ to 1.
- While stack is not empty:
    - pop number off stack and multiply it by $P$,
    - add number to $N$,
    - multiply $P$ by 10.

Your revised program will now have two stacks in it: one for evaluating individual operands, and the other for carrying out the postfix calculation.

6. Further modify your postfix calculator so that it can handle negative integers. In order to do this you will need to distinguish between the binary form of the - operator (signifying subtraction) and the unary form (signifying

negation). You will find it easier to do this if you require that all binary operators are separated by blanks from their operands and other operators, while the minus sign must *not* have a blank between it and the number to which it applies. For example, the expression:

76 –34 –

in postfix is equivalent to 76 – (–34) = 110 in infix.

7. Use inheritance to define a new class called `PriorityQueue` which is a queue in which each item is inserted into the queue at a location determined by its *priority*. To keep things simple, assume that the elements in the queue are simple `ints`. When a new `int` is added to the queue, it moves in front of all other elements in the queue whose values are greater than it. For example, if the number 3 is to be added to the queue:

1 1 2 4 5 5 7 9

where the head of the queue is on the left, it would be inserted between the 2 and the 4. Note that the only difference between a priority queue and an ordinary queue is in the insertion routine, so all other functions may be inherited directly from the queue class given in the text.

8. Modify the priority queue from the previous question so that the data structure being stored in the queue is a user-defined class containing at least two data fields. One field should be an `int` field giving the priority of that element. The other field may be anything you like (for example, a character string giving a person's name). Modify the class functions so that they can handle this user-defined class.

# CHAPTER 8

# Templates

## 8.1 Generalizing a stack

The code for stacks and queues presented in the last chapter suffered from a serious flaw. As was illustrated by the two stack programs, one for reversing a character string and the other for evaluating postfix arithmetic expressions, if we want to use a stack for storing objects of a different data type than that for which the stack was originally designed, we need to write out the class definition (and many of its function definitions) again, replacing only the references to the data type stored in the stack.

Let us examine the `charstack` class from the previous chapter again to illustrate the point:

```
class charstack
{
protected:
  int StackSize;
  char *Element;          // Stores stack's data
  int StackPointer;
public:
  BOOL Empty() const;
  BOOL Full() const;
  charstack(int stacksize = 10);
  virtual ~charstack();
  virtual BOOL Pop(char& TopElem);
  virtual BOOL Push(const char& NewElem);
};
```

The three places where the data type of the objects being stored in the stack occur have been highlighted in boldface type **(char)**. As we did when we designed the `intstack` class in the previous chapter for use with postfix arithmetic, to define a stack that stores a different type of data, we need to replace these three keywords with the new data type. We also need to replace the keyword in the `Pop()` and `Push()` function definitions, which occur outside the class definition.

It would be convenient to be able to define a class template in which the data type(s) used in the class are, essentially, variables that can be filled in later when a version of that class with a particular data type is required. Fortunately, C++ provides just such a feature, and they are called just what you would expect: *templates*.

## 8.2 Definition of a template

Templates can be defined in C++ to generalize the data types in both classes and functions. We will deal with class templates first.

A template is defined in a C++ program using the keyword `template` followed by the definition:

```
template<template_parameter_declarations>
class ClassName
{
  statements
}
```

First, we should point out that because the designers of C++ were running short of ASCII symbols to use for the new features in the language, the angle brackets < > have now been introduced as part of the language. In many computer textbooks, angle brackets are used to delimit statements that must be filled in with specific code, but are not themselves written in the code. In this case, the angle brackets are actually part of the code, and must appear in the program.

For example, the `charstack` class from the previous section could be generalized to a stack template and stored in the file `stack.h`:

```
#ifndef STACK_H
#define STACK_H
#include <iostream.h>
typedef int BOOL;
enum{FALSE, TRUE};

template <class Type, int maxsize> class stack
{
protected:
  Type Element[maxsize];
  int StackPointer;
public:
  BOOL Empty() const;
  BOOL Full() const;
  stack();
  virtual ~stack();
  virtual BOOL Pop(Type& TopElem);
  virtual BOOL Push(const Type& NewElem);
};
#endif
```

Here, the type of data stored by the stack is given as the first template parameter (`Type`). Note that this parameter is used in various places in the definition of the class to specify the data type being used. The array `Element` is declared to be of data type Type, as are the arguments of the Pop() and Push() functions. We have just replaced the occurrences of the char data type in charstack with the Type parameter in the template.

The second template parameter maxsize is used directly to determine the size of the array Element. Note that there is no longer any need to declare a separate StackSize data field in the class since this field is now included in the template. There is also no need to initialize the array in the constructor, since the template will do this for you.

The functions in this class template are defined in a similar way to those for an ordinary class, except that the function signature gets a bit ungainly. The general syntax is:

```
template<template_parameter_declarations>
Return_Type
ClassName<template_parameters>::
   FunctionName(parameter_declarations)
{
   statements
}
```

The function definitions for the stack template may be located in a file stacktem.h. (The template function definitions are stored in a header (.h) file rather than in a source code (.cpp) file for reasons that will be covered a bit later.)

```
#ifndef STACKTEM_H
#define STACKTEM_H
#include "stack.h"

// Constructor
template <class Type, int maxsize>
stack<Type,maxsize>::stack() : StackPointer (-1)
{
}

// Destructor
template <class Type, int maxsize>
stack<Type,maxsize>::~stack()
{
}

template <class Type, int maxsize>
BOOL stack<Type,maxsize>::Empty() const
{
   return StackPointer == -1 ? TRUE : FALSE;
}

template <class Type, int maxsize>
BOOL stack<Type,maxsize>::Full() const
```

```
{
   return StackPointer == maxsize - 1 ? TRUE : FALSE;
}

template <class Type, int maxsize>
BOOL stack<Type,maxsize>::Pop(Type& TopElem)
{
   if (Empty()) {
      cout << "Stack empty: Pop failed.\n";
      return FALSE;
   }
   TopElem = Element[StackPointer--];
   return TRUE;
}

template <class Type, int maxsize>
BOOL stack<Type,maxsize>::Push(const Type& NewElem)
{
   if (Full()) {
      cout << "Stack full: Push failed.\n";
      return FALSE;
   }
   Element[++StackPointer] = NewElem;
   return TRUE;
}
#endif
```

Notice that the bodies of the functions are the same here as they were in the original non-template version, or at least they appear to be on the surface. The reason this qualification is added is that templates hide a fair bit of working from the user, working of which the user should be aware. Consider, for example, the Push() function. It looks simple enough: a reference to the data item to be pushed onto the stack is passed to the function, and this item is copied into the correct location in the array as determined by the stack pointer. However, if Type is a user-defined class, the = operator in the assignment statement must be an overloaded assignment operator, as discussed in Chapter 5. If the user has neglected to provide a custom version of the overloaded = operator, the compiler will provide one. Recall the cautions given in Chapters 4 and 5 about default copy constructors and default assignment operators: they only do a shallow copy so that if the class contains any dynamically allocated memory, only the pointer to this memory will be copied.

Hopefully you can see from this example that although many of the features of C++ reduce the amount of hand coding required by a programmer, they are also capable of introducing subtle errors that may get buried several layers deep in your code. Most of these errors are errors of omission, as in neglecting to define proper argumentless constructors, destructors, copy constructors, overloaded = operators, and so on. It is for this

149

reason that it is a good idea to provide these functions for every class even if you don't plan on directly using them yourself: there are many cases where these functions are called implicitly by other code you have written.

## 8.3 Using templates

Now that we have defined a template class for a stack, let us see how it is used. The definition of variables proceeds in a similar way to that for an ordinary class, except that arguments must be provided for the template parameters. Once the variables have been defined, they are used in exactly the same way as ordinary variables. The following main function makes use of the stack template defined above. The template and associated function definitions are in the file stacktem.h, as described in the previous section.

```cpp
#include"stacktem.h"

int main() {
  stack<int, 10> IntStack;
  stack<float, 4> FloatStack;
  int obj;
  float fobj;

        // Test integer stack
  for (int i=0; i<5; i++) {
    cout << "Enter an integer to push: ";
    cin >> obj;
    IntStack.Push(obj);
  }
        // Test float stack & Full stack check
  for (i=0; i<5; i++) {
    cout << "Enter a float to push: ";
    cin >> fobj;
    FloatStack.Push(fobj);
  }

        // Test pop
  cout << "Popping stuff off the int stack:\n";
  while (IntStack.Pop(obj))
      cout << obj << ' ';
  cout << endl;

        // Test pop  & Empty stack check
  cout << "Popping stuff off the float stack:\n";
  while (!FloatStack.Empty()) {
    FloatStack.Pop(fobj);
    cout << fobj << ' ';
  }
  cout << endl;
  return 0;
}
```

The definition `stack<int, 10> IntStack` defines a stack which stores `int`s and has an array size of 10. The second definition defines a stack of maximum size 4 which stores `float`s. Stacks for storing any other data type, built-in or user-defined classes, can be declared in a similar way.

The remainder of the program tests out the various functions we have defined. Five integers are pushed onto `IntStack`, and five floats onto `FloatStack`. In the latter case, since `FloatStack` was only allocated four elements, the stack will fill up and we test the `Full()` function to see if it works properly. When popping data off the two stacks, we test the return value of the `Pop()` function in the first loop, and the return value of the `Empty()` function in the second. The first loop will produce an error message when the `Pop()` function attempts to pop data from an empty stack. This would look ugly in a 'real' program, but it is a good idea to make sure the error check works, so we have included it here. The second loop illustrates how to produce a 'clean' listing of the contents of the stack: we test the `Empty()` function before attempting to pop the stack.

## 8.4 How templates work

In order to use templates properly in your programming, you need to understand the basics of how the compiler integrates them into your code. Although it may seem that templates use dynamic memory allocation, they actually don't. When the compiler encounters a declaration like `stack<int, 10> IntStack`, it searches for the template definition in the header file(s) and substitutes `int` for `Type` and 10 for `maxsize` everywhere they occur in this definition. It then creates the code for a new class, together with all its associated functions, for a stack variable which stores `int`s and has a maximum size of 10. This code is added to the code you have written manually before the whole batch is translated into machine code. In other words, every variable you define using a template adds a block of code to your program, if that variable uses a new set of template parameters.

The important thing to realize is that *the template definitions that you write are NOT compilable code*; they are instructions that the compiler can use to *create* a class definition if the need arises. This has several consequences:

- You should not put template function definitions in a source code file (one with a `.cpp` suffix), since the compiler is not able to compile these definitions. Always put template function definitions in a header file (one with a `.h` extension).
- You must include the header file containing the template class definition *and* the header file for the template function definitions for that class in *all* source code files that make use of that template. A common error is to include the template class definition file, but not the template function

definition file. The compiler will complain about 'functions not found' in this case.

- If there are errors in either your template class definition, or in the associated template function definitions, the compiler will not find these errors unless you actually declare a variable based on this template. This is because the template definitions are not even consulted by the compiler until such a declaration is made. It is therefore important for you to actually declare variables that use your template definitions when you want to test them; merely including the header file containing the template definitions (with a `#include` statement) in a source code module is *not* sufficient to have the compiler process the contents of these files.

- Every variable declaration based on a template adds a block of code to what you have written manually. Excessive use of templates can therefore increase the size of the source code substantially.

- Class parameters in templates can be of any data type (built-in or user-defined), but if you use it with one of your own classes, you must ensure that all the operations used in the various template functions are defined for that class. For example, if one of your template functions uses an assignment (=) or a comparison (<, <=, >, >=, etc.), it may work fine provided you use it with built-in data types such as `int` or `float`, but die when you try to use it with one of your own classes. You must provide overloaded forms of whatever operators your template functions use in order for the template to work properly with these classes. This usually means that you have to fix the user-defined class, not the template. It is particularly important to ensure that various 'hidden' features, such as copy constructors, overloaded assignment operators, argumentless constructors, destructors, and so on are properly defined for use of a class with a template.

## 8.5 Template functions

Functions not included in a class can be defined using templates as well. The procedure is even simpler than for classes. The syntax for a template function declaration is:

```
template<template_parameter_declarations>
   function_declaration
{
   statements
}
```

For example, a function to determine the maximum of two objects can be declared using a template as:

```
template <class Type>
Type max (const Type a, const Type b);
```

152

and defined, possibly in a different file:

```
template <class Type>
Type max (const Type a, const Type b)
{
    return a > b ? a : b;
}
```

This function template will be used by the compiler to generate a function called max () for any situation in which the two arguments are of the same data type. This generation will take place automatically, without any explicit declaration of the function for that specific data type. For example, the following program based on this template definition will produce the expected results, with the above template definition stored in the file tempmax.h:

```
#include "tempmax.h"
int i,j,k;
double u,v,w;
char a,b,c;

main()
{
    i = 4; j = 5;
    k = max(i,j);
    u = 34.5; v = 23.4;
    w = max(u,v);
    a = 'a'; b = 'b';
    c = max(a,b);
    cout << "Max values: " << k << ' ' << w << ' '
        << c << endl;
}
```

The three instances of the max () function will be created by the compiler during compilation: there is no need to include explicit declarations of the functions such as int max(int num1, int num2), for example.

Note that if you wished to use this template for a user-defined class, that class must have an overloaded form of the > operator.

The automated generation of functions does not always work as you might expect, since *no typecasting is done in template functions*. To understand what this means, consider an ordinary function (not based on a template) for finding the maximum of two numbers:

```
double SimpleMax(const double a, const double b)
{
    return a > b ? a : b;
}
```

If this function is passed any combination of `int`s, `float`s, or `double`s, it will return a `double` value which is numerically equal to the maximum of the two arguments it was given. If the function is called with a statement like `maxval = SimpleMax(num1, num2)`, and `maxval` is an `int` or a `float`, the `double` value returned by the function is automatically converted to the correct data type and stored in the variable `maxval`. This conversion between one numeric type and another is known as *typecasting*, and occurs frequently in most programs because most of us don't give much thought to the fact that we are using different numeric data types. The same thing is true of the arithmetic operators: +, * and so on all type-cast their operands before using them.

Functions based on templates, however, do not do this. The reason for this should be fairly obvious: since a template is a means of defining a function for *any* data type, there should be no need to do any typecasting, since a function for whatever data type is being used can (or should) be derived from the template definition. As a result, if we try using the template version of the `max()` function above on *mixed* arguments, like:

```
int Num1 = 5;
float Num2 = 6.54;

double MaxVal = max(Num1, Num2);
```

we will get an error, because the compiler can't find a template definition which allows the two arguments of the function to be of different types.

There is a way around this, however. We can explicitly declare an instance of the function with particular data types. Once we have done this, the compiler treats that function as if it is a regular function (in other words, it forgets that the function was derived from a template), and will apply typecasting to any calls to that function. For example, suppose we modified the `main()` routine above as follows:

```
#include "tempmax.h"
int i,j,k;
double u,v,w;
char a,b,c;
double max(const double Num1, const double Num2);

main()
{
   i = 4; j = 5;
   k = max(i,j);
   u = 34.5; v = 23.4;
   w = max(u,v);
   a = 'a'; b = 'b';
   c = max(a,b);
```

```
    cout << "Max values: " << k << ' ' << w << ' '
      << c << endl;
    w = max(a,v);
    cout << "Max of char and float: " << w << endl;
}
```

In this case, the explicit declaration of max() that takes two double arguments provides a catch-all for those cases where a specific template match could not be found. The order of action for an instance of max() is:

1. See if a specific version of max() can be generated from the template for the data types given as its arguments.
2. If not, see if an explicit version of this function exists with argument types to which the present argument types could be cast. In this case, a char can be cast to a double (by taking the ASCII value of the char and converting it to a double) so we are OK.
3. If no useable explicit version of the function exists, generate an error message.

# 8.6 A checklist for constructing a project in C++

Since we have now covered most of the features of C++ that we will need in this book, it is useful to summarize the principles of building an object oriented project in C++ at this point. Starting in the next chapter, we will continue our study of data structures and algorithms in earnest. These chapters will provide many examples of the construction and use of C++ classes. You may find the following list of points useful when constructing your own C++ projects:

- Make sure you understand the project you are trying to implement as an object oriented, C++ program. Many people (myself included, from time to time) suffer from an irresistible urge to 'get into the coding' as quickly as possible. This results in badly designed code that frequently must be torn apart and rewritten. Some serious thinking time, preferably several miles from the nearest computer, is well worth the effort.
- Once you feel you have an understanding of the project, write out (on paper, or using a text editor, but do *not* write any C++ code at this point) all the objects that will be used in your project, and list the properties and actions associated with each object. Try to group these lists together so that you have a sensible and coherent division of objects. Read through your lists to make sure that the properties and actions you have attributed to each object make sense.
- Repeat the previous step until you get it right, because you won't get it right the first time. Trust me. Despite all the high-powered object oriented

design tools on the market, you will still produce a bad design if you don't do this initial grouping properly, and that usually takes several attempts. Don't rush this stage. If you do, you will waste even more time in the coding stage when you find that your classes don't fit together in a logical fashion.

- Examine the classes you have decided to use for any relationships that could be represented using inheritance. Remember that inheritance should be used *only* to relate classes where one class is a special type of another class. Don't use inheritance as a back door method for allowing one class access to the private fields of another, unrelated class. If your design requires you to do this, it is faulty and should be redone.

- Decide which fields in each class should be private, protected, and public. In general, *all* data fields should be private or protected, since their values should only be changed by interface functions. Only those functions that will be used by routines external to the class should be public. Public functions should contain only those arguments relevant to the use of the function by an external routine.

- For each class that is serving as a base class in an inheritance relationship, examine each private field to see if it will be required by the derived class. If so, it must be made protected rather than private. Decide which functions will be overloaded in the derived class; such functions should be virtual.

- Provide as many constructors and destructors as you require. Remember that if you provide *any* constructors for the class, there is *no* default argumentless constructor unless you write one yourself. If the class is a base class for another derived class, the destructor should be virtual. Remember the order in which constructors are called: derived class first, then base class. Destructors are called in reverse order to constructors.

- Does your class contain any dynamically allocated memory? If so, you will need to provide a copy constructor and an overloaded = operator if (i) an object of this class is ever passed by value in a function call; (ii) an assignment of one object of this class to another object is made. Also, the destructor must explicitly deallocate any space allocated with the new operator.

- Is the class likely to be a generic form of a common data structure, such as a stack? If so, it may be more useful to write a template for the class. Remember that template function definitions are *not* compiled code: they must be included in all files that refer to an instance of such a function.

- Is the class likely to be used as a data type in another class template? For example, are you likely to declare a stack containing objects of this class? If so, ensure that all relevant operators are overloaded in your class.

- Examine each function declaration to see where the const keyword might make your code safer. Remember that a const variable in an argument list means that the function cannot change the variable, a const after the argument list of a class function means that the function cannot change any data fields in the object that calls that function.

- Determine which function arguments are passed by reference and which by value. Remember that passing by value requires copying the data element to the function, requiring more time for large data structures, and a copy constructor if the object has any dynamically allocated space connected to it. Passing by reference is the most efficient way to pass variables to a function, but any changes made to that variable will be returned when the function exits. If a reference variable should not be altered by a function, protect it with a `const` qualifier.

Finally, remember that C++ is a *big* language, and there are quite a few features we have not covered in this book. If you want to become a C++ guru, you should consult a more comprehensive textbook dealing with the C++ language as its central topic. Before doing so, however, remember that all the ammunition you need to start writing properly constructed object oriented code in C++ has been presented in this book. Some of the other features of C++ may help you write more elegant or compact code, but refrain from using a feature of the language just because 'it's there'. Remember that 'clever' or 'elegant' code is, more often than not, more difficult to understand and maintain than code that takes a few more lines to write and uses more mundane features of the language. The main goal in your programming career should be to produce properly structured, understandable, maintainable code, rather than showing off what obscure features of the language you have managed to learn.

## 8.7 Summary

This chapter completes our survey of the syntax of C++ by examining templates. The main points to be remembered about templates are:

- Templates can be designed for classes and for functions.
- A class template is used for defining a class in which the data type(s) of some of the fields can vary from one instance of the template to another, thus avoiding the necessity of duplicating a class definition for different data types.
- A function template is used for defining a function in which the data type(s) of the arguments can vary.
- A template is not compilable code. The compiler will refer to the template definition only if a variable making use of that template has been declared.
- A template definition (including definitions of the class functions) should be placed in a header file.
- All header files pertaining to a template must be included in any source code file making use of the template.

- Templates may be used with user-defined classes, but you must ensure that all relevant constructors, destructors, and overloaded operators are defined for such classes.

Finally, some guidelines for designing an object oriented project using C++ are given.

## 8.8 Exercises

1. The code below gives a simple class with a single data field, two contructors, and a `Print()` function. Change this class to a template so that the data field `Num1` may have any data type specified by the user. Modify the other class functions if necessary. Add a `main()` function in which two objects based on this template are declared: one using `float` as the data type and one using `char`. The `float` object should have `Num1` initialized to 23.19 and the `char` object should have `Num1` initialized to `'K'`. Use the corresponding `Print()` function to print out the `Num1` field from both objects.

```
class testClass
{
private:
   int Num1;
public:            '
   testClass() {}
   testClass(int num1)  : Num1(num1) {}
   void Print() { cout << Num1 << endl; }
};
```

2. The code below defines a class containing an `int` pointer which is initialized to point to an array of size `ArraySize`. Note that there are two constructors: one simply allocates space for the array but does not initialize the array elements; the second expects two arguments: the array size and the initial value each array element should have. The `Print()` function prints out the elements of the array.

a. Convert the class `testClass` into a template with a single argument: the data type used for the array elements. Provide definitions for all the class functions so that they meet the specifications given in the preceding paragraph. Finally, test your code by writing a `main()` routine which uses all the functions you have written.

```
class testClass
{
private:
   int *Array;
   int ArraySize;
public:
```

```
   testClass(int arraysize=10);
   testClass(int arraysize, int InitElement);
   void Print();
};
```

b. Modify the template from part (a) so that the `ArraySize` variable is a template parameter instead of a class data field. Note that this will mean that you can declare the array directly in the class, so that the constructors will no longer have to reserve the space for the arrays. (See the stacks example in the notes.)

3. The code below attempts to use the template for the `max()` function given in the text for a user-defined class called `dog`. Copy and compile the code as given to verify that there is an error in the code.

Find and correct the error in this program by providing an appropriate overloaded operator for the `dog` class. Make a sensible decision as to what this operator should do for the `dog` class.

```
#include<iostream.h>

template<class Type>
Type max(const Type& a, const Type& b)
{
   return (a > b ? a : b);
}

class dog
{
private:
   float Weight;
   int NumTeeth;
public:
   dog(float weight = 10.0, numteeth = 32) :
      Weight(weight), NumTeeth(numteeth) {}
   void Print() { cout << Weight << ' ' << NumTeeth; }
};

void main()
{
   dog dog1(12.5, 40), dog2(20, 30);
   dog dog3 = max(dog1, dog2);
   cout << "The larger dog is: ";
   dog3.Print();
}
```

4. Write a template for the queue data structure based on the class defined for queues in Chapter 7. The type of data stored in the queue and the size of the array used for storing the queue elements should be parameters for the

template. Write definitions for all the template functions. Test your code by writing a `main()` routine that uses all the template code you have written.

# CHAPTER 9

# Sets

## 9.1 The mathematical set

A *set* in mathematics is an unordered collection of objects of any type. To keep things simple in our introductory examples, we'll consider only sets of integers. The C++ class definitions, however, will be more general.

We can denote a set by the notation $A = \{1,2,3,4,5\}$ where $A$ is the name of the set, and the elements of the set are the integers 1 through 5, enclosed in braces (curly brackets). A set can exist on its own, but it is also possible to define a *universal set*, which is a set that contains all elements from which other sets in the problem you are considering can be taken. For example, we might define a universal set such as $U = \{1,2,3,4,5,6,7,8,9,10\}$ which is the set of all integers from 1 through 10. In this case, any other set would have to contain only integers chosen from the universal set.

The basic operations defined for sets are:

- **Union.** The union of two sets $A$ and $B$ is the set containing all elements in $A$ and $B$. The union is written $A \cup B$. Elements common to both $A$ and $B$ are *not* duplicated in the union. For example, if $A = \{1,2,3,4,5\}$ and $B = \{3,4,5,6,7\}$, the union is $A \cup B = \{1,2,3,4,5,6,7\}$. The elements 3, 4, and 5, which are common to both sets, are not duplicated in the union.

- **Intersection.** The intersection of two sets $A$ and $B$, written $A \cap B$, is the set containing elements common to both $A$ and $B$. For example, with $A$ and $B$ defined as above, the intersection is $A \cap B = \{3,4,5\}$.

- **Difference.** The difference of two sets $A$ and $B$, written $A - B$, is the set of all elements of set $A$ that are not in set $B$. Using $A$ and $B$ from the previous example, we have $A - B = \{1,2\}$.

- **Complement.** A complement of a set can only be defined if a universal set $U$ exists. The complement of a set $A$, written $\overline{A}$, is defined as $U - A$. For example, with $U$ defined as above (the set of all integers from 1 through 10), we have $\overline{A} = \{6,7,8,9,10\}$.

There is a bit more notation that is necessary to understand set terminology:

- **Membership.** An object $x$ (which is *not* a set, merely an object) is a *member* of a set $A$ if $A$ contains $x$. This is written as $x \in A$. If an object $x$ is not a member of the set $A$, this is written as $x \notin A$.

- **Subsets.** A set $S$ is a subset of another set $A$ if all the elements of $S$ are also members of $A$. This is written as $S \subset A$. If $S$ is not a subset of $A$, this is written as $S \not\subset A$.

- **Proper subsets.** A set $P$ is a *proper subset* of a set $A$ if $P$ is a subset of $A$, but there are some elements of $A$ that are not also members of $P$. For example, if $P = \{1,2,3\}$ and $A = \{1,2,3,4,5\}$, then $P$ is a proper subset of $A$ because the elements 4 and 5 are present in $A$ but not in $P$.

## 9.2 Designing the set data structure

A set is a good example to use for defining a C++ data structure, since it has a well-defined collection of operations that can be defined on it, so it is fairly easy to construct a class definition to represent it. To design a set class in C++, we need to identify the data fields and functions, and decide which fields should be public and which private (or protected, if we plan on using the class as a base class).

There are several ways we can implement sets in C++, so we need to consider carefully what we want our set class to achieve.

We would like to declare sets for storing *any* data type: `ints`, `floats`, objects from user-defined classes, and so on. This means that we should use a template. It also tells us something about the mechanism that we should use to store the set elements. From a mathematical point of view, if we know what elements are in the universal set, then to specify a subset of the universal set, all we need to do is say whether or not each element from the universal set is present in the subset. In other words, we could just define an array of Boolean variables with a size equal to the size of the universal set, and then set those elements which are present in the subset to TRUE and the others to FALSE.

Doing things this way, though, means that we have to have some easy way to determine the array index corresponding to the set element we are interested in. If the set elements are consecutive integers, this is easy: we can just map the integers to the range 0...ArraySize. However, for other data types, a mapping to a sequence of integers isn't so easy.[12] We therefore will store the set elements as an array of the actual objects making up the set, rather than just a Boolean array. For large data objects, this will require more memory, but it makes the coding a lot easier.

Now that we know how the set elements are to be stored, we need to consider what operations we want to perform on them. We would like to implement the standard set operations such as union, intersection, and so on. We could do this by defining public functions named `Union()`, `Intersection()`, and so on, but it is more natural to use operator overloading, so we will overload the + operator to implement a union, and

---

[12] Trying to do such a mapping leads us into the topic of hashing, which we cover in Chapter 13.

the * operator to implement an intersection. Other operators can be added later.

Finally, we need to consider how we are going to calculate things like unions and intersections. If we are storing the set elements in an array, then to calculate the union of two sets, we need to construct a third set whose elements contain all elements in the other two sets, but without any duplication. The last qualifier is what causes us some problems. If all we had to do was just copy the elements from the first two sets into the third, we could just pile the elements together into an array without any concern for their order or whether there were duplicate elements.

The easiest way to resolve this is to keep the set elements in *sorted order* within the array. That way, we could use the following algorithm to construct a union of two sets $A$ and $B$:

- Initialize MarkerA to point to element 0 of set $A$, and MarkerB to element 0 of set $B$.
- While (MarkerA < Size of set $A$) and (MarkerB < Size of set $B$):
    - If     A.Element[MarkerA]     <     B.Element[MarkerB],     insert A.Element[MarkerA] into the union and increment MarkerA by 1.
    - Else if     A.Element[MarkerA]     ==     B.Element[MarkerB],     insert A.Element[MarkerA] into the union and increment *both* MarkerA and MarkerB by 1.
    - Else insert B.Element[MarkerB] into the union and increment MarkerB by 1.
- Copy remainder of the set that has not been fully read into the union.

That is, we start at the beginnings of the two sets and step through them one element at a time, ensuring that we copy each element into the union only once. Try this algorithm yourself by hand for a couple of small sets with some common elements to convince yourself that it works.

The algorithm for intersection works similarly, except that we copy elements into the intersection set only if that element occurs in both sets.

The key point for both these algorithms is that we can rely on the set elements being sorted in increasing order. The routines for constructing a set and building unions and intersections must therefore ensure that this is always the case.

Although we haven't studied sorting algorithms yet, we will introduce a simple technique here so that we can guarantee that our set elements are sorted. Before we do so, however, you should realize one important consequence of our requiring the set elements to be sorted. Since we plan on defining the set class as a template, *any class used with this template must have comparison operators defined for its objects.* This is true since we cannot sort a list of objects unless the concepts of 'greater than', 'less than' and 'equal to' have some meaning for these objects. We must therefore ensure that any class we plan on using with our set template has the appropriate overloaded operators to implement these concepts.

The sorting algorithm we will use here is called *insertion sort*. It is not the most efficient general sorting algorithm around, but for sorting arrays that are almost in order already (as the set element array will be), it is one of the best. For a sorted array called `Element` containing `NumItems` elements, to which we wish to add one more item `NewItem`, insertion sort works as follows:

- Initialize Marker to NumItems (remember that arrays are indexed from 0, so element number NumItems is stored at location NumItems - 1).
- While Marker > 0 and NewItem < Element[Marker - 1]:
    - Move Element[Marker - 1] to Element[Marker].
    - Decrease Marker by 1.
- Store NewItem in Element[Marker].

The elements in the array are shifted over one at a time until space is made at the correct location to insert NewItem. Insertion sort can be generalized to sort a completely unordered list, but we won't need that feature here.

## 9.3 C++ code for sets

Finally, let us have a look at the beginnings of a set class. We begin with the header file, `sets.h`:

```
#ifndef SETS_H
#define SETS_H
#include<iostream.h>

typedef int BOOL;
enum {FALSE, TRUE};

template <class Type, int SetSize>
class set {
private:
  Type Element[SetSize];
  Type EmptyElement;
  int Cardinality;
public:
  set();
  set(Type emptyelement);
  BOOL contains(const Type& member) const;
  BOOL insert(const Type& element);
  set<Type,SetSize>        // Union
    operator+(const set<Type,SetSize>& Set2) const;
  set<Type,SetSize>        // Intersection
    operator*(const set<Type,SetSize>& Set2) const;
  void Print() const;
```

```
  void Read();
};
#endif
```

Most of the features in this file should be familiar. A template is used with parameters for determining the data type stored in the set, and the maximum set size (the number of elements in a set is called its *cardinality*) that will be allowed. An empty set is indicated by a cardinality of 0. The `EmptyElement` field is used as a flag value to indicate the end of input when reading in set values from the keyboard. This isn't the cleanest way of reading set values, but the alternatives involve doing a bit of string parsing, which we don't want to get into here.

The interface functions don't include all the set operations (we have to leave something for you to do on your own!), but they should give you a good idea how things are done. There are two constructors: an argumentless constructor, and a constructor which allows you to set up the value of `EmptyElement`. Since we are defining a set *template* and not just a single set class, we can't really combine these two constructors by providing a default value for `emptyelement`, since we don't know what data type is going to be stored in the set. For example, if we are storing integers, we could use a default value of 0 for `emptyelement`, but this wouldn't work if we were storing objects from a user-defined class.

The Boolean function `contains()` tests the set to see if it contains `member`. The function `insert()` attempts to insert `element` into the set. The Boolean return value indicates whether the attempt was successful or not. There are two reasons why an insertion attempt might fail: the set is full (the cardinality is equal to the universal set size) or the element might already be in the set. In either case, `insert()` returns `FALSE`.

The next two functions are overloaded operators implementing the union and intersection operations. The rather verbose declarations of these functions is due to the fact that we are defining a template: the functions return a set, so this return value must be specified using template notation. Similarly, their second operand (the first operand is the set in which they are embedded) is also a set (or rather, a reference to a set, to avoid copying), so the template notation must be used here as well.

Finally, there are I/O functions `Read()` and `Print()` for reading in and printing out the set values, respectively.

The template function definitions are given in the file `settemp.h`:

```
#ifndef SETTEMP_H
#define SETTEMP_H
#include "sets.h"

template <class Type, int SetSize>
  set<Type,SetSize>::set() : Cardinality(0)
```

```
{}

template <class Type, int SetSize>
  set<Type,SetSize>::set(Type emptyelement) :
      Cardinality(0),
    EmptyElement(emptyelement)
{}

// Use + operator for set union.
// Elements added to Union from *this and Set2
// using insertion sort
template <class Type, int SetSize>
  set<Type,SetSize>
  set<Type,SetSize>::
    operator+(const set<Type,SetSize>& Set2) const
{
  set<Type,SetSize> Union;
  int marker1 = 0, marker2 = 0;
  int UnionSize = 0;
  while (marker1 < Cardinality &&
         marker2 < Set2.Cardinality) {
    if (Element[marker1] < Set2.Element[marker2]) {
      Union.insert(Element[marker1]);
      marker1++; UnionSize++;
    } else if
        (Element[marker1] == Set2.Element[marker2]) {
      Union.insert(Element[marker1]);
      marker1++; marker2++; UnionSize++;
    } else {
      Union.insert(Set2.Element[marker2]);
      marker2++; UnionSize++;
    }
  }
  for (; marker1 < Cardinality; marker1++) {
    Union.insert(Element[marker1]);
    UnionSize++;
  }
  for (; marker2 < Set2.Cardinality; marker2++) {
    Union.insert(Set2.Element[marker2]);
    UnionSize++;
  }
  if (UnionSize > SetSize)
    cout << "Error in Union: Union cardinality
      exceeds universal set size.\n";
  return Union;
}

// Use * operator for set intersection.
// Elements added to Intsect from *this and
// Set2 using insertion sort
template <class Type, int SetSize>
  set<Type,SetSize>
  set<Type,SetSize>::
```

```
     operator*(const set<Type,SetSize>& Set2) const
{
  set<Type,SetSize> Intsect;
  int marker1 = 0, marker2 = 0;

  while (marker1 < Cardinality &&
      marker2 < Set2.Cardinality) {
    if (Element[marker1] < Set2.Element[marker2]) {
      marker1++;
    } else if
        (Element[marker1] == Set2.Element[marker2]) {
      Intsect.insert(Element[marker1]);
      marker1++; marker2++;
    } else {
      marker2++;
    }
  }
  return Intsect;
}

// Tests if "member" is in the current set
template <class Type, int SetSize>
BOOL set<Type,SetSize>::
  contains(const Type& member) const
{
  int marker;
  for (marker=0; marker < Cardinality; marker++)
    if (Element[marker] == member)
      return TRUE;
  return FALSE;
}

// Adds "element" to current set;
// returns TRUE if successful
template <class Type, int SetSize>
BOOL set<Type,SetSize>::insert(const Type& element)
{
  if (! contains(element) &&
    Cardinality < SetSize)
  {
    int marker = Cardinality;
    while (marker > 0 && element < Element[marker-1]) {
      Element[marker] = Element[marker-1];
      --marker;
    }
    Element[marker] = element;
    Cardinality++;
    return TRUE;
  } else {
    return FALSE;
  }
}
```

```
// Reads in set elements from keyboard
template <class Type, int SetSize>
void set<Type,SetSize>::Read()
{
  Type NewElement;

  Cardinality = 0;
  cout << "Enter elements, finish with " <<
    EmptyElement << endl << "Element 1: ";
  cin >> NewElement;
  for(int i=0; i < SetSize &&
                  NewElement != EmptyElement; i++) {
    if (contains(NewElement)) {
      cout << "Element already in set.\n";
      --i;
    } else {
      insert(NewElement);
    }
    if (i < SetSize-1) {
      cout << "Element " << (i+2) << ": ";
      cin >> NewElement;
    }
  }
}

// Prints set elements on screen
template <class Type, int SetSize>
void set<Type,SetSize>::Print() const
{
  cout << "Set elements: ";
  for (int marker=0; marker<Cardinality; marker++)
    cout << Element[marker] << ' ';
  cout << endl;
  cout << "Cardinality: " << Cardinality << endl;
}
#endif
```

There are no new features of C++ in these definitions, but a few things may need to be clarified. There are two constructors: an argumentless constructor that only initializes the `Cardinality` field, and a constructor with the `emptyelement` argument for those `set` objects requiring an end-of-input marker.

Note that no copy constructor or overloaded = operator has been declared for this class. We can get away without them here since there is no dynamic memory allocation in constructing an object from this class. The set array size is specified by using a template parameter, rather than allocating the array dynamically in a constructor. Note, however, that if any dynamic memory allocation *is* done in this class, a copy constructor *is* required, since set objects are passed *by value* (in the final return statement) whenever set union or intersection is done. If a copy constructor is not provided, then any pointers in the set object returned to the calling function would point to memory that was allocated when the union or intersection operator was called. Since this memory is deallocated when the function terminates, the pointers could point to memory that is no longer allocated to your program, which could cause all sorts of problems.

Set union is implemented by overloading the + operator. The set template notation needs to be used a record four times in the header for this function (once to let the compiler know this is a template member, once to declare the return value type, once to declare the class to which the function belongs, and finally to declare the type of the second operand of the operator). A local set template variable Union is declared which is used to collect the elements as they are inserted into the union of the two sets. A variable UnionSize is used to keep track of the number of elements we are *attempting* to insert into the union. If the cardinality of the union of the two sets is larger than SetSize, the maximum size of set which the template can store, then the set returned by this operator will not contain all the elements in the union. If this happens, a warning message is printed by the operator+() function.

Other than that, the function implements the algorithm for set unions described in the previous section. The two for loops at the end pick up any elements left over after all the elements from the other set have been included in the union. You should work through it with a couple of small sets to be sure you understand what is happening.

The intersection algorithm is similar to the union algorithm, except here we are only interested in elements that are equal in the two sets. We still must consider the other cases (where the element from set 1 is less than the current element from set 2, and *vice versa*), but only for purposes of adjusting the markers. Once we have processed to the end of one of the sets, there is no need to consider the remaining elements in the other set, so we omit the two for loops present in the union operation. Also, it is impossible for the cardinality of an intersection to exceed SetSize, assuming that the two sets entering into the intersection both have cardinalities that don't exceed SetSize, so there is no need to test this condition here.

The contains() function merely scans the set until it either finds the element being tested or reaches the end of the set. The insert() function implements the insertion sort algorithm described earlier. It will only insert the new element if the element is not already in the set, and if there is room for the element in the set. Its BOOL return value indicates whether it has been successful or not.

The Read() function prompts the user to enter the set elements, tests each element to see if it is already present (to give the user another chance to enter an element) and, if the element is not already in the set, calls the insert() routine to insert it.

The Print() function prints out the set's contents and cardinality.

169

A main routine that makes use of these functions is:

```
#include "settemp.h"
int main()
{
  set<long, 100> Set1(0), Set2(0), Set3;
  Set1.Read();
  Set1.Print();
  Set2.Read();
  Set2.Print();
  Set3 = Set1 + Set2;
  cout << "****Union:\n";
  Set3.Print();
  Set3 = Set1 * Set2;
  cout << "****Intersection:\n";
  Set3.Print();
  return 0;
}
```

The main function declares three long integer sets with a universal set size of 100 elements, the first two of which call the constructor which defines a value for EmptyElement. This is important for any sets that are to be read in from the keyboard, since the Read() function makes use of EmptyElement in order to determine when the last element has been typed in. Since Set3 is only used internally to store intermediate results, it does not need a value for EmptyElement.

The two sets are read in and printed out (to test that they have been read in properly and to see if the Print() function works). The union and intersection are calculated and printed out.

As mentioned earlier, there are many different ways to implement sets (and most other data structures) in C++. The one given here should not be used blindly if another method is more suitable. Some alternative implementations and additions are explored in the problems.

## 9.4 Summary

After a brief summary of the mathematical properties of sets, a C++ set template was designed, illustrating that careful consideration must be given to the interplay between algorithms and data representation when you are designing a class.

The set class designed in this chapter stored the set elements in an array, using insertion sort to keep the elements in order. The set operations of union and intersection were implemented using overloaded operators. These operations are easier to perform if the sets on which they operate are sorted. Finally, a main routine was written to test the features in the set template.

# 9.5 Exercises

1. Add functions to the set template in the text to implement:
   a. set difference (use an overloaded – operator)
   b. a test that a set is a subset of another set (overload the <= operator)
   c. a test that a set is equal to another set (overload the == operator)
   d. a test that a set is a *proper* subset of another set (overload the < operator)

2. Use inheritance to define a class which includes a *universal set* field. The derived class should not be a template, but should store only ints as the set elements. (You may wish to read section 10.3 on inheritance and templates first.) The universal set should be the set of integers from 0 to SetSize − 1. Add a class function which implements the *set complement* operation by overloading the ! (logical NOT) operator.

3. a. Write a program, using the set template in the text, which reads a text file and generates a set of chars giving all the ASCII characters used in the text file.

   b. Modify this program so that it reads two text files and generates a set of chars containing those ASCII characters that are common to both text files.

4. Define a set class (not a template) in which a set of ints is stored using the other method described in the text. That is, a set is represented by an array of Boolean values where each value in the array indicates whether the corresponding element is present or absent in the set. Define class functions for implementing union, intersection, reading, and writing for sets represented in this way.

# Linked lists

## 10.1 Arrays and lists

There are two basic methods by which collections of related data can be stored: as *arrays* or *lists*. An array is a data structure where all elements are stored in contiguous memory; the defining parameters of an array are the memory address of its first element (called the *base address*), the size of each element (e.g. 4 bytes for an integer, 1 byte for a char, etc.), and the number of elements. Arrays allow *random access* to their elements, which means that, given the index of the element required, its location can be calculated by adding an offset to the base address. This calculation involves the same number of steps for all elements of the array, so the access time for any array element is constant. Arrays also require only as much space as is needed to store the data itself; no extra space for pointers or other markers is needed.

The main disadvantage of an array is that its size is fixed, either at compilation or when space is allocated dynamically (e.g. by using the C++ new operator). Sufficient space must be allocated for the largest number of elements that will ever be used in the program, which can result in a lot of wasted space if most applications only require a fraction of that space. Also, certain algorithms are less efficient if used on data stored in arrays.[13]

The main alternative to the array is the *linked list*. A list is a data structure in which the first element is stored on its own, but is provided with a pointer to the location of the second object, which may be stored in a different area of memory. The second object in turn has a pointer to the third, and so on, until the last object has a null or zero pointer associated with it to indicate that it is the end of the list.

The main advantage of a linked list over an array is that the size of the list need not be determined in advance, since extra space can be allocated as needed. Disadvantages are that extra space is needed to store the pointer associated with each element, and that access to internal list elements may take more time than with an array, since finding an internal list element requires starting at the first element and following the chain of pointers until the required element is located.

---

[13] Some languages (and C++ class libraries) support arrays that will dynamically change their size. In such languages, you are required to specify an initial size and an increment for the array. The initial instance of the array will be of the initial size. If the array ever exceeds the initial size, an extra block of elements given by the increment size is allocated to the array. This can be inefficient, since the program must locate a new block in memory that is large enough to store the new, larger array, and in most cases will have to shift all the data from the original array into the new location.

## 10.2 Lists in C++

Although it is possible to implement a linked list using arrays, it is inefficient to do so, so we will concentrate on the pointer form in this chapter. Before we get into this, we need to see how objects with pointer fields are handled in C++.

We have already seen an example of a pointer field in a class when we defined the `atm` class in Chapter 2. A pointer to an `account` class variable was declared, and this pointer was later used as the base address of an array of accounts, with the space being allocated using the `new` operator. However, once we had allocated the space, we could treat the variable as an ordinary array, so we didn't need to worry about using pointers beyond this stage.

With a linked list, we begin in a similar way. A pointer to a *head node*, which is a dummy node that is always present before the first 'real' node in a linked list, is defined. The head node is not used to store any of the actual data present in the list, although it could be used to store information pertaining to the list as a whole, such as the number of nodes. The list pointer plus the head node thus constitutes an empty list (see Fig. 10.1).

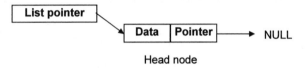

Fig. 10.1. An empty list.

The head node contains a pointer to the first data node in the list (or a null pointer if the list is empty). The space for this first data node, however, is not allocated until the data to be inserted in the node are actually provided to the program. Thus the class function for inserting a new node into a linked list must handle this process.

In Fig. 10.2, a list containing one data node after the head node is to have a new node inserted between the head node and the first data node. The new node must first be dynamically allocated (using the `new` operator). Then its pointer is directed to point to the data node which is to follow it in the list. Finally the pointer from the head node is redirected to point to the new node.

Similarly, when a node is removed from the list, another class function will handle the deallocation of this node.

Since a linked list is a general sort of data structure which should be able to accept objects of any data type as list elements, it makes sense to define the class as a template. In doing this, however, we are faced with a slight problem. If we wish to store objects in a linked list, we don't want to be concerned with the extra pointer that must be attached to each node. Ideally, we would like to be able to declare a linked list of `int`s, say, by giving a declaration like list<int> IntList;. That is, we simply specify the type of object we wish to store in the list and let the internal workings of the list template take care of the details with the pointers. When we defined a template for a set class in the previous chapter, this sort of thing was quite easy to do, since we were storing the set elements in an array. Each element of the array contains an object of the specified data type, and nothing more. With a linked list, however, we need to store not only the data object but its associated pointer, so that the actual data type which makes up a node in the list is a compound data type, even if we are storing built-in data types such as int or float.

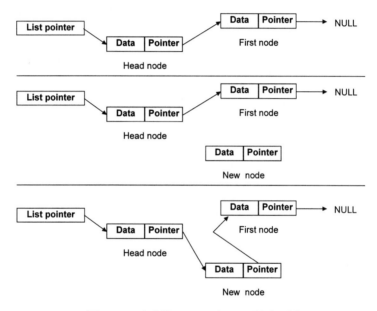

Fig. 10.2. Adding a node to a linked list.

We therefore need to define an auxiliary data type in which the data we wish to store in the list are combined with a pointer field. This is, in principle, easy enough to do, but we should try to do it in an object oriented way.

There are two common ways this is done in C++. The first involves defining a separate class, outside the list class, in which the fields are the data field and the pointer. In order for these fields to be accessible to the list class, however, they either have to be declared as public fields (violating the spirit of OOP), or made accessible to the list class in some other way. C++ provides a method for allowing the private fields of one class to be accessed by functions from another class. This is the *friend* keyword: a class or function can be declared a friend of another class, which allows the second class or function access to all fields (public, protected, or private) of the first class.

The whole idea of data encapsulation, however, is to allow a class to be defined as an independent entity so that it can be transplanted into other programs without any alteration. If a class is a friend of another class, that implies that some of the functions in the friend class require access to the other class, so that a class cannot be transplanted into another program unless all the classes of which it is a friend are allowed to come along too. In this sense, the friend class is something like the infamous goto statement: it should be avoided if at all possible. In most cases, it is possible to do so. However, just like the goto statement, there are cases where the friend attribute can be used properly (otherwise it wouldn't be in the language). We could legitimately use it here, but we will defer its use until we study trees.

The second solution, and the one we shall use here, is to include the definition of the list node as one of the private fields of the list class. C++ allows nested classes, which we will use to implement our solution. Without further ado, here is the skeleton of a list class, in file lists.h:

```
#ifndef LISTS_H
#define LISTS_H
#include<iostream.h>
enum {FALSE, TRUE};
typedef int BOOL;

template <class Type>
class list
{
protected:
  struct ListNode
  {
    Type Element;
    ListNode *Next;

    ListNode() : Next(0) {}
    ListNode(Type Data, ListNode *Node = 0) :
      Element(Data), Next(Node)   {}
  };

  ListNode *Head;
  Type DefaultVal;
public:
  list() : Head(new ListNode) {}
  list(Type defaultval) :
    DefaultVal(defaultval), Head(new ListNode) {}
  virtual ~list();
  BOOL Empty() const;
  virtual void Insert(const Type& NewElement);
  virtual BOOL DeleteElement(const Type& DelElement);
  void Print() const;
  void Read();
};
```

```
#endif
```

Since there are many varieties of linked list possible, we will keep an eye to the future and assume that the class we are defining here will serve as a base class to be inherited by other linked list classes with more bells and whistles on them. For that reason, we have declared the first set of fields as `protected` rather than `private`: this way, they are accessible to derived classes.

The main protected field is `struct ListNode`. A `struct` in C++ is identical to a class with the exception that a `struct`'s fields are `public` by default instead of `private`. By declaring a `struct` as a protected field within the list class, all its fields will be accessible to the class functions, but not to any functions outside this class (except functions in any derived classes). This `struct` forms the basis of the nodes from which the list will be constructed. Note that it contains two data fields: `Element` which is of a data type that is determined by the template, and a pointer `Next` which will point to the next node in the list. By encapsulating the `struct` within the class we keep all parts of the list together, and avoid the need for friend classes.

The constructor associated with the `struct ListNode` is a very clever bit of C++ that you will see often in any code involving linked lists. The two arguments to the constructor are:

1. `Data`: the data field to be added to the new node in the list. The `Element` field is initialized to this value.
2. `Next`: the address of the list node which *follows* the new node. The `Next` pointer of the new node is initialized to this address.

In other words, the constructor stores the data in the `Element` field, and sets the `Next` pointer for the new node. The only operation that remains to be done is to connect the pointer from some other node in the list so that it points *to* this new node. This is also done in a rather clever fashion, which we'll get to below.

The `Head` field is a pointer to the head node. The `DefaultVal` field is a special field containing a data value which is used in the input routine later on.

There are two constructors for the `list` class. The argumentless constructor uses the `new` operator to reserve space for the head node, and initializes the `Head` pointer to point to it. Remember that the `new` operator reserves enough space for the data type which is its argument (`ListNode` in this case) and returns a pointer to this space. Thus the value that is actually being passed to the `Head` field is the pointer to the space where the head node is to be stored, as required.

The second constructor also initializes the head node, but accepts an argument which is used to initialize the default value.

The destructor is declared as `virtual` because the class may be inherited. The `Empty()` function just checks to see if the list is empty. Since it doesn't alter any of the data in its associated object, it is declared as `const`.

The `Insert()` function inserts `NewElement` into the list. There are various ways the new element could be inserted into the list. It might be added immediately after the head node, inserted after some specified list element, or just added at the end of the list. Here, we simply add the new node at the end of the list.

Finally, the two functions `Print()` and `Read()` print out the list contents and read in list elements from the keyboard respectively.

Let us now have a look at the bodies of the functions that are not defined in the class definition above. These functions are stored in file `listtemp.h`:

```
#ifndef LISTTEMP_H
#define LISTTEMP_H
#include "lists.h"

template <class Type>
list<Type>::~list() {
  ListNode *Temp = Head->Next;

  while (Temp) {
    Head->Next = Temp->Next;
    delete Temp;
    Temp = Head->Next;
  }
  delete Head;
}

template <class Type>
BOOL list<Type>::Empty() const
{
  return Head->Next == 0 ? TRUE : FALSE;
}

// Adds NewElement to the end of the list
template <class Type>
void list<Type>::Insert(const Type& NewElement)
{
  for(ListNode *Marker = Head; Marker->Next;
      Marker = Marker->Next);
  Marker->Next = new ListNode(NewElement,
      Marker->Next);
}

template <class Type>
BOOL list<Type>::DeleteElement(const Type& DelElement)
{
```

```
    ListNode *Marker = Head, *Temp;

    for(; Marker->Next &&
        Marker->Next->Element != DelElement;
        Marker = Marker->Next);
    if ((Temp = Marker->Next) &&
        Marker->Next->Element == DelElement) {
      Marker->Next = Marker->Next->Next;
      delete Temp;
      return TRUE;
    } else
      return FALSE;
}

template <class Type>
void list<Type>::Print() const
{
  cout << "Traversal of list: ";
  ListNode *Marker = Head->Next;
  for (; Marker; Marker = Marker->Next)
    cout << Marker->Element << ' ';
  cout << endl;
}

template <class Type>
void list<Type>::Read()
{
  Type NewElement;

  cout << "Input list elements. End with "
    << DefaultVal << "\n";
  cout << "Enter element: ";
  cin >> NewElement;
  while (NewElement != DefaultVal)
  {
    Insert(NewElement);
    cout << "Enter element: ";
    cin >> NewElement;
  }
}
#endif
```

The destructor introduces a new bit of C++ syntax: the -> (arrow) operator. Recall if you have an object variable such as ObjectVar, its fields can be accessed by adding a dot (.) followed by the field name, as in ObjectVar.Member, or for a class function, ObjectVar.MemFunc(). In many cases in C++, you will be dealing not with objects directly, but with *pointers* to objects. For example, in the destructor shown here, Head is a *pointer* to the head node of the list. If you want to access, say, the Next field of the head node through this pointer, you use the notation Head->Next. The general syntax is

```
pointer_to_object -> field_of_object
```

The important thing to remember is that the left operand of the -> operator *must* be a pointer, and the right operand must be a field name (either data field or function) belonging to the class to which the left operand is pointing. (The notation Head->Next is equivalent to (*Head).Next, but is considerably easier to write.)

The destructor uses the temporary pointer Temp to hold the pointer to the node about to be deleted while the pointers around it are rearranged. Starting with the node following the head node, each node in turn is deleted and the pointer from the head node is redirected to point to the node just after the one that was deleted. When the end of the list is reached (at which point the Next pointer will be 0), the loop terminates, and the head node itself is deleted.

Next, we have a brief look at the Empty() function. Since an empty list contains a head node and nothing else, the Next pointer from the head node will be 0 in an empty list. That is all that this functions checks.

The Insert() function locates the end of the list by following the chain of pointers in a for loop. Note that the for loop has no body, so that everything is done in the loop testing conditions. We test the Next field of the Marker pointer, rather than the pointer itself, since we must stop the loop when we have found the node whose Next pointer is 0, in order that we can add on the new node to that location. If we tested Marker itself, the loop would only stop when we had run right off the end of the list, and we would have lost the identity of the pointer to the last list element.

The last line in the function illustrates the 'clever' method of inserting a new node that we referred to earlier. We know that the new node should be inserted directly after the node pointed to by Marker. That is, the Next pointer from the new node should point to where Marker->Next pointed before the insertion, and after the insertion, Marker->Next should point to the new node. If you glance back to the discussion of the constructor for the struct ListNode above, you will see that we must pass Marker->Next as the second argument to this constructor, since that is where the new node's Next pointer must point. The other link, that of redirecting Marker->Next to point to the new node after the insertion, is handled by the return value of the new operator. Remember that new finds space for the new ListNode and returns the address of that location. This address is stored in Marker->Next by the assignment statement.

Finally, we shall consider the DeleteElement() function. This function is designed to delete the *first* occurrence of a node whose data field matches its argument. It does *not* delete the whole list; that is the job of the destructor described earlier.

We search the list until we find a node that matches the target we have given the function as its argument `DelElement`, or until we reach the end of the list without finding it.

The `Marker` pointer is used to step through the list searching for the element to delete. Since we need to redirect the `Next` pointer from the node immediately *preceding* the node being deleted, we must keep a marker to this preceding node, rather than directly to the node we want to delete. This is why we compare `Marker->Next->Element` with `DelElement`, rather than just `Marker->Element` itself. Again, the entire search is done in a single-line `for` loop.

When the loop terminates, we must test to see if a match was found. This is done in the *if* statement. Note carefully that we are *not* testing to see if `Temp` is equal to `Marker->Next`, since we have used only a single = operator, which is an assignment operator and not a comparison operator.[14] Since the precedence of the = operator is lower than the `&&` operator, the assignment must be enclosed in parentheses. The second condition in the `if` statement tests that, if the loop terminated before the end of the list, the marked node is actually the one we want. The idea is to set `Temp` so that it points to the node to be deleted, and then redirect the `Next` pointer from the preceding node so that it skips over the node to be deleted. After this, the `Temp` node is deleted. The return value of the function indicates whether or not a deletion took place.

The `Print()` and `Read()` functions can be designed to suit your personal taste. The `Print()` function just traverses the list and prints out the list elements in order. The `Read()` function reads list elements from the keyboard until the user enters the special `DefaultVal` value specified in the constructor, and calls the `Insert()` function to add these elements to the list.

A `main()` routine that could be used to test the functions that we have written so far is:

```
#include "listtemp.h"

main() {
  list<int> TestList(0);
  int DelElement;

  TestList.Read();
  TestList.Print();
  cout << "Delete a few items.\n";
  for (int i=0; i<5; i++) {
    cout << "Element to delete: ";
    cin >> DelElement;
```

[14] Some compilers flag a warning for statements like this in case you inadvertently use an assignment operator (=) instead of a comparison operator (==). Rest assured that the statement really is correct in this case!

```
    if (TestList.DeleteElement(DelElement))
      cout << "Element deleted.\n";
    else
      cout << "Element not in list.\n";
  }
  TestList.Print();
  return 0;
}
```

This main routine checks the list functions by using a list of integers, but the same functions should work with any user-defined data type as well. As usual in C++, if you use your own classes in a template such as this, you must ensure that all the required fields are present in that class. In particular, the initialization of a new `ListNode` involves initializing the `Element` field, which uses a copy constructor, since the new list element is passed to the `ListNode` constructor by *value*. Hopefully you can see why it is important to consider the environment in which your own defined classes are going to be used, so that you know what functions, constructors, destructors, and operators to define for them.

## 10.3 Inheritance and templates

To demonstrate how a derived class can be defined using a template, we'll consider a simple generalization of the linked list template above. As we stated earlier, we defined the list class with a view to its future inheritance, by using protected fields and virtual functions.

We will define a slight variant of the linked list in which the nodes are sorted in decreasing order, and where no duplicate nodes are allowed. Scanning down the list of fields in the list class, we see that this will require modifying only the `Insert()` and `DeleteElement()` functions, since these are the only functions that depend on the sorting order of the list. The elimination of duplicate nodes can also be handled by the `Insert()` function. The definition of the derived class is stored in the function `declist.h`:

```
#ifndef DECLIST_H
#define DECLIST_H
#include "lists.h"

template <class Type>
class DecreaseList : public list<Type>
{
public:
  DecreaseList() {}
  DecreaseList(Type defaultval) :
    list<Type>(defaultval) {}
  void Insert(const Type& NewElement);
  BOOL DeleteElement(const Type& DelElement);
```

```
};
#endif
```

We include the header file lists.h, since it contains the definition of the base class. The procedure for defining a template for a derived class is almost identical to defining an ordinary derived class. We begin the declaration with a template statement. The derived class is named DecreaseList, and it inherits the list<Type> class. Since list itself is a template, the template parameters on which it depends must be explicitly stated here.

An argumentless constructor is defined; recall that this constructor will automatically call the argumentless constructor in the base class, so the initialization of the head node performed there will still be performed here without any extra work on our part.

The second constructor, in which the default value is specified, must explicitly call the corresponding constructor in the list class, and pass the argument to it. Again, note that the template parameter must be passed to this constructor.

The last two function declarations are overloaded versions of the corresponding functions in the base class. The new functions are stored in the file dectemp.h:

```
#ifndef DECTEMP_H
#define DECTEMP_H
#include "declist.h"
#include "listtemp.h"

template <class Type>
void DecreaseList<Type>::Insert(const Type& NewElement)
{
   ListNode *Marker = Head;

   for(; Marker->Next &&
      Marker->Next->Element > NewElement;
     Marker = Marker->Next);
   if (!Marker->Next ||
      (Marker->Next &&
        Marker->Next->Element != NewElement))
     Marker->Next = new ListNode(NewElement,
        Marker->Next);
}

template <class Type>
BOOL DecreaseList<Type>::
   DeleteElement(const Type& DelElement)
{
   ListNode *Marker = Head, *Temp;

   for(; Marker->Next &&
     Marker->Next->Element > DelElement;
```

```
    Marker = Marker->Next);
  if ((Temp = Marker->Next) &&
      Temp->Element == DelElement) {
    Marker->Next = Marker->Next->Next;
    delete Temp;
    return TRUE;
  } else
    return FALSE;
}
#endif
```

The only difference in the new `Insert()` function is that elements are now sorted in decreasing order, and a test has been added to avoid inserting duplicate elements. A new node is only inserted if either (i) the `for` loop has reached the end of the list or (ii) the loop terminated before the end of the list, but the element stored just after the marker position is *not* the same as the new element.

The `DeleteElement()` function now searches the list until (i) it finds the element to be deleted, (ii) it reaches the end of the list without finding the element to be deleted, or (iii) it finds an element less than the element to be deleted. Since we know that the list is sorted in descending order, there is no need to search beyond the point where we first encounter a node less than the target node.

All of this is straightforward enough, but (as is so often the case in C++) you should be aware of a hidden danger in the new derived class we have defined here. Since the main purpose of defining a class template instead of an ordinary class is to allow that template to be used with *any* data type, we have every right to expect that we should be able to use this template with classes we define ourselves. In the case of the first list template, where each new node is just attached to the end of the list, this is no problem. However, in the derived class we now sort the nodes as they are inserted. In order for nodes to be sorted, it must be possible to compare them so that we can say whether one node is larger than, equal to, or less than another node. This means that we must ensure that the comparison operators (>, !=, and ==) used in the `Insert()` and `DeleteElement()` functions be overloaded in the user-defined class. Just another reminder that you must carefully consider all of the ramifications of any changes or additions you make to established classes!

The `main()` routine that we used for the original list can be used to test these new functions with the only changes necessary being an alteration of the `#include` file so that the new derived class's definitions are available, and a change to the list declaration so that a list of type `DecreaseList` is declared. A suitable function is:

```
#include "dectemp.h"
```

```
main() {
  DecreaseList<int> TestList(0);
  int DelElement;

  TestList.Read();
  TestList.Print();
  cout << "Delete a few items.\n";
  for (int i=0; i<5; i++) {
    cout << "Element to delete: ";
    cin >> DelElement;
    if (TestList.DeleteElement(DelElement))
      cout << "Element deleted.\n";
    else
      cout << "Element not in list.\n";
  }
  TestList.Print();
  return 0;
}
```

## 10.4 Summary

We have introduced the *linked list* data structure in this chapter. A linked list begins with a pointer which points to a *head node*. The head node is a dummy node which is not one of the actual data nodes of the list, but is used to make the algorithms dealing with linked lists easier.

Each data node in the linked list consists of two main parts: the *data* section in which the actual data for that node are stored, and the *pointer* section which contains a pointer to the next node in the list. The end of a list is marked by a zero pointer.

The C++ class template for a linked list illustrates how to deal with *pointers to objects*. To access a field or function in a object represented by a pointer, use the arrow notation: ->, as in `List->Insert(Item)`, where `List` is a pointer to a linked list object, and `Insert()` is the class function which inserts `Item` into the list.

The list template also illustrates how to define an embedded `struct` within a class. This allows the data and pointer sections of a list node to be encapsulated in a class that is accessible only to the list class itself.

Finally, we illustrate how a class template may be defined which inherits another class template.

## 10.5 Exercises

1. Using inheritance, define a new linked list template with the following new functions:

   a. An insertion routine which keeps the list in ascending order by using the insertion sort algorithm (see previous chapter) to insert each new element. Allow duplicate elements to be inserted.

b. A function which deletes duplicates of all elements from the list, so that after running this function, each list element occurs only once.

c. A function which counts the number of elements in the list.

2. Design a template for a stack which uses a linked list to store the stack elements. Provide class functions for the operations of pushing, popping, and testing for an empty stack.

3. a. Design a template for a queue which uses a linked list to store the queue elements. Provide class functions for the operations of adding an element, removing an element, and testing for an empty queue.

b. Using inheritance, define a template for a priority queue (see exercise 7 in Chapter 7) where the elements are stored as a linked list.

4. Design a template for a set in which the set elements are stored in a linked list. Provide class functions (or overloaded operators) for the set operations of union, intersection, difference, testing if an element is in a set, and testing if one set is a subset of another.

5. a. Design a template to implement a *bi-directional* or *symmetric* linked list. Each element in a bi-directional list has two associated pointers: one pointing to the previous element in the list and the other to the following element. Design functions which allow insertion and deletion of elements from such a list, and provide appropriate constructor(s) and destructor(s).

b. One application of a bi-directional list allows a computer to deal with integers of arbitrarily large size. Write a program which uses your bi-directional list template to allow addition of two integers of any size. To do this, remind yourself of how addition of two numbers is done with pencil and paper. To add two numbers such as 176 + 892, for example, you start with the units column, add the two numbers (6 + 2 = 8), write down the answer and proceed to the tens column. Adding 7 + 9 gives 16, so we write down the 6 and carry 1 to the hundreds place. The sum here is the carried digit (1) plus 1 + 8, giving 10. The 0 is written down, the 1 carried to the left, but since we are done, we can just write down the final carried 1 to give the answer: 1068. Use the same technique to add together two very large numbers, except that instead of storing only a single digit as a list node, store a larger block (say numbers from 0 to 999,999) at each node. Then a large number can be read into the list from left to right (in the conventional way), and two numbers can be added by traversing the list from right to left (in the conventional way for addition).

CHAPTER 11

# Searching algorithms

## 11.1 The study of algorithms

An *algorithm* is a precise set of instructions for achieving a particular goal. In a computer program, all data structures have associated algorithms which are used to access and modify the data they contain. Built-in data structures in C++, such as `ints` and `floats`, have built-in algorithms for such things as arithmetic, input and output. User-defined classes have their associated algorithms encapsulated in their class functions.

For many operations performed on data structures, there are several different algorithms that may be used. Different algorithms make different demands on computer memory and running time. In an industrial setting, where the cost of commercial software and staff time become important, the availability and price of off-the-shelf routines that implement the algorithms, and the programming time required to implement the algorithm if no commercial package is available, must be considered.

It is therefore useful to know things like the running time and memory requirements of algorithms so that you can make an informed decision about which algorithm is best for your particular application. The theoretical study of algorithms, known as *complexity theory*, is a highly mathematical branch of computer science. It involves detailed analysis of the number of steps required by an algorithm to process varying amounts of data. For many algorithms, exact results have been derived, but for others, only approximations or averages are available.

Since this book assumes no significant mathematical knowledge on the part of the reader, we won't be going into any detailed studies of the complexities of the algorithms we will be studying. It is still important, however, for you to achieve an understanding of how the complexity of an algorithm is measured, and to develop techniques whereby you can measure these complexities experimentally by actually running programs to calculate them. This is one of the goals of this chapter.

We begin our study of algorithms by looking at a couple of methods for searching a list of items. We use searching algorithms as an introduction because they are commonly used as examples in an introductory course in programming, so there is a good chance you have met them before. They are also fairly simple algorithms, both to code and to analyse, so you shouldn't have to wrestle with the concepts behind the algorithms while you are trying to see how their efficiencies can be measured.

We will consider two searching algorithms: sequential search and binary search.

## 11.2 Sequential search

Both searching algorithms we will consider in this chapter work on one-dimensional lists of data. The data may be stored in an array or a linked list. The examples in this chapter all assume that the data are stored in an array.

A searching algorithm requires a *target* for which to search. The list is searched until either the target is located or the algorithm has determined that the target is not in the list. For simple data types, such as `ints`, a simple comparison is performed between the target and the data stored at each node in the list. For more complex data types such as user-defined classes, often one of the fields is chosen as a *key* field. The target is then compared only to the key field, with the other fields being ignored for the purposes of the search. For example, a database may store customer information for a company. A customer is represented by a class in which the surname, first name, address, phone number, and so on are stored. For searching purposes, an ID number unique to each customer may be defined. This number is then used as the key field in the class, and the searching algorithm would expect the target to be an ID number.

The sequential search is simple: we start at the first array element and compare each key with the target until we have either found the target or reached the end of the list without finding it. The index of the corresponding array element is returned if the search is successful, and some flag value, such as $-1$, is returned if the search fails. We can formalize the algorithm as follows:

1. Read in `Target`; initialize `Marker` to first array index (0).
2. While `Target != Key` at location `Marker` and not at the end of the list:
   3. `Marker++`.
4. If `Target == Key` at location `Marker`, then return `Marker`.
5. Else, return $-1$.

## 11.3 Binary search

There are two forms of the binary search algorithm, both of which are designed to be applied to lists of *sorted* data. The condition that the data be sorted is a constraint not present for the sequential search, and could mean that extra computing is required to sort the list before the binary search is used. Since sorting algorithms are always less efficient than searching algorithms (as we will see in the next chapter), this could mean that even though binary search on its own is much more efficient than sequential search, the combination of (sort + binary search) may actually be less efficient than sequential search on its own. The binary search algorithm is best used on lists that are constructed and sorted once, and then repeatedly searched.

We will only study one form of the binary search algorithm in depth here, and leave the other form for the exercises at the end of the chapter. The form we will look at here is sometimes called the *forgetful binary search* because it doesn't bother to check if the target node has been found until the very end of the algorithm. The forgetful algorithm looks less efficient than it needs to be, but as we will see, it is in most cases more efficient than the other form of the binary search.

The basic idea behind either binary search algorithm is to chop the list in half at each step, so that you only have half as many keys to search at each stage. The forgetful binary search continues to chop the list in half until there is only one element left, and then checks to see if this single remaining element is the target. The more traditional form of binary search checks at each stage to see if the target has been found.

The formal statement of the forgetful binary search algorithm is as follows, where we have a list of `numdata` elements stored in an array with indexes ranging from 0 to `ArraySize` - 1. We use three markers (`top`, `bottom`, `middle`) to mark positions in the list.

1. Set `top` = `numdata` - 1; set `bottom` = 0.
2. While `top` > `bottom` do:
   3. set `middle` = (`top` + `bottom`) / 2 [using integer division]
   4. if key at index `middle` is less than target key, then set `bottom` = `middle` + 1
   5. Else, set `top` = `middle`.
6. If `top` == -1, return -1 indicating that the list is empty.
7. If key at location `top` is the target key, return location `top` indicating that the target has been found.
8. Else, return -1 indicating target has not been found.

You should work through the algorithm by hand on a short list (around 10 elements) for cases where the target is present in the list and where it is not present. If you count the number of comparisons done in the `while` loop (step 2 above) you should see that doubling the length of the list adds, on average, only one extra comparison to the algorithm.

We will return to the discussion of the efficiency of this algorithm later. For now, we will write some C++ templates that can be used for searching.

## 11.4 C++ templates for searching algorithms

Since we have precise statements of both searching algorithms, writing C++ code to implement the algorithms is straightforward. Since we would like to be able to apply these algorithms to any type of data, we will write templates for classes in which the algorithms are implemented.

## 11.4.1 Sequential search

Let us begin with the sequential search algorithm. We can defi
template that contains the basics that will be needed in any class i
searching: the array in which the data are to be stored, the searching function
itself, and input and output functions. We will use this opportunity to show
how to overload the << and >> operators for output and input, so that user-
defined objects can be read from istream objects (such as cin) and written
to ostream objects (such as cout).

We will define a base class called datalist which is a general purpose
array-based list class containing a pointer to a dynamically allocated array
Element, a constructor, destructor, and input/output functions. We will
make use of this class in many algorithms in this and later chapters. The
definition of the class is in the file datalist.h:

```
#ifndef DATALIST_H
#define DATALIST_H
#include "mydefs.h"
#include <iostream.h>

template <class Type>
class datalist
{
protected:
  Type *Element;
  int ArraySize;
public:
  datalist(int arraysize = 10) : ArraySize(arraysize),
    Element(new Type[arraysize]) {}
  virtual ~datalist();
  friend ostream& operator<<(ostream& OutStream, const
    datalist<Type>& OutList);
  friend istream& operator>>(istream& InStream,
    datalist<Type>& InList);
};
#endif
```

The class searchlist inherits datalist and adds a Search() function
which will implement the sequential search algorithm. The definition of the
searchlist class is in the file search.h:

```
#ifndef SEARCH_H
#define SEARCH_H
#include "datalist.h"

template <class Type>
class searchlist : public datalist<Type>
{
public:
```

```
    searchlist(int arraysize = 10) :
        datalist<Type>(arraysize) {}
    virtual ~searchlist() {}
    virtual int Search(const Type& Target) const;
};
#endif
```

Most things (apart from the input/output functions) should look familiar in these classes. Since we are planning on inheriting the `datalist` class, we have made the non-public fields `protected`, and have declared the functions as `virtual`.

Now we must consider the input/output functions in the `datalist` class. We would like to be able to use the `<<` and `>>` operators for output and input of the array elements and other information in this class. You might think that since `<<` and `>>` are just operators, we could overload them in the same way we have been overloading other operators such as `+`, `>`, and so on up to now. In a sense we could do this, but there is a slight problem. If we want to use the `<<` operator to print the contents of a `datalist` object `ListObject` to the output stream `cout`, we would like to be able to say

```
cout << ListObject;
```

Note that `cout` is the *left* operand of the `<<` operator, and the class object `ListObject` is the *right* operand. If we tried to overload the `<<` operator in the same way we have used for other operator overloadings up to now, we would write a declaration like:

```
ostream& operator<<(ostream& OutStream);
```

This declaration, however, assumes that the class object calling the operator is the *left* operand and the output stream `OutStream` is the *right* operand, so that to use this declaration, we would have to say:

```
ListObject << cout;
```

which doesn't look right. It would also make it impossible to chain output of user-defined objects with other built-in variables in the same output statement.

We therefore need a way of overloading an operator so that the object calling the operator is the *right* operand and the external object is the *left* operand. Doing this requires the use of an external function (a function that is not a member of the class). The declaration

```
    friend ostream& operator<<(ostream& OutStream,
        const datalist<Type>& OutList);
```

declares an overloaded << operator whose left operand is an `ostream` object (`cout`, for example) and whose right operand is a `datalist` object. Because this operator will need access to the `protected` fields `Element` and `ArraySize`, the function must be made a *friend* of the class. A friend function is allowed access to all protected and private fields of a class.

As mentioned earlier, the friend concept in C++ should be used sparingly, since it presents glaring opportunities to violate the principles of object oriented programming by allowing any function or class to have access to the private fields of any other class. Because of the way C++ was designed, however, there are some cases where friends must be used, since there is no other way of doing things. The situation here is an example of this. There is no C++ language syntax which allows a class function to overload an operator such that the object calling the overloaded operator is that operator's *right* operand. Perhaps in a future version of the language there will be, at which time the use of friends in this context can be eliminated.

The definitions of these functions are in the two files `datatemp.h` and `searchtm.h`. First, `datatemp.h`:

```
#ifndef DATATEMP_H
#define DATATEMP_H
#include "datalist.h"

template <class Type>
datalist<Type>::~datalist()
{
   delete [] Element;
}

template <class Type>
ostream& operator<<(ostream& OutStream,
   const datalist<Type>& OutList)
{
   OutStream << "Array contents:\n";
   for (int element=0; element < OutList.ArraySize;
       element++)
     OutStream << OutList.Element[element] << ' ';
   OutStream << endl;
   OutStream << "Array size: " << OutList.ArraySize
     << endl;
   return OutStream;
}

template <class Type>
istream& operator>>(istream& InStream,
   datalist<Type>& InList)
{
   cout << "Enter array elements:\n";
   for (int element=0; element < InList.ArraySize;
```

```
      element++)
   {
      cout << "Element " << element << ": ";
      InStream >> InList.Element[element];
   }
   return InStream;
}
#endif
```

The overloaded << operator prints out the heading "Array contents:" and then lists the contents of the array Element separated by blanks. Note that the << operator is also used to print out each array element, so if these elements are objects of a user-defined class, that class must also have an overloaded << operator defined for it (we will see an example of this at the end of this chapter).

The overloaded << operator returns an ostream object to allow chaining of objects to the output stream. For example, if we wanted to print out two objects of type searchlist, we could write:

```
cout << ListObject1 << ListObject2;
```

This statement is constructed left to right. The first operation to be performed is cout << ListObject1. Here, the left operand of the << operator is the standard output stream cout, and the right operand is ListObject1. The various elements in ListObject1 are copied into cout according to the instructions in the operator<<() function given above. At the end of this function call, the stream cout is returned. Thus the return value of the operation cout << ListObject1 is cout. The second operation then becomes cout << ListObject2, which causes the components in ListObject2 to be added to cout. The result is that the operator<<() function is called twice: once to print out the components in ListObject1 and then to print out the components in ListObject2.

Similar considerations apply to the overloaded >> operator for reading input from an istream object.

Finally, the Search() function implements the sequential search algorithm, and is defined in the file searchtm.h:

```
#ifndef SEARCHTM_H
#define SEARCHTM_H
#include "search.h"
#include "datatemp.h"

template <class Type>
int searchlist<Type>::Search(const Type& Target) const
{
   for (int element=0; element < ArraySize; element++)
   {
```

```
    if (Element[element] == Target)
      return element;
  }
  return -1;
}
#endif
```

A main() function that tests these routines is in the file search.cpp:

```
#include "searchtm.h"
const int SIZE = 5;

main()
{
  searchlist<float> List1(SIZE);
  float Target;
  int Location;

  cin >> List1;
  cout << List1;
  for (int i = 0; i < 5; i++)
  {
    cout << "Search for a float: ";
    cin >> Target;
    if ((Location = List1.Search(Target)) != -1)
      cout << "Found at index " << Location << endl;
    else
      cout << "Not found.\n";
  }
  return 0;
}
```

A list of five floats is declared, and read in from the keyboard, using the cin >> List1 statement. The << operator is then tested by printing out the list that has just been read in. Finally, the for loop gives the user five chances to look up some numbers in the list and prints out the results.

### 11.4.2 Binary search

Having laid the groundwork for our searching templates with the sequential search algorithm, we may use inheritance to define a class that implements the binary search algorithm. We can inherit everything from the datalist template defined above, and add a Search() function which implements the binary search algorithm.

The derived class is defined in the file binary.h:

```
#ifndef BINARYH
#define BINARYH
#include "datalist.h"
```

```
template <class Type>
class forgetsearch : public datalist<Type>
{
public:
  forgetsearch(int arraysize=10) :
    datalist<Type>(arraysize) {}
  virtual ~forgetsearch() {}
  virtual int Search(const Type& Target) const;
};
#endif
```

We inherit the datalist class template (remember that the Type
parameter must be included in all references to the datalist template). The
forgetsearch constructor calls the datalist constructor to initialize the
ArraySize field. The forgetsearch destructor will call the datalist
constructor automatically.

The Search() function is defined in the file bintemp.h:

```
#ifndef BINTEMPH
#define BINTEMPH
#include "binary.h"
#include "datatemp.h"

template <class Type>
int forgetsearch<Type>::
  Search(const Type& Target) const
{
  int top=ArraySize-1, bottom=0, middle;

  while(top > bottom) {
    middle = (top+bottom)/2;
    if (Element[middle] < Target)
      bottom = middle+1;
    else
      top = middle;
  }
  if (top == -1)
    return -1;
  if (Element[top] == Target)
    return top;
  else
      return -1;
}

template <class Type>
int targetsearch<Type>::
  Search(const Type& Target) const
{
  int top=ArraySize-1, bottom=0, middle;

  while(top >= bottom) {
```

```
    middle = (top+bottom)/2;
    if (Element[middle] == Target)
      return middle;
    else if (Element[middle] < Target)
      bottom = middle+1;
    else
      top = middle-1;
  }
  return -1;
}
#endif
```

This function implements the algorithm exactly as it was stated in the previous section.

# 11.5 Efficiency of searching algorithms - counting steps

The two searching algorithms presented in this chapter demonstrate that different methods require different amounts of work to achieve the same ends. The sequential search requires a number of comparisons (on average) that is roughly proportional to the size of the list being searched, while the binary search requires only one extra comparison (on average) when the list size is doubled.

Similar situations exist with the various algorithms that are used to perform other common computing tasks, such as sorting, dealing with trees and graphs, and so on. In order for you to make an intelligent choice of which algorithm to use in a given situation, you need to have some idea of how the efficiencies of algorithms are calculated. A full treatment of algorithm efficiency requires a proficiency in mathematics that we are not requiring of any reader of this book. We will try to convey a feel for how the efficiency of algorithms can be measured without using anything more than basic arithmetic, so that you can at least take an educated guess at the efficiency of an algorithm when you first meet it.

## 11.5.1 Best, worst, and average cases

There are three main measures of efficiency that can be applied to most algorithms: the *best*, *worst*, and *average* cases. For example, in the sequential search algorithm, the best case occurs when the target for which you are searching is the first item in the list, since only one comparison needs to be done. The worst case is when the target is either the last item in the list or is not in the list at all, since the target must be compared with every list key in either of these cases. The average case is found by considering all possible outcomes of a search and averaging the number of comparisons over all these cases.

## 11.5.2 Efficiency of the sequential search

Let us try to estimate the best, worst, and average number of comparisons for a list of length $n$. As just mentioned, the best case for the sequential search occurs when the target is the first item in the list, since only one comparison must be done. Thus the best case is always one comparison, independent of the list length $n$.

The worst case occurs when the target is either the last list item or is not present in the list, since both of these cases require $n$ comparisons. Thus the worst case is proportional to the length of the list: double the length of the list and you double the amount of work you need to do.

The average case can be worked out by adding up the number of comparisons that you need to do for all possible outcomes and then dividing by the number of possible outcomes. However, it is more useful if we separate the efficiency estimates for the cases of *successful* and *unsuccessful* outcomes of the search. For an unsuccessful search, we know that we always require $n$ comparisons, so the best, worst, and average efficiencies are all the same. For a successful search, the best case requires one comparison, and the worst case requires $n$ comparisons.

What of the average number of comparisons required for a successful search? If we assume that any of the keys in the list is equally likely to be the target for which we are searching, then we would expect that, on average, we would have to look at half the list before we found the target. Thus we can estimate that the average number of comparisons is about $n/2$.

If you know a bit of algebra it isn't too hard to work out an exact formula for the average number of comparisons. Doing this shows that the value is $(n + 1)/2$, which is very close to our estimate of $n/2$, especially if the list is very long.

It is instructive to test these predictions by actually running the algorithms and counting the number of comparisons for a large number of searches. To this end, we will derive a new class from the `searchlist` template to test the efficiency of sequential search.

In doing our tests, we shall be concerned only with those comparisons between the target and a list element. In the program itself there are several other comparisons that are done (for example, testing termination conditions in `for` loops), but we shall ignore those. We want to find out how much work the algorithm itself is actually doing.

The new class will have some extra data fields for storing things like the number of comparisons done in a search, and the average numbers of comparisons for successful and unsuccessful searches. We will need to modify the `Search()` function to have it count the comparisons.

To calculate an average for the number of comparisons required in a search, we need to run the search a large number of times for various targets and keep some statistics on the outcomes. We will therefore use the constructor for the new class to fill up the array with numbers (rather than reading them in from the keyboard), and then use a random number generator to produce a stream of targets for which we shall search the list and record the number of comparisons required in each case. To separate successful from unsuccessful searches we will do a series of searches for numbers that we know to be in the list, and then another series of searches for numbers that we know are not in the list.

The derived class is in the file srcheff.h:

```cpp
#ifndef SRCHEFF_H
#define SRCHEFF_H
#include "bintemp.h"
#include <stdlib.h>
#include <time.h>
#include <fstream.h>

class sequentialEff : public searchlist<long>
{
protected:
  long Comparisons;
  float AverageSuccess, AverageFail;
  long NumRuns;
public:
  sequentialEff(int arraysize = 100,
    long numruns = 100);
  virtual int Search(const long& Target);
  void TestSearch();
  void SaveResults(const char *FileName) const;
};
#endif
```

This header file includes the file bintemp.h, which contains the template definitions for the binary search class, and also includes in turn the files defining the searchlist class. The other included files are for other features that we shall consider later.

The data fields AverageSuccess and AverageFail are for storing the average number of comparisons required for successful and unsuccessful searches, respectively. NumRuns specifies how many searches should be done to calculate the average values.

The size of the array (recall that the field ArraySize is inherited from searchlist) and number of runs are initialized in the constructor. The Search() function implements the sequential search with additional statements that count the number of comparisons. The function TestSearch() runs NumRuns successful and unsuccessful searches on the list, and calculates AverageSuccess and AverageFail. SaveResults() saves the averages and other data in a file.

The function definitions are:

```
#include "srcheff.h"

sequentialEff::sequentialEff(int arraysize,
  long numruns) :
  searchlist<long>(arraysize), NumRuns(numruns)
{
  for (int count = 0; count < arraysize; count++)
    Element[count] = count;
}

int sequentialEff::Search(const long& Target)
{
  for (int element = 0; element < ArraySize; element++)
  {
    ++Comparisons;
    if (Element[element] == Target)
      return element;
  }
  return -1;
}

void sequentialEff::TestSearch()
{
  int count;

  AverageSuccess = AverageFail = 0.0;
                  // Test successful searches
  for (count = 0; count < NumRuns; ++count) {
    Comparisons = 0;
    Search(random(ArraySize));
    AverageSuccess += Comparisons;
  }
  AverageSuccess /= NumRuns;
                  // Test unsuccessful searches
  for (count = 0; count < NumRuns; ++count) {
    Comparisons = 0;
    Search(random(ArraySize) + ArraySize);
    AverageFail += Comparisons;
  }
  AverageFail /= NumRuns;
}

void sequentialEff::
  SaveResults(const char *FileName) const
{
  ofstream SaveFile(FileName, ios::app);
  SaveFile << NumRuns << ' ' << ArraySize << ' ' <<
    AverageSuccess << ' ' << AverageFail << endl;
  SaveFile.close();
}
```

The constructor loads the `Element` array with consecutive numbers from 0 to `ArraySize`, thus ensuring the list is sorted, as will be required for testing the binary search. The `Search()` function counts the number of comparisons.

The `TestSearch()` function does `NumRuns` successful and unsuccessful searches, using a random number generator to produce the targets. Unfortunately, random number generators are not standardized in C++ libraries, so the procedure for generating random numbers may be different in your compiler. The method used in this example is based on the Borland libraries. The `random(ArraySize)` call generates a random integer between 0 and `ArraySize - 1`, inclusive. Since these are the numbers we loaded into the `Element` array in the constructor, we know that all these searches will be successful. Similarly, in the loop that tests unsuccessful searches, the random numbers are generated in the range `ArraySize` to `2*ArraySize - 1`. We know that none of these numbers is in the array, so the search is guaranteed to fail.

The `SaveResults()` function illustrates how to save data in an external file using C++ streams. First, you must declare and define a variable of type `ofstream`. The `SaveFile` variable in `SaveResults()` is of this type, and may be used in exactly the same way as `cout`, except that data are stored in a disk file instead of being printed to the screen. The `ofstream` constructor takes two arguments: a `char` pointer which points to a string giving the name of the file, and a second flag that indicates how the file is to be accessed. We have specified `ios::app` for this flag, which means that the data are to be appended to the file. If you want to erase the contents of the file and start writing from scratch, use `ios::out` instead of `ios::app`.

Reading data from a file can be done by declaring an `ifstream` object in a similar way. For example, the declaration

```
ifstream InFile("input.dat", ios::in);
```

will initialize an `ifstream` variable `InFile` so that data may be read from the disk file `input.dat`. The format for using an `ifstream` object is the same as that for using the `cin` object for reading from the keyboard.

To use file streams in C++, you must include the system header file `fstream.h`.

Following the opening of the file, `NumRuns`, `ArraySize`, `AverageSuccess`, and `AverageFail` are written to the file, and then the file is closed.

The `main()` function which runs the tests is in the file `srchtest.cpp`:

```
#include "srcheff.h"

int main()
{
```

```
sequentialEff *TestSeq;
int ListSize;

randomize();
for (ListSize = 10; ListSize <= 1000; ListSize += 10)
{
   TestSeq = new sequentialEff(ListSize);
   TestSeq->TestSearch();
   TestSeq->SaveResults("testseq.dat");
   delete TestSeq;
}
return 0;
}
```

A *pointer* to a sequentialEff object is declared, rather than the object itself, because we will be creating a series of objects, each with a different list size. It is more efficient in terms of memory requirements to have only a single list in use at any one time, so we create a list of a specified size using the new operator, use the list to perform the efficiency test, and then delete the list before testing the next one.

One final comment about the random number generator. Most generators must be initialized before they are used. Otherwise, they will generate the same sequence of random numbers every time the program is run. Again, the methods for initializing the generator vary from one compiler to another. The Borland library provides the randomize() function which does the job for you.

This program was run on lists ranging in length from 10 to 1000. The results are shown in Fig. 11.1.

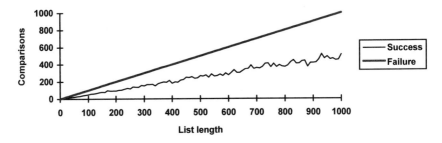

Fig. 11.1. Efficiency of sequential search.

You can see that the predictions of theory are borne out by the experimental runs. The average number of comparisons for a successful search is roughly half the length of the list, while the number of comparisons required to show that a target is not in the list is equal to the list length.

### 11.5.3 Efficiency of binary search

A similar experiment can be done to determine the efficiency of binary search. First, though, let us see if we can predict the results using simple arguments, as we did with the sequential search.

We know that the binary search looks first at the middle element in a sorted list. If the target lies in the upper half of the list, the lower half is ignored for the remainder of the search. Similarly, if the target lies in the lower half, the upper half is ignored. The process is repeated with the half-list and again with half of the half-list, and so on until we have only one element left. Finally, there is a comparison of this last element with the actual target to see if the target has been found.

We can get an estimate of how many comparisons are required by considering lists whose lengths are powers of 2 (2, 4, 8, 16, 32, and so on). The number of comparisons that is done in the first stage of the algorithm, where the list is being chopped in half at each stage, is equal to the number of times 2 divides the list length. For a list of length 8, for example, 3 divisions will be done, since $8 = 2 \times 2 \times 2 = 2^3$. The final comparison with the one remaining element makes a total of 4 comparisons for a list of length 8. For a list whose length is exactly the $n$th power of 2, there will be $n + 1$ comparisons required.

For lists with lengths that are not exact powers of 2, we would expect the number of comparisons to be close to that required for the list whose length is the nearest power of 2. For example, for a list of length 1000, we might expect that 10 comparisons would be needed to divide the list to the point where only one element remains (since the nearest power of 2 is $2^{10} = 1024$), with one further comparison to see if that element is the target we are looking for. We would predict therefore, that about 11 comparisons would be needed to locate an element in a list of length 1000. In addition, we would expect that the number of comparisons should be about the same whether the search is successful or unsuccessful.

We can derive a new class from the `sequentialEff` class above to test the efficiency of binary search. This class is added to the file `srcheff.h`:

```
class binaryEff : public sequentialEff
{
public:
   binaryEff(int arraysize = 100, long numruns = 100);
   int Search(const long& Target);
};
```

The class `binaryEff` will use most of the same fields and functions as the `sequentialEff` class. We need to replace the `Search()` function so that it implements binary search, and counts the comparisons. The functions required for `binaryEff` are added to the file `srcheff.cpp`:

```
binaryEff::binaryEff(int arraysize, long numruns)  :
   sequentialEff(arraysize, numruns)
{}

int binaryEff::Search(const long& Target)
{
   int top = ArraySize - 1, bottom = 0, middle;

   while(top > bottom) {
     middle = (top + bottom)/2;
     ++Comparisons;
     if (Element[middle] < Target)
       bottom = middle + 1;
     else
        top = middle;
   }
   if (top == -1)
     return -1;
   ++Comparisons;
   if (Element[top] == Target)
     return top;
   else
       return -1;
}
```

These functions should be self-explanatory if you have studied the original C++ code for the binary search presented earlier in this chapter.

This code is run with the `main()` function:

```
#include "srcheff.h"

int main()
{
   binaryEff *TestBin;
   int ListSize;

   randomize();
   for (ListSize = 10; ListSize <= 1000; ListSize += 10)
   {
     TestBin = new binaryEff(ListSize);
     TestBin->TestSearch();
     TestBin->SaveResults("testbin.dat");
     delete TestBin;
   }
   return 0;
}
```

The results of running this program on lists ranging in size from 10 to 1000 are shown in Fig. 11.2.

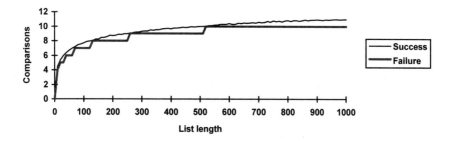

Fig. 11.2. Efficiency of binary search.

You can see that the number of comparisons does increase by 1 each time the list length passes a power of 2 (recall that the powers of 2 are 2, 4, 8, 16, 32, 64, 128, 256, 512, 1024, ...). Also, the number of comparisons is about the same for successful and unsuccessful searches.

You may be wondering why the curve for successful searches increases fairly smoothly while that for unsuccessful searches goes up in steps at each power of 2 boundary. The reason lies in the way the tests were done. The numbers used in testing successful searches were chosen randomly from the range of numbers stored in the list. Those numbers used for testing unsuccessful searches are all larger than the largest number in the list. Thus we never examine what happens in the algorithm when a number for which we are searching lies *between* two numbers in the list. You might like to modify the searching program so that this test is done and see if it smooths out the curve.

The most important thing to notice about these two tests (for sequential and binary search) is how much less work is done by the binary search algorithm, once the list contains more than just a few elements. This seems to indicate that there is some fundamental difference between the two algorithms. We shall explore this idea in the next section.

# 11.6 Efficiency of algorithms - general

## 11.6.1 Classifying algorithms by their efficiency

We saw in the last section that two algorithms for achieving the same result (locating an item in a list) can have very different efficiencies. It is natural to ask whether such differences exist for algorithms in other areas, and whether there is any systematic way of finding and classifying efficiencies.

As you might expect, the answer to all these questions is 'Yes'. There are various approaches to the study of algorithm efficiency, but since we are not assuming any great mathematical proficiency on the part of the reader, we must stick with heuristic and experimental methods. The general sorts of arguments and methods that we will use were illustrated in the last section, where we gave a simple argument to estimate the efficiencies of both the sequential and binary search algorithms. For some algorithms, such arguments are fairly easy to construct, for others, considerably more difficult. One thing we can always do, though, is a series of computer experiments in which we count the number of steps required to run the algorithm on data sets of varying sizes. We used this method in the last section as well, and managed to produce some plots of the number of steps as a function of the length of the list being searched.

We discovered, both by heuristic argument and by computer experiment, that the average number of comparisons required in using sequential search is directly proportional to the length of the list. Using the same methods, we discovered that the average number of comparisons required in the binary search is proportional to the power to which 2 must be raised to obtain the length of the list (that is, if the list length is $2^n$, the number of comparisons is proportional to $n$).

We usually find, either by theoretical argument or by computer experimentation, that the number of steps required by an algorithm depends on some simple expression involving the amount of data being processed. For example, in the case of sequential search, we can say the number $C$ of comparisons is (roughly) equal to half the length $L$ of the list: $C = L/2$. In the case of the binary search, if the length $L$ of the list can be written as $L = 2^n$, then the number of comparisons is roughly equal to $n$: $C = n$.

The most important thing to notice about the efficiency of the sequential search is that $C$ is *directly proportional* to $L$. The fact that the scaling factor is $1/2$, although useful to know, is not the most important fact. Knowing that $C$ is directly proportional to $L$ means that we know that if the length of the list is doubled, the number of comparisons required will double also; if the length is tripled, the number of comparisons also triples, and so on. In other words, what is important is that $C$ is directly proportional to $L$, and not what the actual proportionality constant is. The main point of working out the efficiency of an algorithm is to know how it behaves for large amounts of data; in particular, how fast the amount of work increases as the amount of data increases.

We can therefore make an argument for classifying together all algorithms in which the number of steps increases in direct proportion to the amount of data. Such algorithms are called *linear* algorithms (since the graph of the amount of work versus the amount of data is a straight line, as we saw for the sequential search in the last section).

In a similar way, we can classify together all algorithms that behave like the binary search. These sorts of algorithms are called *logarithmic* algorithms. If you know how logarithms are defined in mathematics, you will see why this is true. If you don't know what logarithms are, a brief description is in order.

Consider an expression like the one we used above for the length of a list in terms of a power of 2: $L = 2^n$. The *logarithm* of $L$ (to base 2) is *defined* to be $n$. That is, $\log L = n$, if $L = 2^n$. In words, the (base 2) logarithm of a number is the power to which 2 must be raised to give that number. The logarithm of 2 is therefore 1 (since $2^1 = 2$), the logarithm of 4 is 2 (since $2^2 = 4$), the logarithm of 8 is 3 (since $2^3 = 8$), and so on.

Logarithms of numbers that aren't exact powers of 2 can also be defined using some mathematical trickery. For example, we can define the logarithm of 5 to be the power to which 2 must be raised to give 5. Since 5 isn't an exact power of 2, but lies between 4 and 8, you would expect that the logarithm of 5 is somewhere between 2 and 3, and you would be right (it is 2.322, to 3 decimal places). For the purposes of this book, don't worry about how such 'weird' logarithms are calculated, since that requires a fair bit of mathematical knowledge. If you remember that a base 2 logarithm of a number is the power to which 2 has to be raised to get that number, that's all you need.

The binary search algorithm has an efficiency that can therefore be written as $C = \log L$, where $C$ is the number of comparisons, and $L$ is the length of the list.

One final note about logarithms: if you want to use a calculator to evaluate a base 2 logarithm, you may have to use a two-step procedure. Most calculators don't have a button for working out base 2 logarithms directly. The most common logarithm buttons are labelled "log" or "ln". The "log" button gives you a *base 10* logarithm, which is the power to which 10 (not 2) must be raised to give a number. For example, the base 10 logarithm of 100 is 2, since $10^2 = 100$, and so on. To get a base 2 logarithm from a base 10 logarithm, divide the base 10 logarithm of the number by the base 10 logarithm of 2. For example, to get the base 2 logarithm of 5, find the base 10 logarithm of 5 by pressing the "log" button on your calculator. The calculator will show the answer as 0.69897. Now divide this number by the base 10 logarithm of 2 (which is 0.30103) to get the base 2 logarithm of 5, which is 2.32193.

## 11.6.2 The big-oh notation

Once you get used to the idea of classifying algorithms by the general way they depend on the amount of data, you will find a shorthand notation for efficiency to be quite handy. We can borrow such a notation from mathematics. We can represent a linear algorithm (one where the number of steps increases in direct proportion to the amount of data) by the notation $O(n)$, which is read "order $n$". This notation means that, for 'large' values of $n$ (where $n$ is a quantity that measures the amount of data being processed by the algorithm; $n$ was equal to $L$ when we were discussing list lengths above, for example), the number of steps taken by the algorithm is directly proportional to the amount of data being processed.

The restriction of this definition to "large values of $n$" is imposed because in some cases the exact form of the dependence of the number of steps on the amount of data implied by the notation $O(n)$ doesn't become accurate until $n$ gets quite large. For example, we mentioned above that the average number of comparisons required by sequential search on a list of length $L$ is $(L + 1)/2$, which expands to $L/2 + 1/2$. The extra term of $1/2$ means that the number of comparisons isn't strictly proportional to $L$. However, when the list gets very long, so that $L$ gets very large, the extra $1/2$ fades into insignificance and saying that the number of steps is proportional to $L$ becomes more and more accurate. The notation $O(n)$ thus means that the term that increases the fastest is the one proportional to $n$. There could be other 'lower order' terms (that is, terms that don't change as fast as $n$ increases), but these will become negligible as $n$ gets large.

In the case of the binary search, the highest order term (the term that increases the fastest) is the logarithmic term, so we say that the binary search is an $O(\log n)$ algorithm.

All algorithms can therefore be classified by giving their order, in the form of big-oh notation. To do this, of course, we must first find an expression for the dependence of the number of steps in the algorithm on the amount of data being processed. This is the hard bit. We may be able to do it by working out a formula analytically, by some form of heuristic argument, or by computer experimentation. However we do it, we are interested mainly in the term in this expression that increases the fastest as the amount of data becomes larger.

The most common orders of algorithms are the following, listed in increasing order of complexity:

- Constant ($O(1)$): the number of steps is independent of the amount of data. The best case result for the sequential search is $O(1)$, since if the element for which we are searching is the first element in the list, only one comparison is required no matter how long the list is. Remember, though, that $O(1)$ means that a *constant* number of steps is required, where the constant number can be any number, not necessarily just one. An algorithm that always requires 15 steps is still an $O(1)$ algorithm.
- Logarithmic ($O(\log n)$): algorithms like the binary search.
- Linear ($O(n)$): algorithms like the average case of the sequential search.
- Log-linear ($O(n \log n)$): algorithms where the leading term is proportional to the product of the amount of data $n$ by the logarithm of the amount of data ($\log n$). The most efficient sorting algorithms are of this type, as we will see in the next chapter.
- Quadratic ($O(n^2)$): algorithms where the number of steps depends on the square of the amount of data. In such algorithms, doubling the amount of data quadruples the amount of work that must be done. Some sorting algorithms are of this type.

Other forms of algorithms exist, but these are the only varieties that we shall meet in this book.

## 11.7 Using a template with a user-defined class - searching a list of names

Finally in this chapter, we will give an example of a programming technique to which we have alluded several times in previous chapters. We have mentioned that one of the advantages of using a template to define a class is that the class may be used with any data type, even a user-defined class. We pointed out that if a user-defined class is used with a template, the user must ensure that all required operators and functions are present in the user-defined class.

As a concrete example of how this is done, we will present a program in which a binary search is done on an ordered list of people's names. The class we shall define to represent a person's name contains two text fields: one for the surname and the other for the first name. A list of names is sorted into alphabetical order using the surname as the principal key. Two names with identical surnames are then sorted using the first name as a secondary key. For example, "Steve Roberts" would come before "Jane Smith" in the list, since "Roberts" precedes "Smith" in alphabetical order. "Jane Smith" would come before "John Smith" since the surnames are the same, but "Jane" precedes "John" in alphabetical order.

The class definition is in the file name.h:

```
#ifndef NAME_H
#define NAME_H
#include <iostream.h>
#include <string.h>
#include "mydefs.h"

class name
{
private:
  char FirstName[20], Surname[20];
public:
  name();
  BOOL operator <(const name& OtherName) const;
  BOOL operator ==(const name& OtherName) const;
  friend ostream& operator<<(ostream& OutStream,
    const name& OutName);
  friend istream& operator>>(istream& InStream,
    name& InName);
};
#endif
```

The class contains the two text fields for first name and surname. Since the class is to be used with the `forgetsearch` template, we must ensure that all required operators are defined in the `name` class. We see that we need the comparison operators `<` and `==`, and the overloaded input and output operators `<<` and `>>`, so we provide these in the class. Since we will be using some functions from the string library to implement these operators, we must include the system `string.h` header file.

The function definitions are in the file `name.cpp`:

```cpp
#include "name.h"

name::name()
{}

BOOL name::operator <(const name& OtherName) const
{
   if (strcmp(Surname, OtherName.Surname) < 0)
      return TRUE;
   else if (strcmp(Surname, OtherName.Surname) > 0)
      return FALSE;
   else       // Surnames the same; compare first names
      return strcmp(FirstName, OtherName.FirstName) < 0;
}

BOOL name::operator ==(const name& OtherName) const
{
   return (!strcmp(Surname, OtherName.Surname) &&
      !strcmp(FirstName, OtherName.FirstName));
}

istream& operator>>(istream& InStream, name& InName)
{
   cout << "Enter surname: ";
   InStream.getline(InName.Surname,
      sizeof InName.Surname);
   cout << "Enter first name: ";
   InStream.getline(InName.FirstName,
      sizeof InName.FirstName);
   return InStream;
}

ostream& operator<<(ostream& OutStream,
   const name& OutName)
{
   OutStream << OutName.Surname << ", "
      << OutName.FirstName << endl;
   return OutStream;
}
```

The overloaded < operator implements the ordering described above. The two surnames are compared using the strcmp() function from the string library. This function returns –1 if the first string is alphabetically prior to the second, 0 if the two strings are the same, and +1 if the first string is alphabetically after the second. We therefore compare the surnames and return TRUE or FALSE if the two surnames differ, depending on which order they are in, and if the two surnames are equal, we then compare the first names.

The overloaded == operator returns TRUE if both the surnames and the first names of the two strings match. Finally, the overloaded << and >> operators provide simple input and output routines for a name object. Note that these functions are friend functions of the name class, so their definitions do not have the name:: prefix before their names.

Finally, we present a main() function which uses the name class as a parameter in the forgetsearch template, reads in a list of names, and then offers the user a chance to search this list for names entered from the keyboard. The function is in the file namesrch.cpp:

```cpp
#include "name.h"
#include "bintemp.h"

const int SIZE = 5;

int main()
{
   forgetsearch<name> NameList(SIZE);
   name NameTarget;
   int Location;

   cin >> NameList;
   cout << NameList;
   for (int i = 0; i < 5; i++)
   {
      cout << "Search for a name in NameList: ";
      cin >> NameTarget;
      if ((Location = NameList.Search(NameTarget)) != -1)
         cout << "Found at index " << Location << endl;
      else
         cout << "Not found.\n";
   }
   return 0;
}
```

Note that we were able to use the forgetsearch template without any modifications, provided that we ensured that all the relevant operators were defined in the name class. The line cin >> NameList; for example, uses the overloaded >> operator in two forms. First, the overloaded form of the operator defined in the forgetsearch template is used to read in the list of names. Each name read in for this list calls the overloaded **>>** operator from the `name` class. The line `cin >> NameTarget;` on the other hand uses the overloaded **>>** operator from the `name` class directly. The other overloaded operators (**<** and **==**) defined in the `name` class are used behind the scenes by the `Search()` function in the `forgetsearch` template.

This simple example demonstrates the power of the C++ template, combined with operator and function overloading. Templates for commonly used operations, such as searching and sorting, can be defined, and user-defined classes can be linked into these templates at a later time.

## 11.8 Summary

In this chapter we have studied two searching algorithms: sequential search and binary search. C++ templates for these algorithms were produced.

The main theoretical concepts covered in this chapter are:

- The efficiency of an algorithm is measured by counting (theoretically or experimentally) the number of steps it needs to process a certain amount of data.
- Different algorithms for accomplishing the same task (such as searching a list) can have very different efficiencies.
- The efficiency of an algorithm is classified by finding a simple expression which describes the number of steps taken by the algorithm as a function of the amount of data it processes.
- The big-oh notation is used as a shorthand for classifying algorithms.
- Algorithms studied in this book range from constant order ($O(1)$) up to quadratic order ($O(n^2)$).

C++ programming techniques described in this chapter are:

- Overloading the **<<** and **>>** input/output operators using friend functions.
- Writing data to and reading data from external files using the `fstream` library.
- Counting the steps in an algorithm as a function of the amount of data it processes. This is an experimental technique that can be used to estimate the efficiency of algorithms.
- Using objects of a user-defined class in a template. This example shows how to ensure that the operators required in the template are provided in the user-defined class.

## 11.9 Exercises

1. a. Write a general data template similar to the `datalist` template in the text, except that the data are stored as a linked list, rather than as an array.

b. Using this new template, write versions of the sequential search and forgetful binary search algorithms.

c. Derive a class from the template in part (b) and use it to calculate the efficiency of the two searching algorithms in a manner similar to that in the text.

2. Redesign the experiment used in the text for calculating the efficiency of the forgetful binary search so that, for unsuccessful searches, numbers less than the smallest number in the list, numbers between numbers in the list, and numbers greater than the largest number in the list are all used. Plot a graph of your results and compare it with the graph given in the text. Do you get a smoother curve?

3. As you will have noticed in question 1, implementing the binary search on a linked list requires many traversals of the list to locate the various elements to use in the comparisons. An alternative algorithm for searching a sorted linked list is as follows:

1. Set pointers `Marker` and `OldMarker` to the first data node in the list.
2. While `Marker != 0`
   3. Compare data at location `Marker` with `Target` data:
   4. If `Target == Marker`, return indicating target found
   5. Else if `Target > Marker`, save current `Marker` in `OldMarker`, advance `Marker` by `step` nodes (`step` is usually `>= 2`; if `step == 1`, this algorithm is equivalent to sequential search) and repeat from step 2.
6. Else if `Target < Marker`, return to location `OldMarker` and compare the `step - 1` nodes forward from that location with `Target`. If a match is found, return indicating that `Target` has been found; if no match is found, or a zero pointer is encountered, return indicating that `Target` has not been found.

The idea behind this algorithm is to use larger steps to do a crude initial search through the list. Once a pair of markers localizing the section of the list where `Target` may be found are identified, that section of the list is searched in detail.

Implement this algorithm for a linked list and run some experiments to calculate its efficiency. Try several values of `step`, and compare your results with the binary search.

4. As mentioned in the text, there is an alternative form of the binary search which tests at each halving of the list whether the node at the division point is equal to the target. If not, the relevant half of the list is then searched in the

same manner. Implement this form of the binary search for an array, and run an experiment to calculate its efficiency. How does it compare with the forgetful binary search? The result is surprising, since it would seem that by checking for the target at each stage of the algorithm rather than only at the end, you should be able to shorten the search for a large number of targets. However, for any list of reasonable size, most of the elements will not be found until you have reduced the list to one or two elements anyway. The gain for a few list elements is more than offset by the fact that you must do two comparisons, rather than one, at each step.

# CHAPTER 12

# Sorting algorithms

## 12.1 Introduction

Since one of the most common uses to which computers are put is the storage and retrieval of information, it is important to use algorithms that maximize the efficiency of such data manipulation. As we saw in the chapter on searching algorithms, the binary search algorithm is, for any but the smallest lists, a much more efficient searching technique than the sequential search. The binary search, however, requires that its data be sorted first. Many other algorithms either require sorted data, or are much more efficient when their data are sorted. Since sorting is such a common operation in computing, it is not surprising that there are a great many algorithms for doing it.

We shall examine four sorting algorithms in this chapter. The first two (insertion sort and selection sort) appear to have much poorer efficiency than the last two (mergesort and quicksort). However, this is only true for data of a particular initial ordering. For example, although insertion sort is an $O(n^2)$ algorithm for randomly ordered initial lists, it is closer to an $O(n)$ algorithm for lists that are almost fully sorted to begin with. It is therefore a very efficient algorithm for checking that lists are correctly sorted. The quicksort algorithm is, on average, an $O(n \log n)$ algorithm for randomly ordered lists, but its efficiency actually *degenerates* to $O(n^2)$ for fully sorted lists. Quicksort is therefore an efficient algorithm for sorting lists whose ordering is random, but hideously inefficient for checking that a sorted list is actually in the right order.

As with our treatment of searching algorithms in Chapter 11, we will take an experimental approach to determining the efficiency of sorting algorithms. We will motivate these experiments with some heuristic arguments along the way.

## 12.2 Insertion sort

The insertion sort algorithm is copied directly from a commonly used technique for hand-sorting objects, such as index cards or forms. If we are presented with a pile of cards, on each of which is printed someone's name, and told to sort them into alphabetical order, with the As on the top and the Zs on the bottom, one way we might proceed is as follows.

Take the first card to form the beginning of our sorted pile. Take the next card and compare it with the first card: if it comes before the first card, place it on top of the first card, otherwise place it underneath the first card. Take the third card and compare it with the top card in our sorted pile. If it doesn't come before the top card, compare it with the next card in the pile, and so on, until you find a card which comes after it. In other words, insertion sort inserts the items into the sorted list one at a time by beginning at the beginning of the list and stepping through the list one item at a time until the correct position is found.

The algorithm can be implemented pretty much as described in the previous paragraph if we use linked lists to represent our data. If we wish to use an array to store the sorted list, perhaps because we wish to use a binary search on the list later on, we need to make a few alterations. Because of the nature of an array, if we wish to insert an item at some point in an array, we need to move over by one space all the items to one side of that point in order to create a space for the new item.

We will see the complete code for implementing insertion sort later, when we give a C++ example. For now, we summarize it in words.

We assume we are given a list with `numarray` elements in some arbitrary order. We take element 0 (since C++ arrays start at zero) to be the first element in the sorted list. To facilitate the shifting/insertion process, we examine the first element after the end of the sorted part of the list, and search *backwards* through the sorted list (rather than forwards from the first element). The reason for this is that we can do the shifting at the same time as the searching. We are using a sequential search here to locate the correct location for each item.

Our algorithm is therefore as follows, for a list `Element` of `L` items stored in an array with elements numbered from 0 to `L - 1`:

1. Initialize `marker1` to 1 (the second element in the list).
2. While `marker1 < L`
    3. If `Element[marker1] < Element[marker - 1]`, store `Element[marker1]` in a temporary location `temp`. Initialize `marker2` to `marker1 - 1` (the location just before `marker1`).
        4. While `Element[marker2] > temp` and `marker2 >= 0`, shift `Element[marker2]` to location `marker2 + 1`. (This slides the element over to make room to its left.) Decrease `marker2` by 1.
        5. Insert `temp` into the location last vacated by a shift.
    6. Increase `marker1` by 1.

Notice that steps 4 and 5 are only done if a shift needs to be performed. If an element is already in the correct location relative to its neighbour, nothing is done. It is this fact that makes insertion sort so efficient for checking that a list is correctly ordered. Each element is compared only with its immediate predecessor, and if these two elements are in the correct relative order, no shifting of data is done.

An example of insertion sort is shown in Fig 12.1.

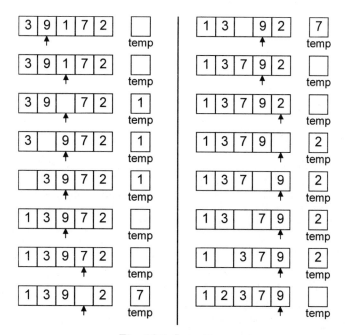

Fig. 12.1. Insertion sort.

The arrow shows the location of `marker1` as we progress through the algorithm. Beginning with array element 1 (the number 9), we compare the element with its immediate predecessor. In this case, 9 > 3 so no data shifting needs to be done. We move `marker2` along to element 2 (the number 1). In this case, 1 < 9 so we need to shift some elements over to the right to make a space into which we can insert 1. We store the 1 in the `temp` location, and then shift the 9 and the 3 over to make a space for 1, into which it is inserted. The process is repeated for the remaining elements in the array (7 and 2) until we achieve a fully sorted list.

## 12.3 Selection sort

Although insertion sort is a straightforward algorithm which is easy to program, it requires a large amount of shifting within the array (although if it is implemented using linked lists, this disadvantage disappears). For large lists, this shifting can be the dominant operation, especially if each item contains a large amount of data that must be moved (as in a personal record with name, phone number, and other data, for example). We will quantitatively analyse the various sorting methods for efficiency later, but for now, it appears that an alternative algorithm in which the amount of shifting was reduced would be an advantage. Selection sort was designed with this in mind.

The idea behind selection sort is that each shift of data moves an item directly into its final, correct place. This is done by starting with a list with numarray elements. In the first step, the largest element in the array is located and swapped with the element at the high end of the list. Then the largest element in the remaining numarray – 1 elements is located and swapped into the second-highest location, and so on. Because selection sort involves accessing the list at various points in a more-or-less random fashion, it is not a good algorithm to use with data stored as a linked list, since a great deal of time will be used traversing the list trying to locate the correct elements at each step, and then reassigning the pointers. It was designed primarily to avoid the excessive number of shifts that occur when insertion sort is used on an array, and so should be used only with arrays.

Selection sort will shift only (at most) two items at each step, and possibly none, if the item is already in the correct location. Its main overhead is in the determination of the maximum element in each sublist. This requires a scan of all remaining unsorted elements at each iteration, but this scanning does not actually move any data and so should be relatively fast.

For a list with L elements numbered from 0 to L – 1, the selection sort algorithm is:

1. Set marker to L – 1 (begin with the last element in the list).
2. While marker > 0:
   3. Find the largest element in the range numbered from 0 to marker;
   4. Swap that element with the element at location marker;
   5. Increase marker by 1.

An example of selection sort is shown in Fig 12.2. The position of the arrow indicates the location of marker at each step. In the first step, marker points to the end of the list, and the maximum value in the entire list is found (9). In the next step, the 9 is swapped with the 2. Note that a swap requires an auxiliary storage location (not shown in the diagram). To swap two values a and b, for example, we must define an extra location temp. Then a is copied into temp, b is copied into a, then temp is copied into b. Thus each swap requires three shifts of data.

In the next step, marker is moved back one step in the list, so that it now points to the second last element (7). The largest element from the beginning of the list up to marker is now found. This turns out to be the value at which marker is currently pointing. We have also not bothered to ask the algorithm to detect when the largest element coincides with marker, so 7 is swapped with itself. This decision is a trade-off between the extra comparison that would need to be done at each stage in the algorithm and the extra swap that may need to be done occasionally if the largest element in the unsorted part of the list happens to be at location marker.

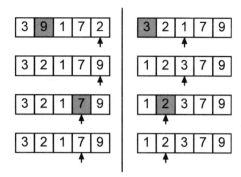

Fig. 12.2. Selection sort.

## 12.4 C++ code for insertion and selection sort

We now present some C++ templates for implementing insertion sort and selection sort. The routines are fairly straightforward to write, since the algorithms are quite simple. We will use the datalist class introduced in the chapter on searching algorithms as the base class for our templates, since sorting algorithms work on the same sorts of lists as searching algorithms. As a reminder of the definition of the datalist template, we present it again here, as stored in file datalist.h:

```
#ifndef DATALIST_H
#define DATALIST_H
#include "mydefs.h"
#include <iostream.h>

template <class Type>
class datalist
{
protected:
  Type *Element;
  int ArraySize;
public:
  datalist(int arraysize = 10) : ArraySize(arraysize),
    Element(new Type[arraysize]) {}
  virtual ~datalist();
  friend ostream& operator<<(ostream& OutStream,
    const datalist<Type>& OutList);
  friend istream& operator>>(istream& InStream,
    datalist<Type>& InList);
};
#endif
```

Refer back to the chapter on searching for definitions of the functions. We will not need to refer to these function definitions here as long as we know what they do.

Templates for insertion sort and selection sort are derived from `datalist`. They are defined in the file `inssel.h`:

```
#ifndef INSSEL_H
#define INSSEL_H
#include "datalist.h"

template <class Type>
class InsertSortList : public datalist<Type>
{
public:
  InsertSortList(int arraysize = 10) :
    datalist<Type>(arraysize) {}
  virtual ~InsertSortList() {}
  virtual void Sort();
};

template <class Type>
class SelectSortList : public datalist<Type>
{
protected:
  void Swap(const int marker1, const int marker2);
  int MaxKey(const int low, const int high);
public:
  SelectSortList(int arraysize = 10) :
    datalist<Type>(arraysize) {}
  virtual ~SelectSortList() {}
  virtual void Sort();
};
#endif
```

Both templates define constructors which call the `datalist` constructor to initialize the array. The destructors will call the `datalist` destructor to delete the `Element` array. Both templates include a `Sort()` function which implements the corresponding sorting algorithm.

The `SelectSortList` template includes a couple of `protected` functions: one for swapping two data elements, and the other for finding the maximum element in a given range of the array.

The definitions of all these functions are in the file `insseltm.h`:

```
#ifndef INSSELTM_H
#define INSSELTM_H
#include "inssel.h"
#include "datatemp.h"

template <class Type>
void InsertSortList<Type>::Sort()
{
  Type temp;
  int marker1, marker2;
```

```
    for(marker1 = 1; marker1 < ArraySize; marker1++) {
      if (Element[marker1] < Element[marker1 - 1]) {
        temp = Element[marker1];
        for (marker2 = marker1 - 1; marker2 >= 0;
          marker2--)
        {
          Element[marker2 + 1] = Element[marker2];
          if (marker2 == 0 ||
            Element[marker2 - 1] < temp)
            break;
        }
        Element[marker2] = temp;
      }
    }
}

template <class Type>
void SelectSortList<Type>::Swap(const int marker1,
    const int marker2) {
  Type temp;

  temp = Element[marker1];
  Element[marker1] = Element[marker2];
  Element[marker2] = temp;
}

template <class Type>
int SelectSortList<Type>::MaxKey(const int low,
    const int high) {
  int marker1, max = low;

  for (marker1 = low + 1; marker1 <= high; marker1++)
    if (Element[max] < Element[marker1])
      max = marker1;
  return max;
}

template <class Type>
void SelectSortList<Type>::Sort()
{
  int marker1, marker2;

  for (marker1 = ArraySize - 1; marker1 > 0; marker1--)
  {
    marker2 = MaxKey(0, marker1);
    Swap(marker2, marker1);
  }
}
#endif
```

Since this file defines functions for templates that inherit another template, the corresponding template functions in the file `datatemp.h` are included here to make them available to any routine that uses the two sorting templates. The functions defined here should all be fairly obvious given the algorithms that they are implementing.

A `main()` function that tests these functions is in the file `inssel.cpp`:

```
#include "insseltm.h"

const int SIZE = 10;

int main()
{
    InsertSortList<int> TestInsertSort(SIZE);

    cin >> TestInsertSort;
    cout << "Testing Insertion Sort:\n"
      << TestInsertSort;
    TestInsertSort.Sort();
    cout << "After sorting:\n" << TestInsertSort;

    SelectSortList<int> TestSelectSort(SIZE);
    cin >> TestSelectSort;
    cout << "Testing Selection Sort:\n"
      << TestSelectSort;
    TestSelectSort.Sort();
    cout << "After sorting:\n" << TestSelectSort;
    return 0;
}
```

The user is asked to read in a list of integers which is then sorted by the insertion sort and selection sort routines. The array is printed before and after sorting (so that you can see that the routines actually work!).

## 12.5 Efficiency of insertion sort and selection sort

### 12.5.1 Comparisons and assignments

We can do a similar sort of experiment as we did for the searching algorithms in the last chapter to determine their efficiencies. In the case of a searching algorithm, we evaluated its efficiencies for successful and unsuccessful outcomes separately. With a sorting algorithm we always expect the outcome to be successful (otherwise we have made a mistake coding the algorithm!). However, there are two types of operations involved in sorting a list of data: comparisons and assignments. Since these two operations require different resources in terms of computing, we need to evaluate them separately.

A comparison requires that those parts of the data structure being used for sorting are compared to determine whether they are in the correct order. Depending on the complexity of the data structures being compared, this can take varying amounts of time. If we are sorting lists of integers (or only using an integer field of a more complex data structure to determine the sorting order) a comparison is relatively fast. If we must compare several fields in a complex data structure, comparisons can take considerably longer.

An assignment requires that data be physically moved within the computer's memory. Assignments are therefore almost always more time-consuming than comparisons. In general, algorithms that minimize the number of assignments are to be preferred.

## 12.5.2 Insertion sort

Before doing the computer experiment, let us see if we can get a heuristic estimate of what order insertion sort will be. For a randomly ordered list, we might expect that we must compare each element with about half of those already sorted before we insert it into its proper place. This, in turn, means that we have to shift about half the data in that portion of the list that has been sorted to insert each new element. This should give us a clue that we expect the number of comparisons and assignments to be about the same. Certainly they should be the same order, even if the constant of proportionality isn't quite the same.

What order will this be? Let us look at the amount of work that is required to insert the *last* element into its proper place. If the list length is $L$, we expect about $L/2$ comparisons *and* $L/2$ assignments to be made. For the first element to be sorted (remember that the first element that actually needs sorting is the second element in the list), we expect that 1 comparison and either 0 or 1 assignments must be made. The average of these two extremes gives us about $L/4$ comparisons and $L/4$ assignments (very roughly) as an *average* number of comparisons and assignments *per element*. Since we have $L-1$ elements to sort (remember that the first element in the list is not actually sorted on its own), we would expect about $(L - 1)L/4$ comparisons and assignments to be made in total. The leading term in this expression is $L^2/4$, so we can predict that insertion sort is an $O(n^2)$ algorithm for both comparisons and assignments, with a proportionality constant of about 0.25 in both cases.

We can test this prediction by writing a program similar to the one that we wrote for testing the searching algorithms in Chapter 11. The program will generate a number of lists of a given length, fill the lists up with randomly ordered numbers, and then apply the insertion sort algorithm to sort the list, keeping track of the number of comparisons and assignments that are made. We will not give the details of the program here, but merely present the results in Fig. 12.3.

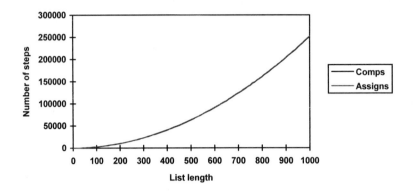

Fig. 12.3. Efficiency of insertion sort.

At first glance, it looks as though our predictions are quite good. The two curves (for comparisons and assignments) are so close that they cannot be distinguished in the graph, and a few checks seem to indicate that the number of steps in each is about $L^2/4$. The curve looks roughly like a parabola, which is what it should be if we have an $O(n^2)$ relationship.

However, we can do better than this. If we believe that the relationship between the number of steps and the list length really does depend on $L^2$, then we can try drawing a graph of the ratio of the number of steps to $L^2$ as a function of the list length. If our prediction is right, we should get (at least as $L$ gets larger) a horizontal line, and the horizontal level of this line should be close to 0.25. If we do this, we get Fig. 12.4.

We can see from this graph that our prediction is definitely true. After an initial flurry above the 0.25 level, the ratios settle down nicely by the time the list length is about 100.

### 12.5.3 Selection sort

Selection sort is unusual amongst sorting algorithms in that, for a given list length, it always performs exactly the same number of both assignments and comparisons. With a bit of elementary algebra it is possible to work out the exact formula, but in keeping with the spirit of this book, we will arrive at an approximate answer through a heuristic argument.

First, consider the number of comparisons. In the first iteration of the algorithm, we must find the largest element in the entire list. With a list of length $L$, we must therefore do $L - 1$ comparisons. To see this, look at it this way. We first compare elements 1 and 2. Then we pick whichever is the larger of these two elements and compare it with element 3, and so on, until we compare the largest element in the first $L - 1$ elements with the last element.

This makes one comparison for the first two elements, and then another comparison for all the remaining elements, for a total of $L - 1$.

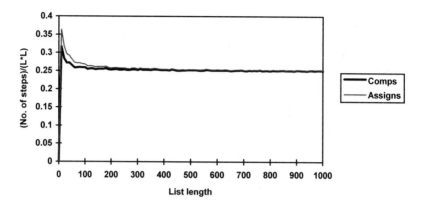

Fig. 12.4. Efficiency of insertion sort (normalized).

In the last iteration of the algorithm, we have a list of length 2 to sort, which requires only a single comparison. Therefore, the average number of comparisons *per element* is the average of $L-1$ and 1, which is $L/2$. The overall average should therefore be $L(L/2)$ or $L^2/2$. Selection sort is therefore an $O(n^2)$ algorithm for comparisons, with the proportionality constant equal to 0.5. It requires twice as many comparisons, on average, as insertion sort.

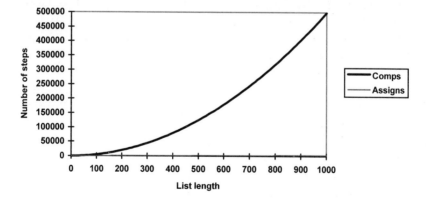

Fig. 12.5. Efficiency of selection sort.

Now consider the number of assignments. If we don't do any checking to avoid swapping an element with itself (as discussed in the previous section), then there will be $L - 1$ swaps. Each swap (as explained earlier) requires 3 assignments, so there will be a total of $3(L - 1) = 3L - 3$ assignments. Selection sort is therefore an $O(n)$ algorithm for assignments, with a

223

proportionality constant of 3. It is a *linear* algorithm for assignments, which is a vast improvement over insertion sort.

To test these predictions, we can try selection sort on lists of various lengths. The results are as shown in Fig. 12.5.

The plot dramatically shows the difference between an $O(n^2)$ and an $O(n)$ algorithm. The number of comparisons curves up quickly, while the number of assignments is scarcely distinguishable from the horizontal axis. The accuracy of our predictions for the two efficiencies could be further verified by plotting the ratio (number of comparisons)/($L^2$) versus list length $L$, and (number of assignments)/$L$ versus $L$, but we trust that the point has been made with the above graph.

## 12.6 More efficient sorting methods

In our study of searching algorithms in Chapter 11, we saw that with a little ingenuity, we could vastly improve the efficiency of the sequential search algorithm by using the binary search. It is natural to ask if a similar improvement can be obtained with sorting algorithms.

How efficient can we expect the best sorting algorithm to be? A full analysis requires a fair bit of mathematics, but we can get a rough idea from the following argument.

Suppose we start by asking: How many different ways can a list of length $L$ be arranged? We can work this out by placing the elements of the list in an array one step at a time. For the first element, we may choose any of the $L$ elements, so there are $L$ ways of filling the first array element. For the second array element, we may choose from any of the remaining $L - 1$ elements, so there are $L - 1$ ways of filling the second array element. However, for each of these $L - 1$ ways, there were $L$ ways of filling the first element, so the total number of ways of filling the first *two* elements of the array is $L(L - 1)$. We can continue the argument in the same fashion for the remaining elements of the array so that we find that there are $L(L - 1)(L - 2)(L - 3)...(3)(2)(1)$ ways of ordering the entire list. There is a shorthand notation for this expression: we can write $L(L-1)(L-2)(L-3)...(3)(2)(1) = L!$ (pronounced "$L$ factorial").

For example, if $L = 2$, there are $2! = (2)(1) = 2$ ways of ordering a list of 2 elements (either *ab* or *ba*). If $L = 3$, there are $3! = (3)(2)(1) = 6$ ways (*abc, bac, acb, bca, cab, cba*), and so on.

At each stage in a sorting algorithm, a comparison between two elements in the list is made and, as a result of this comparison, one of two things is done. Either the two elements are left in the same places in the list, or else they are swapped. Now suppose that, with each swap, the number of final orderings of the list that needed to be considered was reduced by a factor of 2 (in much the same way that the number of elements being considered was reduced by a factor of 2 at each stage in a binary search). This is the largest factor by which the number of choices could be reduced, since there are only two options (to swap or not to swap) at each step in the algorithm. If the total number of possible orderings is a power of 2 (say, $L! = 2^n$), then the number of steps we need to completely sort the list is $n$.

This argument is necessarily a bit vague and imprecise because we are not using a proper mathematical formalism to do the calculation, but the basic assumption that we are making is that there is a sorting algorithm that is capable of eliminating half of the possible orderings of the list at each step in the algorithm. If such an algorithm exists, the number of steps that it should require is around log ($L!$), for the same reason that the binary search algorithm is an $O(\log n)$ algorithm: each step in the algorithm cuts the amount of remaining work in half. Using results from mathematics, the logarithm of a factorial may be approximated by the expression log $(n!) \approx n \log n$. In other words, the most efficient sorting algorithm should be an $O(n \log n)$ algorithm. Since log $n$ increases much more slowly than $n$, an $O(n \log n)$ algorithm is considerably more efficient than an $O(n^2)$ algorithm, which, as you remember, was the efficiency of both the insertion and selection sort algorithms for sorting random lists.

In the remainder of this chapter, we will examine two $O(n \log n)$ sorting algorithms: mergesort and quicksort. Both of these algorithms rely on the 'divide and conquer' technique. The list is split into two parts and the same algorithm is recursively applied to each part until the entire list is sorted.

## 12.7 Mergesort

Mergesort is based on another simple idea: if you are given a pile of cards to sort, divide the pile in half, sort each half independently, and then merge the two piles. This statement looks innocent enough, until we notice that part of the algorithm is to "sort each half independently". How? Do we use selection sort or some other method to sort these smaller piles and then merge the result? We could, but we could also apply the mergesort algorithm again to each half-pile. In other words, we apply mergesort recursively to each half-pile until we encounter the smallest possible pile: a pile of one object. We then 'merge' the sub-piles together one stage at a time until we reach the top level again, at which point the entire list is sorted.

Mergesort therefore has two stages: the initial division of the list into sub-lists of a single element each, and the merging of these sublists to produce the final sorted list. The first stage of mergesort is illustrated in Fig. 12.6.

The second stage merges each of the sublists, starting at the bottom level and working upwards, sorting each pair of sublists to an ordered list at the next higher level at each stage (see Fig. 12.7).

Despite the appeal of mergesort, it has its problems when we attempt to implement it. Suppose first that we try to implement it on data stored in arrays. Since we are dividing the original list in half and sorting each half before we merge the results to produce the final sorted list, we will be (potentially) changing the positions of all the elements in the array before the final merge. This means we need some place to store these sublists while they are being sorted, which means we need to declare a temporary array of the same size as the original list to use as working space.

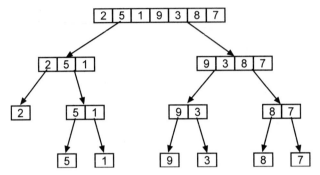

Fig. 12.6. Subdivision of the list in mergesort.

If we attempt to use mergesort for a linked list, we don't need any extra space since we can perform the sorts by redirecting pointers. However, we need to be able to divide a linked list in half, which means we must be able to access the central node. Since the only way we can do this is to follow a chain of pointers from one end of the list, we use a lot of time in continually locating the centre of a linked list.

The C++ code for mergesort is based on the earlier datalist class. The template definition is in the file merge.h:

```
#ifndef MERGE_H
#define MERGE_H
#include "datalist.h"

template <class Type>
class MergeSortList : public datalist<Type>
```

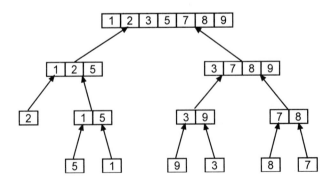

Fig. 12.7. Merging the sublists.

```
{
protected:
  void MergeSort(Type *temp, const int list1,
    const int size);
  void Merge(Type *temp, const int list1,
    const int size1, const int list2, const int size2);
public:
  MergeSortList(int arraysize = 10) :
    datalist<Type>(arraysize) {}
  virtual ~MergeSortList() {}
  virtual void Sort();
};
#endif
```

This class introduces a technique we shall be using frequently with recursive algorithms. The protected function `MergeSort()` has three arguments:

- `temp`: a pointer to the array containing the data to be sorted.
- `list1`: the array index of the first element in the list (or sublist, in recursive calls) to be sorted.
- `size`: the number of elements in the list or sublist to be sorted.

To keep with the philosophy of OOP, the user should not have to be bothered with these arguments when calling the sorting function. A simple call like `MessyList.Sort()` should be all that is required. The `Sort()` function should then call some internal function which does the actual work. The best way to implement this is as we have done here: a public `Sort()` function is declared which (as we shall see) calls the protected `MergeSort()` function which starts the recursion off.

The other protected function `Merge()` is non-recursive, and performs the merging operation on the two sublists. The three new functions in this class are in the file `mergetmp.h`:

```
#ifndef MERGETMP_H
#define MERGETMP_H
#include "merge.h"
#include "datatemp.h"

template <class Type>
void MergeSortList<Type>::MergeSort(Type *temp,
  const int list1, const int size)
{
  int list2, size1, size2;

  if (size > 1) {
    list2 = list1 + size / 2;
    size1 = list2 - list1;
```

```
    size2 = size - size1;
    MergeSort(temp, list1, size1);
    MergeSort(temp, list2, size2);
    Merge(temp, list1, size1, list2, size2);
  }
}

template <class Type>
void MergeSortList<Type>::Merge(Type *temp,
  const int list1, const int size1,
  const int list2, const int size2)
{
  int i = list1, j = list2, k = list1;

  while(i < list1 + size1 && j < list2 + size2) {
    if (temp[i] < temp[j])
      Element[k++] = temp[i++];
    else
      Element[k++] = temp[j++];
  }
  while (i < list1 + size1)
    Element[k++] = temp[i++];
  while (j < list2 + size2)
    Element[k++] = temp[j++];
  for (k = list1; k < list1 + size1 + size2; k++)
    temp[k] = Element[k];
}

template <class Type>
void MergeSortList<Type>::Sort()
{
  Type *temp = new Type[ArraySize];

  for(int i = 0; i < ArraySize; i++)
    temp[i] = Element[i];
  MergeSort(temp, 0, ArraySize);
  delete [] temp;
}
#endif
```

Look first at the third function Sort(), which is the function called by an external user. It declares an auxiliary array temp, and copies the data from the Element array into it. The idea is that successive splits and merges of the list alternate between the temp array and the original Element array. The MergeSort() function is called with the temp array and told to sort a list of size ArraySize beginning at element 0 (the first element).

The MergeSort() function uses the marker list2 to record the position of the first element of the second half of the list. size1 and size2 store the sizes of the two sublists. The first sublist is sorted by a recursive call to MergeSort(), followed by the second sublist. After the two sublists have been sorted, they are merged using the `Merge()` function. Notice that the bottom of the recursion is reached when the list contains only one element.

The `Merge()` function takes the `temp` array and the starting points and sizes of the two sublists that it is to merge. The first `while` loop merges the two sublists until the end of one of the sublists is reached. At this point, either `i == list1 + size1` or `j == list2 + size2`, depending on which sublist was finished first. Thus only one of the two `while` loops following the main loop will actually do anything. This loop simply copies those elements from the unfinished subloop into the `Element` array.

After the merge of the two sublists, the elements are copied back into the `temp` array since the merge that has just occurred may have been at some point deep in the recursion, so further merges are necessary as we climb out of the recursion. This copying operation is unnecessary at the top level where the two sublists each consist of half the original list, but rather than putting in a special check for this one case, it is easier to just do the extra copying anyway.

## 12.8 Efficiency of mergesort

We can run an experiment to count up the numbers of comparisons and assignments in the same fashion as for insertion sort and selection sort earlier in this chapter. The results are shown in Fig. 12.8.

The results are averages over 100 runs for each list length. The first thing we notice is that mergesort does about twice as many assignments as comparisons, which is bad news, since assignments are usually more costly in terms of computer time. However, the actual numbers of each of these operations is considerably less than for insertion sort (where about 250,000 each of comparisons and assignments were done for a list of 1000 items), so we definitely have a more efficient algorithm in mergesort.

To see if we have indeed found the holy grail of an $O(n \log n)$ algorithm, we can plot the ratio of the number of steps required in a list of length $L$ against $L \log L$ for each of comparisons and assignments. The results are shown in Fig. 12.9.

We can see that the number of assignments levels off at around $1.9 \, L \log L$, and the number of comparisons at around $0.9 \, L \log L$. Theory predicts that, in the worst case, the number of comparisons should be $L \log L$, and the number of assignments should be $2 \, L \log L$. Since our experiments would give results closer to the average case than the worst case, we can see that the average case is not far off the worst case for the mergesort algorithm.

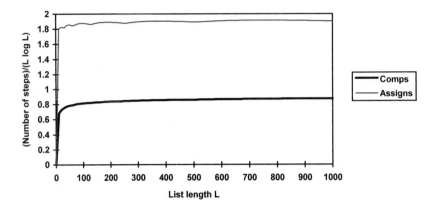

Fig. 12.8. Efficiency of mergesort (normalized).

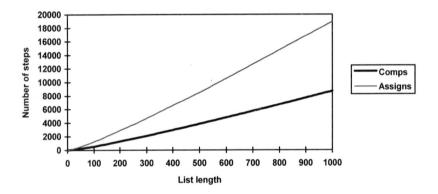

Fig. 12.9. Efficiency of mergesort.

We see therefore that mergesort is an $O(n \log n)$ algorithm overall. Actually, the version we have studied here, using arrays, is not the most efficient form. Mergesort is more efficient if used with linked lists, in which case it comes very close to the theoretically most efficient sorting algorithm possible.

## 12.9 Quicksort

### 12.9.1 Basics

The final sorting algorithm we shall consider is another one that relies on recursive subdivision of the list. The main difference between mergesort and quicksort is that in quicksort, the list is divided into two parts in such a way that all the elements in the first sublist are less than all the elements in the second. The two sublists are then sorted independently as in mergesort, but because of the condition used to separate the list in the first place, the final merge is not required.

The list is divided by choosing one of the list elements and using it as a *pivot*. If we are dealing with lists initially in random order, we can simply choose the first element in the list as the pivot. If the list is known to have some partial order, a different choice may be more appropriate. Ideally, the pivot should be chosen so that it divides the list exactly in half, according to the relative sizes of the keys. For example, if we had a list of the integers from 1 through 10, 5 or 6 would be the ideal pivots, while 1 or 10 would be poor pivots.

Once the pivot has been chosen, it is used to sort the remainder of the list into two sublists: one where all keys are less than the pivot, and the other where all elements are greater than or equal to the pivot. These two partial lists are then sorted recursively using the same algorithm. The final sorted list is then produced by concatenating the first sublist, the pivot, and the second sublist, in that order, into a single list. The first stage in quicksort is the recursive partitioning of the list until all sublists consist of only a single element. This stage is illustrated in Fig. 12.10.

In this example, we use the first element in each list (or sublist) as the pivot for that list (the pivot element is shaded in each sublist). In the first step, the element 5 is used as the pivot, so the list is to be partitioned into two sublists, the first containing elements less than 5, and the second, elements greater than or equal to 5. These two sublists are shown on the second level in the diagram. Note that the pivot itself does not form part of either sublist.

In the second stage of the partitioning, each sublist is partitioned in the same way. The lower sublist uses the element 2 as the pivot and is partitioned into two sublists, each containing a single element, so the partitioning of that portion of the list is now complete. In the upper list (9, 8, 7), 9 is used as the pivot. Since all the other elements of this sublist are less than 9, only one sublist is formed, consisting of the elements 8 and 7. The arrow pointing into empty space at this stage shows that no upper sublist is produced when 9 is used as the pivot.

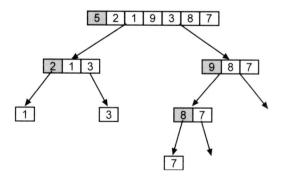

Fig. 12.10. Partitioning the list in quicksort.

The upper sublist requires an extra stage in the partitioning process, with 8 used as the pivot, before the size of the sublist is reduced to a single element. When all sublists have been reduced to this stage, they are concatenated with their respective pivots until the original list is reconstructed in sorted order. This concatenation process is shown in Fig. 12.11.

As we will see when we consider the C++ code for quicksort, the concatenation process does not need to be explicitly programmed, since the partitioning process automatically places the pivot between its respective sublists at each stage, so that when the list has been partitioned to the point where all the sublists contain only a single element, it is already sorted.

This simple example illustrates why it is best to choose the pivot so as to divide the list as nearly in half as possible. The first pivot in the example (5) does just that. In the partitioning of the two sublists resulting from this initial partition, however, we see two contrasting cases. In the lower sublist, the pivot (2) also divides its sublist in half, with the result that this partition is the last one required for that sublist, since both sublists (the 1 and the 3) now contain a single element. In the other sublist, the pivot (9) is the largest element in the sublist, with the result that no division of the list takes place. The only sublist contains two elements, which must be partitioned again.

In the extreme case where the pivot at each stage is always either the largest or smallest element in the sublist, quicksort is actually a very poor algorithm, being even less efficient than some $O(n^2)$ algorithms. For this reason, some variants on quicksort put in a few extra comparisons before each partitioning to ensure that the pivot will actually divide the list as nearly in half as it can.

## 12.9.2 Implementing quicksort in an array

In order to continue building our library of sorting routines we will consider the implementation of quicksort for a list of data stored in an array. The only slightly tricky part of the algorithm is how to partition the array into the two

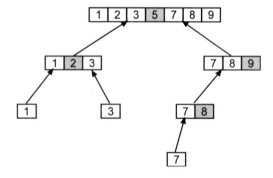

Fig. 12.11.

lists separated by the pivot, without having to declare any auxiliary storage space. Let us suppose that we are using the first element in the list as the pivot. (If we are using some other element, then simply swap it with the first element before proceeding.) We would like to partition the list so that all keys less than the pivot are followed by all those greater than or equal to the pivot. Starting from the element in the array immediately following the pivot, we search for the first element that is greater than or equal to the pivot. We mark this location (call it *s*) as the beginning of the second sublist (the one that will follow the pivot). Now define a marker variable *m* which will be used to point to each location after *s*. For each key after *s*, we compare it with the pivot. If it is greater than or equal to the pivot, we leave it where it is and advance the marker *m* by 1. If it is less than the pivot, we swap it with the key at location *s* and advance *s* by 1 so that it points to the new start of the second list. We continue this process until we reach the end of the list. At this stage, the pivot is still the first element in the array, but we know that the second element is the beginning of the sublist containing elements less than the pivot, and the location marked by *s* is the beginning of the sublist containing elements greater than or equal to the pivot. (If the lower sublist does not exist, then *s* will point to the second list element. If the upper sublist does not exist, *s* should have a value one larger than the sublist length, in order that the next step will work properly.)

Since we would like the pivot to be between the two lists, we swap the pivot with the key immediately before the position *s*. This completes the partitioning of the list. An example of this algorithm which illustrates the first partition in the previous example is shown in Fig. 12.12.

In the first three steps in this diagram, the marker *m* is moved along the array until the first element larger than the pivot is found. This element is labelled with the marker *s* to indicate it is the starting point of the upper sublist. The marker *m* is then moved along from *s*. The next element (3) is less than the pivot, so it is swapped with the element at location *s* (first step in the second column in the diagram) and *s* is advanced by one. In the next two steps, *m* is advanced further, but the remaining two elements (8 and 7) are both larger than the pivot so no further swaps are required. In the final step, the pivot (5) is swapped with the element just prior to *s*. This swap places the pivot between the two sublists, so when these sublists are sorted recursively, it will be in the correct place relative to the sublists. It is this swap of the pivot into the correct location which ensures that the final concatenation step is not required. Note, however, that swapping the pivot into this location alters the order in the lower sublist. In our example above, the lower sublist had the order 2, 1, 3, while here it has the order 3, 2, 1. This will, of course, affect the pivot that is chosen for partitioning the sublist in the next stage of the algorithm. In our case, it will make the second partition less efficient than in our original example, but in other cases, of course, it may improve the

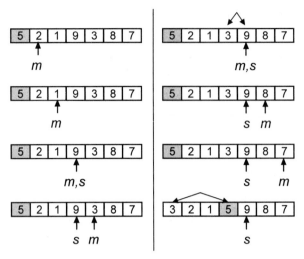

Fig. 12.12.

efficiency so on average, this step will not adversely affect the efficiency of the algorithm overall.

### 12.9.3 C++ code for quicksort

The C++ code for quicksort can be implemented along the same lines as that for mergesort. We define a new derived class in file `quick.h`:

```
#ifndef QUICK_H
#define QUICK_H
#include "datalist.h"

template <class Type>
class QuickSortList : public datalist<Type>
{
protected:
  void Swap(const int i, const int j);
  int Partition(const int low, const int high);
  void QuickSort(const int low, const int high);
public:
  QuickSortList(int arraysize = 10) :
    datalist<Type>(arraysize) {}
  virtual ~QuickSortList() {}
  virtual void Sort();
};
#endif
```

The protected functions implement the stages of the sort (in file `quicktmp.h`):

```cpp
#ifndef QUICKTMP_H
#define QUICKTMP_H
#include "quick.h"
#include "datatemp.h"

template <class Type>
void QuickSortList<Type>::Swap(const int i,
   const int j)
{
   Type temp = Element[i];
   Element[i] = Element[j];
   Element[j] = temp;
}

template <class Type>
int QuickSortList<Type>::Partition(const int low,
   const int high)
{
   int pivotloc, i;
   Type pivotkey;

   // May need to swap pivot into first position here.
   pivotkey = Element[low];
   pivotloc = low;
   for (i = low + 1; i <= high; i++)
     if (Element[i] < pivotkey)
        Swap(++pivotloc, i);
   Swap(low, pivotloc);
   return pivotloc;
}

template <class Type>
void QuickSortList<Type>::QuickSort(const int low,
     const int high) {
   int pivotloc;

   if (low < high) {
     pivotloc = Partition(low, high);
     QuickSort(low, pivotloc - 1);
     QuickSort(pivotloc + 1, high);
   }
}

template <class Type>
void QuickSortList<Type>::Sort() {
   QuickSort(0, ArraySize - 1);
}
#endif
```

The code for quicksort follows our written algorithm fairly closely, except for a few minor points. The variable pivotloc in the Partition() function is the location immediately *previous* to our variable s, which means that it is the location to which the pivot will be swapped at the end of the partitioning (hence the name `pivotloc`). Also, the partitioning algorithm does not do a distinct search for elements after the first which are less than the pivot. Rather, it swaps every element which is less than the pivot to location `pivotloc+1` (which is *s*). This means that if the first few keys immediately after the first element are less than the pivot, they will be swapped into themselves. This is not particularly efficient, especially if we are unfortunate enough to choose a large pivot, so that most of the keys are less than the pivot value. However, adding the extra check would serve to complicate the code for what should be, for most lists, minimal gain.

The `Partition()` function returns the location of the pivot after the partitioning so that the `QuickSort()` function knows the locations of the endpoints of the two sublists, which it then sorts recursively. Since all sorting takes place within the original array, there is no need to explicitly concatenate the sorted sublists: they will automatically be in the correct locations.

These functions may be tested using a similar `main()` routine to that used for the mergesort algorithm:

```
#include "quicktmp.h"

const int SIZE = 10;

int main()
{
    QuickSortList<int> TestQuickSort(SIZE);

    cin >> TestQuickSort;
    cout << "Testing Quick Sort:\n" << TestQuickSort;
    TestQuickSort.Sort();
    cout << "After sorting:\n" << TestQuickSort;
    return 0;
}
```

Note that the actual call to the quicksort algorithm is done by a `Sort()` function call with no arguments. This is in keeping with the philosophy that the user should not have to be concerned with the innards of whatever sorting algorithm is being used. All that is taken care of by protected functions inside the quicksort template.

## 12.10 Efficiency of quicksort

As with other sorting algorithms we will investigate the efficiency of quicksort by running a computer experiment to count the number of comparisons and assignments for various list lengths. The results are show in Fig. 12.13.

The results look very similar to those for mergesort, where the number of assignments is roughly twice the number of comparisons. We can check that quicksort is an $O(n \log n)$ algorithm by plotting the ratio (number of steps)/($L \log L$) (see Fig. 12.14).

For random sequences, quicksort behaves as approximately $O(n \log n)$ for comparisons, and $O(1.8n \log n)$ for assignments. (Theoretical estimates place the order for comparisons around $1.4 \, n \log n$ and for assignments at around $2 \, n \log n$.) However, quicksort is inordinately sensitive to the initial ordering of the list. In particular, if the initial list is already ordered (or nearly so), quicksort is effectively an $O(n^2)$ algorithm, unless extra comparisons are done to ensure that the pivot divides the list in half at each stage.

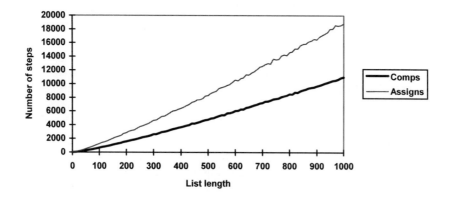

Fig. 12.13. Efficiency of quicksort.

## 12.11 Summary

We have examined four sorting algorithms in this chapter and have seen that they give very different behaviours. Insertion sort and selection sort are both $O(n^2)$ algorithms, while mergesort and quicksort are, for random lists, both $O(n \log n)$ algorithms. However, this doesn't necessarily mean that either mergesort or quicksort is best for all your sorting problems. For example, if you want an algorithm that will check to see if a list is already in order, insertion sort is one of the best algorithms around because it doesn't move any data at all. For initially ordered data, quicksort is one of the worst algorithms because the pivot is always the lowest element in the sublist being partitioned, so no partitioning takes place.

If the elements of the list contain large data records, so that movement is very expensive in terms of computing time, selection sort is probably your best bet, since it is linear ($O(n)$) for assignments. If your data are stored as a

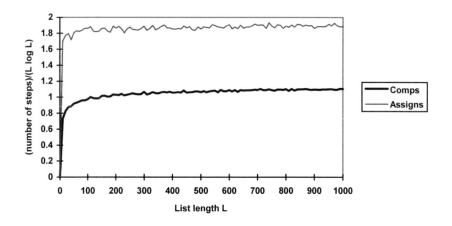

Fig. 12.14. Efficiency of quicksort (normalized).

linked list rather than an array, mergesort is one of the most efficient algorithms for sorting linked lists.

There are many other sorting algorithms in existence, but hopefully the introduction given here has demonstrated that you should investigate which algorithm is best suited to the type and amount of data you wish to process.

The C++ code used in this chapter has not introduced any new features of the language. The main programming technique that is worth remembering is that of hiding the details of the implementation of an algorithm from all functions outside the class in which the algorithm is coded. In our mergesort and quicksort templates, for example, the user should not need to be concerned with the various parameters that these algorithms need (start and end points in the sublists, and so on). A public function called Sort() is defined to provide a simple user interface which allows sorting to be done by simply calling the function for the associated list.

## 12.12 Exercises

1. Sort the following list of numbers:

```
23 19 5 78 12 66 47 32 98 32 24
```

by hand using

    a.   insertion sort
    b.   selection sort
    c.   mergesort
    d.   quicksort.

In each case, count the number of comparisons and assignments that are done. For mergesort and quicksort, draw a tree diagram similar to those in the text (Figs. 12.6, 12.7, 12.10 and 12.11) to show the various levels in the recursive algorithm.

2. Using the linked list data template from exercise 1(a) in Chapter 11, write versions of insertion sort and selection sort for linked lists. Construct computer experiments to measure the efficiencies of these two algorithms when used on linked lists, and draw graphs similar to those in the text to illustrate your results.

3. Write a version of mergesort that operates on a linkedlist. You should handle all assignments by redirecting pointers rather than copying any data elements. Design and run a computer experiment to calculate the efficiency of mergesort when applied to a linked list.

4. Run a computer experiment on the quicksort algorithm when it is applied to fully ordered lists to verify that it is an $O(n^2)$ algorithm in this case.

5. Alter the quicksort algorithm so that the pivot is chosen to divide the list as nearly in half as possible at each step. Design and run a computer experiment to test the effect of this refinement on the efficiency of quicksort. Run your experiment for both randomly ordered lists and fully sorted lists.

6. One of the simplest sorting algorithms is known as *bubblesort*. The algorithm is as follows.

Beginning at the first element of the list, compare each element with the next element in the list. If an element is greater than its successor, swap the two elements. To completely sort the list, you need to perform this process $n - 1$ times on a list of length $n$.

a. Run through the bubblesort algorithm by hand on the list

```
4 9 2 1 5
```

b. Write a C++ program implementing the bubblesort algorithm on an array. Use your program to count the numbers of assignments and comparisons done by the algorithm on lists of lengths from 10 up to 1000, and draw graphs similar to those in the text. Use these graphs to deduce the complexity of the algorithm, and give your answer using the big-oh notation.

c. The bubblesort algorithm may be improved by noticing the following points:

- It is easy to detect when the list is completely sorted, since no swaps will be done on a given pass through the list. You can therefore reduce the number of comparisons required if you stop the algorithm after the first pass where no swaps are done.
- On the first pass, the largest element will be moved to its correct location in the list; on the second pass, the second largest element will be moved to its correct location, and so on. You therefore do not need to scan the entire list after the first pass; rather, on pass $m$, you need compare only elements 1 through $n - m$ with their successors.

Modify your bubblesort program to implement these improvements and do the efficiency checks again. What effects do the changes have?

# Tables and hashing

## 13.1 Alternative methods of storing data

In the last two chapters, we have examined several ways of sorting and searching lists of data. All of the methods we studied required, on average, more computation (comparisons and assignments) to deal with longer lists. You might not be surprised at this, but in fact there is a way of storing data so that the amount of work required to retrieve a particular item is more or less independent of the length of the list. This technique is known as *hashing*.

You have already seen an example of this method of data storage and retrieval, as it is essentially the way arrays are stored and used. The array data type stores data at a location given by the array index. The location at which element *i* of an array is stored is calculated by starting at the base address of an array (the memory address at which the first array element is stored) and adding the size of each element of the array multiplied by *i* to this base address to find the correct location. This method of 'base plus offset' means that the time required to locate any array element is a constant, independent of its location in the array, or even of the overall size of the array.

The important point to remember here is that some formula for converting the array index *i* into a memory location inside the computer must be used to find any given array element. This formula must take the same time to calculate regardless of which array element is sought, or how many elements the array contains. This idea is used in hashing to find efficient ways of storing various types of data.

## 13.2 The `table` data structure

We can generalize the idea behind storing array elements to allow any data to be stored in a one-dimensional form. As an example, suppose we wish to count the number of times each word occurs in a file. We would like to define an array where each element in the array stores the count for a particular word. In doing so, we are faced with two problems:

- The character string forming a word is not an integer and, in C++, cannot be used as an array index.
- There are more than 400,000 words in the English language, only a small fraction of which will be used in any file of moderate length. We do not want to define an array with 400,000 elements; we would rather define an array of a size near, or slightly larger than, the number of different words we expect to encounter in an average file. We will not, in general, know in advance what these words will be.

We therefore need to consider how to transform non-integer data into integer form so that it may be used as an array index. We also need to consider how to map this data into a fairly restricted set of integers. In the word-counting problem, we might define an array of, say, 1000 elements, numbered from 0 to 999. We are then faced with the problem of mapping any of the 400,000 words in English into the integer range 0...999.

To cope with these problems, a new data structure called a *table* is defined. Tables are superficially similar to arrays, but we will reserve the word *array* to refer to the actual data structure found in the C++ language.

A table consists of a function or formula which maps members of one data type *D* (for example, the words in the word-counting problem) onto another type, called the *index I* (usually non-negative integers), which is used to store and access the original data. The properties required of a table data type are:

- A function which calculates the value of the index *I* given the data *D*. (Such a function in the word-counting problem would calculate the array index at which a particular word is stored.)
- Table insertion: a new data item (for example, a word) may be inserted into the table.
- Table retrieval: a table may be searched for a data item and, if present, it, and associated values, may be retrieved. (Given a word, the table is searched to see if that word is present and, if so, the count of the number of times it has been used may be retrieved.)
- Table deletion (optional): a data item may be deleted from the table.

Provided the function which converts the original data into the table index *I* is efficient, a table can, ideally, represent a considerable increase in efficiency over the searching routines we studied earlier. Given the data for which you are searching, its location (if present) is calculated directly from the data, so you need only look in one place in the table to see if the word is there. For example, if the word 'thing' was calculated to have index 39, you need only look at location 39 in the table. If this location is empty, you know immediately that the word 'thing' is not in the table, while if location 39 is occupied, it will be by the word 'thing' and its associated count will be found at that location.

In practice, such clean access to the table is rarely found. This is because you are usually trying to map data from a very large set (such as the 400,000 words in English) into a much smaller space (say, 1000 array elements). Since you don't know in advance what data items will occur, it is very difficult to find a transformation function which will map all the different data items that actually occur into different locations in the array. For example, if the word 'thing' maps into location 39, another word, such as 'computer', might also map into location 39. When this happens, a *collision* is said to occur. We need to establish some method of handling collisions in such a way that both these words can be stored in the array and, of course, can both be retrieved.

Now that we have some idea of the techniques we intend to use and of some of the problems that may arise, we can get down to a more systematic study of the solutions that have been proposed.

# 13.3 Hashing

### 13.3.1 Principles

The process of mapping large amounts of data into a smaller table is called *hashing*, because in the processing the original data gets mixed up, or hashed, as it is stored in the smaller array. The function which provides the map between the original data and the smaller table in which it is finally stored is a *hash function*, and the table itself is called a *hash table*.

The operations defined above in the definition of the table data type are implemented in hashing as follows:

- The hash function provides the map which translates the data $D$ into the index $I$.
- A new data item $D$ is inserted into the table by using the hash function to calculate its index $I$. If this location is free, the item is inserted directly into the table. If not, a procedure for resolving the collision must be given.
- A specific item of data $D$ may be retrieved by using the hash function to calculate its index $I$. Position $I$ in the table is checked. If it is empty, item $D$ is not present. If it is occupied, its contents must be tested to see if they match item $D$. If so, $D$ has been found. If not, the item at index $I$ has the same value given by the hash function as item $D$ and there are two possibilities: (i) item $D$ is not present in the table; (ii) item $D$ is present in the table, but when it was inserted, the other item at index $I$ was already there, causing a collision. In either case, the same procedure used for resolving a collision during insertion of an item must be followed to see if $D$ is located somewhere else in the table. With a properly chosen hash function and collision resolution procedure, there should not be many searches required to resolve the question.
- Item deletion may proceed in a similar manner to insertion, in the sense that the hash function is called to determine the location of the item and if it is present, it may then be deleted. However, if a collision occurred when the item was originally inserted, care must be used in deleting it, as will become apparent later.

In Fig. 13.1, several ice cream flavours are mapped into an array using an unspecified hash function. Note that the two flavours 'raspberry' and 'strawberry' map to the same location, resulting in a collision.

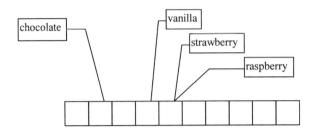

Fig. 13.1. Mapping items into a hash table

## 13.3.2 Choosing a hash function

A good hash function should satisfy two criteria:

1. It should be quick to compute.
2. It should minimize the number of collisions.

Speed of computation means that the function should be fairly simple, and minimize time-consuming operations such as multiplication, division, or more complex functions such as square roots. Speed is an important consideration, because you must remember that the hash function must be used every time the table is accessed for any reason. (For example, look at any program that uses arrays and count up the number of times an array element is accessed.)

Minimization of collisions can best be achieved by choosing a hash function that spreads the incoming data as evenly as possible over the hash table. As an example of a bad hash function from this point of view, in the case of counting words, suppose we have a hash table of 1000 elements, and we choose a hash function that takes the ASCII code of the first character in the word and uses that as an array index. This method would provide only 26 different indexes, so that 974 sites in the table are not directly accessible by the hash function. Any two words beginning with the same letter would result in a collision.

A few examples of commonly used hash functions follow.

- **Truncation**. Part of the key is simply ignored, with the remainder truncated or concatenated to form the index. For example, if we are storing 7-digit phone numbers in a hash table with 1000 elements, we may ignore all but the 2nd, 4th, and 7th digits in the phone number, so that a number such as 731-3018 would be indexed at location 338. This method is quick, as it simply involves accessing a few digits in the input data, but the number of collisions it produces depends on how uniform the input data are. If the table is to contain phone numbers from people all living within a small area, for example, the exchange part of the number (the first three digits) may be the same for all the numbers. In this case, that would mean that all phone numbers would be hashed into indexes beginning with 3 in the table, so that 900 locations would remain unused. This problem could be solved in this case by choosing, say, the last three digits in the phone number instead. In general you should consider what regularities may be present in the data before deciding on a hash function.

- **Folding**. The data can be split up into smaller chunks which are then folded together in some form. For example, a 7-digit phone number could be split into three groups of 2, 2, and 3 digits, which are then added together and truncated to produce an index in the range 000...999. For the number 731-3018, we produce the three numbers 73, 13, and 018, which add up to 104, which may be used as the index. Another number such as 899-6989 would split into 89, 96, and 989, which add up to 1174. Since this number is larger than the highest allowed index in the hash table, we truncate it by saving only the last three digits, giving an index of 174.

- **Modular arithmetic**. Convert the data into an integer (using truncation, folding, or some other method), divide by the size of the hash table, and take the remainder as the index (for example, by using the % operator in C++). For example, modular arithmetic was used in the second example under "folding" above: the phone number 899-6989 produced the index 1174 under the folding procedure, so this number was taken modulo the hash table size (1000) to produce the final index of 174.

There are, of course, many other hash functions that could be used, so you may well think of others on your own. Before using one of your own hash functions it is a good idea to consider the following points:

- Is it fast and easy to compute?
- Will it spread the data to be hashed fairly evenly over the hash table, and therefore minimize the number of collisions?
- Do you have a collision resolution method available? If not, read on...

### 13.3.3 Collision resolution with open addressing

We now examine a few ways in which collisions may be resolved. There are two main ways this can be done: *open addressing* and *chaining*. In open addressing, the amount of space available for storing data is fixed at compile time by declaring a fixed array for the hash table. With chaining, an array is also declared for the hash table, but each element in the array is a pointer to a linked list which holds all data with the same index.

If we are using open addressing, we must deal with a collision by finding another, unoccupied, location elsewhere in the array. In deciding how to do this, we are faced with the same two requirements as in deciding on the hash function in the first place: we would like a method of choosing an alternative location that is fast, and that minimizes the number of additional collisions that will occur as more data are added to the table.

### Linear probing

The simplest method is known as *linear probing*. If a collision occurs when we are inserting a new item into the table, we simply probe forward in the array, one step at a time, until we find an empty slot where we can store our new data. When we wish to retrieve this data, we start by calculating the hash function, test the location given by the index to see if the required data item is there and, if not, examine each array element from the index location until the item is found, or until we encounter an empty site or examine all locations in the table, at which point we know the item is not in the table.

When using linear probing, we assume the array is circular, so that if we search past the end of the array, we start again at element 0.

The disadvantage with linear probing is that data tend to cluster about certain points in the table, with other parts of the table not being used. This gives rise to lengthy sequential searches through the table when attempting to retrieve data. To see why this happens, suppose we have a hash function that distributes data uniformly over a hash table of size $n$. When we insert the first element, the hash table is empty so the first item to be hashed will be placed at exactly the location specified by the hash function. Suppose it is placed at location $i$. For this initial element, all sites in the hash table will be equally likely to be targeted by the hash function, so there is no problem. Consider what happens when the next element is inserted into the table. If it is equally likely to be mapped to any of the table locations by the hash function, then there is equal likelihood that it will be mapped to locations $i$ and $i + 1$. However, site $i$ is full, having been occupied by the first element. Therefore, if the hash function maps the second element to either location $i$ or $i + 1$, the element will be stored in location $i + 1$. Site $i + 1$ therefore has twice the chance of being filled by the second element as any other site in the hash table. If sites $i$ and $i + 1$ are filled by the first two elements, then site $i + 2$ will have three times the chance of any other element of being filled by the third element, and so on. The problem is that any empty site at the end of a sequence of filled sites will receive any item that is hashed to any of the filled sites *as well as* an item that is hashed to that site directly. Thus once a chain of filled sites has started to form, the effect snowballs, causing longer and longer clusters to appear. These long chains of filled sites require long sequences of comparisons in the retrieval process, reducing efficiency.

Fig. 13.2 shows an item being inserted into a hash table using linear probing to resolve the collision. The item is mapped to location 4 by the hash function, but locations 4, 5, and 6 are already full, so the collision resolution method eventually places the item in location 7.

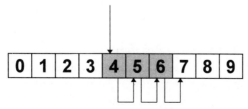

Fig. 13.2. The clustering effect

**Quadratic probing**

One way of resolving the clustering problem is to use a collision resolution function that depends on the index value, or on the number of previous attempts made to resolve the collision. An example of the latter is *quadratic probing*. In this case, if a collision occurs at position $i$, locations $i + 1$, $i + 4$, $i + 9$, and so on, are tested until an empty site is found. Although this method reduces clustering, it does not probe every site in the table. It can be shown that if the table size is a prime number, the maximum number of probed sites in a hash table of size $n$ is $(n+1)/2$, so that approximately half the table is probed. For example, if the table size is $n = 11$, then for an element mapped to location 0, the six sites 0, 1, 4, 9, 5 (16 mod 11), and 3 (25 mod 11) will be probed. The next location to be probed by the quadratic probing algorithm would be site 3 again (36 mod 11), and all further sites produced by this algorithm will be one of the six already visited. For table sizes that are not prime numbers, the number of different sites probed by the quadratic probing algorithm can be less or more than $(n+1)/2$. For example, if the table size is $n = 10$, six sites are still probed (for example, starting at location 0, sites 0, 1, 4, 9, 6, and 5 are probed). For a table size that is a perfect square, very few sites will be probed. For example, if the table size is 16, only the four sites 0, 1, 4, and 9 are probed. It is therefore a good idea to avoid choosing table sizes that are perfect squares (or are divisible by perfect squares), in order to maximize the number of items with the same hash function value which can be stored. A good guide is to choose your table size as either a prime number or a product of two different prime numbers.

**Other collision resolution methods**

One way of resolving collisions by using an item-dependent probe distance is to truncate the data and use the truncated form to calculate the increment. For example, we could take the last digit of a phone number and use that as an increment. Another possibility is to use a *pseudorandom number generator* to generate a 'random' increment. A pseudorandom number generator uses a *seed* value to generate a sequence of integers that appear random, but are actually calculated using a deterministic rule. (We have used pseudorandom number generators in our computer experiments in previous chapters.) However, the property of the random number sequence that makes it useful for generating probe increments is that, provided the same seed is used for successive runs, the same sequence of numbers will be generated. As long as we keep track of the seed and where we are in the sequence of numbers we will always know where to probe next.

## 13.3.4 Deleting elements from hash tables

Having considered several ways of resolving collisions, we will briefly consider the problem of deleting an item from a hash table where open addressing is used. Deletion is very difficult to do efficiently in such a table. The reason is that in any table where collisions have occurred during the insertion of data, there is a chain of items with the same index. If we want to delete any item that is not at the end of the chain, we will remove a link in the chain, thus disconnecting the elements beyond that link. For example, suppose we have stored four items with the same index at sites $i, j, k, l$, and we wish to delete item $j$. We must first locate the item by using the hash function to calculate its index. This will direct us to site $i$, where the first item with that index is stored. This is not the correct item, so we apply whatever collision resolution system we are using to locate the next site, which contains item $j$, the one we are looking for. If we simply delete $j$ from that site, then the site will be empty. A subsequent search for items $k$ or $l$ will start by using the hash function to find their index, which, as before, will start us off in site $i$. Applying the collision resolution system will lead us to the site formerly occupied by $j$. However, since $j$ has been deleted, we will be confronted with an empty site, which is the signal that no more items of that index are present, so the search will terminate with the conclusion that $k$ and $l$ are not present in the table.

There are several solutions to this problem, including shifting the remaining items forward in the list when an item is deleted, or using a special flag which marks an empty cell as 'deleted' rather than just 'empty' so that searches will continue through this cell to see if any more items with that index are present. However, all these methods are rather slow and cumbersome. If you are likely to require item deletion from a hash table, it is better to resolve collisions using the chaining technique, as described in the next section.

### 13.3.5 Collision resolution with chaining

The second method of resolving collisions involves using dynamic data allocation and linked lists. The hash table and associated hash function are defined in the usual manner, except that now the array is an array of pointers to linked lists, one list for each index. If no data are stored at an index site, the corresponding pointer is set to 0. If an item is to be inserted, the hash function is used to find the list to which the item is to be added, and the standard insertion procedures for a linked list are used to insert the item. If a collision occurs, we simply add another node to the end of this list at the corresponding index. When an item is to be retrieved, we use the hash function to calculate its index as usual, and look at the corresponding pointer. If the pointer is 0, the item is not present. If the pointer points to a list, that list is traversed sequentially to see if the desired item is present. With a properly designed hash function, none of these lists should contain more than a few items, so sequential search is an efficient way to search them.

Deletion of an item from a table constructed this way is also quite simple. The hash function is called to determine the index of the item to be deleted. The linked list at that index is searched and, if the item is present, its node is simply spliced out of the list in the usual way. We need not worry about isolating other parts of the table.

The only disadvantage to using chaining is that a linked list requires extra storage space for the pointers connecting the list elements. If the amount of data to be stored consists of a large number of fairly small items, the extra memory required for the pointers could be substantial.

In Fig. 13.3, the array of pointers is shown as the vertical column of boxes on the left, with each box labelled with its hash function value. When a data item (single characters are being stored in this hash table) maps to a particular location, an extra node is allocated and added to the corresponding list. Note that a chained hash table can store more data items than the number of cells in the table. In this case, seven items are stored in a table with six cells.

## 13.4 C++ code for hash tables

### 13.4.1 Abstract or pure virtual classes

Since a hash table should be able to store any type of data, it makes sense to define a template for implementing a hash table in C++. Doing so, however, presents us with a programming problem we haven't faced up to now.

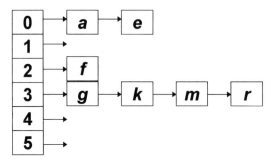

Fig. 13.3. Chaining

The main public interfaces to a hash table are functions for storing and retrieving (and possibly deleting) table entries. Once we have decided on a collision resolution technique (open addressing or chaining), these functions are fairly easy to write, and, through appropriate operator overloading in the classes which are to be stored in the hash table, should be general enough to be used for any data type.

The problem arises when we consider the hash function to be used. The hash function depends in a fundamental way on the type of data that are to be inserted into the table. For example, if we are simply storing integers in the table, we might use a hash function which returns the integer modulo the table size. If we are storing a character string, we might wish to add up the ASCII codes of the characters in the string and return the sum modulo the table size. In other words, we can't define the hash function until we know what sort of data we are storing in the table.

There are several ways around this problem. One solution might be to require all user-defined classes which are to be stored in a hash table to have a `HashFunction()` function as one of their fields, in which a suitable hash function for that data type is defined. This is unacceptable because the hash function should really be a property of the hash table class, not the class which is being stored in the table. As well, the hash function frequently needs access to details of the table (such as the table size) that should not be accessible to the user-defined data class.

A better solution is to recognize that the hash function cannot be defined in the hash table template, and leave it up to the user to define a hash function whenever an instance of the template is used. This may be done by deriving a specialized class from the hash table template for use with a particular data type, and including the `HashFunction()` definition in that derived class.

If we use the second solution, we see that we should *never* declare any objects that are instances of the hash function base class, since that class doesn't have a hash function defined for it. The base class exists only to provide those fields and functions (such as storing and retrieving data) that *can* be defined for all data types, and declaring a HashFunction() field only as a place holder which must be defined in a derived class.

A base class which is never meant to have any objects of its own is known as an *abstract* or *pure virtual* class. Such classes are only useful when they are inherited by another class, which provides the full definitions for all the missing fields in the base class. C++ provides a special bit of syntax that we haven't met yet which allows such abstract classes to be declared. We will see this in action in the code which follows.

## 13.4.2 C++ code for hashing with open addressing

We define an abstract class which may be used for a hash table where the elements are stored in a fixed array, and collisions are resolved by open addressing. The class template is defined in the file openadd.h:

```
#ifndef OPENADD_H
#define OPENADD_H
#include "mydefs.h"
#include <iostream.h>

template <class Type>
class openAddress
{
protected:
  Type *Element;
  Type EmptyCell;
  int TableSize;
  virtual int HashFunc(const Type& Item) const = 0;
public:
  openAddress(int tablesize = 1000);
  openAddress(Type emptycell, int tablesize = 1000);
  ~openAddress();
  virtual BOOL Store(const Type& Item);
  virtual BOOL Retrieve(const Type& SearchItem,
    Type& FoundItem) const;
};
#endif
```

The hash table itself will be stored in the Element array, which is allocated TableSize cells in the constructor. The EmptyCell field is a special value which is stored in those cells which are unoccupied. Such a value is required since the process of collision resolution visits a chain of locations and stops when it encounters a cell that is empty. Since various data types may be stored in a hash table, the EmptyCell value depends on the data type and must be specified in the constructor.

The new feature of C++ which allows us to define an abstract class is illustrated in the declaration of the field HashFunc(). The function is declared as virtual, but the declaration is assigned the value 0 in the class definition (note the "= 0" at the end of the line). This tells the compiler that this function, although declared in the class definition, has no associated definition in this class. It is an *abstract* or *pure virtual* function, which must be defined in another class which inherits the openAddress class. Any class in C++ containing an abstract function is not allowed to be used to declare data objects: the compiler will flag an error if such an attempt is made.

The remainder of the fields in the class are straightforward. The Store() function stores its argument Item in the hash table (if there is room) and returns a BOOL flag indicating whether or not it was successful.

The Retrieve() function searches for SearchItem in the hash table. If SearchItem is found, the corresponding entry in the table is copied into the argument FoundItem (note that SearchItem is declared as const, while FoundItem is not). The reason that Retrieve() has two arguments is that, if SearchItem is a complex data object containing several fields, we may wish to use only one of the fields as a key to search the table. The table itself may be updating the other fields as the program progresses, so that the purpose of retrieving one particular entry is to see what the latest values of these updated fields are. The current entry in the hash table is copied into FoundItem for use outside the table. For example, if we are using the hash table to keep a count of the number of times various words are used in some text, the data class Type may be a compound object containing a text field for the word and an int field for the count. To interrogate the hash table, we would like to pass only the word to the retrieve function and retrieve the full entry for that word which will tell us how many times the word has occurred in the text.

The function definitions for this template are in the file opentmp.h:

```
#define OPENTMP_H
#include "openadd.h"

template <class Type>
openAddress<Type>::openAddress(int tablesize) :
  TableSize(tablesize), Element(new Type[tablesize])
{}

template <class Type>
openAddress<Type>::openAddress(Type emptycell,
  int tablesize) :
  TableSize(tablesize), Element(new Type[tablesize]),
  EmptyCell(emptycell)
{
  for (int elem = 0; elem < TableSize; elem++)
    Element[elem] = EmptyCell;
}

template <class Type>
```

```
openAddress<Type>::~openAddress()
{
  delete [] Element;
}

template <class Type>
BOOL openAddress<Type>::Store(const Type& Item)
{
  int index = HashFunc(Item);
  for (int probe = 0; probe < TableSize; ++probe) {
    if (Element[index] == EmptyCell) {
      Element[index] = Item;
      return TRUE;              // Item inserted
    } else if (Element[index] == Item)
      return FALSE;             // Item already in table
    else
      index = (index + 1) % TableSize;
  }
  return FALSE;                 // Table full
}

template <class Type>
BOOL openAddress<Type>::
  Retrieve(const Type& SearchItem,
    Type& FoundItem) const
{
  int index = HashFunc(SearchItem);
  for (int probe = 0; probe < TableSize; ++probe) {
    if (Element[index] == SearchItem) {
      FoundItem = Element[index];
      return TRUE;              // Item found
    } else
      index = (index + 1) % TableSize;
  }
  return FALSE;
}
#endif
```

The constructors initialize the data fields, with the second constructor initializing all the Element cells to EmptyCell. (Remember that it is always a good idea to define an argumentless constructor even if your own code doesn't use it, since it is often required implicitly by other code.) The destructor deletes the Element array.

Since openAddress is an abstract class, we could have taken the easy way out and simply made all its functions abstract, thus avoiding the need to provide any function definitions. However, since the Store() and Retrieve() functions can be defined in a way that is consistent with all data types, we have chosen to provide versions of them here. In this instance, they implement linear probing to resolve collisions. The method follows the linear probing algorithm exactly, so the code should be largely self-explanatory. We have chosen not to allow duplicate items in the hash table, so a test is made in the `Store()` function to reject `Item` if it is already in the table.

One point that may be worth emphasizing again is that the `SearchItem` and `FoundItem` objects are treated quite differently in the `Retrieve()` function. If `Type` is a user-defined type, we may wish to search for `SearchItem` in the table by comparing only one of its fields with the corresponding field in the items stored in the table. In that case, the `==` operator should be overloaded in the class so that this restricted comparison is made. On the other hand, we wish to copy *all* the fields from the element stored in the table to the `FoundItem` object, in order that all information on that object in the table be returned. In this case, we need an overloaded `=` operator which achieves this.

We have now gone as far as we can in defining the abstract class. To actually use this class, we need to inherit it in another class, and provide a definition for `HashFunc()` appropriate to whatever data type we are using. To illustrate this, we provide a derived class `LinearIntProbe` which tests the hash table functions on integers (`longs` in this case). This class is defined in the file `testlin.h`:

```
#ifndef TESTLIN_H
#define TESTLIN_H
#include "opentmp.h"

class LinearIntProbe : public openAddress<long>
{
private:
  int HashFunc(const long& Item) const;
public:
  LinearIntProbe(long emptycell = 0,
    int tablesize = 1000) :
    openAddress<long>(emptycell, tablesize) {}
};
#endif
```

The only function (apart from the inline constructor definition) that we need to define is `HashFunc()`, which we will take to be a simple modulus function. It is defined in `testlin.cpp`:

```
#include "testlin.h"

int LinearIntProbe::HashFunc(const long& Item) const
{
  return Item % TableSize;
}
```

Finally, we provide a `main()` routine to test out the functions. This is in the file `linprobe.cpp`:

```
#include "testlin.h"

int main()
{
  LinearIntProbe InTable(100);
  long NewItem, GetItem, GotItem;

  for (int i = 0; i < 10; i++) {
    cout << "Enter integer to insert in table: ";
    cin >> NewItem;
    if (InTable.Store(NewItem))
      cout << "Item stored.\n";
    else
      cout << "Item already in table.\n";
  }
  for (i = 0; i < 10; i++) {
    cout << "Enter integer to retrieve from table: ";
    cin >> GetItem;
    if (InTable.Retrieve(GetItem, GotItem))
      cout << "Item " << GotItem << " found.\n";
    else
      cout << "Item not found.\n";
  }
  return 0;
}
```

The main() routine declares a hash table of size 100 and offers the user a chance to store in and retrieve 10 items from the table. When running this program, you should try entering the same item twice to be sure that the program detects that the item has already been stored on the first try.

### 13.4.3 C++ code for hashing with chaining

The main difference between hashing with open addressing and hashing with chaining is that, with chaining, the hash table is an array of *pointers*, where each pointer points to a linked list containing items with the corresponding value of the hash function. Storing an item involves inserting it into the correct linked list, and retrieving an item requires searching a linked list for the item.

The linked list class template that we developed in Chapter 10 may be used to provide the linked lists, but we need an additional Search() function to be able to search a linked list. We therefore inherit the original list template and add this function here. The new list template and the hash table template are in the file chaining.h:

```
#ifndef CHAINING_H
#define CHAINING_H
#include "lists.h"
```

```
// Linked list with search functions added
template <class Type>
class chainList : public list<Type>
{
public:
  chainList() : list<Type>() {}
  BOOL Search(const Type& SearchElement) const;
  BOOL Search(const Type& SearchElement,
    Type& FoundElement) const;
};

template <class Type>
class chainTable
{
protected:
  chainList<Type> *Bucket;
  int TableSize;
  virtual int HashFunc(const Type& Item) const = 0;
public:
  chainTable(int tablesize = 1000);
  virtual ~chainTable();
  virtual BOOL Store(const Type& Item);
  virtual BOOL Retrieve(const Type& SearchItem,
    Type& FoundItem) const;
};
#endif
```

We have provided two `Search()` functions in the `chainList` template. The one with a single argument searches a linked list and returns TRUE or FALSE depending on whether `SearchElement` is in the list or not. No alterations are made either to the list or to `SearchElement`. The second form, with two arguments, searches the linked list and, if `SearchElement` is found, the corresponding element in the list is copied into `FoundElement`. The rationale for this is the same as that in the `Retrieve()` function we considered in the `openAddress` class above: we may be using only one field of a compound data type as a search key, and wish to retrieve the entire, updated, data structure from the list.

The class `chainTable` contains much the same fields as the `openAddress` class. Here, the hash table is represented by the field `Bucket` (some books call each cell in a hash table a *bucket*), which is a pointer to an array of `chainLists`. The function `HashFunc()` is pure virtual, for the same reason as before. Since an empty bucket is marked by a zero pointer, there is no need for a special `EmptyCell` field to mark empty locations in the table.

The function definitions for these classes are in the file `chaintmp.h`:

```
#ifndef CHAINTMP_H
#define CHAINTMP_H
#include "chaining.h"
```

```
#include "listtemp.h"

template <class Type>
BOOL chainList<Type>::
  Search(const Type& SearchElement) const
{
  ListNode *Marker;

  for (Marker = Head->Next;
    Marker && Marker->Element != SearchElement;
    Marker = Marker->Next);
  return (Marker ? TRUE : FALSE);
}

template <class Type>
BOOL chainList<Type>::
  Search(const Type& SearchElement,
    Type& FoundElement) const
{
  ListNode *Marker;

  for (Marker = Head->Next;
    Marker && Marker->Element != SearchElement;
    Marker = Marker->Next);
  if (Marker) {
    FoundElement = Marker->Element;
    return TRUE;
  } else {
    FoundElement = SearchElement;
    return FALSE;
  }
}

template <class Type>
chainTable<Type>::chainTable(int tablesize) :
  TableSize(tablesize),
  Bucket(new chainList<Type>[tablesize])
{}

template <class Type>
chainTable<Type>::~chainTable()
{
  delete [] Bucket;
}

template <class Type>
BOOL chainTable<Type>::Store(const Type& Item)
{
  int index = HashFunc(Item);
  if (Bucket[index].Search(Item))
    return FALSE;
  Bucket[index].Insert(Item);
  return TRUE;
```

```
}

template <class Type>
BOOL chainTable<Type>::
  Retrieve(const Type& SearchItem,
    Type& FoundItem) const
{
  int index = HashFunc(SearchItem);
  return Bucket[index].Search(SearchItem, FoundItem) ?
    TRUE : FALSE;
}
#endif
```

The single-argument `Search()` function traverses the list looking for
`SearchElement` using the `!=` operator (which will need to be provided in a
user-defined class), and returns a flag indicating whether it was found or not.
The double-argument `Search()` function does the same thing except that it
copies the element to `FoundElement` if it is found, otherwise it copies
`SearchElement` to `FoundElement`.

The constructor for `chainTable` creates the `Bucket` array. Note that the
initialization of each list in this array is done by the list constructor (which is
called by the `chainList` constructor), and therefore does not need to be done
here. This program illustrates the advantages of building up a class library, as
earlier modules can be inserted directly into later programs. Extra functions
can be added by inheritance (as with `chainList` being derived from the
`list` class, which we constructed in Chapter 10).

The destructor deletes the `Bucket` array. Again, the destruction of the
individual lists is handled by the destructor for the `list` class, which is called
automatically for each element of the `Bucket` array, so we don't need to
concern ourselves with the details here.

The `Store()` and `Retrieve()` functions are considerably simpler here
than for the open addressing code given earlier, because most of the work is
done by the functions in the `chainList` class (and `list` class, from which it
was derived). The `Store()` function uses the single-argument `Search()`
function to check if `Item` is present in the table and, if not, the `list` class's
`Insert()` function is called to add `Item` to the corresponding list.

The `Retrieve()` function uses the double-argument `Search()` function
to look for `SearchItem` which, if found, is loaded into `FoundItem`.

As before, this abstract class can be tested by deriving another class from it.
The class `chainInt` is in the file `chaintst.h`:

```
#ifndef CHAINTST_H
#define CHAINTST_H
#include "chaining.h"
#include "chaintmp.h"
```

```
class chainInt : public chainTable<long>
{
private:
  int HashFunc(const long& Item) const;
public:
  chainInt(int tablesize = 1000) :
    chainTable<long>(tablesize) {}
};
#endif
```

The definition of `HashFunc()` is the same as before, and is in the file `chaintst.cpp`:

```
#include "chaintst.h"

int chainInt::HashFunc(const long& Item) const
{
  return Item % TableSize;
}
```

Finally, a `main()` function tests out hashing with chaining. It is in the file `chaining.cpp`:

```
#include "chaintst.h"

int main()
{
  chainInt InTable(100);
  long NewItem, GetItem, GotItem;

  for (int i = 0; i < 10; i++) {
    cout << "Enter integer to insert in table: ";
    cin >> NewItem;
    if (InTable.Store(NewItem))
      cout << "Item stored.\n";
    else
      cout << "Item already in table.\n";
  }
  for (i = 0; i < 10; i++) {
    cout << "Enter integer to retrieve from table: ";
    cin >> GetItem;
    if (InTable.Retrieve(GetItem, GotItem))
      cout << "Item " << GotItem << " found.\n";
    else
      cout << "Item not found.\n";
  }
  return 0;
}
```

Except for the included header file and the declaration of the hash table, this function is identical to the one given earlier to test open addressing.

# 13.5 Efficiency of hashing

The main motivation for studying hashing is that it is supposed to give us a method of storing and retrieving data that is equally efficient for any size of hash table. The time has come to see if the method lives up to its promises.

We can do the usual computer experiments to see how the number of comparisons for successful and unsuccessful searches vary with the amount of data stored, but in addition to this there is another factor that we should consider. What is important in hashing is not so much the overall size of the table, but the fraction of sites within this table that are occupied. This fraction, defined as the ratio of the number $N$ of objects in the hash table to the number of buckets $T$ in the table, is called the *load factor L* of the table: $L = N/T$.

For hash tables using open addressing, the maximum load factor is $L = 1$, since each bucket in the table can store only one object. If chaining is used, the load factor can be larger than 1, since each bucket is a pointer to a linked list that can, in principle, store any number of objects. For both methods (chaining and open addressing), we would expect the number of comparisons required for both successful and unsuccessful searches to increase as the load factor increases. The reason is simply that the more objects there are in the table, the more likely it is that collisions have occurred during the storage process, so the more likely it is that more than one comparison will be required to locate an object in the table (or to determine that the object is not present).

We will therefore examine the efficiency of hashing from two viewpoints. In the first, we will show plots of the number of comparisons required for successful and unsuccessful searches on hash tables of various sizes, but with a constant load factor. We expect that the number of comparisons required should be constant for all sizes of hash table in this case.

In the second experiment, we will examine the number of comparisons required for a hash table of a fixed size, but with various load factors. In this case, we expect the number of comparisons to increase as the load factor increases.

First, let us consider the hash table using open addressing, with the linear and quadratic probing methods of resolving collisions. The number of comparisons required is shown in Fig. 13.4.

The graph shows the results of a series of experiments run on tables of various sizes (values at every 10 from 10 to 1000). All tables were filled to load factor $L = 0.9$ before the searching experiments were done. It can be seen that quadratic probing requires significantly fewer comparisons to retrieve an item from the table. The number of comparisons is roughly constant over the range of table sizes used in the experiments, though considerable variation is shown for the linear probing method. This is probably due to the formation of clusters in the linear probing method, something which does not occur to the same extent with quadratic probing.

Next, we consider the number of comparisons required for unsuccessful searches using these two collision resolution methods (Fig. 13.5). Again, the quadratic probing method requires fewer comparisons and shows less fluctuation than the linear probing method.

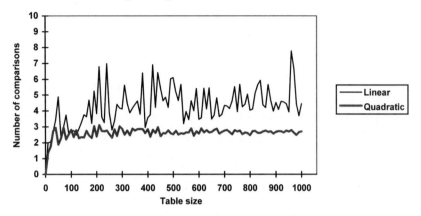

Fig. 13.4. Open addressing - successful search.

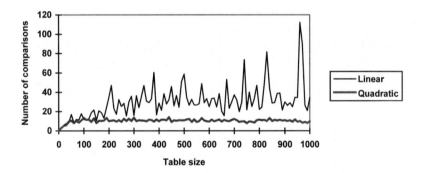

Fig. 13.5. Open addressing - unsuccessful search.

If we examine the number of comparisons for a table of fixed size, but with various load factors, we get the results shown in Figs. 13.6 and 13.7.

These graphs show that quadratic probing performs better than linear probing, especially at high load factors. (The number of comparisons required for a fully loaded hash table using linear probing is, of course, equal to the table size since all locations in the table must be probed. This gives a value of 1000 for the graph in Fig. 13.7, which is off scale in order to allow the other values to show up on the graph.) Perhaps the most striking thing about these plots is the dramatic increase in the number of comparisons when the tables become fully loaded. The moral is that if you plan on using open addressing, you should ensure that the table size is large enough so that you do not approach full loading in practice. If you keep the load factor below about 0.8, the performance of the hash table should be quite good.

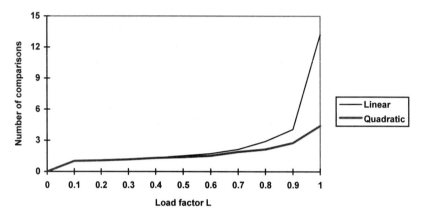

Fig. 13.6. Open addressing - successful search. Table size: 1000.

We can do similar experiments for hashing using chaining to resolve collisions. The results are shown in Fig. 13.8.

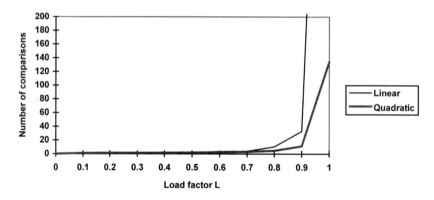

Fig. 13.7. Open addressing - unsuccessful search. Table size: 1000

The graph shows the number of comparisons required for successful and unsuccessful searches on tables of various sizes. The load factor on all tables was $L = 1$. This does not mean that the table was fully loaded since, with chaining, there is in principle no limit to the number of objects that can be stored in the table. It can be seen that significantly fewer comparisons are required using the chaining method than with either of the open addressing methods considered above. This is because the chaining method keeps objects with the same hash function value strictly separate in their own linked lists, so that only those values need be searched. All open addressing collision resolution methods of necessity must store objects in sites other than those to which they are mapped by the hash function if a collision occurs, so that even if *no* items with a particular hash function value are present in the table, some searching may be required to demonstrate this.

The behaviour of chaining as we increase the load factor is illustrated in Fig. 13.9.

We see that the number of comparisons increases as the load factor increases, just as with the open addressing methods. However, the number of comparisons, even at load factor $L = 2$, is still very small compared with those for open addressing methods at high load factors.

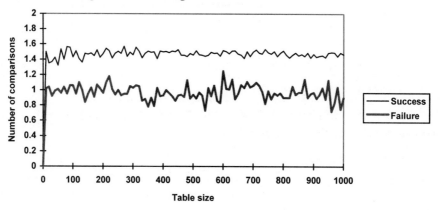

Fig. 13.8. Chaining - load factor 1.0.

Given the significant advantages of chaining over open addressing in all our efficiency experiments, why would you ever use open addressing? The main reason is space: because chaining uses linked lists to store its objects, each object must have an extra field provided for storing its associated pointer. Also, there are some languages (such as most versions of BASIC, including the currently very popular Visual Basic) which do not support pointers as part of the language, so implementing a hash table using chaining is not easy with these languages. If you are using a language that supports pointers easily and are not severely restricted in terms of memory, then chaining is certainly the best method for implementing a hash table.

## 13.6 Summary

In this chapter we have introduced the idea of *hash tables* for storing data in a form in which a search of the table is essentially independent of the table size. Hashing is used primarily for storing data which cannot be used directly as array indices, or for storing samples of data chosen from very large data sets.

Each item of data is mapped to an *index* by using a *hash function*. The index is used to determine the cell in which the data item is stored. If the cell determined by the hash function is already occupied, a *collision* occurs, and some method of *resolving* the collision must be used. Two main methods of resolving collisions are in use: open addressing and chaining. In open addressing, alternative cells in the array are chosen according to some algorithm (such as linear or quadratic probing). In chaining, each cell in the hash table is a pointer to a linked list. Different items with the same index are simply added to the linked list.

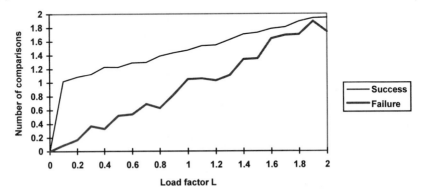

Fig. 13.9. Chaining - table size 1000.

Chaining is more efficient than most forms of open addressing, although it requires extra memory to store the pointer associated with each data item.

A new feature of C++ was introduced in this chapter as well: the concept of an *abstract* or *pure virtual class*. Such a class has one or more of its functions declared as a pure virtual function by prefixing its declaration with the keyword `virtual`, and setting the declaration equal to 0. No instances of an abstract class can be declared; rather another class must inherit the abstract class and provide overloaded versions of the pure virtual functions declared in the abstract class. An abstract class is useful for defining a base class for a set of derived classes when the specific form of some of the functions cannot be determined until the nature of the derived class is known. The example used in this chapter is that of a base class for a hash table. The hash function is declared as a pure virtual function, since the form of the hash function depends on the type of data to be stored in the table.

## 13.7 Exercises

1. a. The integers given below are to be stored in a table with 10 locations (numbered 0 through 9 inclusive) using open addressing. As a hash function use

location = number % tablesize

where % is the modulus operator. Use quadratic probing to resolve collisions. The numbers to be stored are:

```
145  87  477  990  797  878  556  551  965  52
```

b. For the hash table constructed in part (a), calculate (i) the average number of comparisons necessary for a successful search of the table; (ii) the average number of comparisons necessary in an unsuccessful search of the table.

c. Insert the same integers into a hash table with 10 locations using the same hash function, but use chaining to resolve collisions. Calculate the average number of comparisons for (i) a successful search and (ii) an unsuccessful search in this case.

2. Write a C++ abstract class for a hash table in which the collisions are resolved using open addressing with quadratic probing.

3. a. Write a C++ abstract class for a hash table in which the collisions are resolved using open addressing with a pseudo-random number generator (RNG). (Make sure the random number generator in your compiler allows users to specify their own seeds!) The RNG should generate integers which are used as offsets from the starting position, in the same manner as in quadratic probing. Test your class by using it to store integers and retrieve them.

b. Run a computer experiment to test the efficiency of using an RNG to resolve collisions. Follow the examples in the text by finding the number of comparisons required for successful and unsuccessful searches of the table, as a function of table size for a fixed load factor, and as a function of load factor for a fixed table size. Compare your results with the graphs in the text.

4. Using one of the hash classes in the chapter, or one of those from questions 2 or 3 above, write a C++ program which counts the number of times various words occur in a text file. You must first define a class containing a string field and an integer field for storing the word count, together with any overloaded operators required by the hashing class and hash function you are using. A convenient hash function to use for storing a character string adds up the ASCII codes of the characters in the string and uses this sum, modulo the table size, as the array index. The output from your program should be a list of the words in the file followed by the count of the number of times each word occurred. (If you are feeling ambitious, you may want to use one of the sorting algorithms from the previous chapter to sort the list into (i) alphabetical order; (ii) descending order of frequency of occurrence.)

# CHAPTER 14

# Trees

## 14.1 Binary trees

### 14.1.1 Definitions

A *tree* is a data structure consisting of data nodes connected to each other with pointers, in much the same spirit as a linked list. However, each node in a tree may be connected to two or more other nodes, rather than the single node allowed in a linked list. The maximum number of nodes to which any single node may be connected is called the *order* of the tree. The simplest tree is of order 2, and is called a *binary tree*. A diagram of a binary tree is shown in Fig. 14.1.

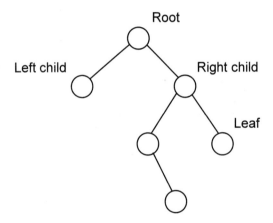

Fig. 14.1. The components of a binary tree

Each node in this diagram contains one or more data fields, and two pointers: one to the left child and the other to the right child. The topmost node in the tree is called the *root node*. A node with no children is called a *leaf*. If we redraw the tree shown above to illustrate the internal structure of its nodes, it would look as shown in Fig. 14.2.

Here, each node is shown with its three main components: the data area, and the pointers to the left and right children. These pointers are used in the same way as pointers in the linked list. When a new node is to be added to the tree, memory is allocated for the new node using the new operator in C++, and the address of this location is loaded into the appropriate pointer (left or right) for the new node's parent. Just as a null pointer indicates the end of a linked list, a null pointer in a tree indicates the end of a branch in that direction. A leaf is therefore a node, both of whose pointers are null.

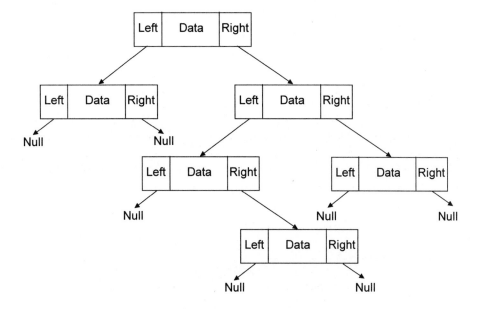

Fig. 14.2. How a binary tree is stored in memory.

## 14.1.2 Tree operations

Trees (binary and otherwise) have much the same basic types of operations as other data structures:

- inserting a new node
- deleting a node
- listing or visiting the nodes of the tree.

The method for doing each of these tasks depends to a large extent on the use to which the tree is being put. To see why this is so, we will consider one of the simplest and most common uses of a binary tree: yet another pair of sorting and searching algorithms.

One way that a binary tree can be used to sort data is as follows. Let us suppose that we have a list of integers, such as 5, 2, 8, 4, and 1, that we wish to sort into ascending order. We can perform a two-stage sorting algorithm. The first stage involves inserting the integers into a binary tree:

1. If the current pointer is 0, create a new node, store the data, and return the address of the new node.

2. Otherwise, compare the integer to the data stored at the current node. If the new integer is less than the integer at the current node, insert the new integer into the left child of the current node (by recursively applying the same algorithm). Otherwise, insert it into the right child of the current node.

We illustrate the process by inserting the integers as shown in Fig. 14.3.

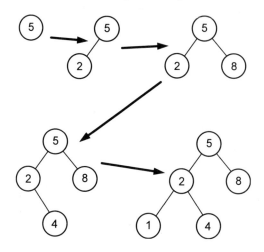

Fig. 14.3. Inserting the integers 5, 2, 8, 4, and 1 into a binary tree.

The first integer (5) is inserted into an empty tree (where the root pointer is 0), so the root node is created and the integer 5 is stored there. The next integer (2) is compared with the value at the root node, found to be less than it, and inserted as the left child of the root. Similarly the third integer (8) is inserted as the right child of the root since it is larger than 5. The fourth integer (4) is compared with the root and found to be less than 5, so the algorithm tells us to insert 4 into the left child. The left child is already occupied, however, so we simply apply the algorithm recursively starting at the left child of the root. The integer 4 is compared with 2, found to be greater than 2, so it is inserted as the right child of 2. The process can be continued as long as we have more data to add to the tree.

Having inserted the numbers into the binary tree, it may not be immediately obvious how that has helped us. In order to produce a sorted list of the data, we need to *traverse* the tree, that is, list the nodes in some specific order.

Various types of tree traversal exist, but the most common is *inorder* traversal, which means that we follow the algorithm:

1. If the current pointer is not 0, then:
2. Traverse the left child of the current pointer.

3. Visit (or print) the data at the current pointer.
4. Traverse the right child of the current pointer.

Steps 2 and 4 in this algorithm use recursion: they call the same algorithm to process the left and right children of the current pointer.

To see how the traversal produces a sorted list, consider the binary tree that we produced in Fig. 14.3 above. We begin the traversal algorithm, as usual, with the root node. The root pointer is not 0, so we must traverse the left child. Its pointer isn't 0 either (it contains the value 2), so we must visit *its* left child. This child's pointer still isn't 0 (it contains the value 1), so we call the algorithm again for the node containing the value 1. The pointer to the left child of this node is now 0, so the recursive call to this node will return without doing anything. We have now completed step 2 in the algorithm for the node 1, so we can now proceed to step 3 for that node, which prints out the number 1. This looks promising, since the first value actually printed from the traversal algorithm is, in fact, the smallest number stored in the tree.

We then complete the algorithm for node 1 by traversing its right child. Since the pointer to its right child is 0, the algorithm is complete for node 1. We can now return to the processing of the next node up, which is node 2. Its left child has been fully traversed, so we now print its value, which is 2. We then traverse the right child of node 2, which takes us to node 4. Since node 4 is a leaf (it has no children) it is printed after node 2.

The entire left subtree of the root node has now been traversed, producing the list 1, 2, 4. The root node may now be printed, giving the value 5. Finally, the right child of the root is traversed, printing out the value 8. The completed list is 1, 2, 4, 5, 8, which is the correctly sorted list.

### 14.1.3 C++ code for a simple binary tree

We can implement these algorithms directly in C++ code. Since we would like to be able to store any data type in the nodes of the tree, we will define a template for the binary tree class. However, as with the linked list, where we had to define an encapsulated `struct` for the list node, we must associate each item of data in the binary tree with the two pointers to the left and right children, so we need an auxiliary class which includes the data to be stored in each node, plus the two pointers.

When we constructed the linked list template, we defined a `struct` as one of the private fields of the list class. This `struct` contained the data and associated pointer for a single node in the list. In principle, we will do the same thing for the binary tree, but there is one complication which causes a few problems for the object oriented design. When we implemented the linked list in Chapter 10, there was never any need to pass a list node pointer as an argument to, or receive a list node pointer as a return value from, any of the class functions. Because many of the binary tree functions are recursive, however, we often need to pass pointers to individual binary tree nodes to and from functions.

The reason this causes problems is that the values in a function's argument list (and the function's return value) are its interface to the outside world. For this reason, it isn't correct to use private or protected data types in argument lists or as return values of class functions. In fact, C++ imposes the following restrictions on the use of encapsulated `struct`s or classes as function arguments and return values:

- An object of an encapsulated class or `struct` may not be used as an argument to a class function unless the encapsulated class or `struct` is a `public` field of the class. (For example, if we had tried to define a function in our linked class in Chapter 10 which contained a list node as an argument, it wouldn't have worked.)
- A class function may not return an object of an encapsulated class, no matter what protection is placed on that encapsulated class (even if it is public).

We therefore must decide how we are going to represent the class for the tree data node. There are several possibilities:

- We could define a `struct` for the data node which is external to the tree class. Remember that all fields in a `struct` are public by default. This option gives us unlimited freedom to use the data nodes in any context: as arguments to functions, return values from functions, and so on. Of course, it also abandons any pretext at object oriented design, since the fields of this `struct` are freely available to any other class or function as well.
- We could define a data node class external to the tree class, and make the tree class a `friend` of the data node class. Remember that friends are allowed access to all fields, whether they be public, protected, or private. In this way, we could restrict access of the data node class's fields to the binary tree class and preserve the object oriented design. This would be the preferable option, except for one *other* problem. If we wish to inherit the binary tree class later on (for example, to add some other tree operations such as deletion of nodes or searching), we discover that the friend classes of the base class are *not* automatically friends of any derived classes. In other words, any functions that we added to the derived class would not have access to any of the fields of the data node class. The only way around this is to define an additional derived class for the data nodes, which inherits the original data node class and adds the derived tree class as a friend. Since we usually don't need to modify the data node class when we derive a new tree class, this can be very annoying.

- The final option is to encapsulate the data node class as a nested *public* class within the binary tree class. This isn't an ideal solution, since the data node is still technically accessible to all external classes and functions. However, at least on some compilers, you will get a warning if you attempt to declare a variable of this nested type outside the class which contains it. This option also has the advantage that the nested class is part of the binary tree class template, so we don't need to use template parameters explicitly whenever we refer to an instance of the nested class.

The binary tree class template is in the file bintree.h:

```
#ifndef BINTREE_H
#define BINTREE_H
#include "mydefs.h"
#include <iostream.h>

template <class Type>
class bintree {
public:
    struct treenode
    {
        int Element;
        treenode *left, *right;
        treenode() : left(0), right(0) {}
        treenode(int item, treenode *leftnode=0,
            treenode *rightnode=0) :
            Element(item), left(leftnode),
            right(rightnode) {}
    };
protected:
    treenode *root;
    Type RefValue;
    BOOL Insert(treenode* &tree, const Type& item);
    void Traverse(treenode *tree, ostream& out) const;
    BOOL Search(treenode* tree, const Type& item) const;
    void destroy(treenode *tree);
public:
    bintree() : root(0) {}
    bintree(Type refvalue) : RefValue(refvalue),
        root(0) {}
    virtual ~bintree();
    virtual BOOL Insert(const Type& item);
    virtual BOOL Search(const Type& item) const;
    friend istream& operator>>(istream& in,
        bintree<Type>& Tree);
    friend ostream& operator<<(ostream& out, const
        bintree<Type>& Tree);
};
#endif
```

The treenode structure contains the data as the field Element, and the pointers to the children (left and right). There are two constructors: an argumentless constructor that initializes the two pointers to 0, and a constructor that stores item in the Element field, as well as allowing the user to specify values for the two pointers. Note that the treenode struct is a public field, but it must come first in the class in order that the treenode data type is available to the other fields in the bintree class.

The remainder of the bintree class defines the binary tree itself. There is a pointer root to the root of the tree. The RefValue field is used only for input: it specifies a value which, when read, halts input of data. It is used in the testing routines later.

The three protected functions implement the insertion and traversal algorithms we described earlier, as well as a function which deletes all the nodes in the tree (used by the destructor). You will notice that there is also a public Insert() function, with only a single argument: the item to be inserted. The reason for two Insert() functions will be described after we have introduced the function definitions. We have added a couple of Search() functions, which search the binary tree for a specified element and return TRUE or FALSE to indicate whether or not the object is in the tree.

The public fields of the bintree contain two constructors, a destructor, the public Insert() function, and the overloaded forms of the I/O operators.

Notice that one advantage of encapsulating the treenode class inside the bintree class is that it is not necessary to define treenode as a separate template. For example, if this had been done, the declaration of root would have to be written treenode<Type> *root, and the protected Insert() function would be declared as void Insert(treenode<Type>* &tree, ...).

The function definitions are in the file bintemp.h:

```
#ifndef BINTEMP_H
#define BINTEMP_H
#include "bintree.h"

template <class Type>
BOOL bintree<Type>::Insert(treenode* &tree,
  const Type& item)
{
  if (tree == 0) {
    tree = new treenode(item);
    return tree ? TRUE : FALSE;
  }
  else if (item < tree->Element)
    return Insert(tree->left, item);
  else
    return Insert(tree->right, item);
}

template <class Type>
```

```
void bintree<Type>::Traverse(treenode *tree,
  ostream& out) const
{
  if (tree) {
    Traverse(tree->left, out);
    out << tree->Element << ' ';
    Traverse(tree->right, out);
  }
}

template <class Type>
BOOL bintree<Type>::Search(treenode* tree,
  const Type& item) const
{
  if (tree) {
    if (tree->Element == item)
      return TRUE;
    else if (item < tree->Element)
      return Search(tree->left, item);
    else
      return Search(tree->right, item);
  }
  return FALSE;
}

template <class Type>
void bintree<Type>::destroy(treenode *tree)
{
  if (tree) {
    destroy(tree->left);
    destroy(tree->right);
    delete tree;
  }
}

template <class Type>
bintree<Type>::~bintree()
{
  destroy(root);
}

template <class Type>
BOOL bintree<Type>::Insert(const Type& item)
{
  return Insert(root, item);
}

template <class Type>
BOOL bintree<Type>::Search(const Type& item) const
{
  return Search(root, item);
}
```

```
template <class Type>
istream& operator>>(istream& in, bintree<Type>& Tree)
{
  Type item;

  cout << "Construct binary tree:\n";
  cout << "Input element (end with " <<
    Tree.RefValue << "): ";
  in >> item;
  while (item != Tree.RefValue) {
    Tree.Insert(item);
    cout << "Input element (end with " <<
      Tree.RefValue << "): ";
    in >> item;
  }
  return in;
}

template <class Type>
ostream& operator<<(ostream& out,
  const bintree<Type>& Tree)
{
  out << "Inorder traversal of binary tree.\n";
  Tree.Traverse(Tree.root, out);
  out << endl;
  return out;
}
#endif
```

The two Insert() functions are defined for much the same reason as we defined two sorting functions in quicksort and mergesort in Chapter 12. The public Insert() function is the interface to the outside world: it requires the user to specify only the item to be inserted into the tree. The public Insert() function calls the protected version of the function, passing it the root node (which is 0 if the tree is empty) along with the item to be inserted. The protected version of the insertion routine is a recursive function. If the tree pointer passed to this function is 0, a new node is allocated. (If this node is allocated a 0 pointer, no space is left in memory, and the function returns a FALSE value to indicate that it could not perform the insertion.) Thus if we begin with an empty tree, a 0 pointer is passed to the recursive insertion function and a new node is created, becoming the pointer to the root node. Note that the treenode pointer is passed to the Insert() function *by reference*, which means that the pointer itself may be modified within the Insert() function, with any change being retained after the function finishes.

If the root node already exists, the value of the new item is compared with the Element stored at the root node. If this value is less than Element, Insert() is called again (recursively), this time with tree->left as the pointer. If the tree contains only the root node, the pointer tree->left will be 0, so the recursive call will create a new node and assign the address of this new node to `tree->left`. The tree now contains two nodes.

Successive nodes can be inserted in the same way. A search through the tree is done until a 0 pointer is encountered, the `new` operator is used to allocate a new node, and this node is attached to the tree when the bottom recursive call returns. The success or failure of this operation is passed back up the chain of recursive calls until the top level returns the boolean value to the public `Insert()` function so that it knows whether or not the insertion succeeded.

The pair of `Search()` functions work on the same principle: the user need only be concerned with the public `Search()` function, which requires only the item for which the tree is being searched. This public function calls a recursive, protected version of `Search()`, which scans the tree in a similar way to the `Insert()` function.

The overloaded input operator `>>` allows the user to read in some data from the keyboard and store this data in the tree using the `Insert()` function. The user enters `RefValue` to stop input.

The `Traverse()` function follows the recursive traversal algorithm described above very closely. In this function, the `Element` fields are output to the `ostream` variable `out`, but the same principle applies if the nodes are to be used in some other fashion. The `Traverse()` function is called by the overloaded `<<` operator to print the tree.

The destructor for this class uses recursion to delete all the nodes in the tree, starting with the leaves. The destructor calls the protected `destroy()` function. This function is essentially a tree traversal function, except that it traverses the tree in what is known as *postorder* fashion: first the left subtree is traversed, then the right subtree, and finally the node itself. Deletion must be done in this order so that we don't lose the pointers to lower layers in the tree before these layers have been visited. You should trace through this function by hand for a small binary tree (or else insert in the `destroy()` function a statement that prints out the node just before it is deleted) to see the order in which the nodes are visited.

## 14.1.4 Deletion from a binary tree

We now consider an algorithm for deleting a node from a binary tree in such a way that the remaining nodes still have the same inorder traversal.

There are three categories of nodes we may wish to delete:

1. Leaves. These are the easiest, since all we need to do is delete the leaf and set the pointer from its parent (if any) to 0.
2. Nodes with a single child. These too are fairly easy, since we redirect the pointer from the node's parent so that it points to the child, then delete the node itself.

3. Nodes with both children. These can be fairly tricky, since we must rearrange the tree to some extent. The method we shall use is to replace the node being deleted by the *rightmost* node in its *left* subtree. (We could equally well have used the leftmost node in the right subtree.) Because of the rules for inorder traversals, this method guarantees the same traversal.

The actual implementation in C++ rearranges only the pointers to nodes, and thus avoids any actual copying of the data stored at the nodes. A function which accepts a single data argument item, searches for the item in the tree, and then deletes the node (if found) is given below. You can add this to the bintree class above directly, or else define a new class which inherits bintree, adding this routine to the derived class.

```
template <class Type>
BOOL bintree<Type>::Delete(const Type& item)
{
   treenode *marker=root, *parent=0, *child=root;
   treenode *temp;

   while (marker && marker->Element != item) {
     parent = marker;
     if (item < marker->Element)
       marker = marker->left;
     else
       marker = marker->right;
   }
   if (!marker) return FALSE;
   if (!parent) {                      // Delete root node
     if (!marker->right)
       root = marker->left;
     else if (!marker->left)
       root = marker->right;
     else {
       for (temp = marker, child = marker->left;
         child->right;
           temp = child, child = child->right);
       if (child != marker->left) {
         temp->right = child->left;
         child->left = root->left;
       }
       child->right = root->right;
       root = child;
     }
   } else if (!marker->right) {
     if (parent->left == marker)
       parent->left = marker->left;
     else
       parent->right = marker->left;
   } else if (!marker->left) {
     if (parent->left == marker)
```

```
      parent->left = marker->right;
    else
      parent->right = marker->right;
  } else {
    for (temp = marker,child = marker->left;
      child->right;
      temp = child, child = child->right);
    if (child != marker->left) {
      temp->right = child->left;
      child->left = marker->left;
    }
    child->right = marker->right;
    if (parent->left == marker)
      parent->left = child;
    else
      parent->right = child;
  }
  delete marker;
  return TRUE;
}
```

This function looks rather complicated, but isn't really, since it just treats all possible cases. The actual steps within each case are fairly simple. The description below is much more easily followed if you draw a binary tree and trace the steps as this function proceeds.

The first thing to note about this function is that it is *non-recursive*, which in itself is something of an oddity for binary tree routines. Recursion works well if we are attempting to locate one site in a tree and restrict our activities to that site once it is found. Node deletion, however, requires action at various places within the tree, so we need to be able to store several locations in memory. This is most easily done with a non-recursive function.

The first part of the function (the `while` loop) does a non-recursive search for the first node whose `Element` field matches the argument `item`. The search is straightforward, except that we also keep track of the `parent` of each node checked. We need the parent since one of its pointers must be redirected if its child is being deleted. If the required node is not found, `marker` will be 0 after the `while` loop finishes, and the function returns straight away with a FALSE value.

Assuming the node to be deleted is present in the tree, we are faced with two possibilities: the required node is the root node, or it is some other node. These must be treated as separate cases, since the root node has no parent.

Let us consider deletion of the root node first. In this case `marker` will be pointing to the root node. We must now deal with the three cases listed above: the root node has (i) no children, (ii) one child, or (iii) both children. The cases of either no children or only a left child are handled by the first section of the `if` statement. In this case, the `root` of the tree is set to the left child of the old root (the actual deletion of the node is done for all cases at the end of the function).

If the right child of the root exists, we next check to see if there is a left child. If not, the second section of the `if` statement assigns `root` to the right child of the old root.

The final `else` deals with the case where the root has both children. Two temporary pointers are used to keep track of things here. The `temp` pointer starts off pointing to the root, and `child` points to the root's left child. The termination condition of the `for` loop tests whether `child` has a right child itself. If not, we have found the rightmost node in the left subtree of the root. If a right child *does* exist, we move both `temp` and `child` one step down the right side of the left subtree. We continue until the rightmost node in the left subtree is found. This node is the one we want to move up to replace the root node.

To do this, we need to redirect several pointers (much more easily visualized if you draw a picture - see Fig. 14.4). Exactly which pointers are redirected depends on whether or not the left child of the root has a right child. If it doesn't, it will be the node that is moved up to the root position. In this case, (where `child` is still `marker->left` after the `for` loop has finished) we must assign `child->right` to point to the same node that the old right child of the root (`root->right`) did, and assign `root` to be `child`. No other redirections are necessary. In particular, we do *not* need to redirect any pointers from `child`'s parent, since that parent is the old root node, and is going to be deleted anyway.

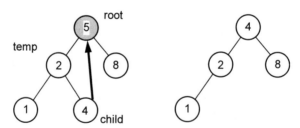

Fig. 14.4. Deleting the root node when the root has two children. In the left diagram, the positions of the variables temp and child when the rightmost element in the left subtree has been located. In the right diagram, the situation after the root has been removed is shown.

If the search for `child` progressed past `marker->left`, however, we *do* need to redirect the pointer from `child`'s parent, since that parent will still be in the tree after `child` is relocated to become the new root node. We know that `child` must have been the right child of its parent (because we are finding the *rightmost* node in the left subtree), and that `child` can have at most a left child (since it is the rightmost node in its subtree) we must redirect the *right* pointer of its parent to point to its *left* child, which is done by the statement `temp->right = child->left`. Finally, we need to ensure that `child`'s left pointer is also correctly assigned.

An example of deleting the root node is shown in Fig. 14.4.

The remainder of the function deals with the case where a node other than the root is deleted. The steps are very similar, except now we must make sure that the parent of the deleted node has its pointers correctly reset. You are urged to trace this function through for several test binary trees to see how it works. An example of what happens in this case is shown in Fig. 14.5.

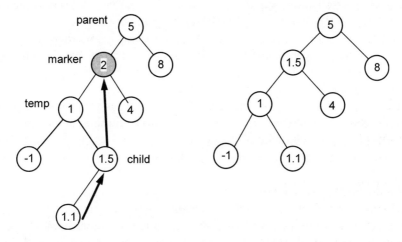

Fig. 14.5. Deleting an internal node with two children. In the left diagram, the shaded node is the one to be deleted, and the positions of the variables parent, marker, temp, and child are shown when the rightmost element in the left subtree of this node has been found. The arrows indicate the rearrangement of nodes that takes place. The position after the deletion is shown in the right diagram.

Finally, we present a `main()` routine which links together these routines. It is stored in the file `bintree.cpp`.

```
#include "bintemp.h"

int main()
{
   bintree<int> TestTree(0);
   int TestItem;

   cin >> TestTree;
   cout << TestTree;
   cout << "Delete some items.  (End with 0): ";
   cin >> TestItem;
```

```
    while (TestItem) {
      cout << "Item " <<
        (TestTree.Delete(TestItem)  ? " " : "not ")
          << "found.\n";
      cout << "Enter element: ";
      cin >> TestItem;
    }
    cout << TestTree;
    return 0;
}
```

The tree `TestTree` stores `int`s, and a value of 0 is specified as the `RefValue`, used for indicating the end of input. The overloaded `>>` operator is used to read in elements from the keyboard and insert them into the tree. The tree is then printed out to show that the numbers have been properly stored (the listing should show the numbers in ascending order). The `Delete()` function is then tested by reading in some numbers to delete from the tree. The `Delete()` function tests if the number is present in the tree and, if so, deletes it. A message is printed indicating whether or not the number was found and deleted. Finally, the tree is printed again to show that the chosen numbers have in fact been deleted.

## 14.1.5 Efficiency of binary trees

The binary tree routines above illustrate a way of using trees to sort and search data. The treesort and treesearch algorithms work well if the initial data are in a jumbled order, since the binary tree will be fairly well *balanced*, which means that there are roughly equal numbers of nodes in the left and right subtree of any node. Balanced trees tend to be 'bushy': they have few levels and spread out width-wise. This makes for efficient sorting and searching routines, because both these routines work their way vertically through the tree to locate nodes. Trees that are wide and shallow have only a few levels, so the insertion and searching routines have relatively few steps. In fact, in these cases, the sorting routine is $O(n \log n)$, so it is of comparable efficiency to mergesort and quicksort. The searching routine is essentially a binary search, and so is $O(\log n)$. (We will leave it up to the reader to construct some computer experiments to verify these results.)

However, if the list is already in order (or very nearly so), the tree formed by this insertion algorithm will be essentially linear, meaning that any searches performed on the tree will be essentially sequential. This simple insertion routine is therefore a disaster if fed a list that is already sorted, or contains a significant amount of order. If we wish to use a binary tree in searching and sorting, we would therefore like a way to ensure that the tree is reasonably balanced, no matter what the order of the input data.

You may be wondering why, with all the searching and sorting algorithms we have studied, we need to consider yet another way of doing these operations. The treesort and treesearch routines, however, offer distinct advantages over other methods in certain circumstances. We see from the above routines that it is easy to insert items into a binary tree, and equally easy to use binary search to look for them. Insertion of items into an already sorted list is slow and painful if we have used mergesort or quicksort, since these methods operate on the list as a whole, and if more data are added, the methods must be reapplied to the entire data set again. As well, mergesort works best on linked lists, on which it is difficult to use binary search, while quicksort works best on arrays, where it is difficult to insert items into a sorted list efficiently. Thus the tree algorithms are suited to cases where data are continually arriving and we want to maintain a sorted list (which can be searched efficiently) at all times.

There are two main approaches which may be taken to decrease the depth (the number of layers) of a binary tree:

1. Insert a number of elements into a binary tree in the usual way (using the algorithm given in the previous section). After a large number of elements have been inserted, copy the tree into another binary tree in such a way that the tree is balanced. This method of 'one-shot' balancing works well if the tree is to be fully constructed before it is to be searched. However, if data are to be continually added to the tree, and searching takes place between additions, the second method is to be preferred.

2. Balance the tree after each insertion. The *AVL tree* is the most popular algorithm for constructing such binary trees. It is considered in the next section.

## 14.2 AVL trees

### 14.2.1 Construction of an AVL tree

An algorithm for constructing balanced binary trees in which the trees remain as balanced as possible after every insertion was devised in 1962 by two Russian mathematicians, G. M. Adel'son-Vel'sky and E. M. Landis (hence the name *AVL tree*). An AVL tree is a binary tree in which the left and right subtrees of any node may differ in height by at most 1, and in which both the subtrees are themselves AVL trees (the definition is recursive). Fig. 14.6 shows some examples of trees that are and that are not AVL trees. In these diagrams, the number in each node is equal to the height of the right subtree minus the height of left subtree. An AVL tree must have only the differences –1, 0 or 1 between the two subtrees at any node.

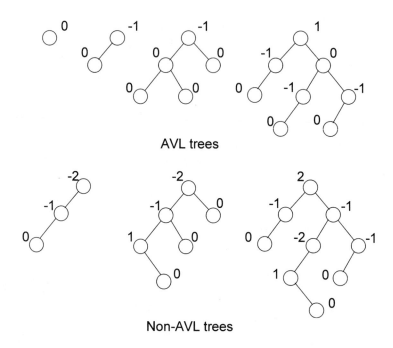

AVL trees

Non-AVL trees

Fig. 14.6. Comparing AVL trees with non-AVL trees.

An AVL tree is constructed in the same manner as an ordinary binary tree, except that after the addition of each new node, a check must be made to ensure that the AVL balance conditions have not been violated. If all is well, no further action need be taken. If the new node causes an imbalance in the tree, however, some rearrangement of the tree's nodes must be done. The insertion of a new node and test for an imbalance are done using the following algorithm:

1. Insert the new node using the same algorithm as for an ordinary binary tree.
2. Beginning with the new node, calculate the difference in heights of the left and right subtrees of each node on the path leading from the new node back up the tree towards the root.
3. Continue these checks until either the root node is encountered and all nodes along the path have differences of no greater than 1, or until the *first* difference greater than 1 is found.
4. If an imbalance is found, perform a *rotation* of the nodes to correct the imbalance. Only one such correction is ever needed for any one node. (We will describe rotations below.)

To see how these modifications work, it is easiest if we give an example of the construction of an AVL tree. We will therefore construct a tree by inserting integers into it. We begin by inserting the integer 10 into the root:

Since this node has no children, the difference in height of the two subtrees is 0, and this node satisfies the AVL conditions.

We now add another node (20):

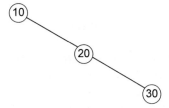

Beginning at the new node (20) we calculate differences in subtree heights. The node 20 has a difference of 0, and its parent (10) has a difference of +1. This tree is also an AVL tree.

We now insert a third node (30):

Beginning at the new node (30), we find a difference of 0. Working back towards the root, the node 20 has a difference of +1, which is OK, but the root node 10 has a difference of +2, which violates the AVL conditions. We therefore must rearrange the nodes to restore the balance in the tree.

As mentioned above, we perform an operation known as a *rotation* when the tree goes out of balance. There are two types of rotation used in AVL trees: *single* and *double* rotations. The rules for deciding which type of rotation to use are quite simple:

1. When you have found the first node that is out of balance (according to the algorithm above), restrict your attention to that node and the two nodes in the two layers immediately below it (on the path you followed up from the new node).
2. If these three nodes lie in a straight line, a *single rotation* is needed to restore the balance.

3. If these three nodes lie in a 'dog-leg' pattern (that is, there is a bend in the path), you need a *double rotation* to restore the balance.

In our example here, the three nodes to consider are the only three nodes in the tree. The first node where an imbalance was detected was the root node (10). The two layers immediately below this node, and on the path up from the new node, are the nodes 20 and 30. These nodes lie in a straight line, so we need a single rotation to restore the balance.

A single rotation involves shifting the middle node up to replace the top node and the top node down to become the left child of the middle node. After performing the rotation on this tree, we obtain:

A check shows that the AVL structure of the tree has been restored by this operation.

We continue by adding two more nodes: 25 and 27. After adding 25, a check shows that the AVL nature of the tree has not been violated, so no adjustments are necessary. After adding 27, however, the tree looks like this:

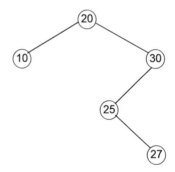

Tracing a path back from the node 27, we find height differences of 0 at 27, +1 at 25, and −2 at 30. Thus the first imbalance is detected at node 30. We restrict our attention to this node and the two nodes immediately below it (25 and 27). These three nodes form a dog-leg pattern, since there is a bend in the path at node 25. We therefore require a double rotation to correct the balance. A double rotation, as its name implies, consists of two single rotations. These two rotations are in opposite directions. The first rotation occurs on the two layers below the node where the imbalance was detected (in this case, it involves the nodes 25 and 27). We rotate the node 27 up to replace 25, and 25 down to become the left child of 27. The tree now looks like this:

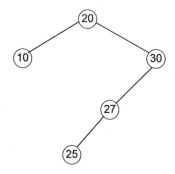

This operation obviously has not corrected the imbalance in the tree, so we must perform the second rotation, which involves the three nodes 25, 27, and 30. Node 27 rotates up to replace 30 and node 30 rotates down to become the right child of 27:

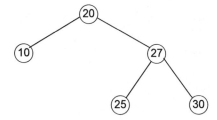

The AVL structure of the tree is now restored. We continue by adding the nodes 7 and 4 to the tree. Adding the 7 doesn't upset the balance, but adding the 4 does:

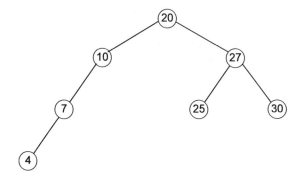

In this case, the first imbalance is detected at node 10, where a difference of −2 occurs. Considering this node and the two immediately below it, we see that the nodes 10, 7, and 4 lie in a straight line, so a single rotation is needed. Applying the rotation balances the tree:

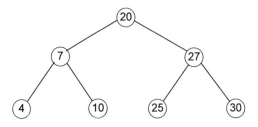

One final example, before we consider the general case. We add the nodes 23, 26, and 21 to the tree (the 23 and 26 do not disturb the balance, but the 21 does):

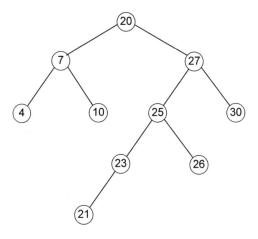

Working back from node 21, we find differences of 0 at 21, −1 at 23, −1 at 25, and −2 at 27. Node 27 is therefore the first node where an imbalance occurs. We examine this node and the two layers immediately below it on the path to the new node. This gives us the three nodes 27, 25, and 23, which lie in a straight line, so a single rotation is indicated. The middle node (25) rotates up to replace node 27 and node 27 rotates down to become the right child of 25. What happens to node 26, which is the old right child of 25? It must swap over to become the new *left* child of node 27. Making these modifications, we obtain:

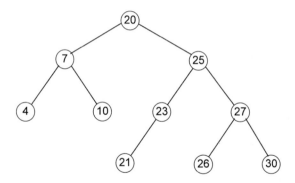

In summary, the steps involved in inserting a new node in an AVL tree are:

1. Insert the node in the same way as in an ordinary binary tree.
2. Beginning with the new node, trace a path back towards the root, checking the difference in height of the two subtrees at each node along the way.
3. If you find a node with an imbalance (a height difference other than 0, +1, or −1), stop your trace at this point.
4. Consider the node with the imbalance and the two nodes on the layers immediately below this point on the path back to the new node.
5. If these three nodes lie in a straight line, apply a single rotation to correct the imbalance.
6. If these three nodes lie in a dog-leg pattern, apply a double rotation to correct the imbalance.

The single rotation can occur towards either the left or the right: one is just the mirror image of the other. Which direction to go should be obvious from the nature of the imbalance. Similarly, double rotations can be either left first, then right, or right first, then left. The first rotation should always be *into* the bend in the dog-leg.

We may describe single and double rotations in general as follows. First, consider the single rotation. Suppose the state of the tree before the new node which causes the imbalance is as shown in Fig. 14.7. The capital letters indicate nodes in the tree, and the rectangular boxes indicate subtrees whose structure doesn't concern us. The letter $h$ indicates the height of the subtree. It is possible that $h = 0$, in which case the nodes B, D, and E are zero pointers. If $h > 0$, then these three nodes are actually present in the tree.

The structure of this tree satisfies the AVL conditions if all the subtrees in the rectangular boxes are AVL trees, since the height difference is 0 at node C and +1 at node A.

Now suppose that we insert a node into the subtree under node E, in such a way that the height of this subtree increases. We now have the situation shown in Fig. 14.8.

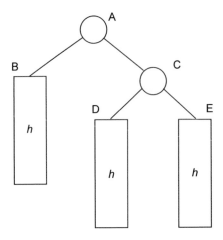

Fig. 14.7.

The tree is now unbalanced at node A, since the height difference there is now +2. Following the rules that we outlined above, we examine the node where the imbalance first occurs (A), and the two nodes immediately below it, on the path to the new node. This gives us the nodes A, C, and E. These three nodes are in a straight line, so we need a single rotation. We rotate C up to replace A and A down to become the left child of C. Node D must swap over to become the new right child of A. The situation after the rotation is shown in Fig. 14.9.

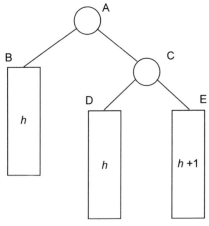

Fig. 14.8.

The balance is now restored, as can be checked by calculating the differences at each node. Note that a single rotation might involve two or three nodes, depending on whether the value of $h$ is zero or greater than zero.

The same technique works in both cases. The example shown here was a single rotation to the left. An example of a single rotation to the right can be obtained by looking at the diagrams in a mirror!

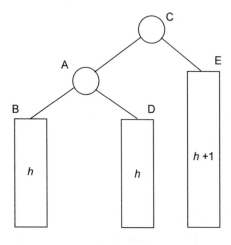

Fig. 14.9.

The double rotation *always* involves three nodes. Suppose a binary tree looks like this before an insertion:

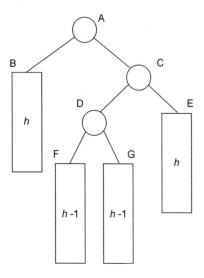

Fig. 14.10.

This tree is an AVL tree, assuming all subtrees in the rectangular boxes are AVL trees. The height differences are 0 at node D, 0 at node C, and +1 at node

A. The value of $h$ must be at least 1, in which case the two subtrees F and G are empty, and node D is a leaf. If $h > 1$, then all four subtrees in the rectangular boxes are actually present in the tree.

Now suppose we insert a new node into subtree F or G (it doesn't matter which) in such a way that the height of the corresponding subtree increases. Suppose we choose subtree G. The situation is now as shown in Fig. 14.11.

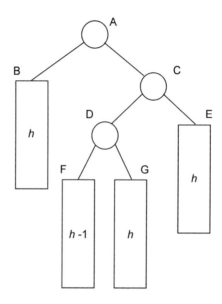

Fig. 14.11.

The tree is now unbalanced, since the height differences are +1 at D, −1 at C, and +2 at A. Node A is therefore the first node where an imbalance is detected. Considering this node and the two nodes immediately below it, on the path to the new node, gives us nodes A, C, and D, which form a dog-leg pattern. A double rotation is therefore needed.

The first rotation involves nodes C and D: node D rotates up to replace C and C rotates down to become the new right child of D. Subtree G swaps over to become the left child of C. The result of this is shown in Fig. 14.12. As can be checked from the diagram, this first rotation does not solve the imbalance problem, since the height differences are still +2 at both nodes A and D.

We therefore perform the second rotation, which is in the opposite direction to the first one, and involves nodes A, D, and C. Node D rotates up to replace node A, node A rotates down to become the left child of D, and subtree F swaps over to become the new right child of node A. The result of this is shown in Figure 14.13.

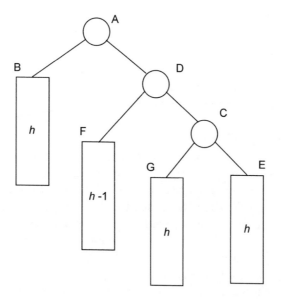

Fig. 14.12.

Note that the first rotation of the double rotation involves a single rotation with two nodes, and the second rotation involves a single rotation with three nodes.

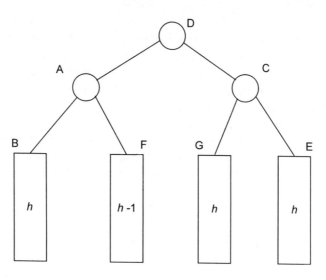

Fig. 14.13.

The final tree is now balanced, since the height differences are now 0 at node C, −1 at node A, and 0 at node D.

Although both of these examples (the single and double rotations) were done with trees where the first imbalance occurs at the root node, exactly the same procedures would be applied in those cases where an imbalance occurs within a tree. The structure of the tree above the node where the first imbalance occurs is irrelevant: all the changes occur at the level of that node and in the two layers immediately below.

### 14.2.2 C++ code for AVL trees

As the AVL tree is essentially an ordinary binary tree with a balancing operation added to the insertion routine, it may seem logical to design an AVL tree template by inheriting the template we designed earlier for the binary tree and overloading the `Insert()` functions. However, there is more to it than this. The balancing operation requires that we calculate the heights of the two subtrees arising from each node on the path from the newly inserted node back up to the root. The height (or depth, as it is sometimes called) of a binary tree is a fairly easy thing to find using a recursive function, but it is also quite costly in terms of computing time. The reason for this is that a *doubly recursive* algorithm is required for finding the height of a tree: we must explore both the left and right branches of all nodes to be sure we find the deepest branch, so if all nodes from the starting point to the leaves have two children, the number of branches that must be explored increases exponentially with the depth of the tree.

It is therefore highly inefficient to calculate the depth of each subtree every time we add a new node. It is a better plan to store some information about the relative sizes of a node's two subtrees as a field in the node itself, so that we don't have to recalculate the information every time a new node is added.

Let us consider what information we need to store. In an AVL tree, each node can be in one of three balance states. The height difference between the left and right subtrees can be 0, −1, or +1. We will refer to these states as balanced, left-high, and right-high, respectively. Given this information, there are two cases in which action must be taken to rebalance the tree after a new node is added: if a left-high node's left subtree increases in height, or if a right-high node's right subtree increases in height. All other possibilities will result in the state of a node changing, but without any balancing being necessary.

The conditions are summarized in Table 14.1.

How do we implement these conditions in C++ code? The recursive method for node insertion that we used in constructing ordinary binary trees offers an almost ready-made solution to this problem. Recall that the way we determine where a rotation is necessary to restore balance is by starting with the node that has just been inserted and working our way up the tree towards the root, checking the balance of each node along the way. This path is stored automatically for us by the recursive insertion routine when it is locating the

Table 14.1. AVL tree actions

| State of node | Effect of new node | Action or new state |
|---|---|---|
| Balanced | Increase left subtree height | Left-high |
| Balanced | Increase right subtree height | Right-high |
| Left-high | Increase left subtree height | **Left balance** |
| Left-high | Increase right subtree height | Balanced |
| Right-high | Increase left subtree height | Balanced |
| Right-high | Increase right subtree height | **Right balance** |

position where the new node is to be inserted. When a new node is to be inserted in a binary tree, the insertion routine begins by examining the root node and comparing its value with that of the new node. If the new node is, say, less than the root node, the insertion routine pushes the root node onto a stack and recursively calls itself to examine the root's left child. That node in turn is pushed onto the stack and one of its children is then examined by another recursive call to the insertion routine. In this way, a complete record of all the nodes visited by the insertion routine on its way to finding the correct position for insertion of the new node is stored on the stack. In an ordinary binary tree, this information is never used: once the node is inserted, the job is finished and the chain of recursive calls simply returns without doing anything else.

In constructing an AVL tree, however, we *can* make use of this information. After the new node has been inserted into the tree, we can examine each node as we climb out of the recursion to check its balance and adjust it, if necessary, to take account of the effect of adding the new node. If an imbalance occurs, we can then apply a rotation routine.

The C++ routines we present here make use of this idea. We modify the tree node data type to include a field for storing information on the balance state of each node. We then modify the insertion routine so that it checks the state of each node after a new node has been inserted. If an imbalance is found, the appropriate rotation routine is called to restore the balance.

Before we present the details of the code, we should say a few words on the object oriented nature of the AVL classes. As we mentioned at the beginning of this section, a logical object oriented approach would suggest that we should be able to inherit the `bintree` class we defined earlier and just modify the insertion routine. Having to change the data structure of the tree node, however, makes this difficult. In practice, it is easier to just start the AVL class from scratch.

If we were ambitious, there is a more sophisticated way of defining a suite of different types of binary tree. We could identify those functions (mainly functions which merely access the data in the tree without altering it) which *are* identical for all types of binary tree and define a base class template containing them. One of the template parameters would then be the type of data node (for example, nodes for use in an ordinary binary tree or in an AVL tree) so that several derived class templates could then construct the specific routines and data types required for each type of binary tree. This all seems a bit too much trouble for our purposes here.

The AVL tree class template is defined in the file `avltree.h`:

```
#ifndef AVLTREE_H
#define AVLTREE_H
#include "mydefs.h"
#include <iostream.h>

enum {LEFTHIGH, BALANCED, RIGHTHIGH};

template <class Type>
class avltree
{
public:
  struct avlnode
    {
    Type Element;
    avlnode *left, *right;
    int balance;
    avlnode() : left(0), right(0), balance(BALANCED) {}
    avlnode(Type item, avlnode *leftnode=0,
      avlnode *rightnode=0) :
      Element(item), left(leftnode), right(rightnode),
      balance(BALANCED) {}
    };
protected:
  Type RefValue;
  avlnode *root;
  BOOL Insert(avlnode* &tree, Type item, BOOL& taller);
  void RotateLeft(avlnode *Tree, avlnode* &NewTree);
  void RotateRight(avlnode *Tree, avlnode* &NewTree);
  void LeftBalance(avlnode* &Tree, BOOL& taller);
  void RightBalance(avlnode* &Tree, BOOL& taller);
  void Traverse(avlnode *Tree, ostream& out) const;
  int Depth(avlnode *Tree) const;
public:
  avltree() : root(0) {}
  avltree(Type refvalue) :
    RefValue(refvalue), root(0) {}
  BOOL Insert(Type item) { BOOL taller;
    return Insert(root, item, taller); }
  friend istream& operator>>(istream& in,
    avltree<Type>& Tree);
  friend ostream& operator<<(ostream& out,
    const avltree<Type>& Tree);
  int Depth() const;
};
#endif
```

The data type definition is contained in the nested `struct` called `avlnode`. Besides the standard data fields and `left` and `right` pointers, it contains a field `balance` which stores one of the three values defined in the `enum` statement: BALANCED, LEFTHIGH, or RIGHTHIGH. The protected fields of the `avltree` class itself contain the recursive `Insert()` function, several functions for implementing the rotation and balancing algorithms, a routine for traversing the tree, and a function for calculating the depth of the tree. We will return to these later when we examine their definitions.

The public functions of the `avltree` class contain the public `Insert()` function, the standard overloaded I/O operators, and public function for finding the depth of the tree.

Since this class contains somewhat more than most of the other classes we have studied so far, we will break up the various functions and store them in separate files. Let us look at the insertion routines first. They are stored in the file `avlins.h`:

```
#ifndef AVLINS_H
#define AVLINS_H
#include "avltree.h"

template <class Type>
BOOL avltree<Type>::Insert(avlnode* &tree,
  Type item, BOOL& taller)
{
  BOOL success;

  if(!tree) {
    tree = new avlnode(item);
    success = tree ? TRUE : FALSE;
    if (success)
      taller = TRUE;
  } else if (item < tree->Element) {
    success = Insert(tree->left, item, taller);
    if (taller)
      switch(tree->balance) {
      case LEFTHIGH:
        LeftBalance(tree,taller);
        break;
      case BALANCED:
        tree->balance = LEFTHIGH;
        break;
      case RIGHTHIGH:
        tree->balance = BALANCED;
        taller = FALSE;
        break;
      }
  } else {
    success = Insert(tree->right, item, taller);
    if(taller)
```

```
            switch(tree->balance) {
            case LEFTHIGH:
               tree->balance = BALANCED;
               taller = FALSE;
               break;
            case BALANCED:
               tree->balance = RIGHTHIGH;
               break;
            case RIGHTHIGH:
               RightBalance(tree, taller);
               break;
            }
      }
   return success;
}
#endif
```

The recursive Insert() function implements the idea we described earlier: using the recursive nature of the insertion to check the balance of each node as we climb out of the recursion. If Insert() is passed a zero pointer, it attempts to create a new node and store the data there. The boolean variable success records whether or not sufficient memory for a new node was found, and is the return value of the Insert() function. If a new node was allocated, the parameter taller is set to TRUE. This flag is set to indicate that the subtree of which this node is a member has increased in height. Clearly this must be true for the branch onto which the new node is added, so the taller flag is set to TRUE when a new node is added.

To see how the balance is checked by the Insert() routine, we will examine what happens in the first else block, which handles the case of the new item being less than the current Element. The first thing that happens in this block is that Insert() is called recursively to explore the left child of the current node. This part is exactly the same as in the ordinary binary tree. The recursion will explore the tree until it finds the correct location to insert the new node. Then, starting from the new node itself, the recursion will start to return. On the first level up from the new node, taller will be TRUE. The if(taller) statement handles what to do in this case. It examines the current state of the balance field for that node and takes the action specified in the table above: if the node is LEFTHIGH, the tree must be balanced, so it calls the LeftBalance() function (to be defined in a minute). Otherwise, it simply adjusts the balance label of the current node. The exploration of the right branch is done in the same way.

Now let us examine the balancing routines, stored in the file avlbal.h:

```
#ifndef AVLBAL_H
#define AVLBAL_H
#include "avltree.h"
```

```cpp
template <class Type>
void avltree<Type>::LeftBalance(avlnode* &Tree,
  BOOL& taller)
{
  avlnode *leftsub = Tree->left;
  avlnode *rightsub;

  switch(leftsub->balance) {
  case LEFTHIGH:
    Tree->balance = leftsub->balance = BALANCED;
    RotateRight(Tree, Tree);
    taller = FALSE;
    break;
  case BALANCED:
    cout <<
      "LeftBalance error: Tree already balanced.\n";
    break;
  case RIGHTHIGH:
    rightsub = leftsub->right;
    switch(rightsub->balance) {
    case LEFTHIGH:
      Tree->balance = RIGHTHIGH;
      leftsub->balance = BALANCED;
      break;
    case BALANCED:
      Tree->balance = leftsub->balance = BALANCED;
      break;
    case RIGHTHIGH:
      Tree->balance = BALANCED;
      leftsub->balance = LEFTHIGH;
      break;
    }
    rightsub->balance = BALANCED;
    RotateLeft(leftsub, Tree->left);
    RotateRight(Tree, Tree);
    taller = FALSE;
  }
}

template <class Type>
void avltree<Type>::RightBalance(avlnode* &Tree,
  BOOL& taller)
{
  avlnode *rightsub = Tree->right;
  avlnode *leftsub;

  switch(rightsub->balance) {
  case RIGHTHIGH:
    Tree->balance = rightsub->balance = BALANCED;
    RotateLeft(Tree, Tree);
    taller = FALSE;
    break;
  case BALANCED:
```

297

```
      cout <<
        "RightBalance error: Tree already balanced.\n";
      break;
    case LEFTHIGH:
      leftsub = rightsub->left;
      switch(leftsub->balance) {
      case RIGHTHIGH:
        Tree->balance = LEFTHIGH;
        rightsub->balance = BALANCED;
        break;
      case BALANCED:
        Tree->balance = rightsub->balance = BALANCED;
        break;
      case LEFTHIGH:
        Tree->balance = BALANCED;
        rightsub->balance = RIGHTHIGH;
        break;
      }
      leftsub->balance = BALANCED;
      RotateRight(rightsub, Tree->right);
      RotateLeft(Tree, Tree);
      taller = FALSE;
    }
  }
#endif
```

The `LeftBalance()` function is called when a `LEFTHIGH` node's left subtree increases in height. At the time that `LeftBalance()` is called, it is not known whether a single or double rotation is required, so that is the first thing that `LeftBalance()` must discover. Remember that to discover which type of rotation is needed, you must examine the node at which the imbalance occurs, and the two layers below that. If those three nodes are in a straight line, a single rotation is needed, while if they are in a dog-leg formation, a double rotation is needed.

`LeftBalance()` sorts this out by examining the `balance` condition of the current node's left child, since it is known that the new node was inserted into either the left or right subtree of the left child. If the new node was inserted into the left subtree of the left child, then the three nodes (current node, left child, and left subtree) all lie in a straight line, so a single rotation is needed. This is handled by the `case LEFTHIGH` section. The `RotateRight()` function (see below) is called, the balance of the two nodes involved in the rotation is restored, and the `taller` flag is switched off to prevent any further rotations later on.

The current node's left child cannot be in the `BALANCED` state (you should convince yourself this is true), so an error message is printed if this option is ever chosen.

Finally, if the current node's left child is in the `RIGHTHIGH` state, this means that the new node was inserted into the right subtree of the current node's left child, so that the current node and the two layers immediately below it form a dog-leg. A double rotation is therefore required. Before the double rotation is actually done, the balance labels must be adjusted, and this depends on which actual branch of the tree the new node was inserted into (you should draw out a few examples to convince yourself that the code is correct). Finally, the double rotation is done by calls to RotateLeft() and RotateRight().

The RightBalance() function is identical to LeftBalance() except all lefts and rights are interchanged.

The routines for doing the actual rotations are in the file avlrot.h:

```
#ifndef AVLROT_H
#define AVLROT_H
#include "avltree.h"

template <class Type>
void avltree<Type>::RotateLeft(avlnode *Tree,
  avlnode* &NewTree)
{
  NewTree = Tree->right;
  Tree->right = NewTree->left;
  NewTree->left = Tree;
}

template <class Type>
void avltree<Type>::RotateRight(avlnode *Tree,
  avlnode* &NewTree)
{
  NewTree = Tree->left;
  Tree->left = NewTree->right;
  NewTree->right = Tree;
}
#endif
```

The pointers are swapped in the correct order to implement the rotation. Note that the first argument in each function is the topmost node in the group of two or three pointers to the nodes being rotated, and is passed by value to the function. The second argument in each function is a pointer passed by reference, and contains the pointer to the new top node after the rotation.

The routine for finding the depth of the tree (useful for checking that the AVL routine is actually producing balanced trees) is in the file avldepth.h:

```
#ifndef AVLDEPTH_H
#define AVLDEPTH_H
#include "avltree.h"

template <class Type>
int avltree<Type>::Depth(avlnode *Tree) const
{
```

```
    if (Tree) {
      int LeftDepth = Depth(Tree->left);
      int RightDepth = Depth(Tree->right);
      return 1 + (LeftDepth > RightDepth ? LeftDepth :
        RightDepth);
    } else {
      return 0;
    }
}

template <class Type>
int avltree<Type>::Depth() const
{
  return Depth(root);
}
#endif
```

The recursive version calculates the depth by finding the depths of the left and right subtrees (recursively) and then adding 1 to the greater of these two. The double recursion in this function can make it very inefficient for large trees.

The I/O routines are very similar to those for the ordinary binary tree. They are stored in the file avlio.h:

```
#ifndef AVLIO_H
#define AVLIO_H
#include "avltree.h"

template <class Type>
istream& operator>>(istream& in, avltree<Type>& Tree)
{
  Type item;

  cout << "Construct AVL tree:\n";
  cout << "Input element (end with " <<
    Tree.RefValue << "): ";
  in >> item;
  while (item != Tree.RefValue) {
    Tree.Insert(item);
    cout << "Input element (end with " <<
      Tree.RefValue << "): ";
    in >> item;
  }
  return in;
}

template <class Type>
void avltree<Type>::Traverse(avlnode *Tree,
  ostream& out) const
{
  if (Tree) {
    Traverse(Tree->left, out);
```

```
    out << Tree->Element << ' ';
    Traverse(Tree->right, out);
  }
}

template <class Type>
ostream& operator<<(ostream& out,
  const avltree<Type>& Tree)
{
  out << "Inorder traversal of AVL tree.\n";
  Tree.Traverse(Tree.root, out);
  out << endl;
  return out;
}
#endif
```

A single header file named `avltemp.h` includes all these template files so that other routines may include them with a single statement. The file is:

```
#ifndef AVLTEMP_H
#define AVLTEMP_H

#include "avlins.h"
#include "avlrot.h"
#include "avlio.h"
#include "avlbal.h"
#include "avldepth.h"

#endif
```

A `main()` function which tests out these routines is in `avltree.cpp`:

```
#include "avltemp.h"

int main()
{
  avltree<float> TestAVL(0);

  cin >> TestAVL;
  cout << TestAVL;
  cout << "Depth of AVL tree: " << TestAVL.Depth()
    << endl;
  return 0;
}
```

The routine uses the overloaded >> and << operators to read in and store the data, and then traverse the tree so that you can see that the numbers have been stored correctly. Finally, the depth of the tree is calculated so that you can check that the tree has been properly balanced.

### 14.2.3 Efficiency of AVL trees

As you can see, the improved efficiency of AVL trees comes at a rather severe cost in terms of the amount of effort required to program them. However, there are several C++ libraries in existence that implement AVL trees for you, so you can often obtain the benefit of their efficiency without having to do the work of writing the code yourself.

The AVL insertion algorithm is sufficiently complicated that it is very difficult to do much in the way of quantitative analysis of such things as running time or average behaviour, except by running simulations. As with the ordinary binary tree, we leave it as an exercise to run these experiments and produce a plot of the average depth of an AVL tree for various numbers of nodes. A theoretical analysis shows that, in the worst case, the height $h$ of an AVL tree containing $N$ nodes should be about 1.44 log $N$. A perfectly balanced tree should have a height of around log $N$, so we see that, even in the worst case, an AVL tree is still quite good. Running actual simulations shows that most AVL trees have depths that are only 2 or 3 greater than a perfectly balanced tree, even for several hundred or thousand nodes.

The computational overhead involved in using the AVL algorithm as opposed to the simple insertion algorithm is small enough to justify its use if the resulting tree is expected to be large and data accesses frequent. Most new nodes do not require rebalancing, and even if they do, there can be at most one rebalancing of the tree (using either single or double rotation) for each item added, since the first balancing restores the balance in the subtree containing the new node, and the rest of the tree was balanced from previous insertions. Thus besides the possible single call to one of the balancing functions, the only extra work is a few comparisons to test that the tree is properly balanced.

Before we leave AVL trees, we should say a few words about deleting nodes from them. You may recall that, even for a simple binary tree, the computer code for deleting a node was fairly involved. The situation with AVL trees is even worse. Due to the requirement that the AVL tree be balanced at all nodes, the deletion of a node presents us with the dual problem of maintaining the same inorder traversal of the remaining nodes, and of retaining the AVL structure of the tree.

Faced with these problems, many authors recommend that if deletions are fairly infrequent (they may be due to an error in typing in a node, for example), the best method to use is so-called *lazy deletion*. Using this method, the deleted node is not actually removed from the tree; rather it is *marked* by either changing the data stored at that node to some value recognized as an indication that the node should be ignored (the special value `RefValue` that we used in the C++ class above may be used for this purpose), or by adding an extra field to the data node class which can be used as a flag to indicate that the node has been deleted. Any functions which access data in the tree would then have to be modified to ignore deleted nodes, but this usually requires only a single `if` statement.

Lazy deletion obviously preserves the traversal of the tree, but it does not preserve the AVL structure. However, provided that deletions are uncommon, this is a small price to pay to avoid having to understand and code the 'proper' AVL deletion algorithm.

## 14.3 Heaps, heapsort, and priority queues

### 14.3.1 The heap data structure

The final application of a purely binary tree that we shall examine is a data structure called a *heap*. Heaps are unusual in the menagerie of tree structures in that they represent trees as arrays rather than linked structures using pointers. To see how a binary tree can be represented as an array, consider Fig. 14.14. Here we have drawn a binary tree and numbered the nodes in order starting with the root node as node 1 and progressing across each level in turn. This numbering is not the order in which the nodes are traversed in any standard traversal pattern, but the purpose of a heap is not to traverse a tree, so this doesn't matter.

If we use the number of a node as an array index, this technique gives us an order in which we can store tree nodes in an array. The tree may be easily reconstructed from the array by noticing that the left child of node number $k$ has index $2k$ and the right child has index $2k + 1$. Thus the root node is always stored in position 1 (the 0 element with which all C++ arrays begin is not used), and its two children are in positions 2 and 3. The children of node 2 are in locations 4 and 5, and so on.

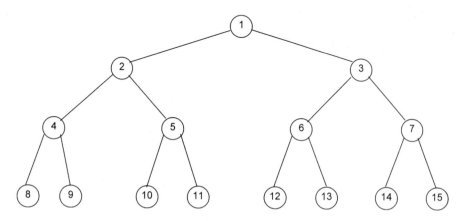

Fig. 14.14. Numbering of a tree's nodes for storage in an array.

Any binary tree can be represented in an array in this fashion if we leave blank those array elements where no corresponding tree nodes exist. This is not an efficient way to store just any binary tree, however, since for most trees there would be many array elements that are left empty, wasting a great deal of space. A heap, however, is a special kind of binary tree that leaves no gaps in an array implementation.

The definition of the heap data type is as follows. A heap is a binary tree satisfying the restrictions:

1. All leaves are on two adjacent levels.
2. All leaves on the lowest level occur at the left of the tree.
3. All levels above the lowest are completely filled.
4. Both children of any node are again heaps.
5. The value stored at any node is at least as large as the values in its two children.

The first three conditions ensure that the array representation of the heap will have no gaps in it. The last two conditions give a heap a weak amount of order, in that in progressing from the root down to a leaf, the keys must not get any larger, and may get smaller. However, the order in which the elements are stored in the array will, in general, not be a sorted representation of the list, although the largest element will be stored at location 1. An example of a heap is shown in Fig. 14.15.

In this figure, note that the largest element (50) is the root node, and that the value stored in each node is larger than both of its children. The leaves of the heap occur on two adjacent levels (the third and fourth), and the nodes on the lowest layer fill that layer from the left. We could remove node 9, for example, and still preserve the heap property, but if node 9 remains where it is, we cannot remove any other node in the bottom layer without violating heap property 2 in the list above.

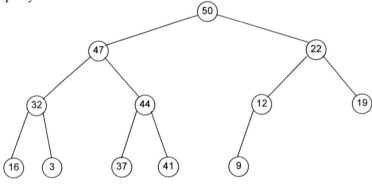

Fig. 14.15. A heap.

The elements of this heap would be stored in an array in the order 50, 47, 22, 32, 44, 12, 19, 16, 3, 37, 41, 9.

Since heaps have only weak ordering of their elements and their traversals don't, in general, give us any useful information, you might wonder what heaps are used for. The most useful property of a heap is that the largest node in the tree is always at the root. If the root is extracted from the heap, there is a simple algorithm (which we will examine below) which can be used to restore the heap condition in the remaining nodes, so that the largest of the remaining nodes is again at the root position. In other words, a heap offers us a way to process its contents in a sorted order by extracting one element at a time and not bothering to fully sort the remainder of the data until it is needed. The most common application of a heap is as a *priority queue*.

Recall that a queue is a data structure in which items are inserted at the tail of the queue and extracted from the head, in first-in first-out, or FIFO, order. A priority queue is similar in spirit to an ordinary queue, except that each item in the queue has an associated *priority*. Items with higher priority will get processed before items with lower priority, even if they arrive in the queue after them.

We could implement a priority queue by using one of the sorting methods from Chapter 12, but since we only need to process one item at a time, a heap turns out to be more efficient. When the current item is being dealt with, we don't care what order the other items in the queue are in: when we make a request for the next item it just has to be the one with the highest priority. Although heaps are fairly sloppy in keeping their members in strict order, they are very good at finding the maximum member and bringing it to the top of the heap.

## 14.3.2 Constructing a heap

In practice, a priority queue may begin with a list of unsorted data. The first step, then, is to organize this initial data so that it has the heap properties. Once we have made our initial heap, we may deal with the priority queue in a continuous fashion by extracting the item at the top and processing it, or inserting another item into the queue while maintaining the heap property. Let us begin by inserting some integers into a binary tree in random order (Fig. 14.16).

This tree is clearly not a heap, since there are several nodes that are smaller than one or both of their children.

The method of constructing a heap from this scrambled tree begins by considering the last node that is not a leaf. Remember that these numbers are stored in an array by reading across each layer in the tree from left to right, so the last non-leaf node is 50. We compare this node to its children (or child, in this case). If the node is larger than its children (as it is in this case) then it satisfies that heap condition, so no change is required.

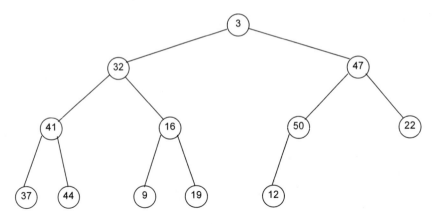

Fig. 14.16.

We move backwards through the tree, examining each node in turn. Looking at node 16, we see that it is larger than 9, but smaller than 19, so it does *not* satisfy the heap condition. To correct this, we swap the node with the larger of its two children, to obtain the tree shown in Fig. 14.17.

Proceeding backwards, we see that we must swap the nodes 41 and 44. We then consider the node 47. Comparing it with its two children, we see that it must be swapped with 50, giving the result shown in Fig. 14.18.

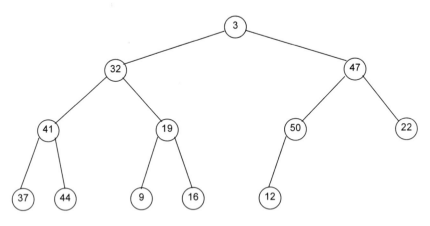

Fig. 14.17

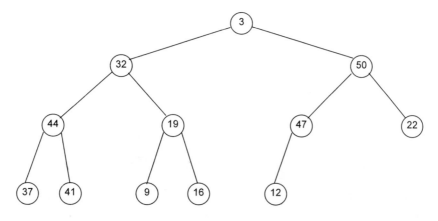

Fig. 14.18.

We must also check that 47 is acceptable in its new position by comparing it with its children at that location. We see that 47 is larger than 12, so we are OK here.

Proceeding back to node 32, we must swap it with 44. Having done that, we now see that the two children of 32 are 37 and 41, both of which are larger than 32. We therefore must swap 32 with the larger of its children (41), giving the result shown in Fig. 14.19.

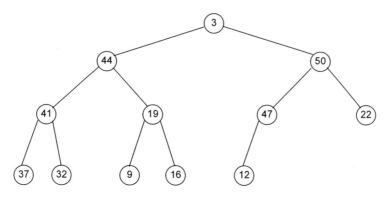

Fig. 14.19.

Finally, we must consider node 3. It is swapped with the larger of its two children (50), then with 47, and finally with 12, giving the final, properly constructed heap (Fig. 14.20).

### 14.3.3 Heapsort and priority queues

Having created the heap, we may now use it in applications. As mentioned above, the main use of a heap is as a priority queue, in which the largest element is extracted from the root node (and used externally), with the remaining elements being rearranged to form a smaller heap.

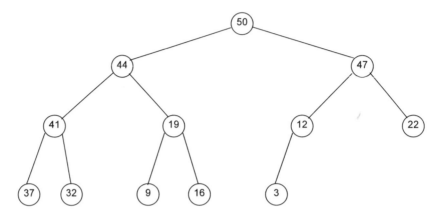

Fig. 14.20.

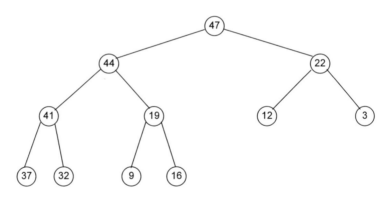

Fig. 14.21

A variation on the priority queue provides us with yet another sorting method, known as *heapsort*. Heapsort makes use of the fact that a heap is stored in an array. With the heap shown above, the numbers are stored in the array in the order 50, 44, 47, 41, 19, 12, 22, 37, 32, 9, 16, 3 (a total of 12 numbers). In heapsort, the last number in the array (3) is stored in a temporary variable, the root of the heap is transferred to this vacated location, and the temporary variable is reinserted into the heap starting at the root position. This reinsertion follows the same procedure as that used in constructing the original heap above: when the 3 is inserted at the root position, its two children are 44 and 47. It is swapped with the larger of the two children, which places 47 at the root and moves 3 down to be the right child of 47. Here, 3 is compared with its two children (12 and 22), and the larger of these two is swapped with 3 to give the final heap shown in Fig. 14.21. The size of the heap is reduced by 1.

The contents of the array are now  47, 44, 22, 41, 19, 12, 3, 37, 32, 9, 16, 50, and the heap size is reduced to 11. Note that the last array element now contains the largest number (50) in the array, and that this number has been removed from the heap.

If we repeat the process with the new root (47), we obtain the heap shown in Fig. 14.22.

The last element in the previous heap (16) was stored in a temporary variable, the 47 was removed and placed just after the end of the heap in the array, and the 16 was reinserted from the root position. The array contents are now 44, 41, 22, 37, 19, 12, 3, 16, 32, 9, 47, 50, with a heap size of 10. The last two numbers in the array are no longer part of the heap, and contain the two largest numbers in sorted order.

The process continues in the same manner until the heap size has been reduced to zero, at which point the array contains the numbers in sorted order.

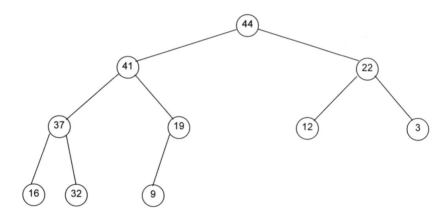

Fig. 14.22

If a heap is used purely for sorting, the heapsort algorithm turns out to be an $O(n \log n)$ algorithm, although it is only about half as efficient as quicksort or mergesort for randomly ordered initial lists. However, we may use the same technique to implement a priority queue. Rather than carry the sorting process through to the bitter end, we can extract the root node (which is the item with highest priority) and rearrange the tree as we did above so that the remaining nodes form a heap with one less element. We need not process the data any further until the next request comes in for an item from the priority queue, at which point we perform the second step in the heapsort, and so on. The heap guarantees that the item with highest priority is always ready and waiting, but makes no promises about the ordering of the remainder of the tree.

A heap is an efficient way of implementing a priority queue since the maximum number of nodes that need to be considered to restore the heap property when the root is extracted is about twice the depth of the tree. This is so because we need to examine the two children of a node in each layer in the tree to decide which number to promote to the next higher level. If we located the largest number in the list by straightforward comparisons, we would need to do $N - 1$ comparisons for a list of size $N$, as we saw when we studied selection sort in Chapter 10. A heap reduces the number of comparisons to around $2 \log N$, which is a significant improvement.

### 14.3.4 Heaps and heapsort in C++

We now show how the basic heap algorithms can be coded in C++. Although a heap is really a binary tree, we can't really make use of any of the tree code developed earlier, since a heap is implemented by representing the tree as an array, and not a linked structure using pointers. We therefore start from scratch with the heap class (in file heap.h):

```
#ifndef HEAP_H
#define HEAP_H
#include "mydefs.h"
#include <iostream.h>

template <class Type>
class heap {
protected:
  Type *Item;
  int HeapSize;
  virtual void Insert(Type NewItem, int start,
    int maxheap);
public:
  heap(int heapsize = 10);
  virtual ~heap();
  virtual void MakeHeap();
  virtual void Sort();
  friend istream& operator>>(istream& in,
    heap<Type>& InHeap);
  friend ostream& operator<<(ostream& out,
    const heap<Type>& OutHeap);
};
#endif
```

The template declares only a pointer to the array Item. The actual space for the array will be allocated by the constructor when an instance of a heap is defined. The Insert() function inserts an item into the heap of size maxheap, beginning at array element `start`. It is protected because it is only accessed by other class functions. We have not provided a public `Insert()` function for inserting a single element into the heap, but have left this as an exercise.

The public functions contain routines to create the initial heap (`MakeHeap()`), perform a heapsort (`Sort()`), and read in and print out the heap's array. The function definitions are in the file `heaptmp.h`:

```
#ifndef HEAPTMP_H
#define HEAPTMP_H
#include "heap.h"

template <class Type>
heap<Type>::heap(int heapsize) : HeapSize(heapsize),
  Item(new Type[heapsize+1]) {}

template <class Type>
heap<Type>::~heap()
{
  delete [] Item;
}

template <class Type>
void heap<Type>::MakeHeap()
{
  for (int i = HeapSize/2; i >= 1; i--)
    Insert(Item[i], i, HeapSize);
}

template <class Type>
void heap<Type>::Insert(Type NewItem, int start,
  int maxheap)
{
  int marker = 2*start;

  while(marker <= maxheap) {
    if (marker < maxheap &&
      Item[marker] < Item[marker+1])
      marker++;
    if (NewItem >= Item[marker])
      break;
    else {
      Item[start] = Item[marker];
      start = marker;
      marker = 2*start;
    }
  }
  Item[start] = NewItem;
}

template <class Type>
void heap<Type>::Sort()
```

```
{
   Type TempItem;
   int maxheap = HeapSize;

   while (maxheap > 0) {
      TempItem = Item[maxheap];
      Item[maxheap] = Item[1];
      Insert(TempItem, 1, --maxheap);
   }
}

template <class Type>
istream& operator>>(istream& in, heap<Type>& InHeap)
{
   cout << "Enter " << InHeap.HeapSize <<
      " heap elements:\n";
   for (int i = 1; i <= InHeap.HeapSize; i++) {
      cout << "Element " << i << ": ";
      in >> InHeap.Item[i];
   }
   InHeap.MakeHeap();
   return in;
}

template <class Type>
ostream& operator<<(ostream& out,
   const heap<Type>& OutHeap)
{
   for (int i = 1; i <= OutHeap.HeapSize; i++)
      out << OutHeap.Item[i] << ' ';
   return out;
}
#endif
```

Note that the array size is one greater than `HeapSize`, since we shall not be using element 0. The heap is stored in locations 1 through `HeapSize`.

In our example, the heap is read in using the overloaded `>>` operator, which calls `MakeHeap()` to construct the initial heap.

Since the first node we must consider when constructing the initial heap is the last non-leaf node in the tree, we can begin with the node `HeapSize/2` (using integer division). Recall that the two children of node $k$ occupy array locations $2k$ and $2k + 1$, so the first non-leaf node will be at location `HeapSize/2`. For each node from this point back to the root, we are using the insertion algorithm to place it in its proper place in the heap. Thus `MakeHeap()` simply calls `Insert()` for each of these nodes.

The `Insert()` function's arguments are:

- `NewItem`: the item to be inserted into the heap;
- `start`: the first node in the array into which `NewItem` will try to be placed;

- `maxheap`: the highest element in the array that can be used for storage.

The `Insert()` function follows the insertion algorithm above quite closely. If we are inserting `NewItem` beginning at location `start`, we must compare it to its two children, which are located at positions `2*start` and `2*start + 1`. We define `marker` as `2*start`, so that it points to the location of the left child of `start`. To see if `NewNode` is the largest, we first locate the larger of its two children, using the first `if` statement inside the `while` loop. This is done by assigning `marker` to point to the larger child, after first checking that the node has two children rather than just one.

With the larger child identified, we check to see if `NewItem` is larger than (or equal to) this child. If so, it is already in the correct place, so we break out of the `while` loop. If not, we move the larger child up to position `start`. We now redefine `start` to point to the position formerly occupied by the larger child, set `marker` to point to the left child of this new location, and continue the process until either `NewItem` is placed correctly, or we reach a leaf in the tree. When either of these two things happens, we have found the correct location at which `NewItem` should be inserted, so the final statement in `Insert()` performs this insertion.

The `Sort()` routine is elegantly simple, since it can make use of the `Insert()` routine to do most of the work. It follows the algorithm described above very closely. The item at position `maxheap` is stored in a temporary variable `TempHeap`, the item at position 1 (the root) is shifted to location `maxheap`, and `TempHeap` is reinserted into the tree starting at the root position, after decrementing `maxheap` by 1. The process continues until the heap is empty, and the list is sorted.

A sample `main()` routine which reads in some integers, constructs a heap, and then applies heapsort to sort the list, is in the file `heap.cpp`:

```cpp
#include "heaptmp.h"

int main()
{
  heap<int> TestHeap(15);

  cin >> TestHeap;
  cout << "Initial heap:\n" << TestHeap << endl;
  TestHeap.Sort();
  cout << "Sorted:\n" << TestHeap << endl;
  return 0;
}
```

# 14.4 B-trees

### 14.4.1 Multiway search trees

The trees that we have considered so far in this chapter have all been binary trees: each node can have no more than two children. Since the main factor in determining the efficiency of a tree is its depth, it is natural to ask if the efficiency can be improved by allowing nodes to have more than two children. It is fairly obvious that if we allow more than one item to be stored at each node of a tree, the depth of the tree will be less, but does this necessarily mean that fewer comparisons will be required to insert or locate an item in the tree?

Let us consider an extreme case where we allow, say, 127 items to be stored at each node in the tree. Then the second layer of the tree will contain up to 128 nodes, since a branch is possible on either side of any item in the root node. Then we can store 127 items in a tree of depth 1, $128 \times 127 + 127 = 16383$ items in a tree of depth 2, and so on. However, to locate an item in the root node will require searching a list of 127 objects. The number of comparisons required for this search depends on how the items are stored: if they are sorted as they are stored, we could use a binary search, but if they are stored in unsorted order, a sequential search is needed. The same process must be repeated at each layer in the tree.

In general, then, any attempt to increase the efficiency of a tree by allowing more data to be stored in each node is compromised by the extra work required to locate an item within the node. To be sure that we are getting any benefit out of a multiway search tree, we should do some calculations or simulations for typical data sets and compare the results with an ordinary binary tree.

All of this assumes that we are dealing with a program which runs entirely within main memory. That is, when the program is started, it and all the data on which it operates are loaded into RAM, and no disk accesses are required from that point on. In many large-scale databases, however, such as those maintained by governments or libraries, the amount of data being stored is so great that it would not be feasible to load all the data into RAM. These databases may contain hundreds or thousands of megabytes of data. In these cases, the data are stored on other media, such as hard or floppy disks, or magnetic tape. The access time for such media is many times slower than for dynamic memory, such as RAM chips.[15] Since disk accesses are so slow, we

---

[15] Anyone with a home computer whose only external storage is on floppy disk will verify this point. One way of speeding up access is to install a *ramdisk* on your home computer. A ramdisk is a section of your computer's RAM that is reserved for storing files in the same way as on a floppy disk, except that the memory is in a chip rather than on a plastic disk. If you have ever used a ramdisk, you will know how much faster they are.

would like some form of data storage that minimizes the number of times such accesses must be made.

A single disk access allows a certain amount of data, called a *block*, to be read into RAM. A typical block size is usually fairly large compared to the size of a single data item stored in the database. If the total amount of data is large enough that it cannot all be loaded into RAM at once, we therefore want a way of searching through the data on disk while satisfying two conditions:

- The amount of data read by each disk access should be close to the block size;
- The number of disk accesses should be minimized.

If we use a binary tree to store the data on disk, we must access each item of data separately since we do not know in which direction we should branch until we have compared the node's value with the item for which we are searching. This is inefficient in terms of disk accesses, since we are only reading in a tiny fraction of what we could read with a single disk access.

The main solution to this problem is to use a multiway search tree in which to store the data, where the maximum amount of data that can be stored at each node is close to (but does not exceed) the block size for a single disk read operation. We can then load a single node (containing many data items) into RAM and process this data entirely in RAM to determine if the item for which we are searching is present in that node, or, if not, in which direction we should branch for the next node to be searched. Although there will be some overhead in the sorting and searching operations required to insert and search for data within each node, all of these operations are done exclusively in RAM and are therefore much faster than accessing the hard disk or other external medium.

For example, if we store 127 items of data in a binary tree, we will require a tree of depth 7 (if the tree is perfectly balanced), so we may need as many as seven disk accesses to locate any given item. If we stored the same data in a balanced multiway tree which allowed up to, say, 15 items to be stored at each node, we would require a tree with a depth of only 2, requiring at most two disk accesses.

## 14.4.2 The B-tree: a balanced multiway search tree

It is customary to classify a multiway tree by the maximum number of *branches* at each node, rather than the maximum number of items which may be stored at each node. If we use a multiway search tree with $M$ possible branches at each node, then we can store up to $M - 1$ data items at each node. A binary tree is a special case of this: each node can have up to two children, and a single item is stored at each node.

Since multiway trees are used primarily in databases, the data that are stored are usually of a fairly complex type. For example, a typical database entry for personal data may contain the person's name, address, telephone number, some unique identification number, and various other details. It is usual to use one or two of the fields in this data structure as *keys* for searching purposes within the tree. If a personal data record contains an identification number as one of its fields, that may be used as the key by which the record is stored in a tree.

In each node of a multiway search tree, we may have up to $M - 1$ keys labelled $k_1, k_2, ..., k_{M-1}$, and $M$ branches $b_1, b_2, ..., b_M$. If we are searching for key $k_s$, then at each node we compare $k_s$ with each key in turn. If $k_s < k_1$, we follow branch $b_1$. If $k_s = k_1$, our search is over. If $k_1 < k_s < k_2$, we follow branch $b_2$, and so on.

To get the greatest efficiency gain out of a multiway search tree, we need to ensure that most of the nodes contain as much data as possible, and that the tree is as balanced as possible. There are several algorithms which approach this problem from various angles, but the most popular method is the *B-tree*. The definition of the B-tree data type is:

1. A B-tree is a multiway search tree with a maximum of $M$ branches at each node. The number $M$ is called the *order* of the tree.
2. There is a single root node which may have as few as two children, or none at all if the root is the only node in the tree.
3. At all nodes, except the root and leaf nodes, there must be at least half the maximum number of children.
4. All leaves are on the same level.

A B-tree is shown in Fig. 14.23. This B-tree is of order 5, which means that up to five branches (and therefore four data items) may occur in each node. Each node other than the root must contain at least $5/2 = 2$ (using integer division) data items, and all leaves must occur on the same level. It can be seen that this tree satisfies these conditions.

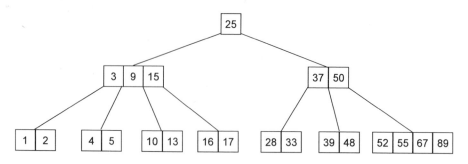

Fig. 14.23. A B-tree.

As an example of how a B-tree (or any multiway tree) is searched for an item, let us search this tree for the item 13. We begin at the root, and compare the target (13) with the root's value (25). Since 13 < 25, we branch to the left, and arrive at the node with elements 3, 9, and 15. Depending on how these items have been stored in the node, we must use an appropriate searching technique to locate the branch between 9 and 15, since our target lies between these two numbers. Having found this branch, we follow it to the node containing values 10 and 13, where another search locates the target.

Had we searched for a key that was not present in the tree, for example the key 12, we would follow the same steps as above until we reached a leaf. A search in this leaf would not locate the target, but would find the branch between the two data values where the target would lie. This branch would be represented by a zero pointer, indicating that the key is not in the tree.

For the purposes of calculating the efficiency of a B-tree, we usually count only the number of nodes visited in a search, and not the number of individual comparisons within each node. This is because B-trees are used primarily in those situations where reading a node requires a disk access, which is much slower than the in-RAM calculations that are required to locate a particular branch or data item within a node.

We can divide up the efficiency calculations into the number of node accesses required for successful and unsuccessful searches, just as we did with the searching algorithms in Chapter 11. For the B-tree shown above, the average number of node accesses required for a successful outcome is $(1 \times 1 + 5 \times 2 + 16 \times 3) \div 22 = 2.68$, since there is one data item on level 1, five items on level 2 and 16 on level 3. Since all leaves in a B-tree are on the same level, the number of node accesses required for any unsuccessful search is always just the depth of the tree, in this case, three.

### 14.4.3 Constructing a B-tree

The insertion method for a B-tree is somewhat different to that for the other trees we have studied, since the condition that all leaves be on the same level forces insertion into the upper part of the tree. It is easiest to learn the insertion procedure by example, so we will construct an order-5 B-tree from the list of integers:

    1 7 6 2 11 4 8 13 10 5 19 9 18 24 3 12 14 20 21 16

Since each node can have up to five branches, each node can store up to four keys. The first four keys can therefore be placed in the root, in sorted order, as shown:

| 1 | 2 | 6 | 7 |
|---|---|---|---|

The fifth key, 11, will require the creation of a new node, since the root is full. From your experience with binary trees, you might think that the procedure would be to compare the new key with those already present in the root, discover that $11 > 7 = k_4$, so we should insert a new node as branch $b_5$ from the root. However, we cannot do this, since it violates one of the conditions on a B-tree: the root is not allowed to have only a single child.

Instead, we split the root at its midpoint and create *two* new nodes, leaving only the middle key in the root. This gives the tree shown:

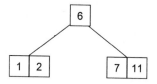

We can now add the next three keys without having to create any more nodes:

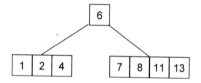

When we wish to add key 10, though, it would fit into the right child of the root, but this node is full. We therefore split this node, putting the middle key into the node's parent (which happens to be the root), giving the tree shown:

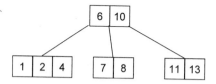

We can now insert the next four keys without any problems:

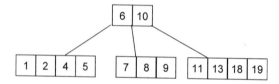

Inserting the key 24 causes another split and increases the number of keys in the root to three:

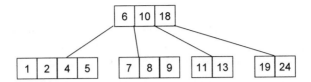

We can insert the next five keys with another split, resulting in the root being full:

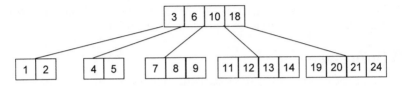

Insertion of the final key, 16, causes the fourth leaf from the left to split, and pushes its middle key, 13, upwards. However, the parent node is also full, so it must split as well, following the same rules. This results in a new root node, and increases the height of the tree to three levels. The completed B-tree is shown in Fig. 14.24.

The algorithm for insertion into a B-tree can be summarized as follows.

1. Find the node into which the new key should be inserted by searching the tree.
2. If the node is not full, insert the key into the node, using an appropriate sorting algorithm.
3. If the node is full, split the node into two and push the middle key upwards into the parent. If the parent is also full, follow the same procedure (splitting and pushing upwards) until either some space is found in a previously existing node, or a new root node is created.

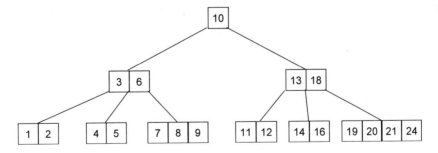

Fig. 14.24. The completed B-tree.

Although the algorithm for insertion may look straightforward on paper, it contains quite a few subtleties which only come out when you try to program it. A program implementing this insertion routine is a non-trivial affair, and could be used as the basis for a programming project. Because B-trees are used primarily when writing databases for handling very large amounts of data, we will not present any stand-alone C++ code for implementing them. For most smaller-scale applications where all the data fits into RAM when the program is running, some form of binary tree is usually adequate from the point of view of efficiency.

As with the AVL tree, the algorithm for deleting a node from a B-tree while preserving the B-tree properties is fairly complex. If deletions are expected to be infrequent, lazy deletion is probably the best option.

## 14.5 Summary

We have introduced the *tree* data structure in this chapter. A tree has a single *root* node. Each node may have one or more branches to other nodes in the tree. A node at the end of a branch is called a *child* of the node at the beginning of the branch. A node with no children is called a *leaf*. The maximum number of branches emanating from any one node is called the *order* of the tree. The most common form of tree is the *binary tree* (a tree of order 2).

We considered algorithms for inserting nodes into a binary tree in such a way that when the nodes of the tree are *traversed* in *inorder* fashion (the left subtree is traversed, followed by the root node, and then the right subtree, and so on recursively), the nodes will be listed in sorted order. These routines were then coded in C++. A routine for deleting items from a binary tree was considered.

Since the efficiency of a binary tree improves if the tree is *balanced* (the left and right subtrees of any node are roughly the same height), we studied the AVL algorithm for constructing a binary tree by balancing the tree, if necessary, after each node is added. The AVL algorithm requires that a few nodes in the tree be rearranged using either a single or double rotation, if the tree loses its balance after an insertion. C++ code was given for inserting nodes into a tree using the AVL algorithm.

We then considered the *heap*. A heap is a binary tree which is stored as an array, rather than as a linked structure. The nodes in a heap are arranged so that the largest element is always at the root. The main use of a heap is as a *priority queue*, that is, a queue in which items are processed in order of priority rather than strictly in the order in which they were added to the queue. Algorithms for constructing a heap from randomly ordered data and for extracting the root element and rearranging the remaining nodes to retain the heap property are given and coded in C++.

Finally, we considered the B-tree, which is a *multiway* search tree. Each node in a B-tree of order $N$ may have up to $N$ branches and store up to $N - 1$ data items. Although the depth of a B-tree is much less than that of a binary tree storing the same data, the fact that several data items are stored at each node means that extra work is required to store and find a data item at each node. However, the main use of B-trees is in large database systems where the entire data set is too large to store in RAM. Blocks of data are read from the hard disk and then searched in RAM. Since a disk access is much slower than processing in RAM, a B-tree is used to minimize the number of disk accesses. The algorithm for constructing a B-tree is given but no C++ code is given since B-trees are not often used in small or medium sized programs.

Most of the programming techniques used in this chapter should be familiar from earlier chapters. However, as discussed in the first section of this chapter, it is difficult to construct a proper object oriented representation of a binary tree in C++. Several solutions are possible, but none of them is ideal. This would seem to indicate a deficiency in the language.

## 14.6 Exercises

1. a. Insert the following numbers, in the order given, into an ordinary binary tree:

342 206 444 523 607 301 142 183 102 157 149

b. For the tree constructed in part (a), calculate the average number of nodes visited for (i) a successful search; (ii) an unsuccessful search of this tree.

2. a. Design a computer experiment to calculate the average number of comparisons required for successful and unsuccessful searches of a binary tree for tree sizes from 10 to 1000 nodes. Generate the binary trees by using a pseudo-random number generator.

b. Extend your experiment to calculate the average number of comparisons and assignments to sort a list of data by inserting them into a binary tree and then traversing the tree.

c. Compare the results from parts (a) and (b) with those for other sorting and searching methods.

3. Write a *non-recursive* C++ function which inserts a new node into an ordinary binary tree.

4. a. Insert the following numbers, in the order given, into an AVL tree:

342 206 444 523 607 301 142 183 102 157 149

b. For the tree constructed in part (a), calculate the average number of nodes visited for (i) a successful search; (ii) an unsuccessful search of this tree. Compare your answers with those for the ordinary binary tree in question 1.

5. Repeat question 2 for AVL trees. Compare the results of questions 2 and 5.

6. Write a `DeleteNode()` function for an AVL tree using the lazy deletion method suggested in the text. That is, use the special `RefValue` to label a node as a deleted node without actually removing it from the tree. Alter the other AVL tree functions, as necessary, to deal with deleted nodes.

7. a. Insert the following numbers into an array:

```
342 206 444 523 607 301 142 183 102 157 149
```

Apply the algorithm in the text to convert this array into a heap.

b. Use the heapsort algorithm to sort this array. Count the number of comparisons and assignments required by the algorithm for this list of numbers.

8. Design a computer experiment to measure the efficiency of heapsort. Generate pseudo-random lists of integers of lengths from 10 to 1000 and calculate the numbers of assignments and comparisons required to sort them. Compare your results with other sorting methods.

9. Write a C++ function which may be used as a `RemoveItem()` function in a priority queue. The function should extract and return the root node from a heap and rearrange the remaining nodes so that the heap structure is restored.

10. Write a C++ function which adds a single node to an already-constructed heap, provided that there is enough space in the array.

11. a. Insert the following numbers into a B-tree of (i) order 3; (ii) order 5:

```
659 767 702 157 728 102 461 899 920 44 774 264 384 344
973 905 999
```

b. Calculate the average number of (i) node accesses; (ii) comparisons within nodes for a successful and unsuccessful search of these B-trees.

c. Insert the same list of numbers into an ordinary binary tree, calculate the quantities in part (b) for this tree, and compare the results with the values for the two B-trees.

CHAPTER 15

# Graphs

## 15.1 Definitions

The graphs we shall study in this chapter are not the type where a curve is drawn on a pair of axes. The term *graph* as used here has an entirely different meaning, though these kinds of graphs also comprise a branch of mathematics.

A graph is a generalization of a tree, in the sense that it consists of nodes connected together by line segments, but many of the restrictions imposed on the construction of a tree are removed when building a graph. To talk clearly about graphs, we need to introduce a bit of notation.

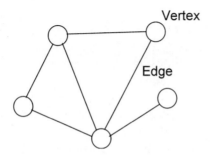

Fig. 15.1. Connected, undirected graph.

A graph (see Fig. 15.1) is a collection of nodes, each of which is called a *vertex* (plural: *vertices*), which may be connected in pairs by line segments called *edges*. The edges in a graph may be of two types, though usually the edges in any one graph will be all of one type. Graphs in which the edges have no specific direction are called *undirected* (Fig. 15.1), while graphs in which each edge has a direction are called *directed* (Fig. 15.2). Directed graphs are sometimes called *digraphs* for short.

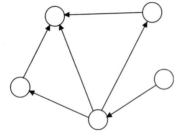

Fig. 15.2. A connected, directed graph.

A graph where there is a path along the edges between any two vertices is said to be *connected* (Figs 15.1 and 15.2). A graph where this is not true is *unconnected* (Fig. 15.3).

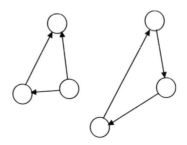

Fig. 15.3. An unconnected digraph.

Like trees, graphs may be used as diagrams that illustrate the relationship between pairs of elements in a set of objects. You may have seen maps of a country in which airline routes are shown as lines connecting pairs of cities, for example. If each line indicates that scheduled flights connect the two cities at either end in both directions, such a map may be represented as an undirected graph, with the cities as the vertices and the lines connecting them as the edges.

A street map of a city may also be represented as a graph, with the road junctions as vertices and the roads themselves as the edges. If the city contains one-way streets, the graph needs to be a digraph, since some edges permit traffic flow in only one direction. A two-way street connecting two junctions A and B would be represented on a digraph by two edges: one from A to B and one from B to A.

Typical problems which graphs can help us solve are those concerned with finding the shortest or most economical route between two vertices, or the smallest set of edges which connect all the vertices in a graph.

There are a great many graph algorithms: far too many for us to study them all in this book. We shall therefore restrict ourselves to describing how graphs can be implemented in a computer and describing a few of the more common graph algorithms.

## 15.2 Implementing graphs on a computer

In order to define a graph, we need a list of its vertices and another list of its edges. In computer languages such as Pascal, in which an explicit representation of sets is supported, a graph may be represented as two sets: one of vertices and one of edges. Most languages do not support sets directly, however, so we must consider how to implement graphs in such languages.

In C++, we have two options. First, we could use the set class that we defined in Chapter 9 but we will see that we do not need it to implement graphs.

The other option is to use more conventional data structures such as arrays and linked lists to implement graphs, which is what we will do here. There are various ways this might be done.

The first possibility is to use a two-dimensional square array. The dimension of the array is the largest number of vertices we allow our graph to have. We shall number the vertices from 0 upwards, to be consistent with the array indexing convention in C++. In the simplest implementation of a graph, the array contains Boolean elements. In a graph represented by an array named graph, the element graph[i][j] is then TRUE if vertex $i$ is connected to vertex $j$ by an edge and FALSE if it is not. An undirected graph is represented by a symmetric array, meaning that the values of graph[i][j] and graph[j][i] are always equal, since in an undirected graph, two vertices are either connected or they are not, regardless of the order in which they are listed. A digraph need not be symmetric, since it is possible for vertex $i$ to be connected to $j$ without $j$ being connected to $i$.

A purely array-based representation of a graph is called an *adjacency table*. It is a list of which vertices are connected to which other vertices. The number of vertices in the graph is given by the dimensions of the array. An adjacency table is a clear representation that allows random access to the information for any vertex. However, for *sparse* graphs, that is, graphs where there may be many vertices but few edges connecting them, it can be wasteful of space, since most of the entries in the table will be FALSE. In such cases, it may be useful to bring in a representation based either wholly or partially on linked lists.

A representation based entirely on linked lists is called an *adjacency list*. First, a linked list of all the vertices is constructed (Fig. 15.4). Each of these vertices has a pointer which points to a list of edges originating at that vertex. Since each edge connects a vertex with another vertex, each node in the list also points back to a node in the vertex list corresponding to the other end of the edge. Such a linked representation of a graph is efficient from a space-saving point of view, but as you can see from Fig. 15.4, the representation can produce a complex tangle of pointers. All of this is not really a problem provided that the graph has been constructed properly, but debugging such a tangle of links can be extremely difficult. In addition, many graph algorithms require random access to the set of vertices, and this purely linked version requires a traversal of the vertex list to find any single vertex and its associated edges.

Another solution to the implementation problem is to combine arrays and linked lists, in a fashion similar to that used in the chaining method of resolving collisions in a hash table (see Chapter 13). Here, we define a one-dimensional array in which each element corresponds to a vertex (Fig. 15.5). Each of these elements contains a pointer to a list of edges which originate at that vertex. Such an arrangement still allows us to trace a path through the graph since each entry in the list of edges contains the index number of the vertex which corresponds to the other end of the edge. We can then jump to the corresponding array element and search the list of edges originating from there to continue our traversal of that path.

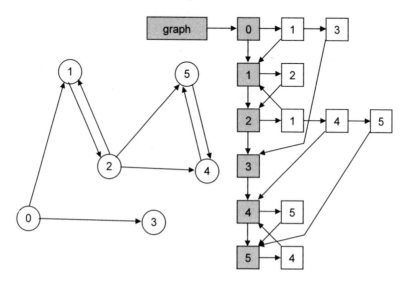

Fig. 15.4. A digraph represented as an adjacency list. The main list of vertices is shaded.

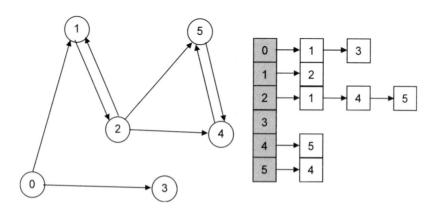

Fig. 15.5. A combined array-linked list representation of a graph. An array of pointers (shaded) represents the vertices in the graph.

# 15.3 Graph traversal

Just as with trees, many graph algorithms require us to visit all the vertices in the graph. With a tree, however, there is one special root node from which our algorithms start. In most graph algorithms, the nodes are all 'created equal', so the starting point is left up to us. There are two commonly used methods of traversing a graph: *depth-first traversal* or DFT, and *breadth-first traversal* or BFT.

## 15.3.1 Depth-first traversal

The traversal algorithms in this chapter are easier to understand (and to work through on paper) if we first construct an *edge table* for the graph. An edge table is built by listing all the vertices of the graph in a vertical column. Next to each entry in the column we list all vertices to which that entry is connected directly (that is, by a single edge). For example, consider the undirected graph in Fig. 15.6.

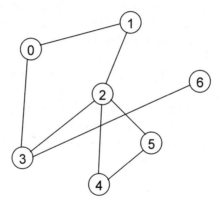

Fig. 15.6. An undirected graph.

The edge table for this graph is shown in Fig. 15.7.

| 0 | 1 | 3 | | |
|---|---|---|---|---|
| 1 | 0 | 2 | | |
| 2 | 1 | 3 | 4 | 5 |
| 3 | 0 | 2 | 6 | |
| 4 | 2 | 5 | | |
| 5 | 2 | 4 | | |
| 6 | 3 | | | |

Fig. 15.7. The edge table for the graph shown in Fig. 15.6.

The order in which the connections are listed in the edge table isn't really important, but it is conventional to list them in ascending order for each vertex. Since graph vertices need not be labelled with numbers, however, the meaning of 'ascending order' may have to be redefined for other graphs.

The graph in the figure is an undirected graph, so we list all vertices that are connected to each vertex by any edge. In a directed graph, we would list only those vertices that have a directed edge from the starting vertex pointing to them.

To do a depth-first traversal of this graph, we first choose a starting vertex. Again, the choice of vertex may depend on the context of the problem. We start with vertex 0 here.

The idea of a depth-first traversal is to follow the chain of edges as far as we can into the graph before we backtrack to pick up other vertices. As we visit each vertex, we cross it off everywhere it appears in the edge table. Since we are starting with vertex 0, we cross it off everywhere it appears (which is in the rows corresponding to vertices 1 and 3). We now begin the traversal. For this graph, starting at vertex 0, we move to vertex 1 since it is the first vertex listed as one of those to which vertex 0 is connected. We cross off vertex 1 everywhere it appears in the table. We now look at the row in the edge table corresponding to vertex 1, ignoring for the moment the fact that vertex 0 is also connected to vertex 3. We see that vertex 1 is connected to vertices 0 and 2. However, vertex 0 has already been visited and is crossed off, so we move along to vertex 2. The depth-first traversal has so far visited vertices in the order $0 \rightarrow 1 \rightarrow 2$ (it is important to keep track of the order in which the vertices are visited, since we may need to backtrack later on), and the edge table is as shown in Fig. 15.8.

| | | | | |
|---|---|---|---|---|
| *0* | *1* | 3 | | |
| *1* | *0* | *2* | | |
| *2* | *1* | 3 | 4 | 5 |
| 3 | *0* | *2* | 6 | |
| 4 | *2* | 5 | | |
| 5 | *2* | 4 | | |
| 6 | 3 | | | |

Fig. 15.8. The edge table after vertices 0, 1, and 2 have been visited. Visited vertices are shown in **bold italic**.

To continue, we examine the row corresponding to vertex 2. The first unvisited vertex in this row is vertex 3, so we add that to our traversal, cross it off everywhere it appears in the table, and go to the row corresponding to vertex 3. This leads us to vertex 6. We have visited vertices $0 \rightarrow 1 \rightarrow 2 \rightarrow 3 \rightarrow$

6, the traversal so far is 0 1 2 3 6, and the state of the edge table is as shown in Fig. 15.9.

$$
\begin{array}{c|cccc}
0 & 1 & 3 \\
1 & 0 & 2 \\
2 & 1 & 3 & 4 & 5 \\
3 & 0 & 2 & 6 \\
4 & 2 & 5 \\
5 & 2 & 4 \\
6 & 3 \\
\end{array}
$$

Fig. 15.9. The edge table after vertices 0, 1, 2, 3, and 6 have been visited.

If we visit the row corresponding to vertex 6, we see that there are no unvisited vertices listed. We therefore must backtrack until we find the last row already examined that has an unvisited vertex listed on it. Recall that the order in which we have traversed the table so far is: $0 \rightarrow 1 \rightarrow 2 \rightarrow 3 \rightarrow 6$. We backtrack by going backwards one vertex at a time in this list until we come to a vertex that has some untraversed edges arising from it. Backing up from vertex 6 to vertex 3, we see from the edge table that all its vertices have been visited, so we back up one more step to vertex 2. Here the first unvisited vertex is 4, so we add that to our traversal, and visit row 4, where we find that the only remaining unvisited vertex, 5, is listed. We add that to our traversal, which completes the exercise. The final traversal is then 0 1 2 3 6 4 5. Had we encountered a dead end again, we would have repeated the backtracking procedure.

Note that depth-first traversals of a graph are not unique. If we had listed the vertices in each row of the edge table in a different order, we would get a different traversal. You should try this yourself: change the order of the rows in the table, or use a different starting vertex, or change the orders of the vertices within each row.

This algorithm (using an edge table) also takes account of disconnected graphs. If at any point we run out of vertices to add to the traversal, and there are still rows in the edge table that have not yet been visited, we move to the next unvisited row in the table and start again. For example, suppose we add some rows to the edge table above to get the result shown in Fig. 15.10. (You should draw the graph corresponding to this edge table.)

After starting at vertex 0 and applying the above algorithm for a depth-first traversal, we obtain the same sequence (0 1 2 3 6 4 5) as before, and the edge table looks like Fig. 15.11.

The three extra vertices (7, 8, 9) form a disconnected subgraph. We therefore continue our traversal by moving down to row 7 and applying the algorithm again to yield the final traversal 0 1 2 3 6 4 5 7 9 8.

| 0 | 1 | 3 | | |
|---|---|---|---|---|
| 1 | 0 | 2 | | |
| 2 | 1 | 3 | 4 | 5 |
| 3 | 0 | 2 | 6 | |
| 4 | 2 | 5 | | |
| 5 | 2 | 4 | | |
| 6 | 3 | | | |
| 7 | 9 | | | |
| 8 | 9 | | | |
| 9 | 7 | 8 | | |

Fig. 15.10. The edge table for the graph in Fig. 15.6 with added vertices.

Looking forward to our C++ implementation of DFT, we note that the algorithm is recursive. As each node is visited, it is recorded in the traversal, and the same algorithm is called for the first unvisited vertex arising from that point. If a dead end is reached, backtracking is done automatically as the recursive calls return in the reverse order to that in which they were invoked, until a vertex with an unvisited edge is found.

| *0* | *1* | *3* | | |
|---|---|---|---|---|
| *1* | *0* | *2* | | |
| *2* | *1* | *3* | *4* | *5* |
| *3* | *0* | *2* | *6* | |
| *4* | *2* | *5* | | |
| *5* | *2* | *4* | | |
| *6* | *3* | | | |
| 7 | 9 | | | |
| 8 | 9 | | | |
| 9 | 7 | 8 | | |

Fig. 15.11. The edge table after traversing vertices 0 through 6.

### 15.3.2 Breadth-first traversal

Breadth-first traversal, or BFT, can be implemented on paper using an edge table in a similar way to depth-first traversal. The idea here is to list *all* vertices connected to each vertex before moving on in the edge table. Consider the same edge table as before (Fig. 15.7).

We begin, as before, with vertex 0. Also, as before, we cross off each vertex as it is added to the traversal. However, this time we add *all* the vertices in each row visited to the traversal. The easiest way to handle this is to use a queue. Each time we add a vertex to the traversal, we add to the queue all unvisited vertices listed in the row corresponding to the added vertex. We then add the vertex at the head of the queue to the traversal, and add any unvisited vertices in *its* row to the tail of the queue. We continue until all vertices in the graph have been added to the traversal, at which point the queue should be empty.

Adding vertex 0 to the traversal, we add vertices 1 and 3 to the queue. Vertex 1 is at the head of the queue, so it is the next vertex to be added to the traversal. Looking at row 1 in the edge table, we see that the only unvisited vertex in that row is vertex 2, so it is added to the queue. The vertex at the head of the queue is now vertex 3, so it is added to the traversal, and the only unvisited vertex in row 3 of the table is added to the queue. At this point, the traversal contains vertices 0 1 3, and the queue contains the vertices 2 and 6. The edge table is now as shown in Fig. 15.12.

$$
\begin{array}{c|cccc}
0 & 1 & 3 \\
1 & 0 & 2 \\
2 & 1 & 3 & 4 & 5 \\
3 & 0 & 2 & 6 \\
4 & 2 & 5 \\
5 & 2 & 4 \\
6 & 3
\end{array}
$$

Fig. 15.12.

Note that vertices are crossed off when they are added to the queue *or* to the traversal. We now continue by removing vertex 2 from the queue and adding it to the traversal, which now contains 0 1 3 2. The vertices 4 and 5 which are present in row 2 of the edge table are added to the queue, so that the queue now contains the vertices 6 4 5. All vertices have now been crossed off in the edge table, so the remainder of the traversal simply removes the items from the queue in order, and adds them to the traversal, giving the final traversal 0 1 3 2 6 4 5.

As with the depth-first traversal, disconnected portions of the graph are handled by starting the algorithm again at the first untouched row in the edge table. With the same extension to the graph as given above, the extra three vertices would be added in the order 7 9 8 to the traversal.

## 15.4 Topological sorting

As an example of the two forms of graph traversal, we shall consider a *topological sorting* or *topological ordering* of the vertices in a digraph. In any digraph without cycles (a *cycle* is a path in the graph where you may start at one vertex and return to that vertex by following the edges in the graph), it is possible to list the vertices so that, as we progress from left to right through the list, we travel only in the direction of the edges connecting the vertices, never against the direction. For example, for the digraph shown in Fig. 15.13, one possible topological ordering is 9 6 3 4 8 2 0 5 1 7. For most digraphs, several different orderings are possible.

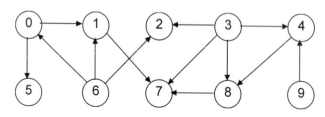

Fig. 15.13.

Various applications of topological orderings exist. For example, the courses in a university degree programme must usually be taken in some definite order, with some courses requiring other courses as prerequisites. We could draw a graph in which each vertex is a course and each directed edge indicates that the course at the starting end of the edge is a prerequisite for the course at the finishing end. A topological ordering of this graph would show a possible order in which the courses could be taken.

A computer program can also be represented as a directed graph, in which each vertex is a function call. If the program contains no recursive or mutually recursive calls (cases where function A calls function B which in turn calls function A, creating a cycle), we can connect the vertices by directed edges showing which functions are called by which other functions. A topological ordering of this graph would then show one possible order in which the functions could be declared in a program so that each function is declared before it is called by another function.

The algorithms for topological sorting can be worked out on paper using edge tables, just as depth- and breadth-first traversals.

### 15.4.1 Depth-first topological sort

Consider the directed graph shown above. Its edge table is shown in Fig. 15.14. The depth-first topological sort is a recursive procedure, similar to the depth-first traversal described earlier. The procedure here, however, works in the opposite direction to the DFT we studied earlier. The idea behind a depth-first topological ordering is to find those vertices that have no successors *first*, so that we build up the traversal from right to left, rather than the more usual left to right. We can use the same recursive procedure, except that we record a vertex in the topological ordering when the recursive call *returns*, and not when it is first called.

```
0 | 1  5
1 | 7
2 |
3 | 2  4  7  8
4 | 8
5 |
6 | 0  1  2
7 |
8 | 7
9 | 4
```

Fig. 15.14.

We begin with vertex 0, and using the depth-first algorithm, locate a vertex that has no successors. Following the chain of directed edges, we go from 0 to 1 to 7. Vertex 7 has no successors, since there are no vertices listed in row 7 of the edge table. We therefore write vertex 7 down at the *right* side of the topological sort. Note that we cross off vertices *when they are visited*, and *not* when they are added to the traversal, in order to avoid visiting a vertex more than once. As with the DFT, it is important to remember the order in which the vertices have been visited: so far we have $0 \rightarrow 1 \rightarrow 7$. The edge table at this point is shown in Fig. 15.15.

```
0 | 1  5
1 | 7
2 |
3 | 2  4  7  8
4 | 8
5 |
6 | 0  1  2
7 |
8 | 7
9 | 4
```

Fig. 15.15.

We now back up one stage to vertex 1. Vertex 1 now has no unvisited successors, since vertex 7 is crossed off. We may therefore write down vertex 1 to the left of 7. Backing up one more step, we encounter vertex 0 again. It has one other unvisited successor, namely vertex 5, so we must trace this path until we encounter a vertex with no successor. Vertex 5 itself is an endpoint in the traversal, so we can write it down to the left of vertex 1 in the traversal. Since vertex 0 now has no unvisited successors, we write it down next. At this point, the topological sort contains the vertices 0 5 1 7, and the edge table looks like Fig. 15.16.

| | | | | |
|---|---|---|---|---|
| **0** | **1** | **5** | | |
| **1** | **7** | | | |
| 2 | | | | |
| 3 | 2 | 4 | **7** | 8 |
| 4 | 8 | | | |
| **5** | | | | |
| 6 | **0** | **1** | 2 | |
| **7** | | | | |
| 8 | **7** | | | |
| 9 | 4 | | | |

Fig. 15.16.

Since we have returned to the top level in the recursion, and there are no more vertices left to process in row 0 of the edge table, we proceed to the next unvisited row, which is row 2. Vertex 2 is itself an endpoint without successors, so we can add it directly to the traversal and cross it off. The next unvisited row is row 3. We do a depth-first trace starting from vertex 3, which leads us through vertices 4 and 8. Vertex 8 is now a dead end, since vertex 7 has already been included in the traversal. We may therefore add vertex 8 to the left of vertex 2. Backing up to vertex 4, we see it has no further successors, so we can add vertex 4 to the left of 8. Backing up one more stage we arrive back at vertex 3 again, which now has no further successors, since vertex 8 has been used. We now add vertex 3 to the left of vertex 4. The topological sort at this stage looks like this: 3 4 8 2 0 5 1 7. There are still two unvisited rows in the edge table: rows 6 and 9. Neither row has any successors remaining, so we may add these two rows in either order to complete the topological sort: 9 6 3 4 8 2 0 5 1 7.

### 15.4.2 Breadth-first topological sort

The breadth-first topological sort is similar to the breadth-first traversal discussed earlier, but we must include an additional check to ensure that topological order is preserved. Rather than search for vertices without successors, as in the depth-first sort, we search for vertices without predecessors.

When we construct the edge table, we add an extra column to the left in which we note down the number of immediate predecessors each vertex has (that is, the number of incoming edges). For the same graph as before, we obtain the table shown in Fig. 15.17.

| 1 | 0 | 1 | 5 | | |
|---|---|---|---|---|---|
| 2 | 1 | 7 | | | |
| 2 | 2 | | | | |
| 0 | 3 | 2 | 4 | 7 | 8 |
| 2 | 4 | 8 | | | |
| 1 | 5 | | | | |
| 0 | 6 | 0 | 1 | 2 | |
| 3 | 7 | | | | |
| 2 | 8 | 7 | | | |
| 0 | 9 | 4 | | | |

Fig. 15.17. An edge table with an added column on the left showing the number of predecessors for each vertex.

We search for all rows in which the corresponding vertex has no predecessors, and begin a queue by adding these vertices to the queue. In this case, the queue begins with vertices 3 6 9.

The main part of the algorithm now begins. We remove the vertex at the head of the queue, add it to the topological sort, and adjust the predecessor count of all vertices of which this vertex was a predecessor. When vertex 3 is removed from the queue and added to the topological sort, we observe from row 3 in the edge table that vertex 3 is a predecessor of vertices 2, 4, 7, and 8, so we decrement the predecessor counts of these four vertices. Any vertices whose predecessor count is reduced to zero by this decrement are added to the queue. In the case of vertex 3, all its successor vertices had two or more predecessors, so no new vertices are added to the queue at this stage.

We now remove the next vertex from the queue and repeat the procedure. Removing 6 and adding it to the traversal requires us to decrement the predecessor counts of vertices 0, 1 and 2. This reduces the predecessor counts of vertices 0 and 2 to zero, so they are added to the queue. The traversal at this point contains the vertices 3 6, and the queue contains vertices 9 0 2. Removing 9 from the queue and adding it to the traversal reduces the predecessor count of vertex 4 to 0, so it is added to the queue. The process continues until the queue is empty. In this case, the topological ordering produces the list 3 6 9 0 2 4 1 5 8 7.

Note that it is not necessary to cross off any vertices in the edge table since the sole determining factor as to when a vertex is added to the queue is when its predecessor count is reduced to zero. This algorithm works equally well for connected or disconnected graphs.

# 15.5 C++ code for graph traversal

## 15.5.1 Iterators

Before we present C++ code to implement some of the graph algorithms described so far, we need to consider one final programming technique. We have dealt in this book with several data structures, such as sets and linked lists, that contain a collection of data items. Often such data types are used as fields in other classes. In some cases, these other classes use algorithms that require us to loop through the data items in a set or a linked list, and use each item in some way. If we have followed proper object oriented design techniques when we wrote the set and linked list classes, however, the actual data fields themselves will be private or protected fields, and therefore not accessible to the functions of that class which has included, say, a set or a linked list object as one of its fields.

An example may make this a bit clearer. Suppose that we are writing a database class which contains, as one of its fields, a linked list of 'person' objects, where each person object contains such information as the name, address and phone number of some person. The data fields of the person object should be private fields within the class of which the person object is an instance, and as such, are not directly accessible to any functions within the database class. Therefore, if we tried to write a database class function which loops through the elements in the linked list (to print out a list of mailing labels, for instance), the compiler will complain about an attempt to access the private fields of another class.

One solution to this problem might be to add some functions to the linked list class (using inheritance) which allow an external class to step through the list one item at a time. For example, we might define a function `Start()` which returns the first item in the list, a function `Next()` which returns the next item in the list, and a Boolean function `End()` which returns TRUE if we are at the end of the list. The new derived list class would also need a marker field so that it could keep track of where it was in the list. The database functions can then make use of these list functions to access the elements of the list in a loop.

This solution works well enough, provided that we don't try nesting two or more loops. Since there is only one marker field defined in the derived list class, if we try writing a nested loop where both the outer and inner loops cover the *same* list, the marker will get confused between the two layers of the loop. For example, if we wanted to write a database function which searched the list to see if any two entries contained the same address, we need to write a nested loop where the outer loop steps through the list one item at a time and the inner loop traverses the *same* list, comparing the address of each item with the current item from the outer loop. If we are using the special list functions to step through the loop, we would need two different markers to keep track of where we were in the two layers of the nested loop.

The generally accepted solution to this problem is to provide what is called an *iterator* class for the linked list. The iterator class contains functions such as `Start()`, `Next()`, and so on, as well as a marker to keep track of the location in the list. The iterator class is made a friend of the original list class. A *separate* iterator object is defined for each iteration over the list. In the nested loop example, we would define one iterator for the outer loop, and a different iterator for the inner loop. Since we are using separate iterator objects for the two levels of the loop, two separate markers are used for keeping track of the locations in each loop, so there is no confusion.

As an example of how an iterator could be defined and used, we present an iterator for a linked list. First, we define a derived class based on the list template we used in Chapter 10. Then, we define the list iterator. These are defined in the file `listiter.h`.

```
#ifndef LISTITER_H
#define LISTITER_H
#include "lists.h"

template <class Type>
class ListIterator;

template <class Type>
class linklist : public list<Type>
{
public:
  linklist() : list<Type>() {}
  linklist(Type defaultval) : list<Type>(defaultval) {}
  friend ListIterator<Type>;
};

template <class Type>
class ListIterator
{
private:
  linklist<Type> *LocalList;
  list<Type>::ListNode *CurrentNode;
public:
  ListIterator(linklist<Type> &List);
  Type Next();
  BOOL End();
};
#endif
```

Since the `ListIterator` class is to be made a friend of the `linklist` class, we must declare it before the `linklist` class is defined. The `linklist` class itself is derived from the list class that we introduced in Chapter 10. Other than defining a couple of constructors which simply call the original list constructors, the only addition we have made is to declare the ListIterator class as a friend.

The ListIterator class has two private data fields. LocalList is a pointer to the linked list over which the iterator will iterate. The other field, CurrentNode, is the marker that keeps track of where the iterator is within the list. Besides the constructor, there are only two functions in ListIterator: Next(), which returns the value of the next node after CurrentNode (if any), and End(), which is TRUE if we are at the end of the list.

The function definitions are in the file itertemp.h:

```
#ifndef ITERTEMP_H
#define ITERTEMP_H
#include "listiter.h"
#include "listtemp.h"

template <class Type>
ListIterator<Type>::
  ListIterator(linklist<Type> &List) :
  LocalList(&List), CurrentNode(List.Head)
{ }

template <class Type>
Type ListIterator<Type>::Next()
{
  if (!End())
    CurrentNode = CurrentNode->Next;
  return End() ? LocalList->DefaultVal :
    CurrentNode->Element;
}

template <class Type>
BOOL ListIterator<Type>::End()
{
  return CurrentNode ? FALSE : TRUE;
}
#endif
```

The constructor expects the name of a linklist object, and assigns LocalList as a pointer to this object. The marker CurrentNode is set to the head node of the list.

The Next() function tests to see if we are at the end of the list and, if not, advances CurrentNode by one node, and returns the Element field stored at that node. The End() function tests if CurrentNode is a null pointer, which can only happen if the end of the list has been reached.

A sample `main()` routine illustrates how the iterator can be used. It is in the file `iterator.cpp`:

```
#include "itertemp.h"

int main()
{
    linklist<int> TestList(0);

    TestList.Read();
    TestList.Print();
    ListIterator<int> Source(TestList);
    for (int TempItem = Source.Next(); !Source.End();
        TempItem = Source.Next() )
        cout << 2 * TempItem << ' ';
    cout << endl;
    return 0;
}
```

A `linklist` object which stores `int`s is declared, read in, and printed out using the `Read()` and `Print()` functions inherited from the `list` class. At this point, a `ListIterator` is defined, and passed `TestList` as the list over which it will iterate. This declaration calls the `ListIterator` constructor, which initializes the `CurrentNode` marker in the iterator to the head node of `TestList`.

The `for` loop illustrates how the iterator may be used to access and use the individual elements of the list. The variable `TempItem` receives each `int` stored in the list in turn. The loop simply multiplies each item by 2 and prints it out.

Had we needed a nested loop, we would declare a second `ListIterator` object for the inner loop and used that to iterate over the same list. The two iterators use separate markers, so a nested loop will work properly.

Of course, we could have avoided the need for iterators by simply making all fields in the original `list` class public, so that any other class could access the list elements directly. However, doing this violates the fundamentals of object oriented programming, since the data fields of a class should not be accessible to any outside class except through an interface function. The iterator class provides this interface and therefore should be used whenever iteration over the elements of a data type is required.

## 15.5.2 C++ code for topological ordering of a graph

We now introduce some C++ code which defines a graph class and implements the two topological sorting algorithms described above. (The ordinary traversals are left as exercises.)

Unlike the other data structures we have considered in this book, we will not define a template for a graph, since doing so would require some extra

C++ programming techniques that are beyond the scope of this book. To see why this is so, we must remember that most representations of a graph use an array (the adjacency table uses a two-dimensional array, and the representation we use in the following code uses a one-dimensional array of linked lists). The array index is the label used for the graph vertex. If this label is of a complex data type (that is, it is not an int), we must have a way of translating this data type into an int, since only ints are allowed as array indices in C++.[16]

We begin by defining a minimal directed graph class (in file digraph.h):

```
#ifndef DIGRAPH_H
#define DIGRAPH_H

#include "mydefs.h"
#include "itertemp.h"
#include <string.h>
#include <stdlib.h>

class digraph {
protected:
  linklist<int> *Edge;
  int NumVertex;
public:
  digraph(int numvertex = 10);
  friend ostream& operator<<(ostream& OutStream,
    const digraph& OutGraph);
  friend istream& operator>>(istream& InStream,
    digraph& InGraph);
};
#endif
```

The representation we are using here for a graph is the combination of the adjacency table and adjacency list mentioned earlier in this chapter. An array Edge of linklist objects represents the vertices of the graph. Each list in the Edge array contains the edges arising from the corresponding vertex. Since we are representing a vertex by an int, the data type stored in the linklist objects is int.

The public functions consist of the constructor and the usual overloaded I/O operators. The input operator, however, illustrates how we construct the graph. The function definitions are in the file graph.cpp:

---

[16] The array index notation (the square brackets []) is actually an operator which can be overloaded in C++. We could, therefore, define a graph template by overloading this operator so that if complex data types are used to label the graph vertices, this óperator extracts and returns an int which may then be used as the array index. Since the graph algorithms and their associated C++ code are already complex enough, however, we will not pursue this further.

```
#include "digraph.h"

digraph::digraph(int numvertex) :
  NumVertex(numvertex),
  Edge(new linklist<int>[numvertex])
{}

istream& operator>>(istream& InStream,
  digraph& InGraph)
{
  char line[80], *nextvertex;
  int finish;

  cout << "For each vertex, enter vertices to
    which it is connected.\n";
  for (int start = 0;
    start < InGraph.NumVertex; start++)
  {
    cout << "Vertex " << start << ": ";
    InStream.getline(line, sizeof(line));
    if (nextvertex = strtok(line, " ")) {
      finish = atoi(nextvertex);
      InGraph.Edge[start].Insert(finish);
      while (nextvertex = strtok(0, " ")) {
        finish = atoi(nextvertex);
        InGraph.Edge[start].Insert(finish);
      }
    }
  }
  return InStream;
}

ostream& operator<<(ostream& OutStream,
  const digraph& OutGraph)
{
  OutStream << "List of vertices and edges.\n";
  for (int start = 0;
    start < OutGraph.NumVertex; start++)
  {
    OutStream << "Vertex " << start << ": ";
    ListIterator<int> Source(OutGraph.Edge[start]);
    for (int Vertex = Source.Next();
      !Source.End(); Vertex = Source.Next() )
      OutStream << Vertex << ' ';
    OutStream << endl;
  }
  return OutStream;
}
```

The input function uses the standard string library to parse the input line. Doing things this way allows the user to type in all edges arising from a particular vertex on one line, and to leave the line blank if no edges arise from a particular vertex. The `strtok()` function in the standard string library accepts two arguments: the first is a pointer to the string to be parsed, and the second is a string containing a list of parsing characters. On the first call to `strtok()`, the string is searched until one of the parsing characters is found. That character is replaced with an ASCII null character and a pointer to the beginning of that segment of the string is returned. On subsequent calls to `strtok()`, if the first argument (the string pointer) is zero, the function will pick up where it left off in the same string.

Thus, in the call `strtok(line," ")`, the string `line` is searched until a blank is found. The blank is replaced with a null and a pointer to the first word ending in the blank is returned. `strtok()` will return a null pointer when no more words are found in the string.

The function `atoi()` converts an ASCII string to its `int` equivalent, if the ASCII string contains numeric characters. For example, if the ASCII string "352" is fed into `atoi()`, the `int` value of 352 is returned.

Once the value of the vertex to which an edge is connected is read and evaluated by these functions, it is inserted into the corresponding `linklist` object using the `Insert()` function inherited from the original `list` class.

The overloaded output operator uses an iterator to loop through the elements of each `linklist` object and print out a table of the edges in the graph. The example is very similar to that given earlier in the section on C++ iterators.

A `main()` routine demonstrating how these routines are used is in the file `traverse.cpp`:

```
#include "digraph.h"

int main()
{
  digraph TestGraph(5);

  cin >> TestGraph;
  cout << TestGraph;
  return 0;
}
```

We can now define a derived class which inherits the basic `digraph` class defined above, and which adds functions to implement the two forms of topological sorting. The derived class is in the file `topsort.h`:

```
#ifndef TOPSORT_H
#define TOPSORT_H
#include "digraph.h"
#include "qtemp.h"

class topsort : public digraph
```

```
{
private:
  int *TopOrder;
  void Sort(int vertex, int& place, BOOL *visited);
public:
  topsort(int numvertex = 10)  :
    digraph(numvertex), TopOrder(new int[numvertex]) {}
  void DepthSort();
  void BreadthSort();
  void PrintTopSort();
};
#endif
```

The array `TopOrder` (initialized in the constructor) is used to construct the topological ordering of the vertices. The private function `Sort()` is used in conjunction with the public `DepthSort()` function to implement a recursive depth-first sort of the graph. The `BreadthSort()` function implements the breadth-first sort. The functions are in the file `topfunc.cpp`:

```
#include "topsort.h"

void topsort::Sort(int Vertex, int& place,
  BOOL *visited)
{
  ListIterator<int> temp(Edge[Vertex]);

  visited[Vertex] = TRUE;
  for (int NextVertex = temp.Next();
    !temp.End(); NextVertex = temp.Next() )
    if (!visited[NextVertex])
      Sort(NextVertex,place,visited);
  TopOrder[--place] = Vertex;
}

void topsort::DepthSort() {
  BOOL *visited = new int[NumVertex];
  int Vertex;
  int place;

  for (Vertex = 0; Vertex < NumVertex; Vertex++)
    visited[Vertex] = FALSE;
  place = NumVertex;
  for (Vertex = 0; Vertex < NumVertex; Vertex++)
    if (!visited[Vertex]) Sort(Vertex,place,visited);
  delete [] visited;
}

void topsort::BreadthSort() {
  int *predecessorcount = new int[NumVertex];
  queue<int> vertexq(NumVertex);
  int Vertex, NextVertex, place, TempVertex;
```

```
for (Vertex = 0; Vertex < NumVertex; Vertex++)
  predecessorcount[Vertex] = 0;
for (Vertex = 0; Vertex < NumVertex; Vertex++) {
  ListIterator<int> temp(Edge[Vertex]);
  for (TempVertex = temp.Next();
    !temp.End(); TempVertex = temp.Next())
    predecessorcount[TempVertex]++;
}
for (Vertex = 0; Vertex < NumVertex; Vertex++)
  if (!predecessorcount[Vertex]) vertexq.Add(Vertex);
place = 0;
while (!vertexq.Empty()) {
  vertexq.Remove(Vertex);
  TopOrder[place++] = Vertex;
  ListIterator<int> temp(Edge[Vertex]);
  for (NextVertex = temp.Next();
    !temp.End(); NextVertex = temp.Next()) {
    predecessorcount[NextVertex]--;
    if (!predecessorcount[NextVertex])
      vertexq.Add(NextVertex);
  }
}
delete [] predecessorcount;
}

void topsort::PrintTopSort()
{
  cout << "Topological ordering:\n";
  for (int i=0; i<NumVertex; i++)
    cout << TopOrder [i] << ' ';
  cout << endl;
}
```

These functions follow the algorithms in the notes quite closely. For the depth-first sort, the Sort() function is the recursive routine that searches out those vertices that have no successors and adds them to the sorted list. In the DepthSort() function, the array visited is a Boolean array used to label each vertex that has been visited in a previous pass of the function. The function descends into the edge table by searching as deeply as it can at each vertex. The search is carried out using recursive calls to Sort(). When the bottom of the recursion is reached, the vertex found at that point is copied into the corresponding place in the TopOrder array, and the place marker variable place is decremented. The public function DepthSort() loops over all vertices in the graph to ensure that any disconnected parts of the graph are included in the sort.

The breadth-first sort is carried out by the function BreadthSort(). This function requires a queue, so we use the queue class (generalized to a template here) that we introduced in Chapter 7.

The `BreadthFirst()` function again follows the algorithm in the notes very closely. The array `predecessorcount` stores the number of predecessors for each vertex. It is cleared, then built up by examining the linked list for each vertex to see which vertices follow each vertex in the graph. Then the queue is initialized by inserting all vertices with no predecessors into it, and the `place` marker is set to zero. The main `while` loop continues until the queue is empty. A vertex is removed from the queue and added to the `TopOrder` array. The linked list for that vertex is traversed by the `for` loop, and the predecessor counts adjusted. Any vertex whose predecessor count has dropped to zero is added to the queue. Note that an iterator is used in any situation where a loop over the elements of a list is needed.

Finally, the function `PrintTopSort()` prints out the topologically sorted list of vertices.

A main routine that tests all these functions is in the file `topsort.cpp`:

```cpp
#include "topsort.h"

int main()
{
   topsort TestGraph(10);

   cin >> TestGraph;
   cout << TestGraph;

   TestGraph.DepthSort();
   cout << "Depth first sort:\n";
   TestGraph.PrintTopSort();
   TestGraph.BreadthSort();
   cout << "Breadth first sort:\n";
   TestGraph.PrintTopSort();
   return 0;
}
```

# 15.6 Minimum cost spanning trees

## 15.6.1 Kruskal's algorithm

The graphs we have studied so far have vertices that are connected by simple edges, where an edge serves only to indicate that there is a path from one vertex to another. We can generalize the concept of a graph a bit so that each edge includes a *weight* or *cost* as well. For example, if we represent airline routes as a graph with the cities as the vertices, the weight associated with each edge could be the distance between the two cities, or the cost of a flight between the cities. In such cases, we may need to know the shortest or cheapest route between two cities. The algorithm we consider in this section deals with finding such paths in a graph.

For an undirected, connected graph with $N$ vertices, we can find a set of $N - 1$ edges which connect all the vertices. Such a set of edges is guaranteed not to have any cycles, and is therefore referred to as a *spanning tree*. For a graph where each edge has an associated cost, we define the *minimum cost spanning tree* as the spanning tree where the sum of all the weights on the edges is a minimum.

There are several algorithms for finding minimum cost spanning trees, but we will consider just one representative of them: Kruskal's algorithm. Kruskal's algorithm is an example of a *greedy algorithm*, that is, one which seeks maximum gain at each step. The algorithm, on paper at least, is very simple. Given a connected, undirected graph, we wish to select those edges, one at a time, that comprise the minimum cost spanning tree. We begin by choosing the edge with the minimum cost (if there are several edges with the same minimum cost, we select any one of them) and add it to the spanning tree. In the next step, we select the edge with the next lowest cost, and so on, until we have selected $N - 1$ edges to form the complete spanning tree.

The only thing of which we must beware is that we don't form any cycles as we add edges to the spanning tree. This is fairly easy to ensure for small graphs which we draw on paper, since we can see just by looking at the diagram we are drawing if adding an edge would create a cycle. However, we must find some way of coding this in C++, so we can't rely on pictures.

At each stage in the algorithm, the partially formed spanning tree will consist of several sets of vertices which form connected subgraphs. If we keep a list of these sets, we can use them to determine if a new edge will form a cycle. Suppose that, at some point in the algorithm, vertices 1 and 2 have been connected in the spanning tree, as have vertices 3, 4, and 5, but vertex 0 has not yet been connected to any other vertex. We may write this state of affairs in set notation by saying that the list of sets of connected vertices in the spanning tree is {0}, {1,2}, {3,4,5}. Now suppose that the edge with the next lowest cost is that connecting vertices 2 and 3, which we write as (2,3). Adding the edge (2,3) would connect the second and third of these sets because each end of the edge lies in a different set. The edge (2,3) will therefore not form a cycle, so it is safe to add. After its addition, the sets of vertices in the spanning tree are {0}, {1,2,3,4,5}. If the next edge up for consideration is (3,4), this would connect two vertices that are already inside the same set, so this would provide an alternative path between vertices 3 and 4, thus creating a cycle. We therefore should *not* include the edge (3,4).

Kruskal's algorithm, with the addition of this check for avoiding cycles, is therefore:

1. Initialize the spanning tree $T$ to contain all the vertices in the graph $G$ but no edges.

2. At the start of the algorithm, each vertex will be in its own set, since no edges have yet been added to the tree, so create sets of the tree $T$ with one vertex per set.
3. Choose the edge $e$ with lowest weight from graph $G$.
4. Check if both vertices from $e$ are within the same set in the tree $T$, for all such sets of $T$. If not, add the edge $e$ to the tree $T$, and replace the two sets that this edge connects with their union.
5. Delete the edge $e$ from the graph $G$ and repeat from step 3 until there are no more edges to add or until the spanning tree $T$ contains $N - 1$ vertices.

As an example of Kruskal's algorithm, consider the graph shown in Fig. 15.18.

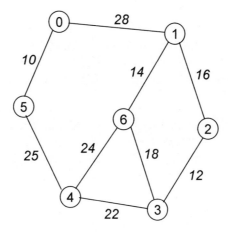

Fig. 15.18. An undirected, weighted graph.

We begin our spanning tree by filling it with the vertices, but none of the edges, in the original graph (Fig. 15.19).

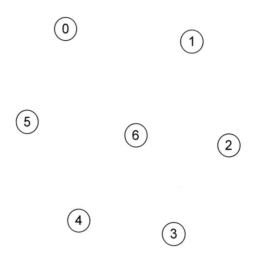

Fig. 15.19. The beginning state for Kruskal's algorithm.

We select the edge with the lowest cost (the edge (0,5)) and add it to the tree (Fig. 15.20).

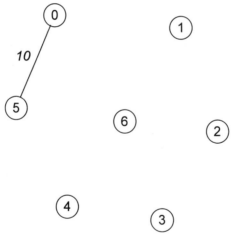

Fig. 15.20. Adding the edge with the lowest cost.

The sets of vertices in the spanning tree are now {0,5}, {1}, {2}, {3}, {4}, {6}. We continue by adding the edges (2,3), (1,6), and (1,2). At this point, the tree looks like Fig. 15.21.

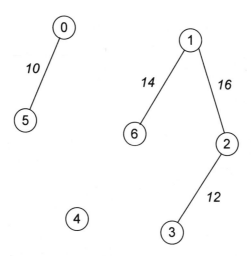

Fig. 15.21.

The sets of vertices now consist of {0,5}, {1,2,3,6}, {4}. Looking at the original graph, the next edge that must be considered is (3,6). We can see from the diagram that adding this edge would create a cycle. We can also see this from the list of sets of vertices, since vertices 3 and 6 are both in the same set. We therefore pass over this edge and add edge (3,4). The next edge that would be considered is (4,6), but this would also create a cycle. Finally, the edge (4,5) is added to complete the tree (Fig. 15.22).

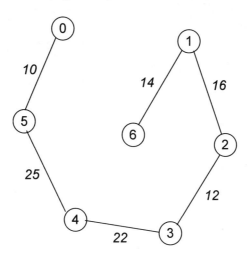

Fig. 15.22. The completed spanning tree.

## 15.6.2 C++ code for Kruskal's algorithm

The addition of costs to the edges in a graph changes most of the structures and functions in the graph class, so it is better to design a new class from scratch rather than try to inherit the old `digraph` class and modify it. We therefore define the class `undigraph` as follows:

```
#ifndef UNDIGRAF_H
#define UNDIGRAF_H

#include "mydefs.h"
#include "itertemp.h"
#include <string.h>
#include <stdlib.h>
#include "settemp.h"
#include <limits.h>

class undigraph {
public:
   struct WeightEdge {
     int start, finish, weight;
     BOOL operator<(const WeightEdge& OtherEdge) const
       { return weight < OtherEdge.weight ?
         TRUE : FALSE; }
     BOOL operator!=(const WeightEdge& OtherEdge) const
       { return (start != OtherEdge.start ||
         weight != OtherEdge.weight ||
         finish != OtherEdge.finish)
         ? TRUE : FALSE; }
     BOOL operator==(const WeightEdge& OtherEdge) const
       { return (start == OtherEdge.start &&
         weight == OtherEdge.weight &&
         finish == OtherEdge.finish)
         ? TRUE : FALSE; }
     friend ostream& operator<<(ostream& OutStream,
       const WeightEdge& OutWeightEdge);
     friend istream& operator>>(istream& InStream,
       WeightEdge& InWeightEdge);
   };
protected:
   linklist<WeightEdge> *Edge;
   int NumVertex;
public:
   undigraph(int numvertex = 10);
   friend ostream& operator<<(ostream& OutStream,
     const undigraph& OutGraph);
   friend istream& operator>>(istream& InStream,
     undigraph& InGraph);
};
#endif
```

The encapsulated `struct` for representing a weighted edge is called `WeightEdge`. Since we will be using objects of type `WeightEdge` in a `linklist` object, we need to provide all the overloaded operators required by the `linklist` class functions. Referring back to the `list` class in Chapter 10, we see that we need `!=` and `==` operators. We also include a `<` operator since we will be forming a sorted list of the edges using insertion sort, which requires this comparison operator. We also provide overloaded `<<` and `>>` operators for `WeightEdge` objects.

The graph itself consists of a linked list of pointers to each vertex, just as with the graphs we used earlier in this chapter. The overloaded I/O functions for `undigraph` must be modified to take account of the costs on the edges, however.

The C++ code for these functions is in the file `undigraf.cpp`:

```cpp
#include "undigraf.h"

ostream& operator<<(ostream& OutStream,
  const undigraph::WeightEdge& OutWeightEdge)
{
  OutStream << OutWeightEdge.start << ","
    << OutWeightEdge.finish << "," <<
    OutWeightEdge.weight;
  return OutStream;
}

istream& operator>>(istream& InStream,
  undigraph::WeightEdge& InWeightEdge)
{
  InStream >> InWeightEdge.start >> InWeightEdge.finish
    >> InWeightEdge.weight;
  return InStream;
}

undigraph::undigraph(int numvertex) :
  NumVertex(numvertex),
  Edge(new linklist<undigraph::WeightEdge>[numvertex])
{}

istream& operator>>(istream& InStream,
  undigraph& InGraph)
{
  char line[80], *nextvertex, *nextweight;
  undigraph::WeightEdge TempEdge;

  cout << "For each vertex, enter (vertex, weight)
    pairs for links.\n";
  for (int source = 0; source < InGraph.NumVertex;
    source++)
  {
    cout << "Vertex " << source << ": ";
```

```
      InStream.getline(line, sizeof(line));
      if ((nextvertex = strtok(line, ",")) &&
         (nextweight = strtok(0, " ")))
      {
        TempEdge.start = source;
        TempEdge.finish = atoi(nextvertex);
        TempEdge.weight = atoi(nextweight);
        if (TempEdge.finish >= TempEdge.start)
           InGraph.Edge[source].Insert(TempEdge);
        while ((nextvertex = strtok(0, ",")) &&
           (nextweight = strtok(0, " ")))
        {
          TempEdge.start = source;
          TempEdge.finish = atoi(nextvertex);
          TempEdge.weight = atoi(nextweight);
          if (TempEdge.finish >= TempEdge.start)
             InGraph.Edge[source].Insert(TempEdge);
        }
      }
   }
   return InStream;
}

ostream& operator<<(ostream& OutStream,
   const undigraph& OutGraph)
{
   OutStream << "List of vertices and edges.\n";
   for (int source = 0; source < OutGraph.NumVertex;
      source++)
   {
     OutStream << "Vertex " << source << ": ";
     ListIterator<undigraph::WeightEdge>
        Source(OutGraph.Edge[source]);
     for (undigraph::WeightEdge Vertex = Source.Next();
        !Source.End(); Vertex = Source.Next() )
        OutStream << Vertex << ' ';
     OutStream << endl;
   }
   return OutStream;
}
```

The I/O functions for the WeightEdge struct read and print the three data fields start, finish, and weight.

The I/O functions for undigraph use the same string parsing techniques described in the last section, except this time an edge is input by typing the finishing vertex number, then a comma, then the weight on the edge. Since we are dealing with an undirected graph, a connection from vertex *A* to vertex *B* implies a connection from *B* to *A* as well. There is no point in storing both these vertices in the edge list, so we only store an edge if it leads to a vertex with an index greater than or equal to the starting vertex. This test is made in the input function.

The output function is similar to that defined for the non-weighted graph in the last section. It uses an iterator to traverse each linked list and print out the edges arising from each vertex.

To implement Kruskal's algorithm, we defined a derived class which adds the required fields to the undigraph class. This definition is also in the file undigraf.h.

```
#ifndef UNDIGRAF_H
#define UNDIGRAF_H

#include "mydefs.h"
#include "itertemp.h"
#include <string.h>
#include <stdlib.h>
#include "settemp.h"
#include <limits.h>

// undigraph class defined here...

class mincostgraph : public undigraph
{
protected:
  linklist<WeightEdge> EdgeList;
  void MakeEdgeList();
public:
  mincostgraph(int numvertex = 10) :
    undigraph(numvertex) {}
  void Kruskal();
};
#endif
```

The header file settemp.h is included to provide access to the set templates we defined in Chapter 9. The header file limits.h is included since we wish to make use of the system defined constants INT_MAX and INT_MIN, which are the largest and smallest integers the int data type will support. We use these in Kruskal's algorithm as well.

The EdgeList field is used to store a list of edges sorted in ascending order of weight by the function MakeEdgeList(). The list is used to decide the order in which edges are examined for insertion into the spanning tree. The function Kruskal() implements Kruskal's algorithm. The code for the class functions is in the file kruskal.cpp:

```
#include "undigraf.h"

void mincostgraph::MakeEdgeList()
{
  for (int vertex = 0; vertex < NumVertex; vertex++) {
    ListIterator<undigraph::WeightEdge>
      temp(Edge[vertex]);
```

```
      for (undigraph::WeightEdge Vertex = temp.Next();
        !temp.End();
        Vertex = temp.Next())
        EdgeList.InsertSort(Vertex);
  }
}

void mincostgraph::Kruskal() {
  mincostgraph spantree(NumVertex);
  set<int,MAXGRAPHSIZE> connected[MAXGRAPHSIZE];
  int EdgesAdded = 0;
  int vertex1, vertex2;
  int SetIndex1, SetIndex2;
  BOOL cycle = FALSE;
  int vertex;

  MakeEdgeList();
  for (vertex = 0; vertex < NumVertex; vertex++)
    connected[vertex].insert(vertex);
  ListIterator<undigraph::WeightEdge> Edges(EdgeList);
  for(undigraph::WeightEdge CurrEdge = Edges.Next();
    EdgesAdded < NumVertex-1 && !Edges.End();
    CurrEdge = Edges.Next())
  {
    vertex1 = CurrEdge.start;
    vertex2 = CurrEdge.finish;
    SetIndex1 = INT_MAX;
    SetIndex2 = INT_MIN;
    for (vertex = NumVertex - 1; vertex >= 0; vertex--)
    {
      if (connected[vertex].contains(vertex1))
        SetIndex1 = vertex;
      if (connected[vertex].contains(vertex2))
        SetIndex2 = vertex;
      cycle |= (SetIndex1 == SetIndex2);
    }
    if (!cycle) {
      spantree.Edge[CurrEdge.start].Insert(CurrEdge);
      EdgesAdded++;
      connected[SetIndex1 < SetIndex2 ?
        SetIndex1 : SetIndex2] =
        connected[SetIndex1] + connected[SetIndex2];
    }
    cycle = FALSE;
  }
  cout << "Minimum cost spanning tree:\n";
  if (EdgesAdded < NumVertex - 1)
    cout << "Warning: spanning tree incomplete.\n";
  cout << spantree;
}
```

The `MakeEdgeList()` function constructs a single linked list by traversing all the individual lists for each vertex and storing the edges in ascending order of weight.

Most of the work is done in the function `Kruskal()`. A local `mincostgraph` variable `spantree` is declared which is built into the minimum cost spanning tree. An array `connected` of sets is declared using our set template.

The calculations begin by calling `MakeEdgeList()` to construct the list of edges sorted according to their weights. Then the sets are initialized by assigning one vertex to each of them, so that initially each vertex is in its own separate set. After these initializations, a local `WeightEdge` variable `CurrEdge` is used with an iterator to traverse the edge list, reading off edges in increasing order of weight. For each edge, the two vertices it connects are saved in the local variables `vertex1` and `vertex2`. We must now determine if these two endpoints are in the same set. The array of sets is scanned, testing each set to see if it contains both vertices. If any set does, the variable `cycle` will become TRUE. (The operator `|=` means to take the logical OR and then assign the result back in the same variable. It is analogous to the `+=` operator.) Thus if `cycle` is TRUE after all sets have been tested, the inclusion of this edge would cause a cycle, so the edge must be discarded. The `if` statement tests the value of `cycle`, and adds the edge to the spanning tree only if `cycle` is FALSE. After the edge is added to the tree, the `EdgesAdded` counter is incremented, and the set with the smaller index is set to the union of the two sets of vertices connected by the edge just added to the spanning tree. At the end of each loop iteration, `cycle` is set back to FALSE to prepare for testing the next edge in the edge list.

At the end of the function, a test is made to ensure that the spanning tree is complete (the number of edges in a spanning tree should always be one less than the number of vertices). Finally, the spanning tree is printed out.

Note that we could have declared the `Kruskal()` function to return a graph as its return value rather than just print it out. Doing so, however, would require that we define a copy constructor and an overloaded `=` operator for the `undigraph` class, since objects in this class contain dynamically allocated memory in their linked lists. The object `spantree` is a local variable in the `Kruskal()` function, so must be passed back by value, and not by reference, since once `Kruskal()` terminates, its space will be deallocated.

A simple main routine using these functions is:

```
#include "undigraf.h"

int main()
{
  mincostgraph TestGraph(7);
```

```
cin >> TestGraph;
cout << TestGraph;
TestGraph.Kruskal();
return 0;
```

# 15.7 Shortest paths in a directed graph

### 15.7.1 Dijkstra's algorithm

We turn now to the problem of finding the shortest or least costly path between two vertices in a graph. It turns out that it is easiest to do this by finding the shortest path from one vertex, called the *source*, to all other vertices in the graph. The algorithm for doing this is also a greedy algorithm, and is generally known as *Dijkstra's algorithm* (pronounced "Dike-stra").

Dijkstra's algorithm is usually used with directed graphs, though it works equally well with undirected graphs if each edge is considered as two directed edges, one in each direction.

The algorithm is as follows:

1. Choose the source vertex.
2. Define a set $S$ of vertices and initialize it to contain only the source vertex. The set $S$ will store those vertices to which a shortest path has been found as the algorithm progresses.
3. Label each vertex *not* in the set $S$ (at this stage, this simply means 'any vertex other than the source') with the minimum distance from the source vertex, but only if this vertex can be connected *by a single edge* with the source. If there is no single edge connection between the source and the vertex not in $S$, label the vertex not in $S$ with a distance of infinity.
4. Add to $S$ that vertex with the smallest distance as determined in step 3 (or step 5 on subsequent iterations of the algorithm).
5. Check the distances to all vertices not in $S$. If the latest addition to $S$ in step 4 provides a *single edge connection* between a vertex in $S$ and the vertex not in $S$, or a shorter path now exists, then adjust the distance to that vertex. Otherwise, do not change the distance.
6. Repeat the algorithm from step 4 until either all vertices are in the set $S$ or all vertices not in $S$ have an infinite distance to them. In the latter case, these vertices are not reachable from the source vertex at any cost.

Let us follow the algorithm for the graph shown below, and find the shortest paths from vertex 6 to the other vertices. Fig. 15.23 shows the graph after steps 1, 2, and 3 in the algorithm above have been executed.

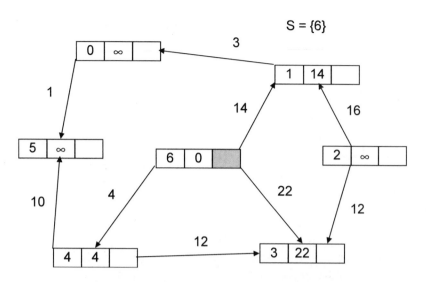

Fig. 15.23. A graph at the beginning of Dijkstra's algorithm. Each vertex is represented by a box with three entries. The first entry is the vertex label, the second entry is the current minimum distance from a vertex in the set *S* to that vertex (or the minimum distance from the source vertex (6) to that vertex if the vertex is in the set *S*), and the last box is shaded if the vertex is in the set *S*.

The first time step 4 is executed, vertex 4 is added to *S*, since its distance of 4 is currently the smallest to a vertex not already in *S*. Adding vertex 4 to *S* opens a path to vertex 5, since vertex 5 has a one-edge link from vertex 4. We therefore adjust the distance to vertex 5 to 14 (4 from vertex 6 to 4, plus 10 from vertex 4 to 5). Vertex 4 also offers an alternative path to vertex 3. The total distance to vertex 3 via vertex 4 is 16, which is less than the direct link from vertex 6 to 3, with a cost of 22. We therefore adjust the distance to vertex 3. The graph now looks like Fig. 15.24.

The shortest distance to a vertex not in *S* is now 14, which occurs for both vertices 1 and 5. It doesn't matter which vertex we choose to add at this stage, so we take vertex 1. This opens up a path to vertex 0, with a distance of 17.

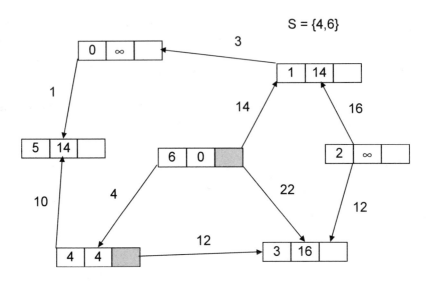

$S = \{4,6\}$

Fig. 15.24.

We continue by adding the vertices 5, 3, and 0, in that order. There is no path from vertex 6 to vertex 2 so the distance to vertex remains infinite after the algorithm finishes. The final state of the graph is shown in Fig. 15.25.

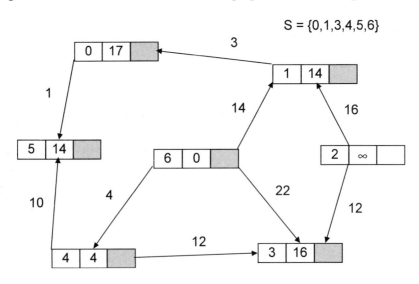

$S = \{0,1,3,4,5,6\}$

Fig. 15.25. The final state obtained from Dijkstra's algorithm.

## 15.7.2 C++ code for Dijkstra's algorithm

We will apply Dijkstra's algorithm to a directed graph with costs on the edges. We can define a class for such a graph quite easily by inheriting the `undigraph` class we used for Kruskal's algorithm. The only change we need to make in the class structure is to remove the condition that only edges leading to a vertex with an index higher than the source will be stored, since a directed graph can (and usually does) have an edge from vertex *A* to vertex *B* without an edge from *B* to *A*.

We define the `digraphweight` class, and a derived class which implements Dijkstra's algorithm, in the file `digrafw.h`:

```
#ifndef DIGRAFW_H
#define DIGRAFW_H
#include "undigraf.h"

class digraphweight : public undigraph
{
public:
   digraphweight(int numvertex = 10) :
      undigraph(numvertex) {}
   friend istream& operator>>(istream& InStream,
      digraphweight& InGraph);
};

class minpathgraph : public digraphweight
{
protected:
   int Weight(int vertex1, int vertex2);
public:
   minpathgraph(int numvertex = 10) :
      digraphweight(numvertex) {}
   void Dijkstra(int start);
};
#endif
```

The only difference between the directed graph class `digraphweight` and the undirected graph class `undigraph` is in the overloaded >> operator.

Dijkstra's algorithm requires that we have access to the weights on the edges in a random access fashion, unlike Kruskal's algorithm, where we needed the edges in ascending order of weight. It is therefore convenient to define a function `Weight()` which, given the endpoints of an edge, returns the associated weight. The function `Dijkstra()` implements Dijkstra's algorithm.

The code for these new functions is in the file `digrafw.cpp`:

```
#include "digrafw.h"

istream& operator>>(istream& InStream,
   digraphweight& InGraph)
{
   char line[80], *nextvertex, *nextweight;
   undigraph::WeightEdge TempEdge;
```

```
    cout << "For each vertex, enter (vertex, weight)
      pairs for links.\n";
    for (int source = 0; source < InGraph.NumVertex;
      source++)
    {
      cout << "Vertex " << source << ": ";
      InStream.getline(line, sizeof(line));
      if ((nextvertex = strtok(line, ",")) &&
        (nextweight = strtok(0, " ")))
      {
        TempEdge.start = source;
        TempEdge.finish = atoi(nextvertex);
        TempEdge.weight = atoi(nextweight);
        InGraph.Edge[source].Insert(TempEdge);
        while ((nextvertex = strtok(0, ",")) &&
          (nextweight = strtok(0, " ")))
        {
          TempEdge.start = source;
          TempEdge.finish = atoi(nextvertex);
          TempEdge.weight = atoi(nextweight);
          InGraph.Edge[source].Insert(TempEdge);
        }
      }
    }
    return InStream;
}

int minpathgraph::Weight(int begin, int end)
{
  ListIterator<undigraph::WeightEdge>
    temp(Edge[begin]);
  for(undigraph::WeightEdge TempEdge = temp.Next();
    !temp.End(); TempEdge = temp.Next())
    if (TempEdge.finish == end)
      return TempEdge.weight;
  return INT_MAX;
}

void minpathgraph::Dijkstra(int start) {
  set<int,MAXGRAPHSIZE> pathfound;
  int mindistance[MAXGRAPHSIZE];
  int tempmin,end,cost;

  pathfound.insert(start);
  mindistance[start] = 0;
  for (int vertex = 0; vertex < NumVertex; vertex++)
    if (vertex != start)
      mindistance[vertex] = Weight(start,vertex);
  for (vertex = 0; vertex < NumVertex; vertex++) {
    int mindist = INT_MAX;
    if (vertex != start) {
      for (end = 0; end < NumVertex; end++) {
```

```
          if (!pathfound.contains(end)) {
            if (mindistance[end] < mindist) {
              tempmin = end;
              mindist = mindistance[end];
            }
          }
        }
        if (mindist < INT_MAX) {
          pathfound.insert(tempmin);
          for (end = 0; end < NumVertex; end++)
            if (!pathfound.contains(end)) {
              cost = Weight(tempmin,end);
              if (cost < INT_MAX &&
              mindist + cost < mindistance[end])
              mindistance[end] = mindist + cost;
            }
        }
      }
    }
    cout << "Minimum distances from vertex " << start
      << " to:\n";
    for (vertex = 0; vertex < NumVertex; vertex++) {
      cout << "Vertex " << vertex << ": " ;
      if(mindistance[vertex] == INT_MAX)
        cout << "No path.";
      else
        cout << mindistance[vertex];
      cout << endl;
    }
}
```

The overloaded >> operator is identical to that for the undigraph class except that we have removed the check that the finishing vertex have a higher index than the starting vertex.

The Weight() function scans the appropriate list until we either find the correct endpoint, in which case the weight is returned, or we hit the end of the list, indicating that there is no edge connecting the two vertices. In the latter case, we return INT_MAX, which is used as a marker that no edge exists. It can also be thought of as an 'infinite weight' between the two vertices.

Dijkstra's algorithm itself is implemented in the Dijkstra() function. A set pathfound is declared which is used to store the indices of those vertices to which the minimum distance has been found. (The set pathfound is equivalent to the set $S$ in the discussion of the algorithm above.) The minimum distances found so far are stored in the array mindistance. Initialization involves inserting the starting vertex into the set pathfound, and setting the minimum distance to the starting vertex at 0. Then the remaining elements of mindistance are initialized by inserting the weights from the starting vertex to the other vertices. Remember that if there is no edge connecting the starting vertex *directly* to another vertex, the value stored will be INT_MAX.

With initialization complete, the main part of the algorithm is done in the central `for` loop. For each vertex in the graph, a test is made to see if it is currently in the set `pathfound`. For all vertices not yet in this set, the vertex with the minimum distance from the starting vertex is found. The index of this vertex is stored in `tempmin`, and the actual distance in `mindist`. If `mindist` is not INT_MAX (that is, if there actually is a path to vertex `tempmin`), this vertex is inserted in the set `pathfound`.

The final stage of the algorithm is to recompute the minimum distances from the starting vertex to all remaining vertices not yet in the set `pathfound`. The distance from the vertex just added to the set (`tempmin`) to each such vertex is found using the `Weight()` function. If there is a direct path from `tempmin` to the vertex (given by the condition `cost < INT_MAX`), and if this distance plus the current distance from the starting vertex to `tempmin` (given by `mindist + cost`) is less than the currently recorded distance from the starting vertex, the corresponding entry in the `mindistance` array is updated.

The algorithm continues until all vertices have been given a chance to enter the set `pathfound`. Any vertices remaining outside this set when the main `for` loop finishes have no path leading to them from the starting vertex, and the corresponding entries in `mindistance` will remain as INT_MAX. The final `for` loop prints out the results: if the entry in `mindistance` is not INT_MAX, the actual distance is printed, otherwise the message "No path." is printed indicating that the vertex is unreachable from the starting point specified.

The `main()` routine which links all this together is in the file `dijkstra.cpp`:

```
#include "digrafw.h"

int main()
{
  minpathgraph TestGraph(7);
  int start;

  cin >> TestGraph;
  cout << TestGraph;
  cout << "Enter starting vertex: ";
  cin >> start;
  TestGraph.Dijkstra(start);
  return 0;
}
```

## 15.8 Summary

This chapter introduced the *graph* data structure. A graph is a generalization of a tree, consisting of *vertices* connected with *directed* or *undirected edges*. The vertices of a graph can be traversed in several ways, including *depth-first traversal*, *breadth-first traversal*, and for a directed graph, *topological ordering*. Algorithms for performing these traversals are given.

Graphs can be represented in C++ using arrays (the *adjacency table*), linked lists (the *adjacency list*) or a combination of the two. C++ classes are defined to represent directed and undirected graphs, and code is given to implement the topological ordering algorithms.

Proper object oriented treatment of graphs requires the introduction of the *iterator* class in C++. An iterator class is a friend of a class containing private array or linked list fields, and allows external classes and functions to iterate over the private arrays or lists without violating the principle of object oriented design.

Graphs can have *weights* or *costs* associated with their edges. A weight represents the cost of travelling from one vertex to another. A *minimal cost spanning tree* is a selection of edges from a weighted graph that spans all vertices in the graph and gives the smallest sum of weights for such a tree. Kruskal's algorithm may be used to find a minimal cost spanning tree. Dijkstra's algorithm may be used to find the shortest or least expensive path from one source vertex to all other vertices in a weighted graph. C++ code is given for implementing both these algorithms.

## 15.9 Exercises

1. Consider the directed graph shown:

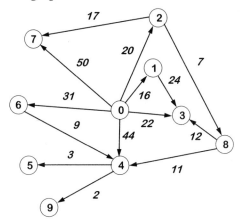

a. Write out an edge table for this graph.

b. Find depth-first and breadth-first traversals of this graph, starting at vertex 0.

c. Find depth-first and breadth-first topological orderings for this graph.

d. Use Dijkstra's algorithm to find the minimum cost paths from vertex 0 to all other vertices in the graph.

2. Consider the undirected graph shown:

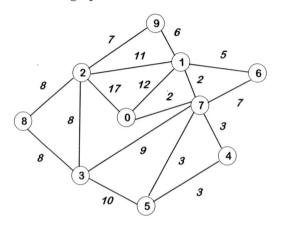

a. Write out an edge table for this graph.

b. Find depth-first and breadth-first traversals of this graph, starting at vertex 0.

c. Use Kruskal's algorithm to find a minimal spanning tree for this graph.

3. Using the `digraph` class in the text, write C++ functions to implement the depth-first and breadth-first traversal algorithms.

4. Define a class to represent an undirected graph, without weights on its edges. Include C++ functions for implementing input and output, and depth-first and breadth-first traversal.

5. Define a C++ class containing a one-dimensional array of `ints` as a private data field, a constructor, and overloaded input and output operators. Provide an iterator for this class which allows the user to iterate over the array elements. Use your iterator in a `main()` function which reads in the array elements, then uses a nested `for` loop to search the array for duplicate elements.

6. Design a C++ class to represent an undirected graph as an adjacency table (a two-dimensional array). Implement depth-first and breadth-first traversal

using this class. Provide an iterator to do the iterations over the array as required by the algorithms.

7. An alternative to Kruskal's algorithm for finding the minimum cost spanning tree in an undirected graph is *Prim's algorithm* (which was also discovered independently by Dijkstra):

Choose a starting vertex (any vertex will do). At the first step, choose the vertex that is connected to the starting vertex by the edge of least cost, and add that vertex to the spanning tree. For the remaining steps, choose that vertex that is not yet part of the spanning tree, but is connected to the partially formed tree by the edge of least cost, and add that vertex to the tree. Continue until all vertices are part of the spanning tree.

a. Use Prim's algorithm on the graph in question 2.
b. Write a C++ function to implement Prim's algorithm which may be added to the undigraph class in the text.

# Index

# Economics

## of the

# Public Sector

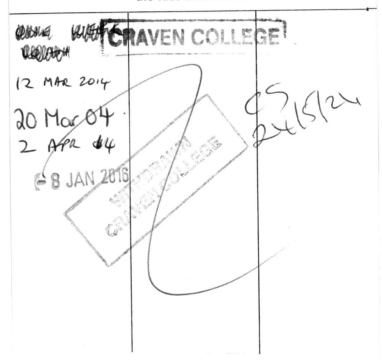